China-India-Japan in the Indo-Pacific

Ideas, Interests and Infrastructure

China-India-Japan in the Indo-Pacific

Ideas, Interests and Infrastructure

Editors

Jagannath P. Panda

Titli Basu

PENTAGON PRESS

China-India-Japan in the Indo-Pacific
Ideas, Interests and Infrastructure
Editors: Jagannath P. Panda and Titli Basu

First Published in 2018

ISBN 978-93-86618-42-9

Published by
PENTAGON PRESS
206, Peacock Lane, Shahpur Jat
New Delhi-110049
Phones: 011-64706243, 26491568
Telefax: 011-26490600
email: rajan@pentagonpress.in
website: www.pentagonpress.in

In association with
Institute for Defence Studies and Analyses
No. 1, Development Enclave,
New Delhi-110010
Phone: +91-11-26717983
Website: www.idsa.in

Printed at Avantika Printers Private Limited.

Contents

Foreword

The regional economic and security dynamics are fast changing, with the term "Indo-Pacific" gaining greater traction among experts and scholars. Although the subtleties of the terms "Indo-Pacific" and "Asia-Pacific" continue to be subject to debate; the cogency of the term "Indo-Pacific" is gaining momentum, underpinned by the vision of a "free and open" regional order that embraces universally accepted democratic values in preference to authoritarianism and a unilateral vision.

The geo-economic power of the world has been shifting, meanwhile, from the north and the west to the south and the east, exemplified by China's rise, and its extraordinary success in lifting almost half a billion people out of poverty within the space of one generation, a feat unprecedented in history. With some attendant delay, the inevitable shift of geopolitics too is happening, with the locus of geopolitical contestation among the great powers moving eastward (towards Asia). Moreover, the bipolar, post-Second World War world has been replaced, first by a description popularised by Samuel Huntington – "uni-multipolar" – and currently by a dynamic and polycentric world order, with shifting strategic allegiances. President Xi Jinping, under his "new era" foreign policy strategy, is leading a number of strategic initiatives that seem to be setting the stage for a Sinocentric order in the region and beyond. Meanwhile, India's judgement to envision a free and open liberal Indo-Pacific region along with likeminded countries like Japan, reflects pragmatism, but India and Japan need to back it up with a well-defined action plan and invest more capital in pursuing their joint initiative. Under the leadership of Prime Minister Shinzo Abe, Japan is offering big investment ideas for connectivity and infrastructural development. This is an area that must invite serious academic discussion and scrutiny. This volume, titled *China-India-Japan in the Indo-Pacific: Ideas, Interests and Infrastructure,* aims to enrich such an academic endeavour.

For India, the Indo-Pacific is emerging as one of the most important strategic theatres. While its maritime economic and security interests are growing, India needs to engage more with the littoral and hinterland states in the Indo-Pacific.India needs to grow faster and invest more in its immediate and extended neighbourhood. As China's geopolitical moves are supported by its economic strength, which it is using to brand infrastructure and other investments under its One Belt, One Road (OBOR) initiative, India too should have a clearer plan of action.

It gives me great pleasure to compliment the editors for bringing out a volume of this length and nature. The volume offers diverse perspectives on the changing environment in the Indo-Pacific region. It brings to the readers' consideration the competing ideas and interests that figure in the foreign policy initiatives of Asia's three biggest economies – China, India, and Japan. Their focus on infrastructural investment is a special feature that makes the politics surrounding the Indo-Pacific region interesting. I would like to compliment the authors for their valuable contribution to this academic exercise. Even if the debates and arguments continue, these will increase our understanding of the complexity of the Indo-Pacific region, where China, India, and Japan are three important actors.

Jayant Prasad
Director General
Institute for Defence Studies and Analyses

Acknowledgements

This Volume is an academic outcome of IDSA's outreach activity with think tanks and academics across the Indo-Pacific region. The initial conception of the Volume can be traced back to a research idea on China's 'Belt and Road Initiative' (BRI). Following several discussions, it was decided to widen the scope and situate the study in the larger Indo-Pacific space by exploring the complex interplay between geo-political and geo-economic variables shaping three Asian power's – China, India and Japan –broader ideas, interests and visions for the region.

The theme of the Volume was decided keeping in mind the changing environment in the Indo-Pacific region that affects India's policy positioning and strategic interests in the region. The collaboration between a wide networks of scholars from across Indo-Pacific region certainly enriched the research project.

The editors would like to sincerely express their gratitude to the Director General, Shri Jayant Prasad, for his continued intellectual guidance and encouragement. We also thank Deputy Director General Maj. General Alok Deb for his support.

We are grateful to each of the contributors for bringing in diverse perspectives into this Volume. Their wealth of experience and in-depth understanding makes this Volume interesting and timely. Any conflict in the national perspective of countries discussed in the Volume is only meant to enrich academic debates, discussions and scholarly deliberations. However, neither editors nor the Institute assumes any responsibility for an author's individual arguments, citations, facts, figures or perspectives. Any errors or factual incongruities in any of the chapters in the Volume are the sole responsibility of the individual author.

We would also like to thank Mr Vivek Kaushik and Ms Nidhi Pant for facilitating the completion of this Volume by providing valuable editorial assistance.

Dr Jagannath P. Panda & Dr Titli Basu

List of Contributors

Justyna Szczudlik is Head of Asia-Pacific Programme and China analyst at the Polish Institute of International Affairs (PISM). She holds a PhD in Political Science from the University of Warsaw (2015), an MA in Chinese Studies from the University of Warsaw (2008) and an MA in Political Science from the University of Wroclaw (2002). She studied Chinese language at the College of Advanced Chinese Training, Beijing Language and Culture University, Beijing, and at the National Cheng-chi University in Taipei. Her research focuses on China's foreign policy, especially China-Central and Eastern Europe relations including China-Poland relations.

Susanne Kamerling is Researcher and Lecturer at the International Relations and International Organisation Department of the University of Groningen and Associate Fellow at the Netherlands Institute of International Relations 'Clingendael' in The Hague. She is finishing her PhD on the role-perception and role-behaviour of China and India in international security issues since the end of the Cold War. She was Visiting Fellow at the Tsinghua University, Beijing and at the Institute for Defence Studies and Analysis (IDSA), Delhi. She has a background in Political Science and International Development Studies (University of Amsterdam, the Netherlands, and SciencesPo, Paris, France). Her research interests include international relations theory, foreign and security policy of China and India, security issues in Asia and EU-Asia relations.

Huang Yunsong is Professor of Law, Coordinator of China Center for South Asian Studies, and Associate Dean at School of International Studies, the Sichuan University. In 2012, he received his PhD in law from the Sichuan University. He has held research scholarships in Pakistan, India and the US. He did his postdoctoral research on international law at the University of Michigan Law School. His research focuses on international law, South Asian studies. His current research projects include improving regional cooperation between China and South Asia, and population change in the China-India Trans-border Region.

Simon Shen is Associate Professor and Associate Programme Director of the Global Studies at the Faculty of Social Science, Chinese University of Hong Kong. A graduate of the University of Oxford and Yale University, he is one of the few international relations scholars originating from Hong Kong who has earned both local and international recognition. He has published over 70 academic articles, including in the prestigious *China Quarterly, China Review* and *Journal of Contemporary China*. He is also Lead Writer (Global) at the *Hong Kong Economic Journal* and International Relations Consultant of the *Bloomberg Business Magazine*.

Ming Shih Shen is Director and Associate Professor at the Graduate Institute of Strategic Studies and International Affairs, War College, National Defence University, Republic of China (Taiwan). He is Adjunct Associate Professor, Tamkang University. He holds a PhD in Political Science from the National Defence University (2005), an MA from the National Chengchi University, Taiwan (1995) and a BA from the Taiwan Military Academy (1985). His research topics include strategic theory, PLA studies, national security, defence organisation and India's national defence.

Christian Wagner is Senior Fellow at the German Institute for International and Security Affairs (SWP) in Berlin. He has held various positions at the Universities of Freiburg and Mainz and the Centre for Modern Oriental Studies in Berlin. From 1996 to 2001, he was Assistant Professor of Political Science at the Rostock University where he submitted his habilitation on India's Foreign Policy. Before he joined the SWP in 2003, he was Senior Research Fellow at the Centre for Development Research, University of Bonn. He was Visiting Fellow at the Observer Research Foundation (ORF), at the Jawaharlal Nehru Institute for Advanced Studies (JNIAS) and at the Institute for Defence Studies and Analyses (IDSA). His main areas of interest are India and South Asia with a special focus on foreign policy and security issues.

Sukjoon Yoon is a retired Captain of the Republic of Korea Navy, and is currently Senior Fellow at the Korea Institute for Military Affairs (KIMA). Captain Yoon's more than 30 years of commissioned service included 13 years at sea as Surface Warfare Officer and several command and staff appointments. He has been Director of Maritime Strategy Studies at the Naval War College, Commanding Officer of the four ROKS, Director of Policy Division, ROKN HQs and Adjunct Professor of the Centre for Chinese Studies, IFANS, KNDA, Korea. He holds a Ph. D in International Politics from Bristol University, UK. His most recent works include *The Korean Maritime Strategy: Issues and Challenges* (2011); "Implications of Xi Jinping's True Maritime Power: Its Context, Significance, and Impact on the Region" (2015); and "Decoding China's Maritime Aspiration" (2017).

Yasuyuki Ishida is a Researcher on International Relations and Asian Studies. His current research interests include Japan's diplomacy in the Asia-Indo-Pacific and Japan-India-China relations. He has been associated with the Japan Institute of International Affairs (JIIA), Institute for Defence Studies and Analyses (IDSA), Australian Strategic Policy Institute (ASPI), Council for Security Cooperation in the Asia Pacific (CSCAP) and Japan-India Association. He has conducted various policy-related researches including "Japan's Diplomacy in the Indo-Pacific Era" (March 2015) and "The East Asia Summit as a Tool for Strengthening the Rules-based Regional Order in the Asia-Pacific" (December 2014). He holds a PhD from the Jawaharlal Nehru University (New Delhi), a BA and an MA from the Keio University (Tokyo) and a diploma from the University of Wales (Aberystwyth).

Takashi Terada is Professor of International Relations at Dôshisha University, Kyoto, Japan. He received his PhD from the Australian National University in 1999. Before taking up his current position in April 2012, he was Assistant Professor at the National University of Singapore (1999-2006) and Associate and Full Professor at Waseda University (2006-2011). He was also Visiting Fellow at the University of Warwick, UK (2011-12) and at the Woodrow Wilson International Centre for Scholars, Washington DC (2012), and Operating Adviser for the US-Japan Institute (USJI) (2011~). His areas of specialty include international political economy in the Asia-Pacific; theoretical and empirical studies of Asian regionalism and regional integration; and Japanese politics and foreign policy. His publications include *East Asian and Asia-Pacific Regional Integration: Institutional and Normative Competitions among Great-powers* (in Japanese, 2013). He is the recipient of the 2005 J.G. Crawford Award.

Ryohei Kasai is Visiting Researcher at the Centre for South Asian Studies, Gifu Women's University, Japan. He holds an MA from the Aoyama Gakuin University, Japan. He has taught courses on international relations in South Asia, Japan-India relations and Indian politics at the University of Tokyo, Waseda University, Komazawa University and Yokohama City University. He previously served as Political Researcher/Advisor at the Japanese embassies in China, India and Pakistan. His recent publications include *Modi Changes India* (in Japanese, 2017).

Satoru Nagao is Visiting Fellow at the Hudson Institute. His research area is Japan-India-US security cooperation. He is also Research Fellow at the Institute for Future Engineering (strategy, defence policy); Visiting Research Fellow at the Research Institute for Oriental Cultures, Gakushuin University; Research Fellow at the Japan Forum for Strategic Studies;

Associate at the Society of Security and Diplomatic Policy Studies; Senior Fellow at the Institute of National Security Studies, Sri Lanka; and Senior Research Fellow of the Indian Military Review. He was Visiting Scholar at the Centre for Strategic & International Studies in Washington DC. He was also Research Fellow at the Tokyo Foundation and the Ocean Policy Research Foundation and Lecturer at the Gakushuin, Aoyama-Gakuin and Komazawa Universities. He received his PhD from the Gakushuin University in 2011 for his thesis entitled "India's Military Strategy", the first research thesis on this topic in Japan.

Takuya Shimodaira is Senior Research Fellow at the Security Studies Department and Policy Simulation Division, National Institute for Defence Studies (NIDS), Tokyo since 2016. He is a Captain in JMSDF. He is also Adjunct Lecturer at the Kokushikan University and Director of the Crisis & Risk Management Society of Japan. He was Visiting Military Professor in Joint Military Operations Department, US Naval War College, from 2014 to 2016. He received his PhD in Political Science from the Kokushikan University in Tokyo. His research focuses on maritime security in the Indo-Pacific region, the Japan-US alliance and non-traditional security. His recent publications include *The Security of Japan: The Maritime Security and The Regional Security* (in Japanese, 2018); *The Complete Picture of the U.S. Naval War College* (in Japanese, 2017); "The Japan Maritime Self-Defense Force in the Age of Multilateral Cooperation" (Spring 2014); and "Cooperating in the South China Sea" (April 2015).

Lee Cordner is Fellow at the Indo-Pacific Governance Research Centre, University of Adelaide, Australia, and former Australian Navy Commodore. He is an international strategic risk analyst with extensive academic and professional expertise in Indian and Pacific Ocean maritime security. He has been Visiting Research Fellow at the US Naval War College, Newport, US; Visiting International Fellow at the Institute for Defence Studies and Analyses (IDSA), New Delhi, India; and Visiting Fellow at the S. Rajaratnam School of International Studies (RSIS), Singapore. Lee was Co-chair of a Council for Security Cooperation in the Asia-Pacific (CSCAP) Study Group on offshore oil and gas safety and security in the Asia-Pacific, and he is a member of the Indian Ocean Research Group (IORG).

Dr. Jagannath P. Panda is a Research Fellow and Centre Coordinator for East Asia at the Institute for Defence Studies and Analyses (IDSA), New Delhi, India. He is an expert on China, East Asia and Indo-Pacific security. Dr. Panda is in charge of East Asia Centre's academic and administrative activities, including the Track-II and Track 1.5 dialogues with the Chinese, Japanese and Korean think-tanks/institutes. He is a recipient of V. K. Krishna Menon Memorial Gold Medal (2000) from the Indian Society of International Law & Diplomacy in New Delhi. Dr. Panda is the author of the book *India-China Relations: Politics of Resources, Identity and Authority in a Multipolar World Order* (Routledge: 2017). He is also the author of the book *China's Path to Power: Party, Military and the Politics of State Transition* (Pentagon Press: 2010). He has also edited many books to his credit. Dr. Panda is a Member of the Editorial Board of the *Journal of Asian Public Policy* (Routledge). Dr. Panda has published in leading peer-reviewed journals like *Journal of Asian Public Policy (Routledge), Journal of Asian and African Studies (Sage), Asian Perspective* (Lynne Reiner), *Journal of Contemporary China* (Routledge), *Georgetown Journal of Asian Affairs* (Georgetown), *Strategic Analyses* (Routledge), *China Report* (Sage), *Indian Foreign Affairs Journal* (MD Publication), *Portuguese Journal of International Affairs* (Euro Press) etc.

Kenneth King was Director of the Centre of African Studies and Professor of International and Comparative Education at the Edinburgh University for many years. He is now Emeritus Professor in its Schools of Education and of Social and Political Studies. His research has focused on the politics and history of international education, aid policy and skills development, especially in the informal sector. He edited *NORRAG News* for 30 years, until 2017. Since 2006, amongst other research activities, he has analysed China's educational aid to Africa, and also authored *China's Aid and Soft Power in Africa* (2013). In 2016, he began to research India's development cooperation with Africa, with a focus on skills and human resource development. His next book is *Education, Skills and International Cooperation: Comparative and Historical Perspectives* (forthcoming).

Titli Basu is Associate Fellow at the East Asia Centre, Institute for Defence Studies and Analysis (IDSA). Her research interests include great power politics in the Indo-Pacific; East Asian security issues with special focus on Japanese security, strategy and foreign policy and India-Japan relations. She has published several research articles on these issues including in the *India Quarterly: A Journal of International Affairs, Tamkang Journal of International Affairs, The Asan Forum, East Asia Forum, Asian Journal of Public Affairs* and *Indian Foreign Affairs Journal*. She completed her doctoral thesis from the Jawaharlal Nehru University in New Delhi. She was Visiting Fellow at the National Institute for Defence Studies, Japan, in 2017. Earlier, she was associated with the University of Tokyo as Visiting Research Fellow, and was recipient of the Japan Foundation fellowship in 2010. She has also been associated with the Institute for Global Environmental Strategies, Japan.

Dattesh D. Parulekar is Assistant Professor of International Relations and Area Studies at the Department of International Relations and the UGC Centre for Latin American Studies, Goa University. His areas specialisation include India's foreign policy and diplomacy, Chinese political economy, strategic maritime affairs in the Indo-Pacific, strategic issues in West Asian security and Latin American and Caribbean (LAC) studies. A Visiting Faculty at the Naval War College, INS Mandovi (Goa), and the College of Defence Management (Secunderabad), he professes expertise in myriad themes of Chinese Studies and broader strategic aspects of Peace and Conflict Studies. He also lectures periodically at public universities and think tanks across China and institutions in South Asia, Europe and Latin America. A former Fulbright Fellow, he completed his doctoral research on the theme of "US-UN Relationship in the Use of Force and Coercive Humanitarian Intervention in the Post-Cold War Era", vide a stint at the School of Advanced International Studies (SAIS), Johns Hopkins University, Washington DC.

Munmun Majumdar is Associate Professor at the Department of Political Science, North-Eastern Hill University, Shillong, Meghalaya. Her area of specialisation is Southeast Asia. Her ongoing research focuses on the ASEAN and Conflict management in the South China Sea. She holds a PhD from the Centre for South, Southeast and Southwest Pacific Studies, Jawaharlal Nehru University, New Delhi. She has been Visiting Fellow at the Institute for Defence Studies and Analysis (IDSA), Visiting Faculty at the Centre for South and South East Asian Studies, Calcutta University, Kolkata, and Visiting Professor at the ASEAN Centre, Chulalongkorn University, Bangkok. She was awarded the University Grants Commission (UGC) Research Award (earlier known as the Career Award and National Fellow) from 1999 to 2002 to pursue postdoctoral research and the UGC Major Project from 2003 to 2006, and has been an Associate at the Institute of Advance Study, Shimla. She has published three books and several articles.

1

Introduction

Jagannath P. Panda and Titli Basu

What This Book Is about

The Indo-Pacific order is entering a new phase of interaction and interface. The major power rivalry in this theatre, reinforcing old and new modes of power alignments and realignments, is stimulating this competition. The grandeur of this power competition is certainly global and cross-continental, and yet very local. The planning and initiatives of Asia's three major countries – China, India and Japan – progressively point to this. Their foreign policies are certainly guided by domestic interests, being closely linked to their national planning, domestic economic development and national perspectives. The policies and perspectives are executed keeping in view the international positioning and rising influence of these countries in Asia and beyond, mainly in the Asia-Pacific or in the newly coined Indo-Pacific paradigm.[1] Moreover, the trajectory of the region is heavily influenced by a range of conflicting subjects. Maritime disputes between China and Japan and China and Southeast Asian countries, land boundary dispute between China and India, demand for energy resources, conflicting connectivity and corridor proposals, and the intent to emerge as stronger maritime powers are the principal issues that are currently at play in the Indo-Pacific.

Among all these, infrastructural development across the Indo-Pacific has recently been one of the high points of discussion. Sustainable growth and connectivity are heavily dependent upon infrastructural development. The true potential of this critical area will remain unfulfilled without cross-border flows of trade and investments, trans-regional connectivity and corridors and people-to-people contacts. A plethora of infrastructural initiatives, especially by China, Japan and India, has shaped the political trajectory and environment in Asia, and largely the Indo-Pacific. China's Belt and Road Initiative (BRI), earlier known as the One Belt, One Road (OBOR) initiative, under President Xi Jinping and Japan's Expanded Partnership for Quality Infrastructure (EPQI) under Prime Minister Shinzo Abe are two striking strategic initiatives that have put the spotlight on infrastructural politics. India has strengthened its foreign policy outreach and envisioned advancing its much-needed domestic infrastructural requirements besides focusing on transnational or trans-regional connectivity. India's competing vision to advance its international positioning in the Indo-Pacific and categorising Japan as a "special partner", without really abandoning China as a partner at various levels, explain the numerous shades of politics that Asia, or the region of Indo-Pacific at large, is currently navigating. Competing national perspectives of China, India and Japan, which influence the future of the Indo-Pacific, underline this politics. This Volume examines the competing and contending national perspectives of these three countries of Asia, particularly taking into account their approaches towards infrastructure development and national interests.

In a nutshell, this Volume aims to analyse the competing policies and perspectives that exist among the three major Asian actors on infrastructural development across the Indo-Pacific. It examines their policies and perspectives on infrastructure developmental initiatives and the commonalities and contradictions between them that shape their ideas and interests. Examining their national perspectives with regard to their approaches on infrastructure and connectivity is critical to the Indo-Pacific region since the future of the Asian century is heavily dependent on the relationship pattern among these three countries. The Volume explores the strategic contention that exists between China's Asia-Pacific strategy, factoring BRI, and Japan's Free and Open Indo-Pacific Strategy and EPQI. It equally takes into account other grand initiatives, such as the Asia-Africa Growth Corridor (AAGC) that Japan and India have envisioned together to enhance their positioning in the Indo-Pacific, while analysing India's policies and perspectives in the region. It also analyses India's national planning and perspectives on connectivity and infrastructure in the geostrategic and geo-economic context of the Indo-Pacific region. In brief, the Volume examines the power politics concerning infrastructure and connectivity that has already brought China, Japan and India into strategic spotlight in the Indo-Pacific region.

China's Ambitions and Interests

China under Xi Jinping is envisioned to emerge as a "new power". This vision combines both national and international objectives as parts of China's grand strategy. If establishing a "fully modern" economy and a "prosperous society" by 2035 continues to be the main short-term target behind this "new power" ambition, then achieving comprehensive national power (CNP) by 2050 to establish China as the "global leader in terms of composite national strength and international influence" remains both the national and international long-term target for Beijing.[2] Debate continues inside and outside China, whether the country would succeed in achieving its intended targets; but China under Xi Jinping will move ahead with a number of domestic and international initiatives to achieve its goals by 2035 and 2050 as part of its grand strategy. Central to this grand strategy is the BRI, a flagship initiative that Xi Jinping introduced to the world in 2013, which is primarily aimed at revitalising the Chinese economic growth by engaging more intently with the outside world by promoting international cooperation through "policy, infrastructure, trade, financial, and people-to-people connectivity".[3]

Focusing primarily on infrastructural investment and promoting connectivity projects, the BRI blends delicately China's domestic and international objectives that will not only help in sustaining its economy but will also raise China's influence internationally. Xi Jinping's statement at the May 2017 BRI Summit in Beijing that "infrastructure connectivity is the foundation of development through cooperation" illustrate this point.[4] As a long-term initiative, domestically, the BRI is clearly linked to address the challenges that China is currently facing while creating opportunities for economic and political advantages. Legitimising the rule of the Communist Party of China (CPC) through sustained economic growth is the key domestic motive behind the BRI. The Chinese economy has been under stress for some time, and the growth rate has slowed down. In 2016, the economy grew at 6.7 per cent, which was the slowest growth rate since 1990.[5] The domestic intent behind the BRI is to revitalise the economy and bring back its impressive growth rate that will improve the CPC's image nationally, if not internationally. In fact, the BRI is an initiative to take advantage of China's US$3 trillion-plus capital reserves to address the structural difficulties in the economy, which the leadership has labelled as a "new normal" economy due to its slower growth rate.

One of the main objectives behind the launch of the BRI is to address the challenges of industrial over-capacity.[6] The BRI will establish a connection between China's domestic industrial output with the neighbourhood and international supply routes that will be helpful in safeguarding employment within China and protecting its industrial units in key areas such as steel, cement and construction industries. The immediate targets are to expand China's export markets, promote the flow of domestic goods outside the country, boost the demand for Chinese products internationally through the promotion of connectivity and corridor projects between China and the outside world,[7] promote the renminbi as an international currency[8] and revitalise state-owned enterprises (SOEs) that have been struggling to contribute to the economy for some time. Attending to trade issues, such as tariffs and costs in the transportation of goods, is another important area that the BRI aims to address for China.

The BRI is further aimed at invigorating the Chinese domestic relationship configuration between different provinces, redirecting the demand-supply chain and empowering the provinces that are land and maritime bound through trade connectivity and corridor routes. Beijing's March 2015 *Vision and Action Plan*, released by the National Development and Reform Commission (NDRC), offers a clear picture on how both soft and hard developmental components, economic development strategies through intergovernmental communication mechanisms, regional cooperation, connectivity and people-to-people contacts are integral aspects of China's BRI.[9] Reforming domestic and foreign policies; addressing the existing gap between urban and rural China; tackling unemployment, poverty and corruption; solidifying the country's international posturing; and bringing forth innovative ideas nationally and internationally while promoting Beijing's national interests are some of China's other current objectives.

Internationally, these objectives are indeed being pursued with a "new era" foreign policy strategy that focuses on a Chinese-envisioned international order through an assertive and active diplomacy. The immediate effect of this diplomacy, rather strategy, is visible in the Asia-Pacific region. Establishing stronger bilateral contacts, signing trade and economic deals, investing in connectivity and corridor projects and promoting stronger Chinese soft and hard power presence are indeed important parts of this strategy. China's approach towards Asia, mainly in the context of the Asia-Pacific, currently reveals this. A multipurpose foreign policy with a focus on Asia has been unfolding for some time under Xi Jinping. Calling for "Asia for Asians" as part of its new security thinking in Asia, Beijing is visualising to establish an Asian order free from the external powers' influence, mainly the US. In the recent past, Chinese advocacy to form a "new type of great power relations" in order to equalise China's international status with the US appears to be one of the key thresholds of its foreign policy arch. But Beijing's overall foreign policy thrust rests on Asia and in the immediate Asia-Pacific region, as it has realised that the region is key to China's international positioning. Under Xi Jinping's leadership, a "new security concept" that is linked with China's Asia-Pacific vision, primarily aimed at establishing a progressively China-driven regional order, is visible.[10] Beijing did not really envision taking a leadership role in the first decade of the current century.[11] Neither was China's action leadership-centric nor was its CNP at a level where it could have envisioned for itself a real leadership role in the region and the world at large. This Chinese reluctance seem to have faded away in recent years, with Beijing aiming to emerge as a leader, immediately at the regional level with global ambitions.

A number of high-profile initiatives exemplify this Chinese intent: (1) BRI; (2) establishment of the Asian Infrastructure Investment Bank (AIIB); (3) taking the lead in the formation of the New Development Bank (NDB) with the cooperation of the BRICS countries (Brazil, Russia, India, China and South Africa); (4) expanding the Shanghai Cooperation Organisation (SCO) by involving new South Asian countries like India and Pakistan; (5) aiming to promote the regional integrative model of the Free Trade Area of the Asia-Pacific (FTAAP); (6) emphasising the Regional Comprehensive Economic Partnership (RCEP); and (7) creating a platform like the Conference on Interaction and Confidence-Building Measures (CICA) in Asia. No doubt, some of these new initiatives and propositions are mainly aimed at overcoming the strategic difficulties that China still faces in the regional and global security and economic environment. Nonetheless, the focus/primary intent is the country's growing ambition to be a "new power". A new mode of multi-textured strategy is visible in China's international approach, forming the core of its "new era" foreign policy diplomacy. Designing a new regional and international environment that is skewed in its favour, by focusing on the immediate neighbourhood of the Asia-Pacific, is one of the hallmarks of this "new era" strategy. Overall, focusing primarily on infrastructure investment, the BRI is an effective medium for China's multi-textured strategy which involves the following "five Cs": *connectivity, corridors, cooperation with neighbours, co-funding multilateral projects, country-specific reach* and *continental* strategy. This multi-textured strategy is imminently visible in the Asia-Pacific region currently.

Promoting *connectivity* with the neighbourhood has been one of the most important aspects of China's new foreign policy under Xi Jinping.

Adequate emphasis is being given not only to strengthen rail, road and highway networks within China but also to strategically link China with the immediate and extended neighbourhood through these connectivity linkages. Both the Silk Road Economic Belt (SREB) and the Maritime Silk Road (MSR) – two important constituents of the BRI – promote connectivity between China and the outside world. The SREB aims to connect China's overland infrastructure and connectivity network with the Eurasia region, particularly with Central Asia. The intent is to empower China's northwest provinces like Xinjiang, Ningxia, Gansu and Shaanxi, the lesser developed provinces, by establishing direct trading routes through rail, roads and highway networks. The MSR will establish direct connectivity for China with the Southeast Asian region that will empower economically coastal provinces like Jiangsu, Zhejiang, Shanghai, Guangdong, Fujian, Shandong and Hainan. This will facilitate China's entry into the Bay of Bengal and Indian Ocean Region (IOR). China's gross domestic product (GDP) used to be heavily dependent upon Shandong, Henan, Jiangsu, Zhejiang and Guangdong, but their performance has slipped over the years. The MSR will help China in promoting this domestic target while facilitating overall connectivity networks with Southeast Asia and the IOR.

Building six *corridors* under the BRI has been central to China's external economic and strategic engagement: China-Pakistan Economic Corridor (CPEC); Bangladesh-China-India-Myanmar (BCIM); China-Mongolia-Russia Corridor; a New Eurasia "Land Bridge"; Corridors from China to Central Asia and Western Asia; and China-Indochina Peninsular Corridor.[12] These corridors constitute an integral aspect of China's Asia-Pacific strategy that would facilitate China's trade, energy and pipeline networks with the different regions.

Cooperation with neighbouring countries is another hallmark strategy of the BRI. Offering lucrative deals, granting cooperative packages to enhance China's own presence and signing trade and economic deals through free trade agreements (FTAs) are all part of this strategy. This strategy is being implemented under three major rubrics: "win-win outcomes", "mutual benefit" and "harmony, openness and inclusiveness", where a China-led regional operating order is unfolding rapidly.

Co-funding China's own projects through multilateral channels, institutions and banks is another important strategy under the BRI. The AIIB, Silk Road Fund (SRF) and NDB help China by not only funding and promoting BRI projects but also providing an international platform to display its leadership role. The AIIB is increasingly being seen as a competitor to the Japan-led Asian Development Bank (ADB). The Chinese leadership has long been involved in designing an effective Asia policy to help China leave a stamp of its authority. The establishment of the Boao Forum for Asia (BFA) in February 2001 was a prelude to this final objective.

Country-specific outreach is another important aspect of the BRI. China today has a stronger network of relations with most countries. The intensity of this policy is Asia-specific, wherein countries in South Asia, Southeast Asia and Central Asia are offered priority. Equally important is effective *continental outreach*. Demographically, the BRI aims to connect China with 4.4 billion people in these three continents, which is almost 62 per cent of the global population.[13] Geographically, the BRI establishes an economic link between the Chinese economy and the rest of the participating economies in Asia, Africa and Europe where the target is to take advantage of the US$2.1 trillion economy. In terms of resource target, both SREB and MSR facilitate the Chinese interest in building economic corridors, acquiring overseas land through infrastructure investment and having a greater control over maritime resources through a stronger maritime diplomacy.

Beijing thus pursues a complex and compound approach that exhibits an accommodative yet aggressive diplomacy through the BRI – what has been described as China's "new diplomacy".[14] Without really endorsing the concept of the Indo-Pacific, Beijing at present pursues a "going global strategy" in the Asia-Pacific and beyond for sealing overseas deals, such as oil and gas contracts by pushing Chinese companies to invest overseas and purchase assets that are critical to China's interests. Establishing partnerships to deny privileges is also a medium that is fast emerging as a convenient strategy for China. The Chinese White Paper on Asia-Pacific Security, released in 2017, and Xi Jinping's BRI initiative reveal a clear picture wherein "connectivity", "partnerships" and "infrastructural development" remain the catch phrases of Beijing's foreign policy strategy; most of the contributors to this Volume have referred to this aspect. Placing security as the centrepiece of its approach, Beijing has gradually pushed "strategic partnership" of a consultative character where building infrastructure in the immediate and extended neighbourhood is a priority. Promoting the BRI remains the central proposition of this priority. The 19th National Congress of the CPC, held from October 18-24, 2017, adopted a new resolution amending the Party's Constitution to include the promotion of the BRI as one of the major future objectives of China. The inclusion of the BRI in the CPC Constitution elucidates that it is a long-term national project. China has brought more policy weight to the initiative and offered legal sanctity to the BRI by mentioning it in the CPC Charter. The inclusion further marks that the BRI is not merely an economic policy proposition;

rather, it is a "political project" that Beijing would like to pursue for its national developmental programme.[15] The constitutional amendment puts together the inclusion of the BRI with China's urge to "build a community of shared interest" and to achieve "shared growth" through "discussion and collaboration". This implies that inherent in the success of the BRI is Beijing's leadership ambition of shaping a world order that slowly positions China as the centre of the world.

The execution of the BRI is being carried out in a way that projects China as a "moderately prosperous society". The BRI is more a national security strategy than a national ambition, and is being pursued keeping in view China's overseas national security interests in securing energy resources, gaining investment deals and crafting bilateral and multilateral deals, eventually contributing to domestic economic stability and China's rise. At the 19th National Congress of the CPC, Xi Jinping stressed on revitalising the SOEs in order to help China in securing stable overseas deals. Building a "moderately prosperous society" and achieving "socialist modernisation" by 2035 are therefore part of a strategy linked to the CPC's overseas interests to secure more energy and financial resources, eventually promote Xi's pet project, BRI, and carry forward the economic development momentum. The aim is to expand China's overseas economic interests through connectivity and corridor projects, by establishing strong trade and economic contacts, and to build a regional and global consensus in Beijing's favour, i.e. positioning China as the driver of globalisation.[16] China's ambitions are growing; its only challenge is how to establish partnerships that would not only be advantageous to its rise but equally also be serving to check the influence of other competing powers. Both Japan and India are seen as competitors of China. Xi Jinping's "new era" foreign policy strategy, which focuses on infrastructure investment and connectivity, illustrates this contention.

In brief, a new grand global strategy under Xi Jinping is unfolding where Beijing's ambition is to emerge as the leader of globalisation and free trade, a role that the US has played for decades. Xi Jinping's repeated stress on making China the leader of globalisation, including in his speech at the 2017 World Economic Forum in Davos, indicates that China's ambition is global, where the immediate focus is to maximise an economic order in the Asia-Pacific region. This Chinese ambition becomes significant at a time when the US foreign policy under Donald Trump has become more "inward" looking.[17] The geopolitical hierarchical order in the Asia-Pacific is becoming divided between an economic and a military order, with China's rise being the looming factor. The US is perhaps still the leader of the military order, but China's growing influence is shaping the economic order that is driving the region, forcing other countries, including India and Japan, to rethink their positioning in the region. Moreover, China's stronger economic policy and increasing influence are encouraging many smaller economies in the Asia-Pacific region to associate with China as partners, which are also slowly distancing themselves from the US security umbrella. Besides, Beijing's security presence in the Asia-Pacific is constantly rising, where China is gradually establishing its overseas military bases, naval stationing points and ports that would facilitate its maritime diplomacy. President Trump's transaction- and bilateral-centric foreign policy in the region is only solidifying the Chinese strength. These emerging geopolitical conditions in the Indo-Pacific are encouraging countries like Japan and India to take a relook into their respective positions and outreach in the region.

Japan's Ambitions and Strategy

Prime Minister Shinzo Abe expanded Japan's strategic canvas and designed the "Free and Open Indo-Pacific Strategy", encompassing the Indian and Pacific Oceans as a unified strategic theatre. This strategy is shaped by Japan's pursuit of geo-economic and geopolitical interests and maintaining stability in this maritime "super-region". Abe's objective is to maintain the US-led order that has served its national interests and project Japan as an effective ally to the US in guarding the global commons. Japan's "Free and Open Indo-Pacific Strategy" aligns with President Trump's National Security Strategy (NSS) that identifies the Indo-Pacific as a strategic priority for the US, where Washington has served as the key patron of a liberal economic architecture and maritime order.

While the Japanese official discourse often refers to Chinese activities as "unilateral actions to change the status quo", the US NSS has identified China as a revisionist power and argued that Beijing "wants to shape a world antithetical to U.S. values and interests". As "China seeks to displace the US in the Indo-Pacific region, expand the reaches of its state-driven economic model and reorder the region in its favour",[18] the NSS strives for more cooperation and contribution from the US allies and partners. In this regard, both the US and Japan envision India's role as one of the anchors of stability in the Indo-Pacific. The US has welcomed India's emergence as a leading global power and a strong strategic and defence partner, and further indicated its support for India's "leadership role in Indian Ocean security and throughout the broader region". Japan's maiden NSS, published in 2013, outlines the need to deepen cooperative ties with its partners, including South Korea, Australia, the Association of Southeast Asian Nations (ASEAN) countries and India, with whom Japan shares universal values and strategic interests. In addition, the 2013 National Defence Programme Guidelines (NDPG) categorically argue: "Japan will strengthen its relationship with India in a broad range of fields, including maritime security, through joint training and exercises as well as joint implementation of international peacekeeping activities."[19]

Prime Minister Abe's Indo-Pacific vision is anchored on the principles of universal values and international norms. Japan's value-led diplomacy is aimed at furthering a stable international order with regard to the rule of law and freedom of navigation that serve the interests of regional stakeholders.[20] There were two key factors which allowed Japan to anchor its grand strategy on universal values and norms: First, following the collapse of the Soviet Union and the end of the Cold War, Japan was in search for a new role within the redefined framework of its alliance with the US. Second, Japan's position as one of the most powerful economies in the world gave it the national confidence to draw from its economic clout and diplomatic investment and work towards a pacifist image. Japan focused on pursuing a value-led foreign policy to demonstrate its commitment to protect the international order based on rules and universal values, including freedom, democracy and the rule of law.

Nobukatsu Kanehara, one of the key intellectuals shaping the debate on Japan's grand strategy and national interests, has argued that invaluable lessons from history have shaped the 21st century Japan into a nation that not only respects universal values but also embraces a leadership role in defending these values. According to him, it was Japan's ethical immaturity that misled the country in the first half of the last century and made Japan miss the unfolding paradigm shift from European imperialism to US-led liberalism.[21] As value-oriented foreign policy gained traction following the Cold War, Tokyo designed several value-based constructs like Taro Aso's "Arc of Freedom and Prosperity", Abe's conceptualisation of "Confluence of the Two Seas", Quadrilateral Initiative, "Asia's Democratic Security Diamond" and the latest articulation of the "Free and Open Indo-Pacific Strategy".

Redefining the alignments, maritime democracies are crafting a shared vision for the Indo-Pacific region underpinned by the convergence of geostrategic, geopolitical and geo-economic interests. To deliver its international responsibilities of upholding universal values and maintaining a rule-based order, Japan aims to operate within the alliance arrangement with the US and further weave action-oriented strategic partnerships with likeminded countries in Asia and Europe. Japan's "Free and Open Indo-Pacific Strategy" aims to tap the dynamism of two continents – Asia and Africa – and achieve greater regional integration along the Indian and Pacific Oceans by promoting high-quality infrastructure building and improved connectivity.

Japan's objective is to offset the expanding Chinese regional influence as President Xi Jinping pursues the Chinese Dream, employing his mega-infrastructure enterprise through the BRI. Chinese assertiveness in the South China Sea, its network of strategic port building in the Indian Ocean and its first overseas base in Djibouti at the crossroads of Africa and the Middle East have raised Japan's anxiety vis-à-vis Chinese ambitions. Japan has underscored the critical importance of maritime security and the rule of law together with freedom of navigation and unimpeded commerce as important pillars of Japan's new strategy in the Indo-Pacific. At the 2014 Shangri-La Dialogue, Abe argued that the case of keeping oceans open as global commons and observing international law which is "not created by any particular country or countries, nor was it the product of some sort of group. Instead, it is the product of wisdom, cultivated over a great many years for the well-being and the prosperity of all humankind".[22]

The NSS of Japan conceptualised Tokyo's role as a "Proactive Contributor to Peace" based on the principles of international cooperation. It is imperative to design and maintain a stable international security environment that favours Japan by proactively engaging in international affairs. Strategic functioning of Japan's "Proactive Contribution to Peace" is witnessed as Tokyo steps up in shouldering the responsibility of delivering "public good in maintaining a free and open Indo-Pacific".[23] The roots of Japan's "Free and Open Indo-Pacific Strategy" can be traced back to Abe's celebrated speech, "Confluence of the Two Seas", in the Indian Parliament in 2007, wherein he argued that the Pacific and the Indian Oceans present a "dynamic coupling as seas of freedom and of prosperity". Pursuing this strategy, Japan has invested in bolstering its alliance with the US and also worked towards building regional networks with maritime democracies for maintaining a maritime order based on international law. India has progressively featured as an important pole in Shinzo Abe's idea of Asia, as echoed in his book *Utsukushii kuni e,* and is perceived as a critical strategic anchor in Abe's latest Indo-Pacific strategy for securing strategic stability and economic prosperity in the Indo-Pacific theatre. Hence, in addition to designing the India-Japan Joint Vision 2025, several trilateral frameworks involving the US and Australia, focusing on maritime security and regional connectivity, have taken shape towards realising a Free and Open Indo-Pacific.

One of the manifestations of Japan's Indo-Pacific Strategy is the formulation of the Quadrilateral Initiative (the "Quad"). The idea of the Quad germinated during the 2004 tsunami when all these four navies engaged in humanitarian assistance and disaster relief (HADR) operations, following which a loose framework was set up among the foreign secretaries of the four countries. In 2006-2007, during Abe's first term as prime minister, Japan instituted the Quadrilateral Initiative involving maritime democracies of Australia, India, Japan and the US. India began featuring in Tokyo's security outline once the US Department of Defence acknowledged New Delhi as an enduring security partner. The May 2007 US-Japan Security Consultative Committee argued the case for nurturing "partnerships with India" since India's sustained growth is "inextricably tied to the prosperity, freedom, and security of the region".[24] Abe's initial attempts at sustaining the Quadrilateral Initiative lost steam because of then Australian Prime Minister Kevin Rudd's decision to pull out following Chinese reservations towards what it perceived as a potential "Asian NATO". Moreover, India's ideological orientation towards strategic autonomy made New Delhi hesitant under the United Progressive Alliance (UPA)-led government. Nevertheless, both Japan and the US continued to nurture India as a security provider in the region. The 2011 US-Japan Security Consultative Committee articulated welcoming "India as a strong and enduring Asia-Pacific partner" and supported India's increasing involvement in regional architecture.

After a decade-long hiatus, the Quad resurfaced in strategic discourse in 2017 with a joint secretary level meeting held in Manila on the sidelines of the ASEAN and East Asia Summits. The focus was on shared universal values and securing global goods in the Indo-Pacific. Japan under Prime Minister Abe is carving out a new role in regional security architecture underscoring the importance of rule-based order in the Indo-Pacific, freedom of navigation and overflight, respect for international law, maritime security, and so on.[25] While Abe's attempts at the Quad during his first tenure were hasty, leading to its unsustainability, this time the Indo-Pacific strategic environment may prove conducive towards realignments.

In pursuit of strengthening maritime security, Japan has bolstered its defence and security cooperation with partners in the Indo-Pacific. In 2016, Japan initiated the "Vientiane Vision" aimed at advancing defence cooperation with ASEAN members furthering maritime security through capabilities for intelligence, surveillance and reconnaissance (ISR) and search and rescue (SAR). Japan's aim is to share with ASEAN its experience on maritime security; build ASEAN's capacity with regard to HADR,

Peacekeeping Operations (PKO), landmine and unexploded ordnance (UXO) clearance and cybersecurity; transfer equipment and technology to ASEAN; develop human resources; and enhance participation in multilateral joint training and exercises.[26] Beyond ASEAN, Japan has stepped in as a permanent member of the Malabar Exercise alongside the US and India to enhance interoperability between the three navies in addition to facilitating synergies for maritime security operations. This joint exercise involving the three democracies is one of the several activities that underscore a robust trilateral cooperation in the Indo-Pacific region.

Geo-economically, Japan is also pursuing its national economic developmental goals by furthering free trade practices and enhancing economic integration in the Indo-Pacific. Japan has demonstrated leadership in shaping regional trade architecture following the US exist from the Trans-Pacific Partnership free trade agreement.[27] Japan remained committed to free trade and navigated difficult negotiations to carve out what is now called the new Comprehensive and Progressive Agreement for Trans-Pacific Partnership (CPTPP, or TPP-11). Japan has pitched the CPTPP as the "engine to overcome protectionism" emerging in parts of the world. While Abe has strongly urged the Trump administration to consider returning to this mega-trade regime, it was certainly a bold step for Japan to proceed without its alliance partner, the US. Beyond TPP's geo-economic goals of trade liberalisation and market reforms, Japan considered this mega-trade agreement as a strategic tool for advancing its national gains. Japan took the opportunity following the US exit to be the rule setter for regional economic cooperation. Abe has invested considerable political capital to overcome resistance from the farm lobby to the TPP. Abe considers the TPP critical for the success of Abenomics and for his trade strategy. World Bank assessments indicate that, with TPP, Japan's growth rate is likely to increase by an additional 2.7 per cent by 2030, with exports rising by US$23.2 billion annually. Japan worries that in case the US refrains from playing a major role in the regional architecture-building process, China will have an easier path creating a Sino-centric regional order. Such a development is likely to prove to be a monumental challenge for Japan as geopolitical and geo-economic uncertainties intensify regional complexity.[28]

One of the key elements of Abe's Indo-Pacific Strategy is infrastructure export. With infrastructure export, Japan pursues the twin objectives of building a new growth engine to revive the Japanese economy and firming up strategic networks with Asian nations to balance the Chinese regional sway.[29] To this effect, Abe launched the AAGC in collaboration with India. The AAGC is aimed at cultivating value chains and integrating and developing a competitive economic bloc, thereby accelerating Africa's and Asia's development trajectory. The AAGC synergises with Abe's EPQI, which aims to consolidate Japan's regional clout among the emerging economies.[30] The goal is to expand their regional influence by catering to the voracious infrastructure appetite of the emerging economies. With the inception of the AIIB, Prime Minister Abe underscored that Japan in cooperation with the ADB will deliver "high-quality and innovative" infrastructure to Asia and committed $110 billion over five years,[31] representing a 30 per cent northward movement from the earlier funding.[32] Subsequently with EPQI in 2016, Japan decided to finance USD 200 billion over the next five years towards infrastructure projects across the world. With regard to infrastructure export, constructive competition between Asia's two biggest economies is welcome since it will eventually serve the larger objective of enabling the emerging economies of the Indo-Pacific to fuel their national growth engines and boost overall ability to compete in the global economy.[33]

To deliver the responsibilities as a Proactive Contributor to Peace, Japan needs a strong economic base. The June 2013 Japan Revitalisation Strategy articulated the significance of creating new frontiers for growth by capturing the international infrastructure market. It argued for tripling infrastructure sales by 2020. The stage is set in the Indo-Pacific. Japan for long has been a key developmental partner to emerging economies, having invested in several projects, including the Master Plan on ASEAN Connectivity, Japan Mekong Connectivity Initiative Projects and Bay of Bengal Industrial Growth Belt (Big-B). In contrast to Chinese infrastructure initiatives and investment models, Japan has strongly argued, in consensus with the US and India, that projects should be implemented "in an open, transparent and non-exclusive manner based on international standards and responsible debt financing practices, while ensuring respect for sovereignty and territorial integrity, the rule of law and environment".[34] As a provider of capital and technical know-how, Japan is increasingly exploring ways to strengthen connectivity and infrastructure along the Indo-Pacific with partners like India and the US. Stepping up engagement by way of joint projects in South Asia (e.g. in Sri Lanka, Myanmar and Bangladesh), Southeast Asia or Africa will enable Japan to perform a deeper role in the Indo-Pacific.

India's Positioning and Policies

Between China's envisioned "Sino-centric" global order and Japan's rejuvenated universal value based politicking through its active and action-oriented foreign policy under Prime Minister Abe, the spotlight of Asia's power politics is equally heavily concentrated on India, a prominent economy in Asia. With an operational foreign policy that is more Indo-Pacific centric, the Indian foreign policy is at present heavily concentrated on the immediate and extended neighbourhood of Asia. If the foreign policy directives of a country make the persona of the nation, the geographic location of a country constitutes the core of that persona. What makes this foreign policy really dynamic is the geographic position of India, which is at the fulcrum of the "Indo-Pacific", the construct approximating the two important Oceans – the Pacific and the Indian Ocean. In fact, unlike China and Japan, Indian economic outreach is yet to arrive at a stage where it can envision playing a leadership role. Yet, the construct of Indo-Pacific certainly offers a range of options and opportunities to India to play a constructive role in shaping a regional order to its favour. Moreover, given the centrality of Indo-Pacific in an evolving global order, India's approach to this region is fundamentally engaging and futuristic. The fundamentalism in India's approach towards the Indo-Pacific is evidenced in its growing contacts with the countries in the IOR, whereas the future goal is to protect economic and energy interests, primarily the marine resources in the region. A number of foreign policy measures that are closely linked to India's domestic and overseas interests explain this Indian approach to the Indo-Pacific construct.

The Indian outlook towards Indo-Pacific is fundamentally cooperative, and is heavily driven by New Delhi's national interests. Stressing for a stable, secure, free, open and liberal Indo-Pacific order, New Delhi pursues an engaging policy across the region without overlooking that a Sino-centric Asian order is fast emerging with China's rising economic and military influence in the Indo-Pacific. India's current China policy explains its pragmatic outlook. The principal reason for this pragmatism is to engage with China without offering it much strategic elbowroom in Asia or the Indo-Pacific at large. Further, this pragmatism comes from a demand that China must treat India as a *peer* partner rather than just a partner.

For India, Asia is currently passing through a multifaceted regional systemic power complexity where the construct of the Indo-Pacific region is becoming more and more relevant. Acknowledging that the "political and military power is diffused and distributed" in today's global strategic configuration, Prime Minister Narendra Modi stated in the second Raisina Dialogue in New Delhi in January 2017 that a "multi-polarity of the world" and an "increasingly multi-polar Asia" is a dominant reality today.[35] Stressing for peace and economic growth in Indo-Pacific, Modi outlined

India's maritime ambitions on the lines of pursuing freedom of navigation and adherence to international law.[36] India's emergence as a stronger maritime power is one of the main defining features of the Indo-Pacific construct. Advocating for a liberal order and supporting a "free and open Indo-Pacific region", New Delhi's current approach is based on the "engagement plus enlargement" strategy. This implies that India's engagement policy across Asia, including China and Japan, aims to enlarge the canvas of India's positioning in the region as a stronger power. The following five correlated policy priorities can be noticed in the Indian foreign policy under Prime Minister Modi, especially in the context of the Indo-Pacific: (1) Pursuing a "neighbourhood first" foreign policy approach by promoting connectivity with the immediate neighbourhood while upgrading infrastructural development and connectivity linkages within the country; (2) pursuing an intensive "Act East" policy, making a transition from the earlier "Look East" policy; (3) pursuing a maritime policy in the Indian Ocean with a stronger "maritime doctrine"; (4) promoting the notion of inter-regional and intercontinental cooperation for greater global governance; and (5) engaging with major powers while promoting India's national interests. Though primarily building on previous foreign policy focuses, each of these priorities sheds new light on India's foreign policy, constituting the core of New Delhi's approach towards the Indo-Pacific. Moreover, the core objectives are to promote inter-regional connectivity, upgrade domestic and neighbourhood infrastructure and secure the country's economic and other national interests.

First, a "neighbourhood first" foreign policy is the key behind India's Indo-Pacific position at present. Since assuming office in 2014, Modi has given special importance to the neighbouring countries. Modi's foreign policy focus has been more on the neighbouring countries, particularly in strengthening India's bilateral ties with the neighbouring South Asian, Southeast Asian and IOR countries. However, India's recent problem with Nepal, the current Maldives crisis and the enduring problematic relations with Pakistan and China may not offer a positive indicator to Modi's "neighbourhood first" approach. Critics may therefore see the approach sceptically. Yet, this approach is not entirely as political-centric as it appears to be. The central tenet of "Neighbourhood first" is to establish better strategic connections with neighbours, from connectivity to information technology linkages. This was aptly reiterated in Modi's speech in Nepal in 2014 where he positioned India's relationship with neighbours, including Nepal, under the "HIT" mantra – Highways, Info-ways and Trans-ways.[37] Likewise, the "neighbourhood first" approach enhances India's outreach in Myanmar and Bangladesh under a multimodal linkage. Kaladan

Multimodal Transit Transport project, which was agreed to be developed between India and Myanmar in 2008, is a fine example of how India is intensifying on neighbourhood connectivity.[38]

Second, while the "neighbourhood first" approach explicates India's foreign policy arc with immediate neighbours, the "Act East" policy constitutes the core of India's Indo-Pacific vision. India's "Act East" policy today comprises a range of institutional, economic, political and security engagements. Contacts with ASEAN-centred multilateral mechanisms have become the main drivers of India's engagement with the East, where India is strongly connected with the East Asia Summit (EAS), ASEAN Regional Forum (ARF) and ASEAN Defence Ministers' Meeting Plus (ADMM+). A further corollary of India's engagement with East Asia is that India shares "strategic partnerships" with all the three main countries in the region, namely China, Japan and South Korea, and the most important institution, ASEAN. If "Look East" was more of a policy that expanded India's presence, then "Act East" is a policy that enhances India's strategic engagement with East Asia.

Third, India's Indo-Pacific outlook is more maritime-centric today than before. While Indo-Pacific has emerged as the centre of gravity of the evolving international system, India's approach to this unified strategic space was articulated in 2004 in the Indian Maritime Doctrine. The Doctrine underscored the "shift in global maritime focus from the Atlantic-Pacific combine to the Pacific-Indian". India is acutely aware that the arrival of China and the churning of "America First" posture will play a crucial role in shaping the contours of the Indo-Pacific order. As host to the world's fastest-growing economies, key choke points for international trade and repository of natural resources, the Indo-Pacific today features as one of the top priorities for India. As the Indo-Pacific region gains strategic salience, India is responding to growing expectations from regional stakeholders to assume a leadership role. While India's role as a "net security provider" in the region is being fiercely debated within the strategic community, New Delhi has designed its outlook towards the Indo-Pacific based on the key principles of maritime order, pillars of global rules and norms that govern freedom of navigation, keeping sealanes free for maritime economic activity and pursuing shared prosperity. As the Indo-Pacific witnesses a flux, the US has identified India as a "net security provider" in the backdrop of Chinese assertiveness in the maritime domain and erosion of the US influence in the Indo-Pacific.

Fourth, for India, promoting outreach in the Indo-Pacific is concurrent with its vision to promote and establish a better strategic connection with other regions. India's collaboration with Japan to establish the AAGC, promoting a stronger relationship with Africa bilaterally and with Africa and Latin America multilaterally through IBSA (India-Brazil-South Africa) and BRICS and BASIC (Brazil-South Africa-India-China), explains this open foreign policy. The AAGC is an envisioned intercontinental framework that complements the two countries' Indo-Pacific vision. Importantly, it promotes the idea of a "free and open Indo-Pacific" order that India, Japan and many other likeminded countries are demanding amidst the growing partisan demand for unilateral and non-democratic measures. Though it is yet to be seen how and to what extent the AAGC will be able to promote a free and open Indo-Pacific narrative, the AAGC's arrival confirms the subtle politics that are rife in the Indo-Pacific region currently.

India understands that the BRI is a unilateral initiative of China that ignores universal values and transparency. It combines China's geo-strategic and geo-economic objectives. It is a Sino-centric initiative attached to Beijing's national interests that is to promote China slowly as the centre of global politics. Centrality behind the BRI is to establish cooperative projects through a "win-win" narrative, which will position China as driver of economic collaboration, and eventually as "leader of globalisation". Connectivity, corridors and collaborative projects in China's immediate neighbourhood are the main crux of BRI that will affect India's interest more than any other country. Given the unilateralism and non-transparency accounts of the BRI, India will be careful and guarded to support and participate on any connectivity, corridor and projects that are parts of BRI. Yet, given the inter-dependency in economic collaboration and the growing developmental partnership between India and China, India may be open to cooperate and collaborate where it will witness a merit after carefully calibrating the sequence according to India's national priorities. In fact, India will compete where it must by lifting the level of its own regional connectivity projects and partnerships.[39] India's opposition to China's BRI is primarily due to security-oriented sovereignty matters and the governance measures that the Chinese flagship initiative overlooks. India's reservations on the BRI are based on the premise that Beijing has overlooked India's sovereignty over Pakistan-occupied Kashmir (POK) by initiating a project like the CPEC in the disputed region. Besides, India's contention is based on the fact that the BRI overlooks the consultative international character and promotes China's unilateral interests, overlooking transparency and governance goals that are universal in nature. This stance of India replicates in other multilateral forums too. India's connection with other continents through IBSA, BRICS and BASIC explains that India's approach to the Indo-Pacific is more governance-centric, implementing universal values and norms that the region demands.

Fifth, Prime Minister Modi has recently argued that the Indo-Pacific region is indispensable to India's future. Even as a great-power rivalry unfolds in this shared strategic space, India's approach is being shaped by its national interests and the fundamentals of its foreign policy orientation. India's approach to geopolitical realities is guided by a balance between engagement and autonomy. Under Modi, it has enunciated greater strategic coordination with likeminded countries, as witnessed within bilateral, trilateral and mini-lateral designs based on shared universal values. India is expected to pursue its quest for multi-polarity and great-power identity and pragmatically engage with all the important players on the global scene to ensure regional peace and stability, which are critical for facilitating development. India's former Foreign Secretary Jaishankar has argued that as India aims to modernise, it seeks resources and technology from global partners. This is the key focus in India's diplomatic endeavours. In his words, "Both the United States and China – and indeed the ASEAN, Japan, Republic of Korea and Europe – can contribute to this transformation. The centrality of this commitment ensures that India will set a positive and interactive agenda with other major powers and groupings."[40] Prime Minister Modi aims to bolster India's leading-power status in the region. There is certainly greater coordination on a few specific regional issues, but Modi has simultaneously engaged with China in building a closer developmental partnership and adopted an approach with regard to the AIIB that is different from that of the US and Japan. India is expected to boldly engage, but certainly not align with, all regional actors to leverage partnerships; it does not subscribe to the practice of alliance formation or a zero-sum game.

The policy contours behind this outlook are to enhance India's strategic positioning as a power, taking advantage of the economic conditions of the region, aiming to maximise the maritime interests and pushing forward India's strategic connections with the region through infrastructure development and connectivity while adhering to liberal values and universal norms. Amidst this, there is an emphasis on the traits of infrastructure, connectivity and development as priorities. The Indian demand is to pursue a consultative process while promoting connectivity and infrastructural development. India's official advocacy is that India favours "not just consultative dialogue but also one based on norms of transparency, good governance, commercial viability, fiscal responsibility and respect for sovereignty and territorial integrity".[41] As Indian economic development becomes resilient, New Delhi has initiated several infrastructure and connectivity projects in the sub-regions constituting the Indo-Pacific. India sees an advantage in partnering with Japan in this regard. India under its "Bharatmala" and "Sagarmala" initiatives has aimed to boost its domestic and neighbourhood connectivity linkages, port modernisation projects, coastal community development programme and energy communication linkages with different sub-regions of Asia and beyond, with a focus on the Indo-Pacific.

Structure of the Volume

Examining the Indo-Pacific theatre complexity is always a daunting task. Each of the issues and subject matters need special attention and close academic analysis. This Volume aims to analyse the growing intricacies in the region and examines the strategic approaches and foreign policy contours of the three main economies in Asia – China, India and Japan – which constitute the core of the Indo-Pacific. Specifically, the Volume examines the politics that surrounds infrastructural initiatives and examines how this is linked with the grand ideas and national interests of China, India and Japan.

Structurally, this Volume is divided into three sections, focusing on the respective approaches of China, India and Japan to the Indo-Pacific with regard to infrastructure investment and promotion of connectivity. It highlights how the subject matters of infrastructure development are closely linked to each of these countries national interests and their leadership visions and ideas. The first section decodes the Chinese strategy, particularly in view of China having tapped the vacuum created by the declining influence of the US and assuming greater responsibility of regional and global leadership. The authors critically analyse the mosaic of Chinese ideas and interests vis-à-vis the Indo-Pacific region. In addition, the authors address several key questions, e.g. how is China pursuing its grand ambitions by employing the BRI as the main tool for promoting Chinese values, economic and political models and the Chinese vision of globalisation? How is Beijing shaping the regional security governance conception and promoting China as the engineer of a new regional security architecture in the making? The section further alludes to Chinese methodology as pursued in multilateral frameworks for agenda setting and testing its new ideas on security cooperation in the region. Furthermore, the authors reflect on the key challenges concerning Chinese designs, for instance, the ambiguity surrounding the strategic objectives of BRI projects and opaqueness on what role China envisions for major regional powers.

They also evaluate the geopolitical, geostrategic and geo-economic implications of China's BRI vis-à-vis the primacy of other regional powers in the Indo-Pacific. In this regard, the case of the CPEC, one of the flagship projects of the BRI, has been closely examined to weigh its prospects as a "game-changer" in the India-Pakistan relationship.

The second section of the Volume examines Japanese foreign policy outreach in the Indo-Pacific. It essentially highlights the vitality of infrastructural investment and leadership vision that Shinzo Abe holds for his country's positioning in the region. With a rich set of contributions from Japanese scholars, this section highlights Tokyo's competing visions, ideas, strategies and policies on how to manage the rapidly altering geopolitical and geo-economic trends in the Indo-Pacific. It essentially analyses Japan's Indo-Pacific strategy, founded on a rule-based order, and aims to strengthen the US alliance network and Japan-India partnership as soft balancing in order to encourage China to play a more responsible and constructive role in the Indo-Pacific region. As the US-led liberal international order has been challenged by China's rise, Japan has pitched the Abe Doctrine based on its "Proactive Contribution to Peace" ideal. Several interesting strands of arguments emerge as authors dwell on Japan's infrastructure strategy, including one narrative cogently articulating the upsurge of Japan's interest in and approach to infrastructure export as reactive to China's initiatives including the launch of the BRI and the establishment of the AIIB. As the authors evaluate Japan's EPQI and the AAGC, there is consensus on the importance of India in Japan's Indo-Pacific strategy, which is aimed at fostering a stable, peaceful and prosperous Indo-Pacific based on a free, open, and equitable rule-based regional order building.

Positioning India's policies and perspectives at the centre, the third part of this volume examines India's approach towards Indo-Pacific. It highlights three aspects in India's policy standing: *first*, how India's maritime policy is heavily influenced by its marine ambitions in the Indian Ocean; *second*, how India foresees China's emergence as a maritime power adverse to its national interests; and *third*, the Indian approach of aligning with Japan as a strategic partner to overcome its national, regional and global infrastructural and connectivity hurdles. This section also examines how India's approach towards the AAGC complements Japan's and other likeminded countries' perspectives, and conflicts with China's unilateral policies and planning in the region. In other words, it investigates critical issues including the strategic implications of maritime infrastructure development and how India has shaped its approach towards the Indo-

Pacific. Maritime infrastructure developments, when viewed through a maritime security strategic lens, present both benefits and challenges. The arguments emerging from this section underscore the importance of the growing need to create and enhance mechanisms for collective and cooperative approaches to maritime security essential to protecting the regional maritime system, including its infrastructure.

This Volume contains a diverse set of arguments and perspectives that are both conformist and non-conformist in nature. It focuses on a theme like infrastructure to bring a more pointed analysis in order to examine the national and international perspectives of China, India and Japan. Infrastructure development in the Indo-Pacific is basically a strategic requirement, and the significance of this must be comprehended within the overall architecture of national interests and ideas of different nations. That makes this Volume distinct from earlier publications on the subject.

NOTES

1. As the title suggests, this volume offers a conceptual preference to the term "Indo-Pacific" over "Asia-Pacific". In some chapters both the terms have been used concurrently due to the respective country perspective or arguments that it generates. China's official use of the term "Asia-Pacific" is a case in reference in this context.
2. Xi Jinping's speech at the 19th National Congress of the Communist Party of China (CPC) listed China's many objectives for the next three decades. By 2035, China aims to emerge as a more "prosperous society" where some of the top priorities are economic and technological strength, improving domestic governance process, promoting the soft power culture and improving environmental standards within China. Similarly, by 2050, China wants to overcome domestic governance difficulties by improving the socialist culture, which will not only improve its domestic conditions but also have a positive impact on the country's international standing. The aim is to improve the overall comprehensive national power (CNP) that would make China a global leader. For a detailed perspective on China's vision for the next three decades, see Xi Jinping, "Secure a Decisive Victory in Building a Moderately Prosperous Society in All Respects and Strive for the Great Success of Socialism with Chinese Characteristics for a New Era", Speech delivered at the 19th National Congress of the CPC, October 18, 2017, at http://www.xinhuanet.com/english/download/Xi_Jinping's_report_at_19th_CPC_National_Congress.pdf (Accessed February 24, 2018).
3. Ibid.
4. "Full Text of President Xi's Speech at Opening of Belt and Road Forum", Ministry of Foreign Affairs of China, May 15, 2017, at http://www.fmprc.gov.cn/mfa_eng/zxxx_662805/t1465819.shtml (Accessed March 1, 2018).
5. Katie Allen, "Chinese Growth Slips to Slowest Pace for 26 Years", *The Guardian*, January 20, 2017, at https://www.theguardian.com/business/2017/jan/20/

chinese-economic-growth-dips-to-67-the-slowest-for-26-years (Accessed March 1, 2018).

6. Cheang Ming, "Mapping out China's Belt and Road Initiative", *CNBC*, February 15, 2018, at https://www.cnbc.com/2018/02/15/belt-and-road-initiative-china-bri-one-belt-one-road-what-cities-and-routes.html (Accessed March 4, 2018).
7. Gabriel Wildeu and Nan Ma, "In Charts: China's Belt and Road Initiative", *Financial Times*, May 11, 2017, at https://www.ft.com/content/18db2e80-3571-11e7-bce4-9023f8c0fd2e (Accessed March 4, 2018).
8. "Belt and Road Boosts RMB Internationalization", *China Today*, January 4, 2018, at http://www.scio.gov.cn/31773/35507/35520/Document/1615654/1615654.htm (Accessed March 3, 2018).
9. *Vision and Actions on Jointly Building Silk Road Economic Belt and 21st-Century Maritime Silk Road*, Issued by the National Development and Reform Commission, Ministry of Foreign Affairs and Ministry of Commerce of the People's Republic of China, with State Council Authorisation, March 28, 2015, at http://en.ndrc.gov.cn/newsrelease/201503/t20150330_669367.html (Accessed March 2, 2018).
10. *China's Policies on Asia-Pacific Security Cooperation*, White Paper, State Council Information Office of the People's Republic of China, January 11, 2017, at http://english.gov.cn/archive/white_paper/2017/01/11/content_281475539078636.htm (Accessed February 19, 2018).
11. Zheng Wang, "China's Institution Building: Leading the Way to Asian Integration", *Georgetown Journal of Asian Affairs*, 2(1), Spring-Summer, 2015, p.16.
12. "Backgrounder: Economic Corridors under Belt and Road Initiative", *Xinhua*, May 9, 2017, at http://www.xinhuanet.com/english/2017-05/09/c_136268314.htm (Accessed March 2, 2018).
13. Diane Regas, "Year-end Review: The Belt and Road Initiative Could Become a Vehicle for Environmental Progress of the World", *CGTN*, December 28, 2017, at https://news.cgtn.com/news/3041544e34637a6333566d54/share_p.html (Accessed March 4, 2018).
14. See Zhiqun Zhu, *China's New Diplomacy: Rationale, Strategies and Significance*, Ashgate, Farnham, 2013.
15. Jagannath P. Panda, "What the Inclusion of BRI in the Chinese Constitution Implies", *IDSA Comment*, November 7, 2017, at https://idsa.in/idsacomments/what-the-inclusion-of-bri-in-the-chinese-constitution-implies_jpanda_071117 (Accessed February 19, 2018).
16. Jagannath Panda, "Xi's 'New Era' Plan Reveals Dragon's Global Ambition", *The Pioneer*, October 21, 2017, at http://www.dailypioneer.com/columnists/oped/xis-new-era-plan-reveals-dragons-global-ambition.html (Accessed February 19, 2018).
17. Iren Chen and Li Mingjiang, "China's Rise and Role in the Asia-Pacific", *The Straits Times*, June 1, 2017, at http://www.straitstimes.com/opinion/chinas-rise-and-role-in-the-asia-pacific (Accessed February 25, 2018).
18. *National Security Strategy of the United States of America*, White House, Washington, DC, December 2017, at https://www.whitehouse.gov/wp-content/uploads/2017/12/NSS-Final-12-18-2017-0905.pdf. (Accessed February 25, 2018).
19. "National Defence Program Guidelines for FY 2014 and beyond", Prime Minister of Japan and His Cabinet, December 17, 2013, at http://japan.kantei.go.jp/

96_abe/documents/2013/__icsFiles/afieldfile/2013/12/27/NDPG.pdf. (Accessed February 25, 2018).

20. Anno Tadashi, "Japan's Value-Oriented Diplomacy: Historical Contexts and Political Implications", *Japan's Values and Foreign Policy: Intangible Power in International Relations*, Japan Forum on International Relations, 2014.
21. Nobukatsu Kanehara, "Japan's Grand Strategy – State, National Interests and Values", Japan's Diplomacy Series, Japan Digital Library, March 2016, at http://www2.jiia.or.jp/en/digital_library/japan_s_diplomacy.php. (Accessed February 25, 2018).
22. "The 13th IISS Asian Security Summit – The Shangri-La Dialogue – Keynote Address by Prime Minister Abe", Prime Minister of Japan and His Cabinet, May 30, 2014, at http://japan.kantei.go.jp/96_abe/statement/201405/0530kichokoen.html. (Accessed February 25, 2018).
23. Tsuneo Watanabe, "Japan's Strategy in the Trump Era", *The Diplomat*, January 16, 2018, at https://thediplomat.com/2018/01/japans-strategy-in-the-donald-trump-era. (Accessed February 25, 2018).
24. Secretary of State Condoleezza Rice, Secretary of Defence Robert M. Gates, Minister for Foreign Affairs Taro Aso and Minister of Defence Fumio Kyuma, "Alliance Transformation: Advancing United States-Japan Security and Defence Cooperation", Joint Statement of the Security Consultative Committee, Ministry of Foreign Affairs of Japan, May 1, 2007, at http://www.mofa.go.jp/ region/n-America/US/security/scc/pdfs/joint0705.pdf (Accessed May 24,2016).
25. "Australia-India-Japan-U.S. Consultations on the Indo-Pacific", Ministry of Foreign Affairs of Japan, November 12, 2017, at http://www.mofa.go.jp/press/release/press4e_001789.html. (Accessed February 25, 2018).
26. "Vientiane Vision: Japan's Defense Cooperation Initiative with ASEAN", Ministry of Defence, Japan, at http://www.mod.go.jp/e/d_act/exc/vientianevision/index.html. (Accessed February 25, 2018).
27. See Koichi Hamada, "The Rebirth of the Trans-Pacific Partnership", *Project Syndicate*, June 29, 2017, at https://www.project-syndicate.org/commentary/tpp-revival-japan-us-by-koichi-hamada-2017-06?barrier=accessreg. (Accessed February 25, 2018).
28. Titli Basu, "Japan's Trump Dilemma", *IDSA Comment*, December 20, 2016, at https://idsa.in/idsacomments/japan-trump-dilemma_tbasu_20122016. (Accessed February 25, 2018).
29. Hidetaka Yoshimatsu, "Japan's Export of Infrastructure Systems: Pursuing Twin Goals through Developmental Means", *The Pacific Review*, 30(4),2017, pp. 494-512.
30. Titli Basu, "Mapping India in Japan's Infrastructure Agenda", East Asia Forum, April 29,2016, at http://www.eastasiaforum.org/2016/04/29/mapping-india-in-japans-infrastructure-agenda/. (Accessed February 25, 2018).
31. "'The Future of Asia: Be Innovative' - Speech by Prime Minister Shinzo Abe at the banquet of the 21st International Conference on the Future of Asia", Prime Minister of Japan and His Cabinet, May 21, 2015, at http://japan.kantei.go.jp/97_abe/statement/201505/0521foaspeech.html(Accessed January 22, 2016).
32. Anthony Fensom, "Japan ups Ante on AIIB", *The Diplomat*, May 23, 2015, at http://thediplomat.com/2015/05/japan-ups-ante-on-aiib/(Accessed January 20, 2016).

33. Titli Basu, "China-Japan Relations: Deciphering the 70th Anniversary Course", in Jagannath Panda (ed.), *China Year Book 2015 – China's Transition under Xi Jinping*, Pentagon Press, New Delhi, 2016.
34. Kenji Hiramatsu, "Challenges and Prospects in the Indo-Pacific Region–in the context of India-Japan relationship", USI, November 2, 2017, at http://www.in.emb-japan.go.jp/Japan-India-Relations/20171102_Hiramatsu_speech_USI.pdf (Accessed February 25, 2018).
35. "Inaugural Address by Prime Minister at Second Raisina Dialogue, New Delhi (January 17, 2017)", Media Centre, Ministry of External Affairs, Government of India, January 17, 2017, at http://mea.gov.in/Speeches-Statements.htm?dtl/27948/Inaugural_Address_by_Prime_Minister_at_Second_Raisina_Dialogue_New_ Delhi_ January_17_2017 (Accessed February 19, 2018).
36. Ibid.
37. Ajay Kaul, "Narendra Modi Outlines Enhanced Commitment to Nepal", *Live Mint*, August 3, 2014, at http://www.livemint.com/Politics/tnRABjAdyFZgRmu7vh6WIL/Narendra-Modi-announces-1-billion-concessional-line-of-cred.html (Accessed February 19, 2018).
38. "Kaladan Multi-Modal Transit Transport Project", Ministry of Development of Northeastern Region, Government of India, at http://www.mdoner.gov.in/content/introduction-1 (Accessed March 5, 2018).
39. Jayant Prasad, "One Belt and Many Roads: China's Initiative and India's Response", DPG Issue Brief, September 2015, at http://www.delhipolicygroup.com/uploads/publication_file/1093_OBOR_Prasad.pdf (Accessed on December 27, 2017).
40. S. Jaishankar, "India, the United States and China", IISS-Fullerton Lecture, July 20, 2015, at https://www.iiss.org/en/events/events/archive/2015-f463/july-636f/fullerton-lecture-jaishankar-f64e. (Accessed February 25, 2018).
41. "Address by External Affairs Minister at Third Raisina Dialogue, New Delhi (January 17, 2018)", Media Centre, Ministry of External Affairs, Government of India, January 17, 2018, at http://www.mea.gov.in/SpeechesStatements.htm?dtl/29362/Address+by+External+ Affairs+Minister+at+ Third+Raisina+Dialogue+New+ Delhi+January+17+2018. (Accessed February 25, 2018).

PART I

DECODING THE CHINESE STRATEGY

2

Belt and Road Initiative: An Effective Future-oriented Instrument of China's Economic Development and Diplomatic Expansion?

Justyna Szczudlik

The aim of this paper is to answer the question whether the Belt and Road Initiative (BRI)[1] could be useful for China's economic development and to what extent it may contribute to Chinese diplomacy. So far, despite Chinese efforts to underscore the success of the concept, in reality, the BRI's effectiveness is in question, both on economic and diplomatic levels. Its vagueness, which in Xi Jinping's mind is supposedly an asset, currently is a barrier. The consequences have varied from stalled market-oriented economic reforms in China to rising concerns in many counties about the real intentions behind the initiative, including unsuccessful projects under the BRI banner. Nevertheless, the BRI's inclusion into the Constitution of the Communist Party of China (CPC) at the 19th Congress indicates that it is a long-term global initiative. It is a main tool for promoting Chinese values, economic and political models and the Chinese vision of globalisation. Combining Chinese principles with economics (state capitalism) and politics (effective authoritarian system) might be attractive for others, especially less-developed and/or unstable countries. At the same time, inconsistent US foreign policy under Trump has created a vacuum, which China is ready to fill. If in the next five years China maintains rather high economic growth and stability and its world status rises, then the BRI might be assessed as a future-oriented tool for China's global ascendance.

A Constant Evolution of the Concept

From the Silk Road Economic Belt and Maritime Silk Road...

When in mid-2013, Xi Jinping for the first time mooted the Silk Road Economic Belt, and a month later announced the 21st century Maritime Silk Road, one may have assumed that it was a thoroughly prepared policy with economic-oriented goals, directed towards China's neighbouring countries. In other words, at that time, this policy was perceived as an idea to boost relations with them. The economic belt would serve this purpose for China's western and inland central Asian states, taking into account the place where this slogan was announced – during Xi's trip to Kazakhstan. While the Maritime Silk Road would do so for the Southeast Asian states – as it was revealed in Indonesia.[2] Conveyed by Xi Jinping in October 2013, the Work Forum on Chinese Diplomacy towards its neighbourhood seemed to confirm the aforementioned thesis about the Silk Road rationales.[3]

The first confusion – about what the concept really is, what instruments it includes, which countries it embraces and what exact goals it assumes – arose in the 2013 fall. On the one hand, it was obvious that this concept became a flagship idea during Xi Jinping's rule, dethroning the "Chinese Dream" (*Zhongguo meng*) – a buzzword number one since December 2012 (after Xi's appointment to the post of the CPC Party Secretary). The first vindication was the third CPC Central Committee Plenum in November 2013. The final document clearly mentions the two slogans Economic Belt and 21st Century Maritime Silk Road, and suggests that the new concept is directed towards the neighbourhood. It reads that there is a need to facilitate openness along the borders and set up or develop regional and neighbouring infrastructure connectivity to promote Silk Road as a new development model.[4]

On the other hand, there were serious problems regarding a clear definition of this concept, even with the distinction whether it is a policy, strategy or something else. It is worth mentioning that since the very beginning, Europe has been included in this notion. There were some hints in Xi's September speech about integrating Europe into the Silk Road concept: "To establish a great transport corridor from the Pacific to the Baltic Sea, and from Central Asia to Indian Ocean."[5] What is more, China included Central and Eastern Europe (CEE) in its Silk Road efforts few weeks after the concept was announced. This was especially visible during Li Keqiang's visit to Romania in November 2013, where he took part in the second China-CEE summit (16+1) and presented new proposals for enhancing relations with the region. Among them was a suggestion for closer cooperation in the transport and infrastructural sectors, which may facilitate economic cooperation. It was highlighted that China's experience in this field might be attractive for CEE, which is facing problems with financing infrastructural projects. In the joint CEE-China declaration (Bucharest Guidelines), both sides declared the intention to construct an international railway transport connection and establish preferential economic areas along them to facilitate trade.[6] This European example only shows an increasing confusion about the newly announced concept.

... via One Belt, One Road (OBOR)...

The next year, 2014, enhanced the aforementioned confusion. This year was held under the banner of internal and external brainstorming about the Silk Road idea such as its rationales, scope, toolkit, etc. However, it was clear that Xi's announcement of the Silk Road slogan in 2013 was a call for experts to "fill" this buzzword with real content, rather than a well-prepared policy. The year 2014 was characterised by manifold conferences organised mainly in China by state institutions, policy think tanks and universities. The main topics of those meetings, to which foreign decision makers, think-tankers and researchers were invited, were questions about their expectations, including what the concept should be.[7] What is more, in mid-2014, another slogan or name for the Silk Road was coined and then aggressively promoted – "One Belt, One Road" (OBOR; *yidai yilu*) – which is used interchangeably with the term "Silk Road". The change of the name was a signal that both Chinese pundits and foreign experts were not clear about Xi's main idea. Official explanation as to why the name had been changed was twofold. The Chinese Ministry of Foreign Affairs (MFA) explained that the new slogan was shorter and easier to use and pronounce – especially in Chinese which prefers four-character expressions (a clear reference to the Chinese *chengyu*). Apart from this, it was also explained that the name "New Silk Road" might be connected with Hilary Clinton's idea announced in 2011 to rebuild Afghanistan, and in that sense it might be confusing.[8]

A domestic and international "Silk Road brainstorming" was used to formulate an action plan or blueprint that was announced by Xi Jinping in late March 2015 at the Boao Forum. Although the document is still nebulous, there are some details which indirectly indicate China's main goals: to be a global superpower which is considering taking more responsibility and, to some extent, abandoning free-riding, the prevalent approach so far; to become a rule-maker in order to make the Chinese voice heard globally; and to contribute to the global economy, e.g. through internationalisation of Chinese enterprises, currency and worldwide politics.

The aforementioned document is trying to defuse doubts about the concept. In fact, sometimes it is easier to quote official arguments about what the Silk Road is not, than what it is. Analysing the blueprint, the striking point is the usage of the words "proposal", "vision" or "framework", instead of "strategy". China has highlighted that the concept has no political goals or is not a political tool to exert pressure on a particular country or countries to behave in line with Chinese interests. To that effect, officially there is neither a list of the countries included in the Silk Road nor an official map which presents the details of the Silk Road routes. What is more, the Silk Road is not a "solo" Chinese idea that the People's Republic of China (PRC) wants to impose on others, but is based on a country's free decision to be part of the concept. Moreover, Chinese officials resolutely reject any links to the so-called Chinese Marshall Plan. They argue that the Silk Road has no similarities to the US-led Cold War plan that was based on ideological, political and security considerations to contain the USSR, and communism, and was seen as a sanctions' tool. In addition, the Silk Road is not any kind of one-way development assistance or donation prepared for a close catalogue of countries as the Marshall Plan assumed (Western Europe) and is not aimed against any other country. Thus, the Silk Road is not an excluding idea based on conditional grants with an aim to augment China's superpower position.[9] Finally, the Silk Road is not just a kind of stimulus package to reinvigorate the Western Development Policy (announced in 2000), and thus there is no one Silk Road starting point. Beijing officially denies that there is domestic rivalry between provinces about being the Silk Road starting point. Moreover, the Silk Road is a comprehensive concept that is being managed and implemented by at least three institutions: National Development Research Commission (NDRC), MFA and Ministry of Commerce (MOFCOM).

Despite the fact that the blueprint is not very concrete, it does present the main rationales behind OBOR. Beyond doubt, it is Xi Jinping's comprehensive foreign policy strategy based on Chinese domestic and foreign interests. China strongly underlines that the main characteristics of the initiative are inclusiveness, openness, equality, voluntariness and win-win principle.

The main reasons for the Silk Road concept might be divided into three groups: politics, economy (including domestic development) and security.

The political rationales are tightly connected with China's perception of the global changes due to financial crisis and rising worldwide interdependence. China, which has coped quite well with the crisis and still has a stable economy, is becoming an indispensable element of the global order. What is more, under Xi Jinping, China's main foreign policy goal to achieve the superpower status (which has been valid since the beginning of the People's Republic) is becoming more visible and clear as Xi is more actively jettisoning Deng's "keep low profile" dictum. In other words, the Silk Road initiative is a tool for Chinese global success which in Xi's eyes is needed due to his negative assessment of Hu Jintao's two terms as head of state and the party. Despite the significance of political rationales, the core areas of cooperation enlisted in the blueprint seem to be economic in nature.

The most important is trade: exports to secure outlet markets for China's products in order to maintain the export-oriented economic model and high gross domestic product (GDP); and imports to acquire raw materials and high technologies. Moreover, the Silk Road is to facilitate Chinese investments by reducing or eliminating barriers, e.g. establishing free trade areas, signing agreements on avoidance of double taxation and expanding the scope of economic cooperation through sectors such as agriculture, maritime, energy and green technologies. Another area is financial cooperation, based on stable currencies, and its internationalisation and new financial institutions such as the Asia Infrastructure and Investment Bank (AIIB), Silk Road Fund, BRICS New Development Bank, etc. to stimulate investments in the region in order to eliminate infrastructure bottleneck, which limits regional development. This cooperation is strictly connected with infrastructural projects to facilitate connectivity such as highways, railways, sea lanes, pipelines, harbours, airports, etc. Those kinds of activities are strictly connected with boosting trade, investments and China's companies and RMB (*renminbi*) internationalisation.

Taking into account the not very stable Chinese neighbourhood such as the Central Asian countries with inter-ethnic conflicts and unstable governments the Silk Road should be a mechanism for securing China's safety on the western borders. Closer and frequent political dialogue and more intimate people-to-people relations, including tourism cooperation, might be perceived as a means to "tie" neighbouring countries with China and to preserve the safety on Chinese borders.

Although there is no detailed map of OBOR, the document presents regions which are involved in this concept, both inside and outside China. Contrary to the initial perception that the Silk Road is mainly created for western China, the blueprint shows that China as a whole has been involved. Document enlists almost all provinces, main cities as well as inland and coastal part of the country, to indicate that this is a comprehensive project aimed at the development of the entire country. OBOR outside China includes three continents: Asia, Europe and Africa. The Economic Belt contains Central Asia, Southeast Asia, Russia to Europe (including the Baltic Sea), the Persian Gulf and the Mediterranean Sea. While, the 21st Century Maritime Silk Road embraces harbours along China's coast, the South China Sea, Pacific Ocean, Indian Ocean and Europe.

The blueprint also presents the OBOR mechanisms and tools. Among them are bilateral, but also multilateral regional and global mechanisms and forums such as the Shanghai Cooperation Organisation (SCO), Asia-Pacific Economic Cooperation (APEC), Asia-Europe Meeting (ASEM), Boao Forum, etc. Moreover, Chinese officials' visits to the countries along the Silk Road, signing deals for cooperation such as investment agreements, and new institutions (AIIB, Silk Road Fund) are also considered as the Silk Road tools.[10]

... to the Belt and Road Initiative (BRI)

Another step in the Silk Road evolution was noticeable in 2016 and 2017. First of all, since early 2016, especially the National People's Congress (Chinese Parliament) session, Chinese officials once again have modified the concept's name. They still use Chinese expressions of *yidai yilu* (一带一路), but the English translation has been changed into the "Belt and Road Initiative" (BRI).[11] Presumably, there are several reasons for this step. Traditionally, Chinese politics uses numbers in its slogans (e.g. "one country, two systems" and "four comprehensiveness"), which explains why the Chinese language name of the Silk Road remains unchanged. The English name was changed to avoid the confusion beyond China about what exactly "one" refers to in the term OBOR. Moreover, the decision to replace OBOR with BRI also signifies a shift from typical Chinese political discourse to a more all-inclusive one.

Moreover, apart from the (English) name, in the Chinese debate, the concept is no longer viewed or promoted as an economic instrument only. Since 2016, the discourse that the BRI is a "public good" has become the main narrative. This means that the BRI is a Chinese contribution to the global governance system and forms a new model for integration, but one that is different from Western notions. The Silk Road aims to create a cooperation network rather than spheres of influence. That is, the initiative is a means to establish Chinese-style leadership based on taking responsibility, setting an example and not exerting pressure on others. It is a kind of Chinese "third way". Chinese leaders stress that this is an open idea and a response to international needs. A good example of this mindset is Chinese efforts to include the BRI into other countries' development strategies. It seems that China is trying to affect the policies of other countries, which are taking part in OBOR.[12] Chinese experts explain the "third way" idea by often underscoring that Western powers were created through hegemonism, imperialism and colonisation, while the Chinese proposal BRI is a voluntary, open and inclusive initiative, which rejects any coercion tactics. The BRI cornerstone is cooperation that is designed to meet the other countries' needs. Moreover, the BRI is to solve problems (e.g. poverty and social inequalities), with which the Western model does not want to or cannot cope. In that sense, as Chinese leaders explain, the BRI does not intend to change the existing global order but to significantly improve it. For example, China is helping remove the remains of colonialism in Africa; facilitating economic and financial cooperation within the BRI, thus eliminating the effects of the recent global crisis; and financing infrastructure projects worldwide that, together with economic cooperation, will create a new model of global integration.[13]

Another significant shift in the perception of BRI has been noticeable since the "Belt and Road International Forum" held in May 2017 in Beijing. The Forum was promoted as the most important international event in China this year. It seems that it marked another step in the BRI evolution – more assertive China's diplomatic agenda and a step forward in the implementation of Xi Jinping's "great power diplomacy with Chinese characteristics". This change might be correlated with a rhetoric of the PRC as a champion of globalisation (marked by Xi Jinping's speech in Davos, in January 2017). To that effect, the BRI is an important tool for introducing the Chinese-led globalisation vision. But despite the very peaceful and inclusive Xi Jinping's opening speech,[14] the Forum preparations and proceeding, showed that BRI is becoming a "hard" tool for implementing China's economic and political interests. Thus, the discourse about the BRI as a "public good" and "third way" has been undermined.

The Forum reflected China's shift from collective efforts of the international community to define the BRI concept – as it was done in the case of setting up of the AIIB[15] – to the "uncritically follow us" approach. The good example were documents prepared by China to be signed at the Forum without prior consultations with other countries or even information about those documents. This was the reason why the European Union (EU) member states did not sign one of the economic-related declarations, arguing that there was no guarantee for projects transparency.[16] What is more, a Forum proceedings published by the Chinese MFA highlighted the existing problem with the BRI definition, including its toolkit. Almost every kind of activity, agreement or topic that was discussed during the Forum, under bilateral and multilateral skims, has been considered as a BRI-related project or result.[17] Further, the Forum also highlighted a severe rivalry between various ministries. They competed with each other in organising additional meetings during the Forum as well as preparing documents and declarations to be regarded as results of this event.[18]

Attempts for BRI Institutionalisation

According to the official Chinese discourse, the first conceptual phase of the Silk Road was accomplished in 2016, and it is now time to reap the first fruits. This was the main assumption after the Politburo meeting devoted to the BRI implementation and assessment, held in Beijing in August 2016.[19] This three-year period marked the launch of the two processes of BRI institutionalisation and implementation.

As far as institutionalisation is concerned, this process was launched about a year after the initiative was announced. It runs at domestic and international levels and takes two forms. The first includes documents which define the BRI as well as implementation plans. While the second includes the creation of new "real" institutions such as banks or funds as BRI tools.

In the domestic dimension, the most important document is the Action Plan announced by Xi Jinping in March 2015, and inclusions BRI into various Chinese strategic documents such as in final decision after the third Plenum in November 2013, government work reports delivered by prime minister Li Keqiang at parliamentary sessions in March, and 13th Five Year Plan (2016-2020) adopted by the parliament in March 2016. As far as "real" institutions are concerned, the most important one is a Small Leading Group for Silk Road Implementation (*tuijing "yidai, yilu" jianshe gongzuo lingdao xiaoxu*) that was set up in March 2015. The Vice Premier and Standing Committee member Zhang Gaoli was appointed as its chairperson; the Secretariat is located within the NDRC and has four departments: general affairs, inland Silk Road, maritime Silk Road and international cooperation.[20]

In the international dimension, China eagerly signs documents related to the BRI such as Silk Road Memoranda of Understanding (MoUs). According to high-level officials' remarks, China has already signed like-minded agreements with more than 60 countries and international organisations, while more than 100 states and other international entities have chosen to take part in the BRI.[21] China also tries to combine the BRI with other countries' development programmes or similar (e.g. infrastructural) projects. For example, it seeks to synergise the BRI and the EU Juncker Plan and cooperate with the South Korean Eurasian Initiative or Russia-led the Eurasian Economic Union. China has also set up international financial institutions such as AIIB, Silk Road Fund and BRICS New Development Bank. Moreover, the decision to hold the BRI Forum regularly, every two years (the second one will be organised in 2019), is another institutionalisation step.

Attempts for BRI Implementation

Apart from institutionalisation, the implementation of the BRI has been launched as well. Chinese sources are trying to, on the one hand, describe all BRI-related projects and activities, and on the other, show this implementation in a systemic and structuralised way. Both tasks are not easy.

Generally, it is argued that implementation embraces four main areas. The first and the most important is infrastructure which includes transport: inland (highways and railways), maritime and air; energy (power stations, transmitting lines); and cyber and IT infrastructure. For example, there are currently about 40 freight trains connecting Europe-China. Chinese state-owned companies have concluded contracts for 38 transport infrastructure projects in 26 countries and participate in 40 foreign energy projects in 19 countries.[22]

The second area refers to trade and investments. Apart from trade, an important dimension is setting up special economic zones, technological parks and economic corridors. The aim is to facilitate trade and investment through integrated customs procedures, tariff reductions, pilot e-commerce programmes, etc. Examples of such activities are free trade zones within China (Manzhouli in Inner Mongolia, Dongxi, Guanxi province) and abroad, through negotiation of free trade agreements (FTAs) and other economic agreements like Regional Comprehensive Economic Partnership (RCEP), such as industrial park in Belarus, Thai-Chinese Rayong Industrial Zone, Indonesia-China Integrated Industrial Parks and special trade and logistics zone in Hungary, Cambodia, Vietnam, Pakistan, Egypt, etc. Economic corridors are also being created: China-Bangladesh-India-Myanmar, China-Pakistan or China-Russia-Mongolia. Further, the rise in trade volume between China and any country or region is also considered as a (successful) BRI result.[23]

The third area refers to financial cooperation. It covers projects financed or co-financed by the AIIB, Silk Road Fund, Chinese Exim Bank and Development Bank. For example, in 2017, the AIIB approved US $ 509 million for the first four infrastructural projects in Bangladesh, Indonesia, Pakistan and Tajikistan. On the other hand, the Fund announced a share in three investments: the hydroelectric plant in Pakistan, acquisition of Italian Pirelli and acquisition of a 9.9 per cent stake in the Russian Yamal LNG project. Until now, the AIIB has approved 28 projects.[24] This category also includes swap agreements – People's Bank of China has agreements with 21 countries of the Road, and offshore transaction centres in the yuan, e.g. in London – and cooperation on financial regulation and supervision such as agreements against money laundering.[25]

The fourth area concerns a very capacious category of people-to-people contacts. China, for example, is planning to launch 10,000 government scholarships for the countries covered by the BRI and aims to encourage 150 million of its citizens to visit the Silk Road countries. As BRI projects are considered e.g. tourism years in various countries, visa-free programmes for Chinese visitors, medical cooperation (such as medical staff training), various other types of scientific cooperation, contacts between Chinese and other countries' political parties, non-governmental organisations (NGOs), think tanks, etc.[26]

As China's every activity at home, and mainly abroad, is considered a BRI activity, it is impossible to thoroughly describe or at least present a list of all BRI projects and activities. In that sense, the Silk Road concept is an umbrella over all Chinese initiatives, which explains the confusion regarding the definition and the lack of a clear-cut understanding of these projects.

International Doubts Arise

Officially, China's assessment of the BRI is positive and enthusiastic. An example is the BRI Forum in Beijing. However, other countries are not buying into China's Silk Road initiative. Their responses are articulated at two levels: the first is at the macro level, such as in the political discourse, regarding the assumptions about the initiative and trust in Chinese statistics; and the second is at the micro level, relating to specific projects and cooperation proposals.

Despite Chinese efforts to give more "substance" to the Silk Road, the initiative remains vague. China's argument that access to the initiative is voluntary, combined with the lack of a list of objectives and tools, reinforces its partners' conviction that it is nebulous. Good evidence of this is the list of activities undertaken in the last four years. Apart from priority areas such as infrastructure, trade, investment and financial cooperation, Silk Road embraces any other forms of state activity, including those in domestic and foreign policy.

Apart from the nebulous BRI concept, China extensively promotes other slogans which are blurred as well, such as "connectivity" – the main slogan used as a BRI tool. But there is no specific explanation as to what China means by this buzzword, stirring doubts in other countries which are trying to define this term by themselves.

There are also doubts about the Chinese statistics. During the BRI Forum, Xi Jinping said that more than 100 countries support and take part in the BRI. But China has not published a list of those countries. The same is with the statistics of projects that are being or have been already implemented. Usually, only access to general, quantitative data is available. It remains unknown when some projects were launched and their stage of implementation. It is highly probable there are only a few real Silk Road projects that began after autumn 2013. However, projects finalised or launched before the initiative's announcement, such as the rail cargo connection between Lódz (Poland) and Chengdu, have been claimed as examples of the Silk Road initiative. The names of the countries taking part in the projects or that are signatories to agreements are rarely made public. As a result, China's enthusiastic assessment of the Silk Road initiative is perceived as arbitrary and cannot be verified. Currently, "Silk Road" is more a label under which China pursues its assertive export, investment and foreign policies while diversifying their directions.

At the micro level, the doubts are connected to the first unsuccessful projects. For example, energy projects in Mongolia have been suspended for environmental reasons, such as threats to Lake Baikal. Some countries also have expressed doubts about their security because of the mode of the Chinese investments. A good example is Thailand, which declined a railway infrastructure project because the Chinese side requested the right to land at the stations and along the tracks. There are also problems with the launch of a similar project in Laos and with the Belgrade-to-Budapest railway. There are also examples of delayed or halted investments in Pakistan, Belarus, Myanmar and Indonesia. The initiative is also wrestling with security concerns that affect project completion, such as terrorism in Pakistan and Middle Eastern countries.[27]

Chinese attempts at infrastructural projects in CEE under the so-called 16+1 formula[28], which is now combined with the BRI, also might be assessed as unsuccessful. The PRC offers assistance similar to the mode exercised in Africa for, in fact, developing countries whose main problem is funding. The Chinese-led projects are based on credits and loans, with requirements for state sovereign guarantees, which shift the burden on the host countries, increasing their public debt, and implementing projects with Chinese workers and contractors. The EU members of this formula do not see this mode as attractive and legal, taking into account the fact that the EU as far as investments are concerned requires public tenders. As a result, there is no any significant infrastructural project in CEE both under 16+1 and BRI skims.

There are no tangible results of the BRI within the EU. In 2015, the EU and China established the so-called EU-China Connectivity Platform to find commonalities between the BRI and EU proposals. The latter includes the Investment Plan for Europe and new work plans within the Trans-European Transport Network (TEN-T) policy, adopted in mid-2015. So far only two meetings have taken place, with no significant outcomes.[29]

Other concerns include the Chinese demand for access to critical infrastructure and the potential for acquiring technologies through investment in the energy and high-tech sectors. This was why the Australian Government rejected the offers of two Chinese companies to lease transmission lines. There also have been concerns in Germany about access to digital data following the China-based firm Midea's acquisition of the Germany-based robotics company Kuka. Another German company, Aixtron, saw its shares fall sharply after the unexpected cancellation of a large order by a Chinese company followed by an offer from another Chinese enterprise to take over the company.

There is also apprehension about whether China, due to its economic slowdown and potential for crises, can finance the projects and how profitable they will be. Concerns about economic sustainability, too, have been raised in connection with, for example, transport projects in Central Asia. These concerns have been strengthened recently due to China's inconsistent policy for BRI projects and their financing. Only in 2017, on the one hand, the Chinese Government revealed plans to curb its foreign investments – which may indicate the problems with the Silk Road initiative implementation.[30] On the other hand, there is also information that the biggest Chinese banks are being encouraged to finance BRI projects, which are rather smoothly accepted.[31]

Further, it seems plausible that there is severe rivalry between ministries (e.g. NDRC, MOFCOM, MFA) – which was noticeable during the BRI Forum in Beijing[32] – as well as between provinces. To some extent this rivalry might be perceived as an asset – it may be a stimulus for value-added projects. But this approach may also result in proposals and projects which will not be based on economic efficiency, but rather on political will to be visible and to become the BRI champion.

Unsuccessful BRI projects, China's economic conditions and other countries' conviction that the BRI as a Chinese project mainly serves the PRC's economic and political interests are among reasons for rising mistrust, which may limit the scope of BRI projects beyond China.[33] A good example is the EU, which, after Chinese attempts to invest in critical infrastructure in 2016, is considering to block these kinds of foreign investments. In February 2017, Germany, France and Italy issued a letter to the EU Trade Commissioner Cecilia Malmström with a proposal to set up EU investment screening mechanism over foreign investments.[34] In September 2017, the President of the European Commission Jean-Claude Juncker in his State of the Union address said: "We are proposing **a new EU framework for investment screening**. If a foreign, state-owned, company wants to purchase a European harbour, part of our energy infrastructure or a defence technology firm, this should only happen in transparency, with scrutiny and debate. It is a political responsibility to know what is going on in our own backyard so that we can protect our collective security if needed."[35] While in May 2017, Frans Timmermans, the first Vice President of the European Commission, had said that "*Europe must help rewrite the global rulebook so that free trade becomes fair trade*".[36] *These two remarks are perceived as directed to, among others, China and the BRI.*

Conclusion

The BRI is China-centric concept, indispensable for the PRC's domestic interests with a key principle to maintain stability. The BRI serves these goals perfectly. Moreover, it aims to promote Chinese exports and investments. In other words, the BRI is a kind of an "insurance" for economic stability in times of unavoidable economic gyrations, because it preserves the default mode of China's current economic model. This model is well known and has proved its validity for almost four decades.

In addition, the BRI is becoming an increasingly important instrument for acquiring technologies that are direly needed for China's economy. The best example of this approach is the "Made in China 2025" strategy, with an aim to base Chinese economy on high-tech. Another example is the process of introducing a social credit system which using big data helps Chinese authorities to effectively manage its economy. In that sense, the Silk Road initiative may help China in implementing the "new normal" economic theory, announced by Xi Jinping in 2014, which says that economic growth should be based on innovation, recognising it as the main economic driver.[37] Moreover, the idea of lifting trade and investment barriers in countries along the Silk Road, by setting up free trade zones and industrial parks and building new or refurbishing existing transport corridors, as per the "connectivity" slogan, might be helpful both for China and other countries. For the PRC, which is under the process of changing its economic model and introducing market-oriented reforms (but after the 19th CPC Congress, these kinds of reforms are in question), while for other countries because they would like to improve their trade value with China and request reciprocity. To that effect, the BRI could become an important tool for the China-led globalisation model, and as a result, in the long term, BRI might become an effective diplomatic tool. Especially, Xi Jinping extensively underscored China's role in globalisation and the BRI as an important tool in this very process.[38] The well-known Chinese scholar Wang Yizhou has already announced that the China-led globalisation 2.0 is in the making. He differentiates between "traditional globalisation" and "new model of globalisation". The former refers to the one-dimensional phenomena based only on trade by lifting barriers and customs; global division of labour between centrums and peripheries, which generally creates a vicious circle (*quanzhihua*); and the process of closing-up – an example of this kind of globalisation is the EU, as 80 per cent of its trade is between member states. The latter is based on the Belt and Road principles such as connectivity, openness, inclusiveness, both inland and maritime development, balanced development between the North and the South and fair share of the globalisation fruits.[39]

However, this "ideal" situation has not materialised yet. The BRI is a rather "one-directional" concept – based on Chinese interests, which seriously limit the Silk Road effectiveness. Despite Chinese efforts to underscore the success of the concept, in reality, the Silk Road stirs doubts both on economic and diplomatic levels. Its vagueness, which in theory and supposedly in Xi's mind, should be an asset – because it gives the Chinese authorities a room for manoeuvre depending on its needs and avoids criteria that may indicate failure – in reality, is a barrier. The consequences is stalled economic market-oriented reforms in China and expanding concerns in many countries about the real intentions behind the Silk Road, including unsuccessful projects under the Belt and Road banner. Moreover, the Chinese discourse about the four years of BRI existence as well as the BRI Forum, suggesting the superiority of Chinese ideas and solutions, including the rhetoric of success – "one big family of Silk Road states"[40] – is also directed at the West, in particular the US. The argument is being used to confirm China's growing status under

Xi Jinping's rule. The BRI Forum strengthens this premise and the convictions that China is not looking for partners but rather followers.

The initiative will remain Xi's flagship political and economic concept and the state's "umbrella" over its domestic and foreign policies. The Silk Road will be a tool for strengthening China's global position under Xi's rule. It is an essential and important instrument to project Chinese power. This was confirmed by the 19th CPC Congress in October 2017. Xi Jinping in his report mentioned the BRI few times,[41] while the party delegates decided to introduce this initiative into the party charter[42]. Thus, now the BRI is openly a tool for promoting Chinese values, economic and political models, state capitalism, which preserves high economic growth, and an effective authoritarian system. Bearing in mind inconsistent US foreign policy and the ongoing debate about the future of European integration, the Chinese model – based on stability, effectiveness and global ascendance – and promoted via the BRI might be attractive for less-developed and not fully stable countries. If China achieves its economic goals such as export expansion of its excessive manufacturing capacities and access to technologies from abroad, then the BRI could be considered effective and successful. At the CPC Congress, Xi Jinping made it clear that the Silk Road idea is a long-term initiative to be implemented beyond his second term.

NOTES

1. The terms "Silk Road", "One Belt One Road" and "Belt and Road" are used interchangeably in the paper.
2. "Hongyang renmin youyi, gongchuang meihao weilai. Zai Nazhaerbayefu daxue de yanjiang" [Enhancement of People-to-People Friendship Creates a Better Future. Speech at Nazarbayev University], *Xinhua*, September 8, 2013, at http://news.xinhuanet.com/politics/2013-09/08/c_117273079.htm; "Guojia zhuxi Xi Jinping zai Yindunixiya guohui fabiao yanjiang (quanwen)" [Chairman Xi Jinping Delivered a Speech in the Indonesian Parliament (Full Text)], *Xinhua*, October 3, 2013, at http://news.xinhuanet.com/politics/2013-10/03/c_117591171.htm.
3. "Xi Jinping zai zhoubian waijiao gongzuo zuotanhui shang fabiao zhongyao jianghua" [Xi Jinping at the Work Forum on Chinese Diplomacy towards Its Neighbourhood Delivered an Important Speech], *Xinhua*, October 25, 2013, at http://news.xinhuanet.com/politics/2013-10/25/c_117878897.htm.
4. "Zhonggong zhongyang guanyu quanmian shenhua gaige ruogan zhongda wenti de jueding (quanwen)" [Central Committee's Decision on Major Issues Concerning Comprehensively Deepening Reforms (Full Text)], Chapter 7, Point 26, *Xinhua*, November 15, 2013, at http://news.china.com.cn/2013-11/15/content_30615132.htm.
5. "Hongyang renmin youyi, gongchuang meihao weilai. Zai Nazhaerbayefu daxue de yanjiang", No. 2.
6. "Li Keqiang chuxi di san jie Zhongguo – Zhongdongou guojia jingji luntan" [Li Keqiang Attended the 3rd China-Central Europe Economic Forum], *Xinhua*,

November 27, 2013, at http://news.xinhuanet.com/world/2013-11/27/c_118305532.htm.

7. Author's personal experience.
8. Personal communication with an official from the Chinese MFA, January 2014; "US Support for the New Silk Road", US Department of State, at https://2009-2017.state.gov/p/sca/ci/af/newsilkroad/index.htm.
9. Zhang Yesui, "Gong jian 'yidai yilu' mouqiu hezuo gongying" [Build Together 'One Belt, One Road' Seeking Win-Win Cooperation], *Qiushi*, 10, 2015, at http://www.qstheory.cn/dukan/qs/2015-05/15/c_1115245697.htm; Wang Yizhou, "'Yidai yilu' juefei Zhongguoban 'Masie'er jihua'" ['One Belt, One Road' is Not a Chinese Marshall Plan], *Qiushi*, 12, 2015, at http://www.qstheory.cn/dukan/qs/2015-06/15/c_1115588162.htm.
10. "Tuidong gongjian sichou zhilu jingji dai he 21 shiji haishang sichou zhilu de yuanjing yu xingdong" [Vision and Actions on Jointly Building Silk Road Economic Belt and 21st-Century Maritime Silk Road], *People's Daily*, March 29, 2015, at http://politics.people.com.cn/n/2015/0329/c1001-26765454.html; Justyna Szczudlik-Tatar, "One Belt, One Road: Mapping China's New Diplomatic Strategy", *PISM Bulletin*, 67 (799), 2 July. 2015.
11. Compare Chinese and English versions of the press conferences of Chinese officials on the sidelines of the fourth Session of the 12th National People's Congress.
12. "Yidai yi lu" guoji luntanhui kaimu, Liu Qibao fabiao zhuzhi yanjiang" [Belt & Road Initiative International Conference Opening Ceremony, Liu Qibao Delivered a Key-note Speech], *Zhongguo Ribao*, September 26, 2016, at http://china.chinadaily.com.cn/2016-09/26/content_26897697.htm; "'Yi dai yi lu': Xi Jinping dakai de 'zhumeng kongjian'" [Belt & Road: Xi Jinping Opened 'Space for Dream Implementation'], Xinhua, September 21, 2016, at http://news.xinhuanet.com/politics/2016-09/21/c_1119594710.htm.
13. "Wang Wen: 'Yidai yi lu', daguo jueqi de disan tiao daolu [Wang Wen: BRI, the Third Way of the Great Powers Rise], *Renmin Ribao*, June 1, 2016, at http://world.people.com.cn/n1/2016/0601/c1002-28402469.html; "Xi Jinping: rang 'yidai yilu' jianshe zaofu yanxian geguo renmin" [Xi Jinping: Let Make Every BRI Country Benefit], Xinhua, August 17, 2016, at http://news.xinhuanet.com/world/2016-08/17/c_1119408654.htm.
14. "Xieshou tuijin 'yidai yilu' jianshe - Xi Jinping zai 'yidai yilu' guoji hezuo gaofeng luntan kaimushi shang de yanjiang" [Work Together to Build BRI – A speech Delivered by Xi Jinping at the Opening Ceremony of the Belt and Road International Forum], Xinhua, May 14, 2017, at http://news.xinhuanet.com/world/2017-05/14/c_1120969677.htm.
15. Yun Sun, "China and the Changing Asian Infrastructure Investment Bank", PacNet#43, Centre for Strategic and International Studies (CSIS), July 28, 2015, at https://www.csis.org/analysis/pacnet-43-china-and-changing-asian-infrastructure-bank
16. Tom Philips, "EU Backs away from Trade Statement in Blow to China's 'Modern Silk Road 'Plan'", *The Guardian*, May 15, 2017, at https://www.theguardian.com/world/2017/may/15/eu-china-summit-bejing-xi-jinping-belt-and-road.
17. "'Yidai yilu' guoji hezuo gaofeng luntan chengguo qingdan (quanwen)" [List of Results of the International BRI Forum], Ministry of the Foreign Affairs of the

People's Republic of China, May 16, 2017, at http://www.fmprc.gov.cn/web/zyxw/t1461873.shtml.

18. Personal communication with a foreign diplomat who personally observed the Forum in Beijing, June 2017.
19. "'Yi dai yi lu': Xi Jinping dakai de 'zhumeng kongjian'", No. 12.
20. "Adhering to the Planning, Orderly and Pragmatically Build the 'Belt and Road'", The Belt and Road Progress Report, Renmin University, September 26, 2016.
21. "Xieshou tuijin 'yidai yilu' jianshe - Xi Jinping zai 'yidai yilu' guoji hezuo gaofeng luntan kaimushi shang de yanjiang", No. 14.
22. "Adhering to the Planning, Orderly and Pragmatically Build the 'Belt and Road'", No. 20.
23. Ibid.
24. See "Approved Projects", AIIB, at https://www.aiib.org/en/projects/approved/index.html.
25. "Adhering to the Planning, Orderly and Pragmatically Build the 'Belt and Road'", No. 20.
26. Ibid.
27. Marcin Przychodniak, "Belt and Road Forum: China's Political Offensive", *PISM Spotlight*, 11, May 13, 2017.
28. This formula was established in mid-2012 and includes China and 16 countries from Central, Eastern and Southern parts of Europe: Albania, Bosnia and Herzegovina, Bulgaria, Croatia, Czech Republic, Estonia, Hungary, Macedonia, Montenegro, Latvia, Lithuania, Romania, Poland, Serbia, Slovakia and Slovenia.
29. "EU-China Summit: Moving Forward with Our Global Partnership", June 2, 2017, at http://europa.eu/rapid/press-release_IP-17-1524_en.htm
30. "China to Curb 'Irrational' Overseas Belt and Road Investment: State Planner", *Reuters*, August 18, 2017, at https://www.reuters.com/article/us-china-economy-odi/china-to-curb-irrational-overseas-belt-and-road-investment-state-planner-idUSKCN1AY0FN.
31. Kane Wu and Julie Zhu, "Exclusive: China's 'big four' banks raise billions for Belt and Road Deal – sources", Reuters, August 22, 2017, at https://www.reuters.com/article/us-ccb-fundraising/exclusive-chinas-big-four-banks-raise-billions-for-belt-and-road-deals-sources-idUSKCN1B20ER; Kane Wu and Sumeet Chatterjee, "Exclusive: China's Belt and Road Acquisitions Surge despite Outbound Capital Crackdown", *Reuters*, August 16, 2017, at https://uk.reuters.com/article/us-china-m-a/exclusive-chinas-belt-and-road-acquisitions-surge-despite-outbound-capital-crackdown-idUKKCN1AW00K.
32. Author's personal communication with a foreign diplomat who observed BRI Forum in Beijing, June 2017.
33. "West Underestimates China's New Silk Road, German Envoy Says", *Channel NewsAsia*, June 8, 2017, at http://www.channelnewsasia.com/news/asiapacific/west-underestimates-china-s-new-silk-road—german-envoy-says-8930082.
34. The letter is available at http://www.bmwi.de/Redaktion/DE/Downloads/S-T/schreiben-de-fr-it-an-malmstroem.pdf?__blob=publicationFile&v=5. Also see Jorge Valero, "Commission Says Proposal to Block Chinese Takeovers Is 'Worth Discussing'", *EurActive*, February 15, 2017, at https://www.euractiv.com/section/trade-society/news/commission-says-proposal-to-block-chinese-takeovers-is-worth-discussing; Sarantis Michalopoulos, "EU Wants to Tackle

Public Procurement 'Imbalance' with Foreign Countries", EurActive, April 4, 2017, at https://www.euractiv.com/section/economy-jobs/news/commission-need-for-an-eu-deal-to-tackle-public-procurement-imbalance-with-third-countries/.

35. "President Jean-Claude Juncker's State of the Union Address", European Commission – Speech, Brussels, September 13, 2017, at http://europa.eu/rapid/press-release_SPEECH-17-3165_en.htm.
36. "Commission Launches Reflection on Harnessing Globalization", European Commission - Press Release, May 10, 2017, at http://europa.eu/rapid/press-release_IP-17-1230_en.htm.
37. "Xi Jinping shouci xitong changshu 'xinchangtai'" [Xi Jinping for the First Time Systematically Elaborated 'New Normal'], *Xinhua*, November 9, 2014, at http://news.xinhuanet.com/world/2014-11/09/c_1113175964.htm.
38. Justyna Szczudlik and Damian Wnukowski, "China as an 'Engine' of Globalisation: More Words than Deeds", PISM Policy Paper, No. 5 (158), September 2017.
39. Wang Yizhou, "Kaichuang 'xin xing quanqiuli'" [To Initiate a 'New Model of Globalization'], *Beijing Ribao*, April 24, 2017, at http://bjrb.bjd.com.cn/html/2017-04/24/content_128134.htm.
40. "Yidai yi lu" guoji luntanhui kaimu, Liu Qibao fabiao zhuzhi yanjiang", No. 12.
41. "Xi Jinping zai Zhongguo Gongchangdang di shijiu ci quanguo daibiao dahui shang de baogao" [Xi Jinping's Report Delivered at the 19th CPC Congress], *People's Daily*, October 28, 2017, at http://cpc.people.com.cn/n1/2017/1028/c64094-29613660.html.
42. "Shouquan fabu: Zhongguo Gongchangdang zhangcheng" [Authorized Release: Charter of the Communist Party of China], *Xinhua*, October 28, 2017, at http://news.xinhuanet.com/politics/19cpcnc/2017-10/28/c_1121870794.htm.

3

China's Security Governance Conception for Asia: Perspectives from India

Susanne Kamerling

Under President Xi Jinping's leadership, China has stepped up its multilateral efforts in taking an active role in international institutions and regional governance. Beijing has buffed its reputation and displayed its leadership by hosting the G20 Summit in 2016, the Belt and Road Summit in May 2017 and the BRICS Summit in September 2017. However, next to shaping the region economically by setting up the Asian Infrastructure and Investment Bank (AIIB) and launching Xi Jinping's landmark foreign policy project of the 'Belt and Road Initiative' (BRI; formerly, One Belt One Road, OBOR), Beijing has moreover aimed at shaping the security governance conception of the region. China has made use of every opportunity in Asia's many regional fora to promote China as the engineer of a new regional security architecture in the making. China's chairmanship of the Conference on Interaction and Confidence Building Measures in Asia (CICA) between 2014 and 2016 and of the Shanghai Cooperation Organisation (SCO) from 2018 onwards provide for agenda-setting testing platforms for China's ideas on security cooperation in the region. In a foreign policy strategy in which infrastructure and connectivity are the major components, China is increasingly drawn into regional security challenges that it cannot evade to address. The CICA and SCO largely evolve around the same themes as the BRI, and can potentially serve as a security complement in which the key partners can address upcoming challenges that the development of infrastructural projects in the various corners of Asia are bound to evoke.

Setting up large infrastructure projects in the region does not automatically lead to more connectivity; it could also flare up tensions. In South Asia, the China-Pakistan Economic Corridor (CPEC), which connects the land and maritime components of the BRI, potentially puts an additional strain on India-Pakistan relations.[1] The CPEC is also one of the main reasons India's response to China's BRI initiative has been lukewarm at best. China has attempted to boost CICA into a regional security platform during its chairmanship, and will most likely use the SCO in a similar manner. But despite having accepted India and Pakistan as full members of the SCO since June 2017, this does not necessarily mean the chances of reaching consensus on security issues in the region have expanded; quite to the contrary – it might weaken the ability of the SCO to act.

Xi's BRI and the Chinese White Paper on Asia Pacific Security Cooperation released in January 2017, however, sketches the contours of a foreign policy in which infrastructure development projects are not only the core of China's economic and political strategy but also of a China-driven regional security governance conception.[2] China however remains opaque on what role it envisions for other major powers in the region in its proposed regional security architecture. What does this imply for the regional security cooperation and potential success of the infrastructure projects in bringing connectivity in the region forward? Moreover, how does emerging power India perceive China's proposals for the Asia Pacific region?

Many observers have identified Sino-Indian cooperation as crucial for the future of Asia, particularly in the context of setting up an effective regional security architecture. At the SCO Summit in June 2017, both leaders recognised that their relations are important for regional stability in a multipolar world. India's Foreign Secretary Jaishankar even characterised the meeting as a 'new equilibrium' in the relationship. Yet in May 2017 Prime Minister Modi decided to send a political signal by not attending the BRI Summit in China, and the summer of 2017 was particularly hot with the Doklam standoff; although the leaders of both countries made sure not to let it fully escalate. As the world's largest emerging markets, with the largest populations, both countries hold aspirations to play a leadership role in Asia. The foreign policies of both countries have become more outward looking since the end of the Cold War, and this process has experienced intensification in the last decade. Their efforts meet in Southeast Asia where both countries have bought into the 'Association of Southeast Asian Nations (ASEAN) Way' – the softly institutionalised regional approach to security governance. China has moreover expanded its role in South Asia, whereas India has taken steps towards closer involvement in the South China Sea and East Asia. It is therefore worthwhile to assess how India perceives China's security governance conception for the region.

As China assumed chairmanship of CICA in 2014 for a two-year term, it has made use of its corresponding agenda-setting privilege to launch several initiatives and attempt to boost CICA up to a template for regional security governance. Although CICA in its current state is a mechanism, not yet a full-fledged organisation, Xi grasped the opportunity at the 2014 CICA to launch his 'New Asian Security Concept' and call for a 'New Regional Security Architecture' to be set up in Asia. A call he reiterated at the Foreign Ministers Meeting of CICA in April 2016 in Shanghai. As a pan-Asian forum, including many countries from West, Central, South, Southeast and East Asia, CICA is the only regional platform next to the SCO in which the US does not participate, and where Japan has only observer status. Covering the whole of Asia, CICA was meant to explore the possibility of a regional security architecture based on security dialogue and security cooperation by increasing the frequency of meetings of foreign ministers and summits, professionalise the CICA Secretariat and set up task forces in confidence building measures and a defense consultation mechanism.[3] Also, cooperation and exchanges in counter-terrorism, business, tourism and environmental protection would be increased.[4]

Xi's foreign policy is perceived within and outside of China as being more proactive than that of his predecessors and the flagship of his foreign policy strategy is the BRI. With this massive plan, China attempts to integrate Eurasia through large-scale infrastructure projects, while at the same time boosting its domestic economy in times of a crucial transition phase from export-oriented to consumption-driven. The fact that the 19th National Congress of the People's of the Communist Party of China enshrined 'Xi Jinping Thought', including the BRI, into the Chinese Constitution in October 2017, has only increased the importance of success of this mega project, not only for the current President but for the reputation of the Communist Party as a whole. Xi's effort to position himself as a paramount leader of China and 'core of the leadership' of the CCP is a factor not to be underestimated in this foreign policy activism. Although Xi's policies are not altogether undisputed, his initiatives, in particular the BRI, have received unprecedented attention worldwide.

But not all actors in the region are similarly enthusiastic about Xi's initiatives, although most countries welcome foreign investments, infrastructural projects and greater connectivity. The same goes for India under Prime Minister Modi. Although New Delhi has joined the AIIB initiated by Beijing, and is on the lookout to attract foreign investments and improve its infrastructure, it has mixed feelings towards the Belt and Road Initiative.[5] Especially the CPEC (part of the BRI) that China invests heavily in, is problematic to India, as it runs through the disputed territory of Jammu and Kashmir.[6] Indian foreign secretary Jaishankar commented on the concept of connectivity in Asia at the 2015 Raisina Dialogue in New Delhi:

> The key issue is whether we will build our connectivity through consultative processes or more unilateral decisions. Our preference is for the former...But we cannot be impervious to the reality that others may see connectivity as an exercise in hard-wiring that influences choices. This should be discouraged, because particularly in the absence of an agreed security architecture in Asia, it could give rise to unnecessary competitiveness. Connectivity should diffuse national rivalries, not add to regional tensions.[7]

In responding to questions following his lecture at the International Institute of Strategic Studies (IISS) in Singapore, the Foreign Secretary was even more outspoken about OBOR: "Where we are concerned, this is a national Chinese initiative. The Chinese devised it, created a blueprint. It wasn't an international initiative they discussed with the whole world, with countries that are interested or affected by it."[8] India's leadership feels that as the other big emerging country, New Delhi should have been consulted by China about initiatives that affect the whole region. Especially China's push into its neighbouring countries in South Asia as well as the Indian Ocean is critically observed by India.

The aim of this analysis is to examine how China's security governance conception, including the 'New Asian Security Concept' and call for a 'New Regional Security Architecture' resonate within the Indian strategic community, and what this implies for the thinking on and prospects for regionalism and security cooperation in the Asia Pacific. These findings are based on fieldwork research between May and August 2016 in which the author conducted roughly 50 interviews among academics, (former) diplomats and military officers in New Delhi, Sonipat and Varanasi, India.[9] The ensuing part first briefly outlines China's evolving security conception and its regional security architecture proposal. The second part assesses how these are perceived within the Indian strategic community. This is followed by concluding thoughts on regionalism and security cooperation in Asia.

China's Evolving Views on Security Governance

With the launch of 'the New Asian Security Concept' at the CICA Summit of 2014, Xi Jinping has put forward his own security concept that is part of Beijing's vision for the Asia Pacific region. With this he has added a new element to China's former 'New Security Concept' (NSC) that originated in the late 1990s and has dominated the government discourse since then. The NSC, which was also the basis of the peaceful development discourse of China, consisted of the three c's: cooperative, comprehensive and common security. The New Asian Security Concept adds 'inclusive and sustainable security' to that equation.[10] Although this new concept also focuses on development as the basis for security, as the NSC did, it goes a step further by stating that security is only durable if it focuses on both development and security that is of equal and inclusive nature, for the whole Asian region.[11] Many interviewees from China's foreign policy elite have recognised this as a new feature of China's security concept, and potentially also a new local norm that China wants to put forward in the international society.[12] A local norm that potentially links together many emerging countries in the Asian region, including India, who have the same pursuit in mind.

Xi's speech at the CICA Summit however also advocated for 'Asian solutions to Asian problems', thereby putting forward a more exclusive form of regionalism that seems to be predominantly aimed at undermining the extra-regional dominance of the US in the Asia Pacific. Although Xi states that Asia is open to countries from other parts of the world, at the same time he claims that: "It is for the people of Asia to run the affairs of Asia, solve the problems of Asia and uphold the security of Asia... China's peaceful development begins here in Asia, finds its support in Asia, and delivers tangible benefits to Asia".[13] With this, the stance on security governance, in specific, and regionalism, in general, have become more pronounced under the current government. Since China's opening-up and reform, and throughout the 1990s, Beijing has taken a more open and constructive approach to multilateralism, especially in the region. For China to grow economically and develop domestically, a regional and international environment that was conducive to China's growth was much needed. Reassuring neighbours in the region as well as long-distance rivals therefore became crucial. This meant being more proactive in multilateral settings, while starting the long road of integration into the international society. Even though Beijing still preferred approaching the more traditional security issues related to territoriality and sovereignty within a bilateral framework, it has nonetheless actively participated in multilateral security fora in the region to foster the relations with its many neighbours. The past decade however, and especially the later period of Hu Jintao's reign, has seen a more assertive foreign policy of China in the region. This is not well received by many neighbouring countries and has led to increasing tensions. Under Xi, the South China Sea disputes have come to the forefront and a debate has started within China's foreign policy establishment about the role of the US in the region.[14]

President Xi, together with other regional leaders, have recognised the need for a more encompassing regional security architecture that goes beyond existing institutions, at least in its current form.[15] Regionalism in Asia has, predominantly because of recent history and Cold War experiences, developed differently than in other regions in the world. As Acharya points out, Asia "...does not offer examples that fit the established models of security multilateralism, such as collective security, collective defence, or even the "common security" model developed in Europe".[16] Although many commentators have been critical of the regional institutional infrastructure, calling it 'talk shops' or 'summitry' rather than multilateral organisations that produce concrete results and outcomes, various scholars have pointed out that this is a one-sided and Eurocentric view on security governance. In contrast, Chinese and other scholars have put forward the idea of 'relational security governance' that fits better the Chinese and other East Asian philosophical and cultural traditions.[17] Moreover, fitting this ideational framework is the norm of non-alliance. Based on the Sino-Indian agreement of 1954, this norm became the basis of the non-alignment movement in which both China and India played a leading role. Elites in China recognise this as a principle that to a large extent still dominates China's foreign policy behaviour. Instead of opting for (formalised) alliances, which are perceived to be aimed at a third party, China is trying to build a partnership network through which it aims to manage its foreign policy priorities and security worries. This preference for a non-binding, softly institutionalised form of regionalism fits the security order that has developed throughout Asia, with ASEAN being the leading example.[18]

By labelling both its security concept as the proposed regional architecture as 'Asian', Beijing claims to be either defining the region's preferences or is at least speaking in its name. This is not well received by other countries in East, Southeast and South Asia that have a troubled relationship with Beijing. In South Asia, India is the most obvious criticaster. The current Chinese Government however continues to pursue this approach to security governance and put it forward as exemplary for the region as a whole. Regional security architecture however cannot be effective or successful in bringing connectivity forward without support in the sub-regions in question. Sub-regions whose support is also needed in making the BRI trade and infrastructure projects work. Therefore, the ensuing part looks into the question how the other major emerging actor in the region, India, perceives this approach.

Perspectives from India

India's post-Cold War reorientation in foreign policy has seen a turn to its eastern neighbourhood predominantly to take part in the new economic dynamism that was taking place in Southeast Asia and grasp the political and diplomatic opportunities at hand.[19] This Look East policy initiated in 1992 also heralded a strategy of increased multilateral involvement of New Delhi in the broader Asian region. ASEAN, as the most coherent regional organisation at the time, was the prime focus of institutional cooperation, and India was soon accepted as an important partner. The early stage of the Look East policy thus focussed primarily on economic relations and institutional involvement, while both sides did not prioritise security issues. It was only at the turn of the millennium that India's agenda towards Southeast and East Asia became broader as to include security issues more prominently.[20] The current Indian Government under Prime Minister Modi has aimed at making this policy even more comprehensive, renaming it the Act East policy.

India, with its Look East and subsequent Act East policy, has thus shown an increased multilateral engagement for over a decade. Like China, New Delhi has bought into the so-called 'ASEAN way', which is characterised by a preference for a non-binding, non-legalised and softly institutionalised regional approach to security governance.[21] As one Indian scholar put it: "The ASEAN way really helps Indian multilateralism...But our approach is not limited to this; our Act East policy is much richer. It is one of our most comprehensive foreign policies. It has become the ASEAN plus 'security provider' thinking."[22] This policy has seen a strengthening of (maritime) security and defence cooperation of India with ASEAN-members in Southeast Asia, most notably the Philippines, Brunei and Vietnam. New Delhi has recently even sent a two-and-a-half month operational deployment of its Eastern Fleet to the South China Sea and North Western Pacific culminating in the Malabar exercise. This was taking it a step further than its traditional perception of a sphere of influence that stretched up to the Strait of Malacca, and has not been well-received by China.[23]

Overall, the perceptions within the Indian strategic community about China are not altogether favourable. Most agree on Beijing's merits in bringing the country's development forward; there is a certain admiration for how China has managed its economy and growth and how it strategies its rise abroad through its foreign policy. The views diverge, however, when it comes to China's increased presence in South Asia and the Indian Ocean and whether or not China is a threat to the region. There is still a deep mistrust stemming from the 1962 War, and former Prime Minister Nehru is criticised by several respondents for putting his trust in China at the time. The majority of interviewees are wary of China and argue that this naivety should not be repeated; India should keenly watch China's advance into the region. The other obvious thorn in the flesh for India is China's close alliance with Pakistan. As Kalyanaraman argues: "India-Pakistan relations should therefore really be studied as a subset of India-China relations."[24] Others state more lightly that China's presence is simply a fact of life and that catching up is not the issue; India really needs to make sure it reaps the benefits of the opportunities offered by China or Beijing's regional initiatives. As one Indian professor in Chinese Studies claimed: "My sense really is: if China is a rising power, you have to give it some space and acknowledge that. If you keep resisting, obviously conflict comes. The conflict is not from China rising, but from the rest resisting."[25]

China's ideas on security governance in the region do not resonate well within the Indian strategic community; they are mostly seen as China-led initiatives that attempt to establish regional hegemony, which undermines multipolarity in the region, and hence India's position. The specific perspectives among the Indian strategic community with regard to China's ideas about and initiatives for the region can be clustered around *five main drivers. First of all*, India's own ideas on regionalism and stance towards the region. Pan-Asian ideas are not new to India. As the prime architect of India's post-independence foreign policy, Nehru devised the ideal of cooperation among Asian nations and Asian unity.[26] In his speech at the first Asian Relations Conference of 1947 in Delhi he stated that Asian nations had come together in a spirit of cooperation to further peace and progress around the world and create a normative international order.[27] This vision of a common Asian identity that should inform regional organisations was the central tenet to his overall foreign policy views.[28] As a former Indian Ambassador to China put it: "In Prime Minister Nehru's time there was a deep faith in Asian unity. If only Asia would come together and all Asia's problems would be solved. But then 1962 happened. We suffered when China invaded. After that we strengthened our military assets and didn't go around trusting people."[29] Besides emphasising that

Nehru's conceptual ideas were put forward in a time when India lacked capacity whatsoever to implement any of it, most interviewees play down the effect that Nehru's foreign policy principles have in India's current foreign policy in any direct sense. India, they argue, has moved from idealism to realism and pragmatism in its foreign policy; and the emphasis is on core interests nowadays instead of ideals and values. As an International Relations-scholar sums up: "We lost a lot of our post-colonial values. The Pan-Asian ideals...we are also past that. Now we would just like to rise economically, and have more say in global institutions."[30] India has greatly valued its participation in multilateral institutions, including fora in Asia, but it has its own preferences as to which mechanisms hold 'regional architecture potential'. Several scholars and (former) diplomats argue that India prefers the empowerment of the East Asia Summit (EAS) to become decisive in security cooperation as well as ASEAN-led mechanism like the ASEAN Regional Forum (ARF), mainly because these are more inclusively Asian-Pacific.[31] The dominant idea is that with the US, Japan and ASEAN at the table, there are much more chances to fair outcomes. So even though China puts its weight behind CICA, this mechanism does not generate much support in Indian foreign policy circles.[32] It must be noted however, that the current policy of India is to be part of any multilateral organisation rather than stay behind. New Delhi has just become a full member of the SCO, and has applied for membership of Asia Pacific Economic Cooperation (APEC) and the Nuclear Supplier Group (NSG). One expert explains: "We want to be part of the thought process... The general idea is that we want to be at the table, part of the decision making to be able to influence and shape it, and be able to check China's actions in the region in the process."[33]

The second driver of India's position is China's recent stance in the South China Sea territorial disputes and towards Southeast Asian states of ASEAN. China's behaviour in the maritime sphere and how Southeast Asian nations have responded to China is reason for most Indian scholars and analysts not only to question China's benign intentions but also to be sceptic about the success of a regional security governance in Asia that is dominated by China. As a former Indian Ambassador stresses: "The way China dealt with the South China Sea and ASEAN completely obliterated the benign face China created through their support during the Asian financial crisis of 1997."[34] There are worries among Indian scholars that the maritime domain will become increasingly securitised and free movement will be affected. While the Indian Government formally does not take a position in the South China Sea disputes, it has taken a firm stance in upholding the freedom of navigation. This is also strongly linked to the concerns about China's presence in the Indian Ocean that is perceived by India as strategic encirclement. A retired military officer states: "All these countries are hedging against China because we are all concerned about the direction China is taking and its strategic behaviour in the South China Sea. The PLA and submarines are in the Indian Ocean, Sri Lanka, Gwadar, Djibouti; all these things create concerns in India. India's reaction is: if we send submarines to the South China Sea: how would you react?"[35] There are moreover questions of how compatible China's notions of governing its neighbouring waters and oceans are with the Maritime Silk Road it has put forward. Observers point to the importance of freedom of navigation and the cooperative venture that is needed in the oceans for economic interconnectedness and trade in a region where so many countries have major interests.[36]

Third, the contested position of the US in the region is a main driver in India's stance. Here, it is of importance to clarify the difference between Asia – the geographical construct of the continental Eurasia region –and the Asia-Pacific; the countries in or near the Western Pacific Ocean; typically much of East Asia, Southeast Asia, South Asia and Oceania. Whereas views diverge among India's security elite on whether America's role in the Asian region should or should not diminish, agreement does exist on the conviction that the US is a legitimate power in the Asia Pacific and therefore should be included in any regional security architecture. A critical shift occurred in the Indian stance towards the US. During the Cold War strong anti-American sentiments dominated Indian politics and the foreign policy establishment. In a way, India used to be much closer to China's views in this regard. The presence of the US has, however, once again become desirable to New Delhi. Another former Indian Ambassador to China, therefore, notes that China has defeated its own objective in that sense.[37] The 'Asia for Asians' idea that China has put forward in the context of its proposal for regional architecture is strongly perceived to be predominantly aimed at pushing the US out of the region. A retired Admiral notes: "That is what you say when you want the US out: Asia for Asians. We are familiar with that: keeping the US out; that was also our reflex during the Cold War. We also opposed the presence of the US on Diego Garcia. But now we have a much more favourable, positive relation with the US."[38] India and the US have indeed drawn closer together, in particular after the nuclear deal that was initiated under former Prime Minister Singh and the Bush-administration in 2005. The visit of Obama to India early 2015 is again seen as a departure, as the joint statement was a testament of shared positions. The statement reads:

> Recognising the important role that both countries play in promoting peace, prosperity, stability and security in the Asia-Pacific and Indian Ocean Region, and noting that India's 'Act East Policy' and the United States' rebalance to Asia provide opportunities for India, the United States, and other Asia-Pacific countries to work closely to strengthen regional ties, the Leaders announced a Joint Strategic Vision to guide their engagement in the region...Further underscoring the importance of implementing infrastructure projects to enhance connectivity and enable freer flow of commerce and energy in the region, the Leaders agreed to develop additional areas in which both sides could work together, including on India's initiatives to enhance its connectivity with the South and South East Asian region... The President and the Prime Minister also welcomed the role of the leaders-led East Asia Summit (EAS) process in promoting open, balanced and inclusive security architecture in the region.[39]

Most interviewees are thus sceptic of China's 'Asia for Asians' construct. For one, because the US is too powerful in the region, and two, because India's elite as well as most countries in the region want the US to stay and play a role. The countries that are in dispute with China or have concerns about China's rise are generally not willing to give up on the one diplomatic tool of bandwagoning that they have and let China take the lead on security issues, or such is the argumentation. The Asia-for-Asians idea therefore does not seem to have many takers. The Indian strategic community seems to be wary of a definition of security and security architecture that is 'Asian' in name, but predominantly put forward by China.

Fourth, India has throughout the decades developed its own ideas of regionalism and expectations of multilateral security cooperation. Key words that are often mentioned within this context are openness, inclusiveness and equality. As one scholar puts it: "India wants equality in the region; we demand an equal role. China and India are in the same league when it comes to leadership in the region."[40] In that sense, India is a proponent of 'cooperative security'[41] – one of the c's of China's security concept. The perceived hierarchy that is implicit in China's proposed regional architecture is not something that India would easily accept. In contrast, New Delhi is trying to balance its position in the initiatives and architecture that are already set up by China. The unilateralism of China's initiatives, which Indian Foreign Secretary Jaishankar explicitly mentioned at the IISS and Raisina dialogue, makes India uncomfortable. India's leadership aspirations are at a stage where it demands to at the very least be taken seriously and given a seat at the tables where the proposals are discussed. However, China has not made it clear how India, or other regional powers for that matter, fit in Beijing's initiatives including the new Asian security architecture China has proposed. This enhances the suspicions that China is striving for a unipolar Asia. Foreign Secretary Jaishankar states in this light: "Asia will no doubt go through some uncertainties before arriving at a new equilibrium. Other factors and other nations will definitely have a say too, among them ASEAN members, Japan or Australia. Shared power, if it works for all parties, will be at the heart of Asia's emerging security architecture".[42]

And finally, India's self-perceived limited role in the region is an important driver. In the end, many interviewees acknowledge, however great the aspirations might be, there is only so much India can do. There is a realisation that New Delhi is bound to its domestic priorities: stimulating its economic growth, elevating its population out of poverty and improving its governance are only some of the issues that will be high on the agenda for some time to come. This will have foreign policy implications as one scholar states: "Even though Southeast Asian nations would welcome a larger role for India in the region, we run into the limits of what we can do. We are not able to deliver; it's a systemic issue."[43] Also, there is no uniform position within the strategic community on whether or not India should even want to be a great power in the first place.[44] The Indian establishment itself moreover knows its challenges; the relative size of its foreign policy bureaucracy is very small, therefore limiting its potential activities. Several scholars acknowledge that India is still an elementary power in Asia and has not been able to implement the construct of leading power yet.[45] National Security Advisor Doval put it aptly when he said: "India has a mentality to punch below its weight. We should not punch below our weight or above our weight, but improve our weight and punch proportionately".[46]

In addition to these views among the strategic community vis-à-vis China's security governance proposals, the idea of 'relationality' and 'relational security governance' – which stems more from East Asian philosophy – in the Chinese approach does not resonate among the Indian security elite. The China experts that do know the concept, think that it is either a deflective strategy or Confucian Sino-centric construct that might be acceptable to East Asia, but not to other parts of the region, including India.[47]

Regional Security Cooperation: Concluding Thoughts

Although India is openly critical of Beijing's BRI, New Delhi is unwillingly wrapped up by it. All of its neighbours receive investments from Beijing for infrastructure development projects in the context of the BRI. Also, India itself has a strong economic connection to Beijing as China is heavily involved in India's economy. The current dynamics that are caused by the BRI in broader Asia, including the CPEC in South Asia, put New Delhi in a difficult position. Despite improved India-US relations, China's forays into Southeast and South Asia limit India's room for manoeuvre in its direct surroundings. Especially since India's neighbours in South Asia closely cooperate with China and increasingly play the 'China card' in their relations with New Delhi.[48] India seems to have no other choice than to join the expanding regional connectivity, engage with China in the process and at the same time strengthen its political presence in the region. India aims at being a driver in reconfiguring South Asia through its 'Act East Policy', Strategic Partnership with Japan and its investments in infrastructure projects like the Chabahar port in Iran. Also, Modi has stressed the importance of the South Asian Association for Regional Cooperation (SAARC) and regional formats like the Bay of Bengal Initiative for Multi-Sectoral Technical and Economic Cooperation (BIMSTEC), the Bangladesh-China-India-Myanmar Forum for Regional Cooperation (BCIM) and the Indian Ocean Rim Association (IORA). China in its turn seems to be more prone to keep India befriended. Xi and Modi reiterated at the SCO Summit of 2017 their relations are a factor of stability in a multipolar world, and that differences should not become disputes. China is trying to build partnerships in the process of developing infrastructure, also with India.

However, the regional security institutions in Asia remain fragile, despite Beijing's efforts in boosting them. The growing multilateral preferences of New Delhi increasingly push the country to be part of regional and international security fora, albeit with diverging success. Indian multilateral practices are also consistent with its preference for multipolarity in the region and globally. Nonetheless, there is a strong divergence in the outlook of India and China on how to upgrade the multilateralism in their foreign policy into a regional security architecture. One that is based on a shared view of the status quo and common ideas on how to move forward. China's proposals for Asian regionalism are not received with enthusiasm or support among the Indian strategic community. This makes the prospects of meaningful progress in security cooperation in the region through multilateral initiatives that are led by China, bleak. None of the interviewees perceived a stable regional order in Asia without the US, and Washington's departure is highly unlikely, whether China wants to or not. The ties between the US and India moreover, and India and Japan are increasingly getting stronger. Also, hope still exists in India and many Southeast Asian countries that the regional security mechanisms lead to moderation on China's side, and a certain binding to shared norms and rules of engagement. As one scholar states: "We need a degree of balance. At least at these fora China is being asked questions, certain concerns are being raised and they have to answer to certain queries. There is a degree of accountability."[49] Despite their wariness of China's security governance proposals for the region, for many countries – including India – their engagement in regional fora like the SCO and CICA is aimed at embedding China in a web of friendly arrangements that makes it less likely for Beijing to act unilaterally.

Beijing aims to bolster economic activity through developing infrastructure and strengthening connectivity in the region while at the same time ease regional tensions in the process. The idea behind the BRI is to overcome political fault lines through so-called 'win-win' partnerships. The projects involved will however undoubtedly run into security challenges; from protection of physical and digital infrastructure through high-risk areas to disputes about contested areas like Kashmir. To bring connectivity in the region forward in the medium to long term, cooperation on security issues will have to be taken to the next level. Despite having been reasonably successful in regional cooperation in the context of BRI projects, China has been less successful with its security governance proposals for the region however. Its calls for a new regional security architecture and boosting of platforms like CICA have not yet resulted in much. Regardless of China's weight behind it, CICA has not blossomed as the new regional security organisation, let alone security architecture. If Beijing is serious about the regional security architecture and bringing connectivity in the region forward, it will have to accommodate grievances that its forays into other sub-regions of Asia evoke.

NOTES

1. Christian Wagner, "The Effects of the China-Pakistan Economic Corridor on India-Pakistan Relations", Stiftung Wissenschaft und Politik, 2016, at http://www.swp-berlin.org/fileadmin/contents/products/comments/2016C25_wgn.pdf.
2. "China's Policies on Asia-Pacific Security Cooperation", The State Council Information Office of the People's Republic of China, 2017, at http://english.gov.cn/archive/white_paper/2017/01/11/content_281475539078636.htm.
3. Yaqing Qin, "International Society as a Process: Institutions, Identities and China's Peaceful Rise," *Chinese Journal of International Politics* 3, no. 2 (2010): 130.
4. Qin, "International Society as a Process: Institutions, Identities and China's Peaceful Rise," 130.
5. Jayant Prasad, "One Belt and Many Roads: China's Initiative and India's

Response", *Delhi Policy Group Brief*, 2015, at http://www.delhipolicygroup.com/uploads/publication_file/1093_OBOR_Prasad.pdf; Jabin T. Jacob, "India's Response to China's 'One Belt, One Road' Initiative", *Nação e Defesa*, 142, 2016, pp. 56-71.

6. Christian Wagner, No. 1.
7. S. Jaishankar, "Speech by Foreign Secretary at Raisina Dialogue in New Delhi", Ministry of External Affairs, March 2,2015, at http://mea.gov.in/Speeches-Statements.htm?dtl/26433/Speech_by_Foreign_Secretary_ at_ Raisina_Dialogue_in_New_Delhi_March_2_2015.
8. Charu Sudan Kasturi, "India Wrinkle on China Silk", *The Telegraph*. July 20, 2015, at http://www.telegraphindia.com/1150721/jsp/frontpage/story_32798.jsp; Jayant Prasad, No. 5.
9. During my visiting fellowship at the Institute for Defence Studies and Analyses (IDSA), New Delhi, between May and August 2016, I conducted roughly 50 interviews among the Indian strategic community, in particular Indian China experts. Moreover, in 2015, I conducted interviews in China.
10. Xi Jinping, "New Asian Security Concept for New Progress in Security Cooperation", Speech presented at the Fourth CICA Summit, Shanghai, China, May 21,2014, at http://www.fmprc.gov.cn/mfa_eng/zxxx_662805/t1159951.shtml.
11. Ibid.
12. Interview of the author with a Chinese associate professor and director, Beijing, China, May 2015; Interview of the author with a Chinese senior military officer (Col.) and director of a think tank, Beijing, China, December 2015.
13. Xi Jinping, No. 10.
14. Interview of the author with a Chinese senior military officer (Maj. Gen.) and secretary-general of a think tank, Beijing, China, December 2015.
15. Shannon Tiezzi, "At CICA, Xi Calls for New Regional Security Architecture", *The Diplomat*, May 22, 2014, at http://thediplomat.com/2014/05/at-cica-xi-calls-for-new-regional-security-architecture/.
16. Amitav Acharya, "Regional Institutions and Asian Security Order; Norms, Power, and Prospects for Peaceful Change", in Muthiah Alagappa (ed.), *Asian Security Order: Instrumental and Normative Features*, Stanford, Stanford University Press, 2003, p. 210.
17. Yaqing Qin, "Relationality and Processual Construction: Bringing Chinese Ideas into International Relations Theory", *Social Science in China*, 30 (4), 2009, at https://www.colwiz.com; Yaqing Qin, "International Society as a Process: Institutions, Identities and China's Peaceful Rise", *Chinese Journal of International Politics*, 3 (2), 2010, pp. 129-53; NivHoresh and Emilian Kavalski (eds.), *Asian Thought on China's Changing International Relations*, Palgrave Macmillan, Houndmills and New York, 2014; Emilian Kavalski, *Central Asia and the Rise of Normative Powers: Contextualizing the Security Governance of the European Union, China, and India*, Bloomsbury Publishing, New York, 2012.
18. Amitav Acharya, "Culture, Security, Multilateralism: The 'ASEAN Way' and Regional Order", *Contemporary Security Policy*, 19 (1), 1998, pp. 55-84.
19. C. Raja Mohan, "India's Role in Asian Security", *Global Power Shifts and Strategic Transition in Asia*, Academic Foundation, New Delhi, 2009.
20. Ibid.

21. Amitav Acharya, No. 18.
22. Interview of the author with a senior research scholar working in a think tank, New Delhi, July 2016.
23. Franz-Stefan Gady, "India Sends Stealth Warships to South China Sea", *The Diplomat*, May 19, 2016, at http://thediplomat.com/2016/05/india-sends-stealth-warships-to-south-china-sea/.
24. Presentation IDSA Fellows Seminar "India's foreign policy options in the Asia-Pacific: A Critical Evaluation", New Delhi, June 10, 2016.
25. Interview of the author with an Indian China Studies professor working in a university, New Delhi, May 2016.
26. Jawaharlal Nehru, "Speech Jawaharlal Nehru at the Asian Relations Conference", Indian Council World Affairs (ICWA), 1947, at http://icwadelhi.info/asianrelationsconference/images/stories/jawaharlalnehru.pdf.
27. Kanti Bajpai, Saira Basit and V. Krishnappa, *India's Grand Strategy History, Theory, Cases*, Routledge, London, 2014.
28. Bhalla, Madhu, "Nehru's Vision of Asian Identity Implications for the Future", *South Asian Survey*, 19 (2), 2012, pp. 283-301.
29. Interview of the author with a former Indian Ambassador and current think tank researcher, New Delhi, June 2016.
30. Interview of the author with an Indian IR-professor working in a university, New Delhi, May 2016.
31. Jagannath P. Panda, "India's Security Outlook and Views on Multilateral Cooperation: The Emerging Asia-Pacific Theater", *Prospects of Multilateral Cooperation in the Asia Pacific: To Overcome the Gap of Security Outlooks*, National Institute for Defence Studies, Tokyo, 2013, pp. 69-86, at http://www.nids.go.jp/english/event/symposium/pdf/2013/E-04.pdf.
32. Interview of the author with a former Indian Ambassador and current think tank researcher, New Delhi, June 2016; interview of the author with a Brigadier (ret.) and current think tank researcher; New Delhi, May 2016; interview of the author with an Indian professor in China Studies, New Delhi, June 2016.
33. Interview of the author with a director of a think tank, New Delhi, May 2016.
34. Interview of the author with a former Indian Ambassador and current think tank researcher, New Delhi, May 2016.
35. Interview of the author with a Brigadier (ret.) and current think tank researcher
36. Ibid; interview of the author with an Indian professor in China Studies, New Delhi, June 2016.
37. Interview of the author with a former Indian Ambassador and current think tank researcher, New Delhi, May 2016.
38. Interview of the author with an Indian Admiral, New Delhi, June 2016.
39. "Joint Statement during the Visit of President of USA to India – Shared Effort; Progress for All", Ministry of External Affairs, January 25, 2016, at http://mea.gov.in/bilateral-documents.htm?dtl/24726/Joint_Statement_ during_ the_visit_of_President_of_USA_to_India_Shared_Effort_Progress_for_All.
40. Interview of the author with a senior research scholar working in a think tank, New Delhi, July 2016.
41. C. Raja Mohan, No. 19, p. 54.
42. S. Jaishankar, "IISS Fullerton Lecture by Dr. S. Jaishankar, Foreign Secretary in Singapore", Ministry of External Affairs, July 20, 2015, at http://mea.gov.in/

Speeches-Statements.htm?dtl/25493/IISS_Fullerton_Lecture_ by_ Foreign_ Secretary_in_Singapore (Accessed July 16, 2016).

43. Interview of the author with an associate researcher working in a think tank, New Delhi, July 2016.
44. The diversity of views on this issue was well represented at the presentation of Bharat Karnad's book *Why India Is Not a Great Power (Yet)*, IDSA seminar, May 18, 2016. Also, the divergent views became apparent in the interviews.
45. Interview of the author with an Indian professor in China Studies, New Delhi, June 2016; interview of the author with a senior research scholar working in a think tank, New Delhi, July 2016.
46. Srinath Rao, "NSA Ajit Doval Underlines Use of Power: India Should Stop Punching below Its Weight", *The Indian Express*, August 5,2015, at http://indianexpress.com/article/india/india-others/ajit-doval-underlines-use-of-power-india-should-stop-punching-below-its-weight/.
47. Two interviews with professors of China Studies at different universities, New Delhi, May and June 2016.
48. Christian Wagner, "The Role of India and China in South Asia", *Strategic Analysis*, 40 (4), 2016, pp. 307-20.
49. Interview of the author with a director of a think tank, New Delhi, May 2016.

4

Reflection on OBOR: A Test of Out-of-the-box Thinking: A Chinese Perspective

Huang Yunsong

For a substantial part of history, China and India were unfamiliar neighbours with fuzzy memories of cultural and economic bondage in ancient time, distinctively different legacies of colonialism and the Great Wars and huge trust deficit due to the brief scuffle in 1962, which has kept the two countries mostly detached from each other for decades in separate confined spaces, physically and mentally, and hence provided grounds for misunderstanding and self-fulfilling suspicion. To strive for economic and political excellence in the world arena, both of the latecomers felt the necessity to outreach beyond their peripheries in a great sense. When unveiling the Belt and Road Initiative in 2013, China did not realise that its breach of India's traditional sphere of influence in an abrupt and decisive way, though primarily in infrastructural and economic terms, was tantamount to seeking an all-out confrontation. Although being attributable to a range of external factors, the strenuous exchange between China and India over One Belt and One Road (OBOR) signifies their loss of focus on convergence in a contemporary and meaningful context, in the aspects of mutually beneficial economic integration, common prosperity and stability in the region and shared responsibilities in solving the pending issues between the two.

OBOR in Relation to India

OBOR is a grand development initiative and framework promoted by China since 2013. This conception has its primary focus on connectivity and economic cooperation with the countries in Eurasia and Africa. Of the two components of OBOR, namely the Silk Road Economic Belt (SREB) and the Maritime Silk Road (MSR), the former is land based and bears little connection to India, while the latter is aimed to establish a highly integrated space along the littoral of Southeast Asia, South Asia, Middle East and East Africa. The midsection of MSR around the subcontinent greatly overlaps with India's traditional sphere of influence.

India's opposition to the OBOR initiative, heavily suspecting its military and strategic implications, caught China by surprise and confusion in the first place. India's preference of geopolitics vigilance over trans-regional economic cooperation has exposed the fragility of its development-oriented relations with China. It also clearly reminded China that India was not ready to reinforce its economic growth before attaining a climate of genuine mutual trust and confidence.

Overriding the potential economic benefits, the divergent ideas on OBOR well debated in New Delhi have left little room for Beijing's further explanation. As general precautions, India's negative interpretation of OBOR seems to be justifiable from the perspective of national security. But it becomes dangerous when the interpretation is built on false reading of the text, or advocates a sense of inevitable rivalry.

Thinking Inside the Box

For the past 70 years, China and India have been everything but trustworthy partners. Even at the initial honeymoon stage, China was quite clear that challenge from India to its sovereignty over Tibet could be a longstanding headache, in one way or another. India was also very grumpy about loss of the buffer zone created by British Raj. Besides, there are many pending problems stalling the development of bilateral relations, to name a few, the territorial dispute, Tibet issue, transboundary water resources controversy and China-Pakistan relations, which have limited the creative thinking of China-India cooperation.

At present time, perhaps the most worrying reality at the bilateral level is that the rise of both countries so far has largely been the achievement of their respective cooperation with the developed economies, rather than a result of embracing each other. While both sides are aware of the positive significance of full cooperation for their own development goals, the lack of trust and confidence is hindering India's will to move forward with OBOR, which has been dismissed by New Delhi as merely a Chinese initiative devised with Chinese interests.

In-the-box thinking for China-India relations on both sides has shown strong influence on a range of issues from trade imbalance to political system, regional power framework and the world order at large, which in turn present major obstacles for them to overcome before reaching a consensus on any mega plan of far-reaching implications. In other words, the standstill between China and India on OBOR is the inevitable outcome of in-the-box thinking and certain external factors beyond their control. But exactly at this moment, getting out of the box and looking at the above issues in a different way appear to be profoundly important.

Misreading of CPEC

As the most frequently mentioned concept, OBOR has become a symbol of all connectivity projects conceptualised by China. For local Chinese authorities, it implies huge economic and political interests to have their own connectivity ambition included in the grand initiative. But at the international level, the Chinese Government exercised extreme caution in specifying its detail and the external links, so as to avoid any misconception especially for the neighbouring countries. Nevertheless, the effort to segregate the China-Pakistan Economic Corridor (CPEC) from OBOR was proven futile in convincing the Indian strategic community, which took for granted the CPEC as an integral part and a flagship project of OBOR. It is undeniable that some unserious Chinese scholars also played the wrong cord and misled the outside world by confusing the true relation between the CPEC and OBOR.

The CPEC is a mega project running through Gilgit-Baltistan, the disputed territory of Kashmir that India firmly believes to be its own. In a strict sense, the CPEC is not qualified as a bilateral issue between China and India until the Kashmir issue is properly resolved through bilateral dialogue between India and Pakistan. However, it has become one of the paramount reasons frequently indicated by Indian decision-makers, scholars and analysts for their opposition to OBOR. To make sure if the argument is sound and valid, two questions need to be raised in relation to India's concern over the correlation between OBOR and CPEC. Firstly, does OBOR really include the CPEC? Secondly, does China take sides on the issue of territorial dispute over Kashmir between India and Pakistan by sponsoring the CPEC?

As for the first question, the CPEC has never been officially announced as an integral part of OBOR, though their close relation was duly recognised by China. Surprisingly, there is a strong tendency in India to regard most of the trans-regional connectivity schemes proposed by China as part of OBOR. Another mistake, for example, is the Bangladesh-China-India-Myanmar Economic Corridor (BCIM) that was a connectivity project conceptualised back in 1999. To be exact, both the CPEC and BCIM are only parallel projects independent of OBOR, as per Section 3 of the Action Plan of the Central Government of China, March 28, 2015:[1]

> ...The China-Pakistan Economic Corridor and the Bangladesh-China-India-Myanmar Economic Corridor are closely related to the Belt and Road Initiative, and therefore require closer cooperation and greater progress...

As for the second question, it is the long-standing position of China not to take sides with either party on the Kashmir dispute, which is subject to the binding principles of China's foreign policy. Similar to the US policy on Kashmir, which has not seen substantial changes despite the profoundly improved Indo-US relations, China does not support Pakistan's agenda for internationalising the Kashmir dispute, and proactively encourages Islamabad to engage with India for a negotiated solution rather than a referendum settlement on the issue. China is even ready to renegotiate with India on border in accordance with the final settlement of the Kashmir dispute. This very neutral stance of China was clearly revealed in Article 6 of the *Boundary Agreement between China and Pakistan (1963)*,[2] and it will not make any difference whether India accepts its legitimacy:

> The two Parties have agreed that after the settlement of the Kashmir dispute between Pakistan and India, the sovereign authority concerned will reopen negotiations with the Government of the People's Republic of China, on the boundary as described in Article Two of the present Agreement, so as to sign a formal Boundary Treaty to replace the present agreement.

It is interesting to note the comparison made by Indian scholars between China's infrastructural development under the CPEC and India's energy exploration in the South China Sea (SCS),[3] where a dispute over maritime rights has already been in place between China and Vietnam for decades. Except for raising protests and demanding India to restrain the investment and marine development activities in the disputed area of the SCS in collaboration with Vietnam, China tacitly allowed the situation to take its natural course, and carefully kept the overall cooperative relation with India insulated from the controversy.

It is Beijing's intention to prevent any dispute involving a third party from undermining its comprehensive engagement with New Delhi. To ensure proper respect for each other's core national interests, both countries have to learn to contain the geopolitical implication of any economic undertakings in a flexible manner. Based on such basic understanding, China has put extra emphasis on separating the CPEC from OBOR, though the appeasement signal did not impress India at all. From a realistic point of view, however, by requesting China to reverse the CPEC as the prerequisite for it to give OBOR a positive consideration, India can hardly achieve any substantial gains on the Kashmir issue, but could possibly create an insurmountable obstacle in the complex fabric of the bilateral relations.

Metaphors of MSR

In regard to India and its immediate neighbourhood, the MSR bears most relevance, and could be of strategic importance to the regional order. Since the introduction of the OBOR initiative, there has arisen a renewed research interest in the "String of Pearls" and the maritime expeditions of Admiral Zheng He in the early 15th century. But several conflicting arguments have been offered in terms of historic evaluation. This is a typical example of the Rashomon effect, where the same event is given contradictory interpretations by different individuals involved, and the objectivity becomes submerged into positional and textual reflexivity. To put it bluntly, China has never being strong in the verbal defence of its motives. Therefore, its publicity outreach on MSR's economic focus was largely overwhelmed by one-sided narratives about its military ambition in the Indian Ocean Region.

The most popular contemporary metaphor of MSR says that it is an attempt at rebranding the "string of pearls",[4] which was a geopolitical hypothesis invented by a US defence contractor in 2005, but most frequently used in Indian media. The theory presents the argument of economic means for military ends, speculating China's intention to expand its naval presence through civilian port infrastructures along the Indian Ocean rim, and implying the military encirclement to the littoral states. This metaphor is almost convincing, considering China's investment in Hambantota (Sri Lanka), Gwadar (Pakistan), Obock (Djibouti), and its deep interests in Sonadia (Bangladesh) and Marao Atoll (Maldives). In the analysis, however, China's motives for economic gains and security of sea lines of communication[5] were only treated as the disguise of vicious calculation. Besides, the rationality for a country of its clout to expand the maritime footprints was inconveniently ignored.

A selective description and analogy of Admiral Zheng He's expeditions in the Ming Dynasty seems to be necessary to bring out a judgemental prediction on a high possibility of repetition of the past pattern of China's quest for maritime influence. From the perspective of some Indian scholars, Zheng's naval expeditions were of aggressive nature, and brought the Indian Ocean under the dominance of a single imperial power that intervened in local politics, instituted regime changes and tried to monopolise all commercial activities related to China.[6] This analysis is partially in resonance with the comment by Richard von Glahn that "Zheng He reshaped Asia", but Glahn's perspective also covers Zheng He's role in building, for instance, Malacca, on the Malayan peninsula, into the great port and hub of a trading network that extended across Southeast Asia and up to China.[7]

Metaphors can be useful as general precautions, but they become dangerous when they convey a sense of historical inexorableness.[8] Painting a picture of China as a hegemonic power both now and in history, these narratives inevitably leave a space blank on viability of the projection in the contemporary context. Firstly, how can it be financially practical for China to create an effective military encirclement against India? Even with a defence budget of approximately US $151 billion for 2017,[9] it is highly doubtful that China can afford this costly game, especially to a rising global power that can become as strong as itself in one or two decades. There are certain quantitative and qualitative requirements for overseas military presence, and so far it can only be effectively done in the American way. In addition to its allies' financial contributions, the US has to spend around US $156 billion annually on its bases abroad.[10] Secondly, what is the rationale for China to use gunboat policy to woo one of its most needed trading partners? The above narratives deliver no answer at all in these two aspects.

Misunderstood Trade Deficit

At the economic front, China has overtaken India in terms of the gross domestic product (GDP) at purchasing power parity (PPP) since 1985, when the figures of both countries were roughly US $640 billion.[11] But within 30 years' time in 2016, India's economy was only one fifth of China's in terms of nominal GDP, or two fifths in terms of PPP GDP.[12] It is the earnest expectation of Indian people that India can match China economically. The reality is that the process can be a lengthy one. According to some authoritative research, the nearest guess is that China can possibly maintain an economy over two times bigger than that of India for another decade or more.

However, the core issue here is not about the size of the economies, but the vast disparity in foreign exchange reserves and the GDP composition between the two countries, which has really put India in a disadvantageous position. Although experiencing a sharp drop in foreign reserves last year, China still has over US $3 trillion in its pocket (until February 2017), while India has only US $364 billion.[13] It means that India cannot afford to compete with China in footing the cost for economic and infrastructural development in their neighbourhood and other parts of the world. Moreover, considering the fact that industry sector accounts for 40.7 per cent of China's 2016 GDP, and only 19.8 per cent of India's,[14] China undoubtedly boasts much higher manufacturing capability and management skills than India, which has been transformed into the discomforting contrast between China's effective delivery and India's abysmal performance[15] in super projects both at home and abroad.

The trade deficit is one of the most debated issues in China-India relations. The ever-increasing figures have swayed most people's judgement, and not many are interested in the truth or courageous enough to admit that the deficit is not an imposed one, and is actually good for India's economy in a certain way. As a matter of fact, it has helped India to improve the overall trade balance. For the past four years, from 2012 to 2016, the trade deficit between India and China increased from US $37.2 billion to US $52.7 billion, a sharp rise by nearly 42 per cent.[16] But at the same time, India's overall trade deficit decreased by over 35 per cent.[17] It is intriguing to explore the link between the two lines of development that are superficially opposite.

A story about the tunnel boring machine (TBM) is very relevant in this case. Due to the complex technology, the TBM market was previously dominated by European, American and Japanese manufacturers. TBM equipment was extremely expensive, and the unit price could be as high as US $45-80 million until 2008, when Chinese manufacturers finally ventured into the market, and compelled the Western competitors to cut down the price by 20 to 40 per cent. And still, many times, they lose to Chinese TBM manufacturers. In 2012, Mumbai imported four TBMs made in China for only US $21 million for its subway project. In April 2016, India obtained another Chinese made TBM for its hydraulic project in Himalaya. In India's foreign trade, China is a crucial cost-saving partner, in a nutshell.

Of China's total 2010 exports of more than US $40 billion to India, more than 60 per cent came from capital goods, such as electrical machinery, nuclear reactors, boilers, iron and steel products, ships and boats and project goods.[18] If the Government of India were to limit imports of Chinese products into its market and switch to the Western suppliers, the trade deficit with China would definitely be lowered, but most possibly at the price of an even bigger overall trade imbalance. Therefore, by importing cheap Chinese capital goods, India is creating an economy that can match with China at a faster pace.

It is worthwhile to note that New Delhi, in order to stabilise the domestic market or preserve natural resources, has made some decisions to restrict raw material exports that were counterproductive per se to narrow the trade deficit with China. For instance, due to the ban on exports of cotton in 2010 and iron ore in 2012, India lost business of billions of dollars in China. In the case of cotton, the exports to China in 2016 shrunk by 79 per cent in comparison with the record surge in 2011.[19] Iron ore exports to China in 2016 decreased alarmingly by nearly 86 per cent compared with the record year of 2009.[20] Although the Government of India has now decided partially to reverse the ban, Chinese manufacturers have become accustomed to alternative supplies, for example, medium- and high-grade iron ore, which is making it even harder for the two countries to scale down the trade imbalance.

Since a nation's trade deficit is determined mainly by the flow of investment funds into or out of the country, blaming the deficits exclusively on differences in trade policy usually misses the reality of investment flows.[21] China is actually more open than India. According to the International Chamber of Commerce, China achieved average score of 3.0 in Open Market Index 2015, while India achieved below average score of 2.6.[22] Therefore, it is very wrong for many Indians to think that the trade deficit proves that China's market is relatively closed to Indian exports. Further, if it is a proven theory that investment inflow can offset any advantage gained by a competitive trading partner, it is self-contradictory for India to complain the trade imbalance on one hand, and on the other hand, turn down the olive branch of OBOR that boasts great potential for generating investment into its market.

Political Systems beyond Compatibility

China and India have nothing in common in terms of political systems except for the bureaucracy. India is the most populous democracy, and China is the most populous one-party system. But not many Chinese believe that India should be responsible to work with other democracies to promote the rule of law and freedom in China, and bring China into the mainstream of the world affairs.[23] Presently, both governments are realistic enough to steer away from this topic in their interactions, because there is no workable ground for both sides to start a dialogue in this aspect.

Echoing Western democracies at various forums, India's political comments from time to time on China are mostly interpreted by Chinese as ideologically exclusive. For instance, in fervently applauding the "Arc of Freedom and Prosperity" proposed by Japan as their common idea,[24] India expressed a deeper meaning that resembles the steadfast opinion of the Western world on the limitation of China's future role. To put it simply, India does not believe that China is fit for global or regional leadership, and that China's overwhelming economic strength and political rigidity could be a threat to the liberal world.

Obviously, not all Indian intellectuals are clear that the demand for democracy in China is more likely to be an expression of discontent, and the democratic impulses of the middle class have been challenged both theoretically and empirically in the Chinese context.[25] Besides, due to the repeated meticulous reports in public media, many Chinese, being aware of the inefficiencies of India's parliamentary system, have developed a good impression of the strong execution of their own political system. More precisely, according to a study by Zhang Mingshu on Chinese discourse of democracy,[26] a pragmatic and contextual approach in discerning various types of democracy has emerged amongst the Chinese. Especially, a majority (50.5 per cent) of young people (between the ages of 18 and 21 years) in China rejected the generalised comment on democracy as a good thing.[27] To follow this line of thinking, in Chinese people's mind, the democratic political system is not indispensable for a country to qualify as part of global leadership. Planning to promote people-to-people bonds with countries along the Belt and Road, amid its five major goals, China obviously hopes to remove the discord in narrating political systems.

Subcontinental Structure for Development

Ever since the departure of British colonisers, India's mindset was centred on its primacy in the subcontinent. After independence, India created a partial picture of its foreign policy as based on non-alignment, Third-Worldism, and so on and so forth. Through the prism of power relations, however, this conception is not entirely true when examining India's approach to navigate through the major powers. As for its periphery and immediate neighbourhood, India's discourse and practice is even more inconsistent.

"Nehru was one man in UN, and he was another man in subcontinent." This behaviour pattern advocating for equality of all nations in international forum while stressing India's supremacy in the Subcontinent applies to India's other supreme leaders as well, and explains why there is a strong urge on the part of India to put other South Asian countries under its supervision umbrella. To the outside world, the first three treaties that Nehru signed with Sikkim, Bhutan and Nepal were reminiscent of those signed with the British Raj, which portrayed India as a protector of the northern neighbours.[28] It becomes even more necessary for India to fortify its role at a time when China is rising and seeking expanded footprint in the subcontinent and its periphery.

India wants to entrench its primacy in the subcontinent and expand its sphere of influence to the whole Indian Ocean Region and beyond. Although Indian nationalists try hard to fulfil India's role as the provider and facilitator of development to its neighbours, it is India's protector role that underpins the structure in South Asia. So the core issue between India and other major powers is how they take on India's primacy in relation to the subcontinent. If the US, the only superpower in the world, has formally ceded power to India and allowed its leadership within the region (except for Pakistan) since 2001, it is then unwise for other major powers to do it differently. The structure in South Asia is not a confusing puzzle to China. In fact, China's role in the subcontinent, though growing, has never surpassed that of the US in terms of impact upon the power framework.

It is difficult for India to sustain this structure at least for two reasons. Firstly, Pakistan has always been the fatal defect of this power structure. It diverts a considerable part of India's resources and attention for running the subcontinent, and weakens India's control over the region with its separatist tendency. Secondly, the primacy sought by India is no longer incumbent upon the enthusiasm or unsubtle diplomacy to protect, guide and control its small neighbours, but essentially the proactive catering to their demands in the aspects of economy and infrastructure.[29] If India is unable to satisfy their thirst for development despite its greater commitment, and keeps failing to deliver on promises, the chances of the structure imploding will grow. The South Asian Association for Regional Cooperation (SAARC) members such as Nepal, Sri Lanka, and Maldives have already learned to exploit alternatives by making use of opportunities such as OBOR. Without effective reconciliation and coordination between China and India, the situation only drives the cost for India to sustain the structure even higher.

From a realist point of view, an ample supply of development opportunities to other SAARC members is unprecedentedly necessary for India to stabilise regional dynamics. If the most visible external supply coming with OBOR is bluntly frustrated, and the alternative from India-Japan consortium is, expectedly, deficient in capacity to match, the mounting pressures from within and outside upon the power framework could turn to be destructive. To avoid the impasse, firstly, China really needs to give due recognition to India's regional primacy commensurate to its absolute and relative strengths; Secondly, in exchange, India also needs to reconsider a more inclusive framework that tolerates China's demand for greater commercial access in the subcontinent. To pessimists, OBOR posts challenges to the power framework in the region. But to optimists, it offers a chance for India to reconstruct a primacy that is based on development and free of colonial impression. In this process, suppressing nationalist sentiments and making full use of certain multilateral financial frameworks, such as the Asian Infrastructure Investment Bank (AIIB) and New Development Bank (NDB), will be extremely important for China and India.

Rewriting the World Order?

Only the major powers capable of providing global public goods, such as protection against a common threat, a secure and stable environment for development and freedom of maritime transport, are entrusted with writing and managing the world order with their allies and partners. The post-Cold War order is mainly about America's centrality and dominance at the global level. Undoubtedly, China has become more concerned about this part of the world order. India's support for a multipolar world probably echoes similar concern.

Although America still upholds its responsibility for global affairs, it has to rearrange the payload in Eurasia and prioritise the tasks at hand due to capability deficiency. Compared to the Chinese Government, Trump administration's efforts to curtail globalisation, favour the rising protectionism, reject the International Court of Justice and United Nations Convention on the Law of the Sea (UNCLOS) and withdraw support from the UN, have posted more severe challenges to the institutions of global governance, especially the UN.

As for India, a closer relation with the US is for the satisfaction of its realistic needs, rather than endorsement of US dominance. It is also helpful to erase America's historic downgrading of India as a regional power. Seeking for permanent membership in the UN Security Council (UNSC), engaging in more active diplomacy and promoting regionalism in South Asia, India's stance on downsizing superpower's dominance and achieving greater influence for itself as a rising power is not that different from China.

The common perception about China being America's arch-rival has evolved from the assumption that China wants a completely different world order, though the fact is otherwise. As an active participant, a major beneficiary and a significant contributor of the current world order, however, China is more interested in the institutions of global governance that produce a fairer world order. The traditional reluctance and incapability of China to get more involved in beefing up the global governance is now replaced by increasing contribution in terms of financial and human resources. On average, China contributes more troops to UN peacekeeping missions than any other permanent member of the UNSC,[30] and bore 10.29 per cent of the cost in 2016.[31]

OBOR was said to be China's strategy for a new world order, with the AIIB being the centrepiece at the financial front. The AIIB, seen as an alternative to the international economic institutions, was in effect the response to the need for infrastructure in the developing countries, and an addition to the global economic governance. Having a consensus with China on this point and expecting economic gains, India joined the AIIB as the second-largest shareholder. The argument about the AIIB being a challenge to the international financial institutions is really a bad exaggeration. Because, firstly, the AIIB cooperates with other major international financial institutions and adheres to international rules that China has no part in creating; secondly, the AIIB, being about half of the World Bank and two thirds of the Asian Development Bank in terms of the capital,[32] is just too weak to be qualified as a challenge.

Conclusion

It is understandable that opportunity and challenge always come together in the age of globalisation. Amongst Indian scholars and strategists, the differences in their focus have led to opposite conclusions on whether to accept China's offer for regional connectivity. While providing a certain opportunity for strengthened regional economic cooperation, better infrastructure, greater trade relations and increased foreign investments, OBOR suggests a possible challenge to India's primacy in South Asian neighbourhood and its confidence in handling competition from China.

The very different or even contradicting discourses on OBOR reflect serious lack of trust between China and India, and show that both countries are very good at in-the-box thinking. Confident with the universal feasibility of its development model, China is determined to lead the second round of globalisation by exporting its model to the states along the Belt and Road. Concerned about the significant power gap with China and the potential security risk of allowing greater Chinese presence in its neighbourhood, India always tends to make the worst possible interpretation of any cooperation deal from China.

Despite being newly endorsed by the UNSC Resolution 2344 as a welcome regional development initiative,[33] introduction of OBOR has triggered more disputes between China and India, and has proven that it is extreme difficult for both countries, particularly India, to propose an unconventional way of looking at bilateral and regional issues. Their failure in thinking outside of the box during the first four years of OBOR's implementation, however, has strengthened the necessity for China and India to shift the focus from divergence to convergence of development in the bilateral relations, and the utter importance of encouraging more objective perceptions of OBOR and other similar development projects.

NOTES

1. "Vision and proposed actions outlined on jointly building Silk Road Economic Belt and 21st-Century Maritime Silk Road", National Development and Reform Commission, March 28, 2015, at http://www.sdpc.gov.cn/gzdt/201503/t20150328_669091.html (Accessed January 15, 2017).
2. *The Boundary Agreement between China and Pakistan, 1963*, at http://people.unica.it/annamariabaldussi/files/2015/04/China-Pakistan-1963.pdf (Accessed January 13, 2017).
3. Rumel Dahiya and Jagannath P. Panda, "A Tale of Two Disputes: China's Irrationality and India's Stakes", *IDSA Policy Brief*, June 29, 2015, at http://www.idsa.in/policybrief/ATaleofTwoDisputesChinasIrrationalityand IndiasStakes _ rdahiya_290615 (Accessed January 21, 2017).
4. Shannon Tiezzi, "The Maritime Silk Road Vs. The String of Pearls", *The Diplomat*, February 13, 2014, at http://thediplomat.com/2014/02/the-maritime-silk-road-vs-the-string-of-pearls/ (Accessed January 21, 2017).
5. Zhou Bo, "The String of Pearls and the Maritime Silk Road", *China-US Focus*, February 11, 2014, http://www.chinausfocus.com/foreign-policy/the-string-of-pearls-and-the-maritime-silk-road/ (Accessed January 25, 2017).
6. Tansen Sen, "The Impact of Zheng He's Expeditions on Indian Ocean Interactions", *Bulletin of the School of Oriental and African Studies*, 79 (3), p. 611.
7. "Zheng He's Voyages of Discovery", UCLA Center for Chinese Studies, April 20, 2004, at http://www.international.ucla.edu/china/article/10387 (Accessed January 27, 2017).
8. Joesph S. Nye, "The Kindleberger Trap", *Project Syndicate*, January 9, 2017, https://www.project-syndicate.org/commentary/trump-china-kindleberger-trap-by-joseph-s—nye-2017-01 (Accessed January 28, 2017).
9. "China's 2017 Defense Budget Rise to Slow Again", March 4, 2017, *Reuters*, at http://www.reuters.com/article/us-china-parliament-defence-idUSKBN16B043 (Accessed March 13, 2017).
10. David Vine, "Garrisoning the Globe: How U.S. Military Bases Abroad Undermine National Security and Harm Us All", *TomDispatch*, September 13, 2015, at http://www.tomdispatch.com/blog/176043/tomgram%3A_david_vine,_our_base _ nation/ (Accessed February 16, 2017).
11. "India vs China GDP", *Statistics Times*, September 12, 2015, at http://

statisticstimes.com/economy/china-vs-india-gdp.php (Accessed February 7, 2017).

12. "GDP (nominal) vs GDP (PPP)", Statistics Times, August 4, 2016, at http://statisticstimes.com/economy/gdp-nominal-vs-gdp-ppp.php (Accessed February 7, 2017).
13. "China Foreign Exchange Reserves", Trading Economics, at http://www.tradingeconomics.com/china/foreign-exchange-reserves (Accessed February 19, 2017).
14. "GDP Composition by Sector of Origin", *The World Factbook*, Central Intelligence Agency, at https://www.cia.gov/library/publications/the-world-factbook/fields/2012.html (Accessed February 11, 2017).
15. Anjelina Patrick, "China Overtaking India in Maldives", Institute of Peace and Conflict Studies, September 15, 2016, at http://www.ipcs.org/print_article-details.php?recNo=5156 (Accessed February 20, 2017).
16. Export Import Data Bank, Ministry of Commerce, at http://commerce.nic.in/eidb/iecnt.asp (Accessed February 22, 2017).
17. Ibid.
18. Anil K. Gupta, "India's Misguided China Anxiety", Bloomberg, March 22, 2012, at https://www.bloomberg.com/news/articles/2012-03-21/indias-misguided-china-anxiety (Accessed February 28, 2017).
19. China Cotton Association, at www.china-cotton.org (Accessed March 2, 2017).
20. Export Import Data Bank, No. 16.
21. Griswold Daniel, "America's Misunderstood Trade Deficit", Cato Institute, July 22, 1998, at https://www.cato.org/publications/congressional-testimony/americas-misunderstood-trade-deficit (Accessed February 28, 2017).
22. *ICC Open Markets Index 3rd Edition 2015*, The ICC World Trade Agenda, September 2015, p. 11, at https://iccwbo.org/publication/icc-open-markets-index-3rd-edition-2015/ (Accessed February 28, 2017).
23. Madhavi Thampi, Bernhard Vogel, Rudolf Dolzer and Matthias Herdegen, *India and China in the Colonial World*, Berghahn Books, New York, 2005, p. 215.
24. Joint Press Release on visit of External Affairs Minister of India to Japan, March 2007, Ministry of Foreign Affairs of Japan, at http://www.mofa.go.jp/region/asia-paci/india/joint0703.html (Accessed February 27, 2017).
25. Gang Wang, "Who Wants Democracy in China? An Empirical Analysis of Chinese Democratization in Perspective", *Asian Journal of Social Science Studies*, 1 (1), 2016.
26. 张明澍,《中国 "政治人": 中国人想要什么样民主》 (Chinese "Political Personality": What Kind of Democracy Do Chinese Want?) 社会科学文献出版社, 2013 年版.
27. "Young Chinese People May Just Not be that into Western-Style Democracy", *The Atlantic*, July 18, 2013, at https://www.theatlantic.com/china/archive/2013/07/young-chinese-people-may-just-not-be-that-into-western-style-democracy/277885/ (Accessed February 19, 2017).
28. Raja Mohan, "India and US policy in South Asia", Speech in IDSA, November 2016.
29. Happymon Jacob, School of International Studies, JNU, "Losing the neighbourhood", *The Hindu*, May 18, 2016, at http://www.thehindu.com/opinion/lead/Losing-the-neighbourhood/article14324718.ece (Accessed February 27, 2017).

30. Courtney J. Fung, "China's Troop Contributions to U.N. Peacekeeping", *Peace Brief*, 212, United States Institute of Peace, July 26, 2016, at https://www.usip.org/publications/2016/07/chinas-troop-contributions-un-peacekeeping (Accessed March 03, 2017).
31. "Financing peacekeeping", United Nations Peacekeeping, at http://www.un.org/en/peacekeeping/operations/financing.shtml (Accessed March 05, 2017).
32. "Why China Is Creating A New "World Bank" for Asia", *The Economist*, November 11, 2014, at http://www.economist.com/blogs/economist-explains/2014/11/economist-explains-6 (Accessed February 18, 2017).
33. "Security Council Authorizes Year-Long Mandate Extension for United Nations Assistance Mission in Afghanistan, Adopting Resolution 2344 (2017)", March 17, 2017, United Nations Security Council, at https://www.un.org/press/en/2017/sc12756.doc.htm (Accessed March 22, 2017).

5

All-rounded Sino-Indian Competition? China's Belt and Road Initiative and its Implications for South Asia

Simon Shen[1]

The OBOR initiative was proposed by China's paramount leader Xi Jinping in 2013. The Silk Road Economic Belt (One Belt) and Maritime Silk Road (One Road) will put China at the centre of the whole network which is intended to extend from East Asia to Central Asia, Europe and North Africa, then via South Asia and back to China. In the past few years, focus has been mainly on infrastructure investment, railways and highways and power grids. South Asia is expected to be a crucial part of the initiative as it is located on the Indian Ocean and in the "backyard" of China. China is actively seeking ways to consolidate the relationships and the One Belt One Road (OBOR) or Belt and Road Initiative (BRI) projects, as Beijing sees this is as a way to weaken the importance of the Straits of Malacca. Among all the OBOR related routes, South Asia as a region, however, is expected to have stronger intention to resist OBOR due to the existence of India. The two countries may share common interests in economic development, but geopolitical influences in neighbouring regions and economic competition in the global market may very likely hinder their cooperation in China's strategic plan, paving ways for future uncertainty and even regional insecurity.

This chapter illustrates the many challenges this initiative faces and previews the implications of OBOR for South Asia in general and India in particular; and concludes by suggesting possible ways through which various countries in the region can extract positive elements from the plan and avoid foreseeable conflicts at the same time.

India: Countering OBOR with Its Grand Strategy

The Sino-Indian War of the 1960s and several subsequent stand-offs in the area, the most recent in 2017, are long-term obstacles preventing both countries from improving their relations and enhancing a partnership in areas other than in trading. Despite being fellow BRICS members (Brazil, Russia, India, China and South Africa), India and China see each other as rivals in the South Asian geopolitics. In particular, the strong relationship between China and Pakistan and the fact that one of the flagship projects of OBOR is the construction of the China-Pakistan Economic Corridor (CPEC) have had a constant adverse effect on China-India relations. The difficult political situation that exists in Kashmir has encouraged the Indian Government to reject the idea of the CPEC going ahead in the area.

China's alliance with Pakistan is, of course, not a new issue for India, but its ambitious plan to develop new strongholds in other ports in the Indian Ocean, including in the faraway continent of Africa, could be most worrisome for Delhi as the Indian Ocean in the past decades had been largely ruled by India and its allies. China's OBOR is not just improving its supportive measures for the economic development of African countries, but also operates with the intention of enhancing its influential role in the area. One frequently attended example is Djibouti: "With the establishment of the military base in Djibouti, a city lacking in economic importance but of great strategic value in allowing Chinese aircraft to access the Middle East, the western Indian Ocean, and central Africa without refuelling."[2] As the de facto status quo defender of the Indian Ocean, to prevent Gwadar of Pakistan being used by Beijing in a similar way as Djibouti, India's sensitivity is well anticipated.

In response, India has sought to build its own geopolitical grand strategy, coming up with the plan of an Asia-Africa Growth Corridor (AAGC) and to cooperate with China's arch-rival Japan, among others. As Panda studies, "The AAGC consists of four main components: development and cooperation projects, quality infrastructure and institutional connectivity, capacity and skill enhancement, and people-to-people partnerships."[3] It has been seen by some in the region as an alternative to OBOR, both having similar plans and focusing on cooperative projects and infrastructure. For instance, under the AAGC, there is a plan to connect ports in Jamnagar (Gujarat) with Djibouti in the Gulf of Aden, which can be further analysed strategically: "AAGC may not entail development of a land corridor, it will essentially be a sea corridor linking Africa with India and other countries of South-East Asia and Oceania, and compete with the Maritime Silk Road of OBOR since they are targeting the same area with similar objectives and plans."[4] The AAGC might well have started out with India and Japan challenging China's OBOR; for indeed, they are complementing each other to see the plan's success.

Interestingly, despite the geopolitical competition, China has never stopped investing in India. As its neighbouring countries like Pakistan, Nepal, Bangladesh and Sri Lanka have been actively involved in OBOR, Delhi is a natural extended target: in 2016, both countries signed 16 agreements in the areas of manufacturing industries, high-speed railway networks, renewable energy and city development.[5] There is a particular focus on developing an industrial park in Gujarat, which is expected to open in 2018.[6] Besides, exporting infrastructure is China's consistent policy, and India would not be a target left alone, as China has also planned to help India build a high-speed railway to link three major cities: Chennai, Bangalore and Mysore.[7] Naturally, these infrastructure projects have attracted other Chinese companies to invest in the area: for instance, Xiaomi and Huawei have already set up offices, factories and research and development (R&D) facilities in India. Many excessively cheap Chinese transportation tools, such as second-hand motorbikes, were also recently offloaded systematically into India and were much welcomed by its population. Of course, the Indians have their own philosophical ways of justifying things: "India does not regard those projects to be parts of OBOR, while China certainly thinks the other way."[8]

Before Modi's notable absence in the global BRI summit in May 2017, some Indian officials had indeed expressed positive views and urged the government to actively participate. For instance, Mukul Sanwal, a senior consultant of the Indian Government, "suggested India should join OBOR so as to avoid being left behind from the fast-growing Asian market, because this is a great opportunity to work together with other OBOR participants to develop a common market, trade partnership and FDIs".[9] Arvind Panagariya, Vice Chairman of the National Institution for Transforming India, also once stated that "India is an open-minded country and welcomes Chinese enterprises to invest; FDIs from China would be useful to help achieve the strategic target of creating more goods that are made in India".[10] Compared with other countries in South Asia, India is more advanced in its economic development and has better infrastructure, making it possible to avoid over-dependency on China while attempting to attract its capital. As Panagariya suggested, "India needs to learn from China about the ways to set up economic zones in coastal areas and attract FDIs to invest in manufacturing industries in the area."[11]

Nonetheless, since May 2017, India has tightened its requirement for China to invest in its power sector: "The new requirements are that companies which are interested in investing in India should have been operating there for at least 10 years, have Indian citizens as top executives, and employees of the foreign firm should have lived in India for a certain period."[12] The reasons behind this are several, with concerns about security overriding those of an economic nature:

> Local firms have long lobbied against Chinese involvement in the power sector, raising security concerns and saying they get no reciprocal access to Chinese markets. The domestic electrical equipment industry has been raising concerns on contracts awarded to Chinese companies for installation of supervisory control and data acquisition systems (SCADA) for power distribution that can lead to foreign control over a sector critical to the country's growth and China can launch any cyber-attacks on the electrical networks easily.[13]

Recently, the Indian Government criticised the delay caused by Chinese enterprises working on a high-speed railway project, alleging that to be "the aftermath and revenge of the issue of territorial disputes".[14] Similar repercussions could be well expected in the future.

OBOR is not a Chinese conspiracy to encircle India – at least it is not primarily targeting India. Delhi, however, has long seen China as its major competitor, despite the fact that the Chinese rarely assign the same importance to India. The rise of nationalist journalism in India has further created an anti-Chinese sentiment in Indian society. As an example, this is the kind of sentiment recorded before the launching of OBOR:

> The survey conducted by Washington-based Pew Research Center in 2012 revealed that roughly 23% of Chinese has a favourable opinion of India, while 62% offer a negative opinion. Also, only 44% of Chinese say their southern neighbour's expanding economy is positive for China, down from 60% in 2010. India has a similar view over China, only 23% of Indians describe their country's relationship with China as one of cooperation and only 24% think China's growing economy is a good thing for India.[15]

A sad projection is that the situation could only have become worse afterwards. China's state media has suggested that "the election of Indian Prime Minister Narendra Modi has fuelled the country's nationalist sentiments, whereas some Indians have the mentality of a zero-sum game on the bilateral relations".[16] The so-called "String of Pearls" strategy of China is a particular target in India, but that is rarely mentioned in the Chinese media. With Hindu nationalism rising, the reluctance of the Indian public to embrace OBOR, partly mobilised by the government, is difficult to see being revised in the foreseeable future. And all neighbours of India in South Asia, an area where India claimed dominance in the previous decades, surely sense the tensions brought upon by OBOR and the Indian response to it, leaving them plenty of opportunities and crises to tackle the latest situation. The good news is the abundance of resources offered by both Beijing and Delhi, but the bad news is the increasing tendency for both sides to view loyalty of smaller South Asian countries in an exclusive manner.

Pakistan: Free-riding OBOR against India?

China and Pakistan have historically strong ties with each other since the establishment of the People's Republic of China. As mentioned, the CPEC is one of the main flagship pillars of the OBOR project. By linking the city of Kashgar to Gwadar through highways and railways, the corridor can be used for oil transportation and is expected to reduce the significance of the Straits of Malacca. As the Chinese embassy in Pakistan proudly reiterated, "Interior Secretary of Pakistan stated that CPEC is a project held by the two closest countries of China and Pakistan, and which has attracted the attention of international society."[17]

To Pakistan, free-riding on Chinese investment has long become a national policy, but the economic diplomacy of the CPEC is still expected to strengthen the Sino-Pakistani relationship further, because of its geopolitical implications. As already mentioned, India, as the key player in the area, has strongly objected to the CPEC going through the Kashmir area and initiated the AAGC to compete with OBOR. China and Pakistan will now have to give their thoughts to the CPEC as this will determine whether OBOR can achieve its pre-set aims and objectives. Under the CPEC, China will provide the infrastructure and resources to Pakistan's economic development and Pakistan will provide access to the ports and let Chinese companies and the government invest in the country and export the surplus from domestic production. To date, China has already committed investing more than US$35 million for the port's fundamental facilities. In return, the port is being leased to China for 43 years; "other surrounding projects, such as the railways and highways from Kashgar to Gwadar, the New Gwadar International Airport, the Development of a Free Zone and the Pak-China Friendship Hospital will cost no less than total of US$46 billion".[18] As the world's largest oil importing country, China has a long-term concern about its lack of influence in the Straits of Malacca area, as the current sea routes used to import Middle Eastern oil are frequently patrolled by the US Navy. The development of Gwadar Port could provide an alternate route for oil imports and, most importantly, it is owned by Pakistan. Figure 1 shows how conveniently placed Gwadar is for oil transportation from the Persian Gulf via the Hormuz Strait: "Oil from the Middle East could be offloaded at Gwadar and transported to China through the corridor, cutting the current 12,000-kilometre journey to 2,395 kilometres and reducing the transport time to the Eastern part of China, such as Shanghai, from around 25-30 days to just 12 days."[19] The plan is supposed to be mutually beneficial; and though the advantageous gains of China would be greater, Pakistan will also earn through freight and cargo handling charges as China, Central Asian states and others use the port for trade: "An industrial free zone is also being established around the port, which will be a hub for manufacturing and port-related business and industry and is expected to generate 40,000 jobs."[20] When Pakistan is

Figure 1: Map of CPEC and Sea Routes for Oil Transportation from the Middle East to China

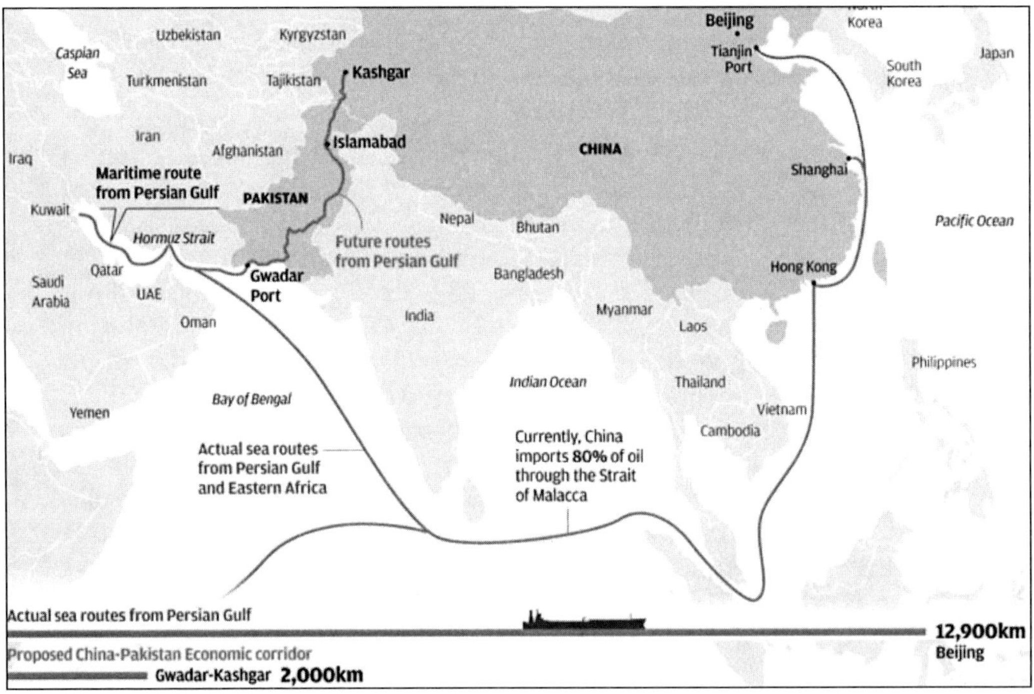

Source: Cargo to Pakistan.[21]

promoting the plan, the emphasis would be shifted to building ports comparable to Mumbai, or strategic strongholds that could be turned into military bases.

Highways and railways are the other infrastructure projects offered by the CPEC which will have a positive effect on the economic development of Pakistan. Such transportation projects enhance the accessibility of remote areas of the country to major cities. For example, the Peshawar-Karachi highways and railways were built, upgraded and renovated under the CPEC: they will go through an area that contributes 90 per cent of Pakistan's gross domestic product (GDP) and contains more than 138 million of its population.[22] This will now be the core part that links northern and southern Pakistan and boosts the economic performance of these areas: "Estimates from the Pakistan Business Council suggest that a combination of all the CPEC projects could account for 20 per cent of the country's GDP over the next five years and boost growth by about 3 percentage points."[23] Furthermore, China is not just giving money, materials and machines to build the infrastructure, but also human resources. This is a typical example:

> On 22 September 2017, China sent the first medical team of 10 staff to Gwadar Port, Pakistan to provide a two-year medical service. The medical team will provide community consultations, training for local medical personnel, teach them about Chinese medical technology and provide medical services to Chinese companies in Gwadar. A study of epidemiology in Gwadar is also about to kick off.[24]

In addition to this, China has also sent a number of workers and engineers to help Pakistan build its highways and railways, something that Pakistan can hardly gain from other potential sources like the US or Japan on the same scale.

As a result, with Pakistan enjoying the help from China to upgrade roads, railways and increasing its energy supply by building new plants, its economic development is now highly reliant on those infrastructures brought by the CPEC – a typical example of strategic reliance. China is now the largest trading partner of Pakistan which accounts for 7.34 per cent of exports and 28.69 per cent of imports during July 2016-May 2017.[25] No matter whether it is the highways or railways stimulating economic activity or the Gwadar Port lowering the cost of oil importation for China and creating jobs for local Pakistan society, the infrastructure has an irreplaceable role. More projects are currently in progress or under construction, and the interaction between the people is increasing at the same time:

According to data from the China embassy in Pakistan, the 43 projects in CPEC have boosted the number of Chinese people in Pakistan three-fold; more than 30,000 Chinese are now living there. The Chinese in Pakistan are largely made up of workers and engineers employed by CPEC projects who need to stay there for a certain period of time and have formed several groups.[26]

Pakistan is certainly enjoying the immediate economic benefits, with China helping Islamabad overcome its financial and technological difficulties in developing those areas, while China can now use the Gwadar port to strengthen its own energy security. The only problem is what can Pakistan leverage on if China withdraws the involvement or if the demanded shares of China significantly increase in the course of building such plans.

Indeed, the CPEC is already being criticised by some stakeholders in Pakistan's local society. "Since it was formally inaugurated in the latter half of 2015, the CPEC project has been the target of Pakistani critics who have drawn parallels with Britain's East India Company that colonized India in the 18th and 19th centuries."[27] Due to the fact that China is planning to send its navy to Gwadar Port to protect the area, reports from Pakistan have suggested that China may also seek an agreement from Islamabad to build a military base at Gwadar.[28] In addition, the financing of CPEC projects provided by Chinese state-owned banks is compounding Pakistan's external debts, "which could reach a much higher than projected US$79 billion, or 66.5 per cent of GDP".[29] According to Senator Usman Khan Kakar, "The people of Balochistan (where Gwadar Port is located) will only get one benefit from this project, which is the water supply, as no electricity or railway projects have been planned for Balochistan as part of the CPEC project."[30] This reflects the diverse opinions among society in Pakistan: the government keeps promoting the CPEC as the way to boost economic growth, while other stakeholders such as the senators are cautious as to whether local people will really enjoy that benefit. Besides, the cost of the CPEC may go sky-high, the national debt is growing, the sovereignty and authority of the Pakistan Government has been weakened with the lease of Gwadar Port, Chinese companies are in the driving seat for the projects and the reliance on the Chinese Government is inexorably increasing.

The socio-cultural factors have raised concerns as the dissimilar backgrounds of the Chinese and the Pakistanis have created cultural tensions that may lead to conflict in the future. For instance, the Chinese have formed associations in cities like Islamabad and Karachi, and although Pakistan may not have big Chinatowns, there are certainly Chinese grocery stores and restaurants.

> This is one of the changes to the local society in Pakistan; when the number of Chinese people keeps growing, the cultural differences become more obvious. Those stores and restaurants are targeting the Chinese; hence the menus or labels are in Chinese characters instead of Urdu.[31]

These changes are often underlying threats which may provoke serious conflict between the Chinese and local Pakistanis, as for example, those grocery stores are now smuggling pork into the country, while most of the Pakistanis are Muslim and forbid the import and consumption of pork. Language barrier is also seen as the factor that most hinders the interaction between China and Pakistan: "Most of the Chinese people in Pakistan don't speak or read Urdu, the language of Pakistan. The local Chinese societies try to serve these groups by publishing Chinese newspapers at 5,000 copies per week to report the news in Pakistan."[32] Chinese characters have also begun to appear in Pakistani television advertisements:

> An ongoing campaign features a Chinese housewife who complains of loneliness to her husband, one of thousands to have arrived in Pakistan to work on CPEC projects. He encourages her to befriend their neighbours in a middle-class suburb of Lahore, but she's unsure how to reach out to them: 'They don't even eat the same food!' She finds a solution in rice, a common staple of the Chinese and Pakistani diets.[33]

Nonetheless, this is aimed at promoting the idea that the harmony between Chinese and Pakistanis can be as easy as sharing food together. But the real situation is much more complicated as most Pakistanis do not know their Chinese neighbours. Pakistani columnist Fasi Zaka argues,

> Pakistanis have a lot of goodwill for China, but most of it is expressed as happiness derived from a transactional relationship. If large numbers of Chinese are to live in Pakistan, people-to-people familiarity needs to increase before cultural tensions do.[34]

The good news for China is that despite all potential crises, the big picture is still looking good. For instance, the strong ties between China and Pakistan remained unaffected despite the death of two Chinese hostages. In June 2017, two Chinese teachers were kidnapped by the Islamic State in Iraq and Syria (ISIS) in Pakistan and were later executed. Foreign Minister of China stated that "the incident would not affect OBOR and appreciated that the Pakistan government had already taken the measures to rescue them and protect other Chinese citizen in the country", also suggested that "since OBOR is exploring the world, it would certain face safety issues and it will rely on the cooperation of various countries to overcome them".[35]

Nepal and Bhutan: Any Realistic Choices of Hedging between India and China?

As a small nation lying between the two big giants China and India, Nepal will have to balance carefully its relationship with them, especially as OBOR faces the challenge of the Indian-led AAGC and also during its territorial disputes. In the past, Nepal was closer to India as the two states were geographically linked with no physical obstacles, while China and Nepal were blocked by the Himalayas. In 1950, Nepal and India signed a Treaty of Peace and Friendship that almost turned the former into an Indian protectorate. The Communist Party of Nepal, which had been backed by China in its efforts to overthrow the Rana regime, was banned between 1952 and 1956. After that, the bilateral relationship was back and forth during the late 1950s to 1970s, as Kathmandu approached Beijing with the Sino-Nepal Treaty of Peace and Friendship which was signed in 1960 and forced the Indian military mission to leave, and both nations began ignoring the treaty provisions. Since then, Nepal has tried to cooperate with both giants on economic development, including after the overthrow of monarchy and the governance of the Communist Part of Nepal: "Nepal is culturally close to India and Nepal relies heavily on imports from India and completely on Indian ports for sea access, with an open border that nationals of the two countries can cross without a visa."[36] In May 2017, Nepal officially signed an agreement to join OBOR; the then Foreign Minister of Nepal Prakash Sharan Mahat said that "the move [was] a major step forward in strengthening Nepal-China relations, and reiterated the need for China to invest more for infrastructure to boost the linkage and economic activities between the two states".[37]

To a small country like Nepal, China's investment in the OBOR era is very substantial. According to figures from Nepal's Department of Industry, China's investment in Nepal in the 2016-17 financial year was about US$81.4 million, or more than four times the US$19.4 million India invested in its neighbour.[38] Under OBOR, the amount China is investing in Nepal is expected to follow an upward trend, with deals on the table to construct border ports, highways and trans-Himalayan railways, and in energy cooperation. Despite the fact that some scholars from Nepal have suggested the country should balance the relationship with China and India and act as a bridge between them after the recent territorial dispute at Doklam, the Indian blockade of Nepal in 2015 has significantly harmed the bilateral relationship, causing Nepal to suffer devastating effects on top of the catastrophe of the magnitude 7.8 earthquake in April 2015:

> Faced with crippling shortages of fuel, cooking gas, and even medicine, the then coalition government led by nationalist communist leader Khadga Prasad Sharma Oli signed agreements with Beijing to secure sea access via Chinese ports and to import petroleum products from China, breaking India's monopoly over Nepal's fuel supplies and access to seaports.[39]

Under these circumstances, Nepal chose to deepen its link with China through OBOR, and Kathmandu is now enjoying assistance from China in several areas, starting from the post-earthquake relief fund: China provided aid from the first moment to rescue the victims, and continuously helped Nepal clean up and rebuild the nation. China International Search and Rescue Team (CISAR) was sent to Nepal once Beijing received a request from Kathmandu.[40] Since then, China has been involved in the rebuilding of houses, schools, hospitals and highways (the repair of the highways between Nepal and China was finished in January 2017).[41] Meanwhile, China has also started to repair temples and other heritage buildings and given RMB3 billion from 2016 to 2018 which is being used to subsidise other redevelopment projects following the disaster.[42]

The question is: does Nepal really have a choice to hedge between Beijing and Delhi? Probably not. Nepal is a developing country with medium human development level – Human Development Index (HDI) at 0.558 and ranked 144 out of 188 countries.[43] This indicates that the administration needs to put greater effort into enhancing the quality of life nationwide. In addition, the earthquakes in 2015 and the floods in 2017 have had a serious adverse effect on the country, including the destruction of infrastructure and economic activities, and the loss of thousands of lives. The cooperation with China is identified as a solution to this, as OBOR will bring the financial resources to rebuild the roads and provide port access. Moreover, Kathmandu is anticipating that this will be the key to stimulate economic performance and enable the nation to recover from the disasters of recent times. "The World Bank estimates that Nepal requires roughly US$13-18 billion directed towards infrastructure in order to maintain its status quo of economic growth, and China has presented itself as an effective donor."[44] Nepal is not just lacking a transportation system and infrastructure, but is also greatly in need of power; China has invested in a US$165 million hydropower plant that is located in the Gandaki area.[45] Although in November 2017, Nepal cancelled the project with the Chinese firm over allegations of irregularities and lack of transparency, the China-led Asian Infrastructure Investment Bank (AIIB) has agreed to invest in two other hydropower plants and it remains to be seen if these two fare better. These plants are expected to improve the stability of the energy supply in Nepal and facilitate the building of other projects and boost economic activities. Thus, Nepal's economy is now heavily reliant on Chinese infrastructure; China is not just investing in the projects itself but is also financing the infrastructure projects through the AIIB: "AIIB has promised to invest in several projects, including a power distribution improvement project, construction of hydropower plants, settlement and urbanization projects and upgrading roads, these projects are worth no less than a total of US$10 billion."[46]

Meanwhile, China is individually footing the cost of many mega projects, such as building a 550-kilometre-long railway from Tibet to Nepal and the second international airport in Nepal, Pokhara International Airport. Pokhara city is located some 200 kilometres west of the capital Kathmandu. It is the second largest city in the country, but has only a small domestic airport, although the government planned to extend and upgrade it nearly 40 years ago. Its interaction with OBOR can be summarised as follows:

> The political instability, social unrest and lack of capital have left the 200 square metres of land vacant for decades. China has decided to finance this project after Nepal's administration officially signed the agreement to join OBOR and made this one of the highlighted infrastructure projects. The new airport will cost approximately RMB 1.5 billion and will take four years to complete. The current airport started operation in 1958 and has outdated runways and terminals; modern planes, such as the Boeing 737, are unable to land and take off at the airport.[47]

After the redevelopment, Pokhara will have the second international airport in Nepal and the potential economic benefit will be huge. The city is a major tourist destination, and the new airport would allow flights from all over the world to land, greatly boosting the tourism industry. Apart from the long-term returns, the immediate impact is on the local community which is learning and working at the same time. Nepali workers learn from Chinese technicians the technical knowledge of construction, while the locals also ask and learn what kind of materials they can use to build houses and other facilities.[48] In short, Nepal is gaining practical knowledge from the Chinese at both local and national levels.

Another example of the OBOR-related mega projects in Nepal is the trans-national railway. Shigatse is a Tibetan city that lies between the boundaries of China and Nepal. The Qinghai-Tibet Railway, opened a decade ago, has linked the city with other parts of China. Kathmandu has seen this as an opportunity to increase the accessibility of the country and improve the efficiency of transportation, particularly the transaction of goods between Nepal and China. Currently, there are only two highways which link the 253 kilometres from Shigatse to the border between the two nations. "Nepal does not have any workable train system at the moment, due to the fact that the nation had never developed or upgraded the railway system and facilities since the British built it back in 1927, and the last station closed in 2014. Kathmandu has requested China to assist in setting up a brand new system, which will connect Shigatse in 2020 and extend to three major cities in Nepal."[49] The government also sees this as an opportunity to join the railway project of OBOR, since China is planning to use railroads to connect countries of Asia with those in Europe, and Nepal is at the middle point. The politicians in Nepal are optimistic about the huge potential returns, which are not possible to be brought about by the Indians.

As with the people in Pakistan, the Nepalese generally have a positive view of the Chinese who live in their country. "The former Prime Minister, Khadga Prasad Oli has said that 'All Nepalese are friends of the Chinese', while a driver said that 'the Chinese are the top favourites of the Nepalese'."[50] They are from different social classes and backgrounds, but are of the same opinion that China has helped Nepal a lot in rebuilding the country and boosting its economic performance, and has also provided the opportunity to reduce its dependence on India, especially since the 2015 blockade. Of particular note is the following:

> Nepal agreed to eliminate the visa requirement for Chinese nationals in 2016 and the tourist numbers have increased sharply since then and caused changes in socio-cultural fields. In Bhaktapur, located 14 kilometres east of Kathmandu, there is a pottery market that accepts RMB and most of the shop owners speak Mandarin. The shop owners learnt the language from the waiters of Chinese restaurants in the city, while the waiters learnt Nepali from them.[51]

The influence of China in Nepal is not just in the tourist spots or service sector, but also in the field of education. According to China's CCTV, currently in Nepal, around 60 elementary and middle schools teach Chinese to their students; and at Kathmandu's Tribhuvan University, Chinese has replaced Japanese as the most popular foreign language subject. The University now has two Chinese teachers teaching 300 students the composition of characters, how to have a daily conversation and how to write essays.[52] Being able to speak Chinese is an attractive asset in the nation's job market. Local society has changed considerably under China's influence and power. Of course, as mentioned above, there are scattered suspicions against the Chinese influx into Nepal, as seen from the cancellation of some infrastructure building projects. But Nepal just does not have the capacity to leverage, nor is India providing sufficient alternatives to OBOR for the Nepalese. Unless India pairs with the US or Japan to compete with Chinese influence in Nepal, it can be expected that the economy of Nepal will eventually be absorbed into the Chinese economic orbit. (Similar situations can be found in another Himalayan country Bhutan, which did not attend the 2017 BRI Summit together with India. But owing to the limitation of space and the relative smallness of the kingdom, its role is not extensively discussed in this chapter.)

Bangladesh: Regaining Strategic Importance with Indian Edging

If Nepal is looking for a balance in its relationship with China and India, with Beijing having the edge, by the same token, Bangladesh might find itself in a similar situation but with India having the edge. Bangladesh is surrounded by India and only connected to Myanmar in the south-east; it became a part of Pakistan as a consequence of the Partition of India and then became an independent state with Indian support in 1971. The two countries were in close alliance during this period as they had a common enemy, Pakistan. However, territorial disputes and the decision by Bangladesh to develop closer ties with Islamic countries by joining the Organisation of the Islamic Conference had cooled the bilateral relationship. This situation was overturned in 2015 when Indian Prime Minister Narendra Modi visited Dhaka, signing 20 treaties and memoranda with Prime Minister Sheikh Hasina, which included resolving disputes over territory, the financing of infrastructure, enhanced trading and signing civil cooperation agreements on health and education. Discussion on the Teesta River dispute also took place. Bangladesh agreed to let Indian ships dock at Chittagong and Mongla Port. The Indian Parliament ratified further treaties to exchange 68 enclaves with Bangladesh. The bilateral relationship reached a new high with these agreements, and "India played a key part in persuading Bangladesh to give up the plan to purchase two submarines from China."[53]

India may have formed a better relationship with Bangladesh in recent years, but China has also worked hard and put in a lot of effort to include Bangladesh in OBOR. An official diplomatic relationship between Dhaka and Beijing was started in 1975, and since then both countries have interacted with each other, especially over trade. "In 2006, China agreed to lift the tariff on 84 types of goods from Bangladesh and the total trade value has reached US$12.54 billion, but with China enjoying a huge trading surplus."[54] As China wants to maintain its ties with Bangladesh and avoid trading deficit as a problem, "the government invested money back into Bangladesh, including US$1.2 billion worth of economic aid and invested into those infrastructure projects that fit into the aim of OBOR".[55] As a result, "Bangladesh formally declared its joining in China's OBOR initiative during the visit of China's President Xi Jinping in 2016. China wishes to build mega infrastructure projects within the Belt and Road areas to increase trade and service, offering substantial prospects for Bangladesh".[56] China's state-owned enterprises recently signed agreements with Dhaka on the construction of a number of power plants, eight bridges between the two countries, railways and an upgrade of existing highways.

However, Bangladesh has also attracted other countries' interest because of its strategic location near the Indian Ocean and it owning the port of Chittagong. Apart from China and India, Japan is another key player: "There are 245 Japanese companies currently investing in Bangladesh and the Minister for Foreign Affairs, Shahriar Alam, suggested Japanese investment will be the key to unleashing the economy's long-term potential."[57] The geopolitical outcome, as a result, would be further complicated: "Japan and China came head to head in competing for the contracts to help Bangladesh build the first ever deep-water port in Matarbari, which is located in the southern part of the country and near to the Indian Ocean."[58] Japan has beaten China in the race, and the control of the port is an important sign that Japan is keen to join the competition in the area. The deal could also mark a setback for China in South Asia, where it is seeking to establish economic and military ties in a region that carries about 80 per cent of its oil imports. For China and Japan, the Indian Ocean ports are valuable. Besides carrying most of the world's oil trade, the seas provide access to some of the world's most populous and fastest-growing markets. Bangladesh has about 166 million people, the fifth-most in Asia. For India, Bangladesh is one of its closest neighbours and has a major role to play in countering OBOR and avoiding China from becoming too involved in the Indian Ocean. Therefore, Bangladesh is currently enjoying the aid and foreign direct investments (FDIs) from India, China and Japan.

Losing the competition for the contract to build Matarbari has not stopped the progress of cooperation between China and Bangladesh on infrastructure. Under OBOR, there is development of water conservancy facilities, building of bridges (e.g. Padma Bridge) and railways, electricity plants, communication facilities and energy facilities. In 2012, China promised to fund a highway connecting Yunnan to Chittagong via Myanmar. Bangladesh is a country that is full of potential, but the government is lacking the funds and technological know-how to turn such potential into results. According to the report from the World Bank,

> Bangladesh has made substantial progress in reducing poverty, supported by sustained economic growth, but increased the demand for energy, transport and urbanization. The Dhaka government will have to reduce the infrastructure gaps and create more and better jobs to maintain the upward trend of the economy in last few years.[59]

Hence, the OBOR initiative is a best-served plan for China and Bangladesh, as one needs to export its excess production and the other one needs help in building infrastructure. Energy is one of the most crucial resources for economic and social development. China has invested in two power plants which are located in the Gazipur and Patuakhali Districts: "Gazipur District is around 30 kilometres from Dhaka, and this plant is expected to take nine months in construction."[60] As the capital is always the centre of the country and the main business hub, the power plant is aimed at enhancing the stability of energy supply in the area and to stimulate economic development. The Payra power plant is a significant project, as the city is not yet fully urbanised. Patuakhali District is in the southern part of Bangladesh and 330 kilometres away from Dhaka. Most of the people here are farmers or fishermen as it is only a small village. According to the Belt and Road Portal, the plant is not being built by China alone, but national enterprises from both countries have formed a joint venture named Bangladesh-China Power Company Limited (BCPCL) for this project. The plant will cost around US$2.2 billion and aims to improve both the 40 per cent access rate of electricity in rural area and the quality of life of its farmers and fishermen.[61]

Apart from the power plant projects, China is also involved in the construction of Bangladeshi highways and railways as in other countries that joined OBOR, but with some differences with its plans in Nepal and Pakistan. Due to the fact that Nepal and Pakistan have common borders with China, and Bangladesh does not, with India surrounding the country, China has chosen to focus on domestic highways and railways. As the Belt and Road Portal elaborates:

> There will be trains from Dhaka to Narayanganj, one of the most important industrial cities; and the highway from Dhaka to the metropolitan area of Sylhet will be upgraded at a cost of US$2.1 billion and is aimed at boosting the economic activities and business sector

> in the areas along the highway ... Dhaka will be on the top of the list with three major projects to improve the transportation system and reduce commuting time because the capital has a serious traffic issue; the average commute time will be reduced from 21 kilometres an hour in 2007 to just seven in 2017.[62]

These three projects are the Bus Rapid Transmit (BRT), Dhaka Airport highway and Metro Rail. They are carrying the hopes of the government and citizens to improve conditions in Dhaka and provide incentives for multinational corporations to invest there.

Compared with the Pakistanis and Nepalese, Bangladeshis have diverse political viewpoints on China and OBOR, while the socio-cultural impact is more or less the same as in the other two countries. Government officials have reiterated that the relationship between Dhaka and Beijing is very important and OBOR will bring loads of opportunities to the country. Chinese enterprises have brought numerous new infrastructure projects to Bangladesh – from bridges and railways to a BRT system and power plants. All of these have certainly enhanced the quality of life and provided a good foundation for long-term economic and social development. The Payra power plant is built by a joint venture of both countries' companies and the Bangladeshi staff state that they have learnt a lot from Chinese workers and have a good relationship with them. "Those Chinese workers have done more than expected and helped the locals to build roads, houses and shops."[63] In addition, the local business sector also favours Chinese people. Montaz, a businessman who trades rice, said that "the country can never repay the kindness shown by the Chinese government as it has removed all of their business and communication inconveniences".[64]

Nevertheless, Bangladesh always aims to achieve a balance in its international relationship, particularly between China and India. "Local experts agreed the links with Beijing are strong but India is still an important partner and Bangladesh is destined to depend on other big countries but not be over dependent."[65] China usually uses economic diplomacy as a means to improve or maintain its good bilateral relationship with certain states; this was successfully achieved in Africa and recently in Pakistan, Nepal and some other nations that are included in OBOR. However, Bangladesh may be a special case. Quite a few Bangladeshis have strongly opposed the development plans in their areas. For instance, in April 2016, "the villagers who lived in the coastal town of Gandamara near Chittagong gathered to protest against the two power plants. These are expected to force the eviction of several thousand people in fertile coastal farming areas and the demolition of temples and schools".[66] The event also turned violent:

"The police admitted killing four people after the villagers' demonstration was banned, but the protesters claimed that at least five people had died, 20 were injured and four others were missing."[67] This was the worst ever protest in the country since 2006, and one of a few that Chinese infrastructure projects have faced in the OBOR initiative. Those infrastructure projects may have brought benefits to the country in different areas of life, but the locals may not be willing to give up their current places of residence for these projects, and they are disappointed that the country is forcing them to leave their hometowns and sacrifice their lands.

Short Summary: Grand Strategy of China

As mentioned above, India is quite strongly opposed to OBOR and is coming up with its own version (AAGC) and partnering with Japan to counterbalance the influence of China in Asia and Africa. Territorial disputes have been one of the major reasons that have forced Modi's government to reject joining OBOR. Regardless of whether this is because of the sovereignty of the southern part of Tibet or that the CPEC passes through Kashmir, Delhi is not going to make any concession on the issue. Moreover, Delhi feels a sense of insecurity as Beijing strengthens its power around the Indian Ocean and its links with African countries. It formed the AAGC as a consequence and is using it to improve its own bilateral relationships with other countries, particularly with Japan and the countries in Africa to compete with China.

The friendship between Pakistan and China has been described as stronger than steel, and China had invested in numerous highways and other infrastructure projects prior to OBOR as well. Now, China is using the Gwadar Port as a direct solution to enhance energy security. Nepal and Bangladesh are two small countries which come within China's orbit and whose governments constantly need to find ways to balance the relationship with the big powers so as not to upset the other "giants". After India's blockade of Nepal in 2015, Nepal has leaned more and more towards China; even the Himalayas cannot impede the links between Kathmandu and Beijing. Bangladesh has a different relationship with India, which has a stronger influence. Dhaka enjoys its reliance on the help it receives from India, China and even Japan, but does not over-rely on them. Bangladesh's strong economic growth in recent years and its location in the north of the Indian Ocean has made its seaports strategically important. Not only is China interested in gaining Dhaka's support and access to those seaports, but Japan also has been drawn to this facility and has beaten China in winning the contract of building a new port in the area. India has used its influence on the Dhaka Government and encouraged it to turn its back on China towards other countries; so OBOR may in fact find a challenging situation here. Nevertheless, the economic reliance of Pakistan, Nepal and Bangladesh on China has increased significantly. Pakistan has relied on help from China for some time, while Nepal has recently switched its focus from India to China, and Bangladesh has increased its reliance to a certain degree as investment from Chinese enterprises may move from setting up factories to financing the constructions of various infrastructure projects. Although the cultural differences between the Chinese and the Muslims of the area are huge, the strategic importance of these countries will negate any obstacles.

So, what can we learn from all the above? According to the grand strategy of China, OBOR is not only an economic policy but also a geopolitical policy that could be compared with the Marshall Plan of the US after the Second World War. Offloading excessive resources from the local economy; solving domestic problems of unemployment by exporting manpower to build overseas infrastructure; using renminbi as the currency of transaction during the infrastructure building process in the hope of turning it into an equal-footing competitor of dollar; and creating structural reliance of its neighbours towards the Chinese economic orbit like the ancient tributary system, in turn restraining the anti-Chinese lobbies in these countries by skilfully utilising "sharp power", as designed by *The Economist* in December 2017, are just a few of Beijing's strategic thoughts. The immediate neighbours of China in South Asia are naturally within the road map of the strategy. If structural reliance of Pakistan, Nepal, Bhutan, Bangladesh, Sri Lanka, Maldives, Afghanistan and the likes are secured, India will find itself facing a brand new situation in which the regional hegemony in South Asia is already challenged by Beijing. India might have to accept the fait accompli and treat China similar to how Western Europe treated the US during the Cold War. It is naturally positive news for Beijing, and not necessarily a bad option for Delhi, too, but the long process leading towards that conclusion, if that is the way ahead, will be full of uncertainties, twists and perhaps also challenges.

NOTES

1. The author acknowledges research assistants Vincent Chan, Marco Kwan and Eugene Lo for their assistance in preparing the draft.
2. M. Wirtz, "India: Hedging China in Africa", *International Policy Digest*, July 11, 2016, at https://intpolicydigest.org/2016/07/11/india-hedging-china-africa (Accessed October 30, 2017)/.
3. J. Panda, "The Asia-Africa Growth Corridor: An India-Japan Arch in the

Making?", *Focus Asia Perspective & Analysis*, 21, August 2017, at http://isdp.eu/content/uploads/2017/08/2017-focus-asia-jagannath-panda.pdf (Accessed October 30, 2017).

4. A. Nair, "To Counter OBOR, India and Japan Propose Asia-Africa Sea Corridor", *The Indian Express*, May 31, 2017, at http://indianexpress.com/article/explained/to-counter-obor-india-and-japan-propose-asia-africa-sea-corridor-4681749/ (Accessed October 30, 2017)..
5. X. Wu, "China and India Increased Bilateral Investments, India Is Unwilling to only be the Commodity Market of China", China Economic Net, October 13, 2016, at http://intl.ce.cn/sjjj/qy/201610/13/t20161013_16724599.shtml (Accessed October 30, 2017).
6. "China Industrial Park in India Has Officially Started Construction", Xinhua, June 20, 2016, http://news.xinhuanet.com/fortune/2016-06/20/c_129077075.htm (Accessed October 30,2017).
7. X. Wu, No. 5.
8. Z. Liu, "The Three Attitudes of India on OBOR", Xinhua Silkroad Net, 2016, at http://silkroad.news.cn/Views/8512.shtml (Accessed October 30, 2017).
9. H. Qu, "Indian Expert: India Should Actively Support and Coordinate OBOR Initiative", *China Daily*, May 11, 2017, at http://china.chinadaily.com.cn/2017-05/11/content_29309125.htm (Accessed October 30, 2017).
10. H. Xu, "Vice Chairman of National Institution for Transforming India: Very Welcome Investment from China", China Economic Net, 2017, at http://intl.ce.cn/specials/zxgjzh/201702/28/t20170228_20570055.shtml (Accessed October 30, 2017).
11. Ibid.
12. S. Varadhan and N. Dasgupta, "Exclusive: Taking Aim at China, India Tightens Power Grid, Telecoms Rules", *Reuters*, August 17, 2017, at https://www.reuters.com/article/us-india-china-business/exclusive-taking-aim-at-china-india-tightens-power-grid-telecoms-rules-idUSKCN1AX1KW (Accessed October 30, 2017).
13. S. Singh, "Security Concerns: India's New Rules Will Bar Chinese Companies in Power Sector", *The Times of India*, May 22, 2017, at https://timesofindia.indiatimes.com/business/india-business/security-concerns-indias-new-rules-will-bar-chinese-companies-in-power-sector/articleshow/58783285.cms (Accessed October 30, 2017).
14. "Chinese Enterprise Suddenly Changed Attitudes, Indian High-speed Railway Upgrade Project Is Being Delayed", *DW News*, 2017, at http://news.dwnews.com/global/news/2017-10-16/60017525.html (Accessed October 30, 2017).
15. S. Bhadoria, "Why Chinese Hate Indians!", *IndiaTimes.com*, October 19, 2012, at https://www.indiatimes.com/asia/why-chinese-hate-indians-44333.html (Accessed October 30, 2017).
16. N. Yu, "Hindu Nationalism Risks Pushing India into War with China", *Global Times*, July 19, 2017, at http://www.globaltimes.cn/content/1057147.shtml (Accessed October 30, 2017).
17. "CPEC Is the New Role Model of International Relationships", PRC Embassy in Pakistan, 2017, at http://pk.mofcom.gov.cn/article/jmxw/201709/20170902647081.shtml (Accessed October 30, 2017).

18. CPEC Gwadar Project Updates, CPEC official website, 2017, at http://cpec.gov.pk/gwader (Accessed October 30, 2017).
19. M. Yeung, "China-funded Gwadar Port Started Operation. As the Important Part of OBOR, Safety Is the Top Concern", HK01, 2016, at https://www.hk01.com/%E5%85%A9%E5%B2%B8/54263/%E4%B8%AD%E8%B3%87%E7%93%9C%E9%81%94%E7%88%BE%E6%B8%AF%E9%96%8B%E9%80%9A-%E7%82%BA-%E4%B8%80%E5%B8%B6%E4%B8%80%E8%B7%AF-%E9%87%8D%E8%A6%81%E4%BD%88%E5%B1%80-%E5%AE%89% E5%85%A8%E6%88%90%E9%A6%96%E8%A6%81%E5%95%8F%E9%A1%8C (Accessed October 30, 2017).
20. K. Munir, "Short Takes: Benefits of Gwadar Port - An Explainer", *South Asian Voices*, January 10, 2017, at https://southasianvoices.org/short-takes-benefits-of-gwadar-port-an-explainer/ (Accessed October 31, 2017).
21. "China to Rule Arabian Sea via Gwadar Port, Cargo To Pakistan", April 23, 2015, at http://www.cargotopakistan.co.uk/blog/china-to-rule-arabian-sea-via-gwadar-port/.
22. "CPEC's Largest Transportation Infrastructure Is Starting to be Built in Pakistan", PRC Central Government, 2016, at http://big5.gov.cn/gate/big5/www.gov.cn/xinwen/2016-05/07/content_5071154.htm (Accessed October 31, 2017).
23. Henny Sender and Kiran Stacey, "China Takes 'Project of the Century' to Pakistan", *Financial Times*, May 17, 2017, at https://www.ft.com/content/05979e18-2fe4-11e7-9555-23ef563ecf9a (Accessed October 31, 2017).
24. W. Xu, "First Ever China Medical Team Supporting Pakistan Has Arrived in Gwadar Port, They Will Provide Medical Services for 2 Years", Belt and Road Portal, 2017, at https://www.yidaiyilu.gov.cn/xwzx/hwxw/28962.htm (Accessed October 31, 2017)
25. External Trade Statistics Tables, Pakistan Bureau of Statistics, 2017, at http://www.pbs.gov.pk/trade-tables (Accessed October 31, 2017).
26. T. Yeung, "CPEC Made Chinese Society in Pakistan be Prosperous, Import Pork and Speak Chinese, Copy China to Pakistan", HK01, 2017, at https://www.hk01.com/%E5%9C%8B%E9%9A%9B/117117/%E4%B8%AD%E5%B7%B4 %E7%B6 %93%E6%BF%9F%E8%B5%B0%E5%BB%8A%E5%B8%B6%E6%97%BA%E5% 94% 90% E4% BA %BA%E5%9 C%88%E5%AD%90-%E9%80%B2%E5%8F%A3% E8%B1%AC%E8%82%89%E8%AC%9B%E4%B8%AD%E6%96%87-%E8%A4%87%E8%A3%BD%E4%B8%AD%E5%9C%8B%E5%88%B0%E5%B7%B4%E5%9F%BA% E6%96%AF%E5%9D%A6 (Accessed October 31, 2017).
27. T. Hussain, "$55b Trade Route, and a Rekindled China-Pakistan Love Affair", *South China Morning Post*, May 13, 2017, at http://www.scmp.com/week-asia/geopolitics/article/2093736/highway-sell-how-55b-trade-corridor-rekindled-china-pakistan(Accessed October 31, 2017).
28. "China Battleship Will Stay at Gwadar Port to Prevent Terrorist Attacks and Pirates, Pakistan Pointed out that China May Construct a Military Base", *Ming Pao*, 2016, at https://news.mingpao.com/pns/dailynews/web_tc/article/20161129/s00013/1480356649814 (Accessed October 31, 2017).
29. T. Hussain, No. 27.
30. S. I. Raza, "'CPEC Could Become Another East India Company'", *Dawn*, October 18, 2016, at https://www.dawn.com/news/1290677 (Accessed October 31, 2017).
31. T. Yeung, No. 26.

32. Ibid.
33. T. Hussain, No. 27.
34. Ibid.
35. "Chinese Murdered by ISIS in Pakistan, Beijing: It Would Not Affect OBOR, The SCO Member States Agreed Joint Anti-Terrorism Statement", *Ming Pao*, 2017, at https://news.mingpao.com/pns/dailynews/web_tc/article/20170610/s00013/1497030894849 (Accessed October 31, 2017).
36. "Nepal Joins China's 'One Belt, One Road' Initiative, Possibly Alarming India", *South China Morning Post*, May 12, 2017, at http://www.scmp.com/news/asia/diplomacy/article/2094091/nepal-joins-chinas-one-belt-one-road-initiative-possibly (Accessed October 31, 2017).
37. S. Giri, "Nepal, China Sign Deal on OBOR", *The Kathmandu Post*, May 12, 2017, at http://kathmandupost.ekantipur.com/news/2017-05-12/nepal-china-sign-framework-deal-on-obor.html (Accessed October 31, 2017).
38. S. Zheng, "Nepal's 'Balancing Act' Continues as Deputy PM Heads to Beijing", *South China Morning Post*, at http://www.scmp.com/news/china/diplomacy-defence/article/2110020/nepals-balancing-act-continues-deputy-prime-minister (Accessed October 31, 2017).
39. "Nepal Joins China's 'One Belt, One Road' Initiative, Possibly Alarming India", No. 36.
40. "Rescue Nepal's Earthquake: China Is in Action", Xinhua, 2015, http://news.xinhuanet.com/world/2015-04/26/c_127734524.htm (Accessed October 31, 2017).
41. "Major Transportation Links between China and Nepal Are Fully Repaired", Xinhua, 2017, at http://news.xinhuanet.com/2017-03/03/c_1120566331.htm (Accessed October 31, 2017)
42. "China Will Help Nepal Repair Heritages that Were Damaged by earthquake", Xinhua, 2016, at http://news.xinhuanet.com/world/2016-09/22/c_1119605497.htm (Accessed October 31, 2017)
43. "Nepal: Human Development Indicators", Human Development Reports, United Nations Development Programme, at http://hdr.undp.org/en/countries/profiles/NPL (Accessed October 31, 2017).
44. W. Shepard, "How India Got Wrapped Up in China's Belt and Road Initiative, Despite Opposing It", *Forbes*, June 25, 2017, at https://www.forbes.com/sites/wadeshepard/2017/06/25/china-now-has-india-wrapped-up-in-its-belt-and-road/#75518220227f (Accessed October 31, 2017).
45. "China Power Construction Corporation's finished the construction of Nepal Kaligadaki A Power Station", *People's Daily*, 2017, at http://ccnews.people.com.cn/n1/2016/0928/c141677-28746689.html (Accessed October 31, 2017).
46. "AIIB Promises Huge Investments in Nepal's Infrastructure Development", *The Himalayan Times*, June 19, 2017, at https://thehimalayantimes.com/nepal/aiib-promises-huge-investments-nepals-infrastructure-development/ (Accessed October 31, 2017).
47. S. Zou, "Chinese Enterprise Constructs 'Role Model' Infrastructure, Pokhara New Airport Will Help Nepal Connect with the World", Belt and Road Portal, 2017, at https://www.yidaiyilu.gov.cn/xwzx/hwxw/24315.htm (Accessed October 31, 2017).

48. Ibid.
49. "Nepal Hopes OBOR Will Bring Railways to the Country, Indian Media Is Jealous", *DW News*, 2017, at http://news.dwnews.com/global/big5/news/2017-08-05/60005263_all.html (Accessed October 31, 2017).
50. "Nepalese: We Love Chinese the Most. I Am Telling the Truth!", *Global Times*, 2017, at http://oversea.huanqiu.com/article/2017-09/11242439.html (Accessed October 31, 2017).
51. "Under China-Indian Standoff, China and Nepal Became Closer", *FT Chinese*, 2017, at http://www.ftchinese.com/story/001073850 (Accessed October 31, 2017).
52. "Chinese Language Popular in Nepal", CCTV, April 17, 2013, at http://english.cntv.cn/program/asiatoday/20130417/107808.shtml (Accessed October 31, 2017).
53. Q. Zhang, "Sino-Bangladesh Relations under Xi Jinping's Neighboring Diplomacy (First part)", *South Asia Watch*, 2016, at http://southasiawatch.tw/sino-bangladesh-relation%E3%80%80%E7%BF%92%E8%BF%91%E5% B9% B3% E5% 91%A8%E9%82%8A%E5%A4%96%E4%BA%A4%E4%B8%8B%E7%9A% 84% E4% B8% AD% E5% AD%9F%E9%97%9C%E4%BF%82%E4%B8%8A/%E3%80%82 (Accessed October 31, 2017).
54. Ibid.
55. Ibid.
56. N. Zahan, "Bangladesh Joins China's 'One Belt, One Road' Initiative: Meeting Challenges, Building the Future", *Shanghai Daily*, February 28, 2017, at https://www.shine.cn/archive/opinion/foreign-perspectives/Bangladesh-joins-Chinas-One-Belt-One-Road-initiative-meeting-challenges-building-the-future/shdaily.shtml (Accessed October 31, 2017).
57. M. Obe, "Bangladesh's Alam: Japanese investment can feed 'new Asian Tiger'", *Nikkei Asian Review*, June 15, 2017, at https://asia.nikkei.com/magazine/20170615/Future-of-Asia-2017/Bangladesh-s-Alam-Japanese-investment-can-feed-new-Asian-Tiger (Accessed October 31, 2017).
58. N. O. Pearson, "Japan Beating China to the Port in Bangladesh", *The Japan Times*, July 05, 2015, at https://www.japantimes.co.jp/news/2015/07/05/national/politics-diplomacy/japan-beating-china-to-the-port-in-bangladesh/#.WfiMtFtL-Ul (Accessed October 31, 2017).
59. "The World Bank in Bangladesh", World Bank, at http://www.worldbank.org/en/country/bangladesh/overview (Accessed October 31, 2017).
60. "Chinese Enterprise Won the Bid of Bangladesh's Oil Power Plant, It Will Significantly Improve Power Supply in Dhaka Area", Belt and Road Portal, 2017, at https://www.yidaiyilu.gov.cn/xwzx/hwxw/27822.htm (Accessed October 31, 2017).
61. "Chinese Enterprises Agreed to Build the Payra Power Plant, Help Bangladesh to Achieve Energy Self-Sufficiency", Belt and Road Portal, 2017, at https://www.yidaiyilu.gov.cn/xwzx/hwxw/16191.htm (Accessed October 31, 2017).
62. "Chinese Enterprise Joined Bangladesh Transportation Projects, Help Improving Traffic Condition of the Capital", Belt and Road Portal, 2017, at https://www.yidaiyilu.gov.cn/xwzx/hwxw/26073.htm (Accessed October 31, 2017).
63. Ibid.
64. "Bangladesh Indebted to China for Friendship Bridges, Eyes More Infrastructure

Projects: Locals", *Xinhua*, 2017, at http://news.xinhuanet.com/english/2017-07/20/c_136458431.htm (Accessed October 31, 2017).

65. Q. Zhang, No. 53.
66. J. Vidal, "Bangladesh Coal Plant Protests Continue after Demonstrators Killed", *The Guardian*, April 06, 2016, at https://www.theguardian.com/environment/2016/apr/06/bangladesh-coal-plant-protests-continue-after-demonstrators-killed (Accessed October 31, 2017).
67. "Bangladesh Power Plant Protest: Four Dead and Three Held", *BBC News*, April 5, 2016, at http://www.bbc.com/news/world-asia-35967762 (Accessed October 31, 2017).

6

Beijing's OBOR Initiative and Taiwan: Beyond the Infrastructure Gambit

Ming-Shih Shen

The concept of the *Silk Road Economic Belt and the 21st Century Maritime Silk Road* (well known as *One Belt One Road*, or *OBOR*) covers various aspects and a wide-ranging scale. To the extent that it is poised to overtake the American hegemony, OBOR has been referred to as a *Grand Strategy*,[1] while other scholars characterise it as *stratagem* or *strategy* in the conventional sense. Scholars on the Chinese side, however, tend to see OBOR as an initiative.[2] The above labels given to OBOR reflect varied interpretations about its nature and different expectations regarding its future. As a matter of fact, when some scholars take OBOR as a grand strategy, they link it to Xi Jinping's sound bites, such as the *Chinese Dream*, *Two-century Goals*, and the *Great Renaissance of Chinese People*. OBOR for them is an important blueprint of Chinese long-term development of geopolitical situations and economic cooperation. The Asian Infrastructure Investment Bank (AIIB) is therefore a supporting mechanism to substantiate OBOR as an initiative, through which more than 30 sovereign states along the one Belt and the one Road are contracted into various frameworks for economic cooperation. In 2017, the OBOR Summit was held in Beijing, where 130 state representatives and 29 national leaders got together. It was Beijing's moment against American hegemony – a striking image reminiscent of the Middle Kingdom that used to command suzerainty from the geographic centre.[3]

In line with the new situation, some scholars perceive the development of OBOR as a necessarily lineal process. They claim that by the year 2050, China would be a socialist power in the world, where Chinese culture would enjoy a golden moment of renaissance.[4] This development of OBOR holds significance for Taiwan, a political entity that is economically deeply linked to mainland China. In view of the cooperation schemes envisaged by Beijing with its regional partners, Taiwan has to understand the challenges from these regional schemes so that it can weather their potential ill impacts. At the same time, Taiwan can also seize the windows of opportunity to maximise its economic benefits. Between the risks and the opportunities, there is no need for Taiwan to be pessimistic, or feel marginalised on the world stage faced by Beijing's current long-term development plan. Nor should Taiwan follow blindly a policy that remains premature and filled with uncertainties at this juncture of Xi Jinping's tenure. Having said that, however, this chapter does not deny that there are opportunities for Taiwan. If Taiwan fails to seize the opportunities offered, it may eventually force Taiwan to lose out with regard to geopolitical and economic interests. Therefore, the following questions cannot be taken lightly: Given the opportunities opened up by OBOR, what kind of benefits could Taiwan possibly garner? What steps should Taiwan take when seeking these benefits? Does a trade-off between national sovereignty and integrating itself into the current regional framework of economic cooperation masterminded by Beijing make sense for Taiwan? These questions constitute vital reference points in the policymaking process of Taiwan. Because most significant will be the direct impact from China's big infrastructure plans under OBOR. These plans are tremendously relevant for economic sustainment in Asian-European areas, of which Taiwan is a part.[5] Thus, Taiwan clearly has to find the right balance between grasping opportunities for further development and taking preventive measures to withstand any negative impact in the future.

Potential Risks in OBOR

There are five deep-rooted risks embedded in OBOR related to geopolitics, security, economics, legal issues and morality.[6] These potential risks are discussed as follows:

Geopolitical Risks

Geopolitical risks increase in the context of geopolitical conflicts and competition for strategic interests among major powers. The geopolitical risks, refer to political concerns of countries identified as part of the OBOR initiative and the intervention from countries outside of the geographic arrangement mapped by OBOR. In accordance with the manifesto *Vision and Actions on Jointly Building Silk Road Economic Belt and 21st Century Maritime Silk Road*,[7] the Belt brings together China, Central Asia, Russia and Europe (the Baltic region) – linking China with the Persian Gulf and the Mediterranean Sea through Central Asia and West Asia; and with Southeast Asia, South Asia and the Indian Ocean. The Road connects the Chinese coasts via the South China Sea and Indian Ocean to Europe, and also connects China via the South China Sea to the South Pacific region.[8] Thus, although there are potential gains to the countries along the OBOR routes, not all the neighbouring countries are willing to concur with the so-called interests. Vietnam and India have expressed their apprehension.[9] States in the Arabic world tend to be free riders to get their interest but not much burden.[10] Russia has pressed clear its concerns over the possibility that geopolitical interests could be re-defined by OBOR.[11] Worse still are the waves of grave instability across the political map of OBOR.[12]

Security Risks

Some countries in the regions covered by OBOR are unstable for the crisis of constant civil wars and local conflicts. Without security assurance, the further development of OBOR bodes ill for future prospects.[13] Uncertainties also include terrorist threats (ISIS and Taliban),[14] ecological deterioration (deforestation and river pollutions as a result of over-development),[15] marine security (pirates harassing the sea lines)[16] and water scarcity (excess use of water and ill effects from retaining dams).[17] As OBOR Watch, a self-funded watchdog over the environmental impacts from OBOR, reported,

> China's business practices are already facing local pushback in several countries where its state-owned enterprises have built energy and infrastructure projects. Some firms have been accused of cutting corners, ignoring safety standards, using secondhand or low-quality materials and equipment.[18]

The bad governance of engineering qualities from the Chinese enterprises will also bring the security risks, and indicate that facts are more complicated than what first meets the eye.

Economic Risks

It must be mentioned that the majority of states located along the OBOR routes are "developing countries". They have weak financial systems and not-so-transparent capital flows, and are vulnerable to changes in the monetary policies of developed economies. Countries such as Indonesia, Turkey and Russia suffer from current account deficits and credit-policy over-extension. Although their local bond markets indeed attract foreign investments in great proportions, their overall protective measures against financial exploitation and other risks are not up to expectation. In short, China and its partners in OBOR are subject to uncertainties caused by fleeting monetary policies of major international actors, such as the Europe, US and Japan. In the medium terms, all the countries in the world are facing economic growth rate dropped and seeking to adjust their economic structure. Especially the developing countries are facing the weak cycle of economic rise and the negative effect of foreign capitals. In order to avoid the impacts mentioned above, these countries must change their economic structure in time. But these changes will also bring the risks of development to China and partner countries of OBOR.

Legal Risks

Because many countries along the OBOR routes suffer from political difficulties, financial crises and debt problems, Chinese enterprises must increase their investments to help these countries. But these countries have their own different legal system, like Civil Laws, Common Laws and Muslim law. As a result of different legal systems in application, there are uncertainties with respect to interpretation of the terms as well as application of the contents.[19] Given the current protectionist moves as an emotional consequence of growth recessions, the issues of legal risks have to be underlined here. If foreign investors are unfamiliar with the local laws in practice, or do not have legal experts available on their teams and, instead, exclusively abide by international customs without reference to local law, they may unknowingly violate the local laws. This is where the legal risks lie. Generally speaking, the difference among the systems of law and the legal disputes will inevitably arise over issues including foreign investment, labour and capital, environmental protection, business management, trade agreement and legal remedy.[20]

Moral Hazards

Moral hazards of the OBOR initiative can be divided into three levels – inter-state, enterprise and individual.[21] At the inter-state level, Beijing invests in the states covered by OBOR for its interest. The other regional power also want to get the same investment opportunities and compete with China. But China often funds interest-free loans to these developing countries in Africa, South Asia and South East Asia as its last resort. However, being aware of the rivalries from Europe Union, U.S. and Japan in the international markets, the countries covered by OBOR may likely use their mutual suspicion of each other as a bargaining chip and ask for more investments from Beijing. These economic competitions between

China and other regional power may transfer to be diplomatic game. This would certainly raise uncertainties about the efficiency of contracts co-signed in the OBOR framework. One significant example is the Colombo Port, Sri Lanka.[22]

At the level of enterprises, moral hazards can be attributed to the negative perception of Chinese companies concerning practices such as monopoly, illegal competition, credit default, breech of contracts, fraud, illegal risk-shifting, evading debts, trade dumping and prohibited subsidies, to name a few. The consequences imply risks of being boycotted or excluded from closer cooperation. Once OBOR enters into the operational phase, the risks faced by these Chinese enterprises may include pollution of natural resources, ideological impact on local cultures and traditional customs, complaints about the degree of transparency with respect to developmental policies as well as bureaucratic bribery. These can also be considered societal risks, for once news regarding corruption malpractices is relayed to the public, it will certainly lead to strong social protests.[23]

At the individual level, risks mainly come from differences in belief systems, patterns of rationality, cultural awareness and working culture. For these risks from state, enterprise and the individual, will make OBOR initiative still filled with uncertainties. These uncertainties are risk factors to not only Beijing but also Taipei. Therefore, not until the risks mentioned above can be effectively toned down or partially resolved, can Taiwan take a definitive step towards OBOR and see it as a booming opportunity.

Opportunities and Challenges

At first glance, we find that Taiwan is not on the list of preferred states and Taiwan will not face the direct benefits or threats quickly. However, a closer reading will show that the prospect may be more of losses than gains. In other words, Taiwan's economy may have already been forced into a dangerous situation where there is no opportunity at hand but more risks ahead.[24] To start with, the primary aim of OBOR is to address overproduction. This aim is to be fulfilled by stimulating domestic demand in mainland China. This means that there are limited opportunities for Taiwanese enterprises that, if any, may refer to those with production lines based in mainland China. In any case, the Taiwanese enterprises will not be able to compete against Chinese companies for infrastructure bids. Moreover, profits in such projects are often minimal and do not appeal to the Taiwanese businesses. Perhaps even more complicated is the possibility that the infrastructure bids as well as the funds allocated for the OBOR initiative are more for Beijing's interests than for practical needs of the locals. Given the fact that the bids are not market-oriented and do not have a transparent mechanism, neither Taiwanese enterprises nor those based in China have active or fair roles to play.

To say that Beijing's campaign for OBOR is characterised by a twofold aim – economic and geopolitical – would not be unfounded. Beijing witnessed economic recession in the past three years. During this period, some enterprises had excess capacity and were under pressure of being phased out. So OBOR was initially started as an economic means to relocate those conventional capacities that were pressurised to close down. The focus on infrastructure projects in developing countries along the route are an alternative to Chinese conventional capacities that are activated by foreign loans and relevant funds through the AIIB. In the future, Beijing expects that once the infrastructure projects in these OBOR countries become functional, there will be a considerable rise in income and demand for goods and services in these countries. And in this manner, through its economic links, China would be able to reap the fruits of its efforts. The media has dubbed the OBOR initiative the Chinese version of Marshall Plan, as doubts regarding its extended geopolitical influence can hardly be dispelled. Beijing is cautious on this metaphorical naming. It immediately denied any link to an idealist philanthropist act, which indicated nothing but Beijing's pragmatist line that is always in pursuit of political interests, economic benefits and military interests.

A closer examination of OBOR also triggers doubts about whether this grandiose project will deliver low-utility goods and whether it could deepen the already serious degree of economic imbalances. It is somewhat ironic to point out that among the developing economies along the OBOR routes, many are plagued by bad governance. Sudden grants and dumping loans from the international front only lead to corruption, including waste, operational inefficiency and bribery. Such scandalous cases have happened quite frequently, even as these loans are masterminded and monitored by the Asian Development Bank or the World Bank. OBOR projects to these countries can certainly not be the exception.

It also needs to be pointed out that despite the OBOR promotional campaign that has garnered much attention, statistics show that foreign direct investment from China to OBOR countries dropped 2 per cent in 2016. It again dropped 18 per cent in the first quarter of 2017. The China Development Bank, the mainstay of the three non-commercial, policy banking institutions in mainland China, reported that its balance of loans to the countries identified as part of the OBOR initiative reduced US $1 billon. This is a reverse trend in development that is worthy of note. It clearly indicates that OBOR, in terms of opportunities and attractiveness, has left much room to be called a real success.

The issue here is on the continuity of these international loans. The AIIB was just set up in 2016 with a register capital of nearly US $100 billon. It therefore makes sense for Beijing to expect some fruitful policy outcomes from the loan strategy. Hence, inference can be made that loans for infrastructure projects to the countries related to OBOR may not come to a halt all of a sudden. This can be also confirmed by the declaration made by Xi Jinping at the 2017 Summit that Beijing would add 400 billion (Renminbi, RMB) to strengthen its support for OBOR. Xi's declared move suggests that the strategy of loans may not change significantly during his tenure. It also indicates that lower levels of direct investment can be interpreted as tentative. Potential gains and economic prospects remain rosy, and will be exploited at any time after they mature.

However, if in the performing process of OBOR, because of the low standards, or worse still, ill-governance over loans occurs, we can anticipate that planned economic outcomes will not be achieved. Nonetheless, OBOR looks to act as the engine of regional economic growth. But the risks for Beijing and the banks lie in moments when the goals are interrupted by a setback or subsequent economic utilities that proves to be unsustainable. Having said that, we also have to admit that funds provided through OBOR are an important opportunity to countries with poor infrastructures or slow economic growth. The loans via OBOR are instrumental for the economic development of these developing countries. This is indeed an asymmetric, one-sided game. On the one side, as long as governments and enterprises from these countries succeed in getting the loans in the forms of projects, construction plans and acquisition programmes, they seize the opportunities for gains. On the other side, the leading banks and the host country, China, that offer the loans run the risks. On the Chinese side, the logic applies as well. As long as a Chinese enterprise wins a construction contract or succeeds in winning the bid for a project, it means commercial interests will be obtained by Chinese enterprise only. It does not matter what happens to the projects once they are completed. The funds get received and risks are minimal. But this is not a healthy market mechanism."

Do these distorted phenomena also apply to Taiwanese enterprises? Perhaps, the opposite reflects the reality. Due to the tension across the Straits, Taiwan is not on the AIIB's guest list, nor a part of the OBOR initiative. It is true that Beijing did send the invitation, welcoming Taiwan on board. Yet, it was only lip service, because only a minority of Taiwanese enterprises were entitled to a shred of symbolic interests. In any case, the OBOR initiative can hardly be taken as a window of opportunity by Taiwan to resolve its economic situation. Instead, the initiative is likely to be filled with more risks for Taiwan than it can cope with, let alone overcome.

These risks are real and substantial. From a short-term perspective, Taiwan enterprises has been excluded from the economic benefits and commercial opportunities of OBOR initiative by China's political condition. If Beijing succeeds in forming a semi-regional economic and trade organisation based on the OBOR framework, an excluded Taiwan will face the negative impact and pressure even more. In the current context when Washington has withdrawn from the Trans-Pacific Partnership (TPP) and Beijing is seeking the control of the Regional Comprehensive Economic Partnership (RCEP) with its unceasing effort in the OBOR initiative, Taiwan, with no access to the East Asian Community (EAC) because of Beijing's opposition, has been marginalised and its future risk of economic development is increasing. Under this situation, Taiwan has to observe the OBOR initiative with different dimensions. It is all right to talk about prosperity, but the opportunities and risks cannot be taken into account like a bystander. Taiwan should take more concern the derivative risks from OBOR.

Taking an exclusively optimistic view on economic benefits, we can assert that there will be tremendous prospects for commercial gains. The industrial sectors in Taiwan are rich in technical competence. Finance, construction, transportation, telecommunications and the Internet are all sectors that can reap the benefits of joining OBOR.

Beijing's attitude towards Taiwan on the OBOR initiative is also one of the signposts for policy-making. Beijing is seeking ways to have a breakthrough in the Cross-Straits deadlock, one of which is building the economic links across the Straits and via the Asia Pacific. It has been argued that if Taiwan takes part in the OBOR initiative, it can help reduce the negative perception about China overall and increase its chance to be a part of regional economy in the Asia Pacific. The OBOR initiative is an extension of China's follow-up development plan. The OBOR initiative is the follow-up trend from China's *West Plan Programmes*, some Taiwan enterprises already invested to this program. This experiences have created investment opportunities for Taiwan in infrastructure projects, local staples and manufacturing goods in China's Great West areas and the developing countries along the OBOR routes. As two sides across the Straits have a comparative advantage in the IT industry, they can establish manufacturing bases and expand market shares in the OBOR countries. In fact, Beijing is making tremendous efforts to transform its economies towards an outgoing pattern creating a China first model. This economic pattern and model will change the direction of cross strait economic cooperation and global value chain (GVC). In light of this, Taiwan has the opportunity to adjust its industrial structure and stimulate a rise in exports. One example this paper refers to is the free-riding opportunity regarding the Maritime Silk Road that could be potentially realised through two Free Trade Zones in Shanghai and Fujian. The starting point of building Fujian as a Free Trade Zone is to "address Taiwan", as Fujian is taken as a new frontier to deepen Cross-Straits economic relations. Ideally speaking, Fujian is the engine to move the Maritime Silk Road, and Taiwan can seize the geographical proximity and become be a free-rider on OBOR. If Fujian is successfully linked to the OBOR initiative, Taiwan could expand more new market alongside the Maritime Silk Road.

Similarly, deploying Taiwanese enterprises into the Shanghai Free Trade Zone also seems promising. Having been selected as the first targeted area for a pilot experiment on a free trade zone speaks about the potential of Shanghai. Shanghai is currently the hub of economics, finance, trade and transportation inside mainland China. It is destined for a key nodal point of foreign investment and global commerce, which is surely becoming the main fulcrum as well as distribution centre of varied resources in the OBOR initiative.

From the perspective of the rate of return on investment, the investment projects, are helping strengthen a quicker integration into the greater Chinese market, where energy and natural resources and utilisation energy are readily available. The speed and convenience offered by this wave of market integration will inevitably work out a new form of division of labour and economic relations. It can be expected that there may be more Taiwanese businesses going into mainland China, seeking lucrative markets in those developing countries involved in infrastructure building. In other words, a thriving wave of investment fever from Taiwan into Mainland is a business trend by nature.

However, there seems to be a gap between hopes and realities. The long-term effects of the OBOR initiative for Taiwan are full of risks, in the market shares of semi-products exported from Taiwan to China will drop and eventually be replaced by the alternatives. The fact is that Beijing is under heavy pressure from rising labour cost in recent years and is keen to switch its industrial bases abroad. With the promotion of OBOR, sustained by loans granted for infrastructure projects overseas by the AIIB, Beijing has already witnessed the immediate outcomes, i.e. a dramatic reduction of cost over transportation and logistics. These developing countries, sustained by international loans, have reaped considerable benefits by making basic spare parts as they serve an important role in the overall supply chain and GVC.

It is perfectly all right for them to satisfy themselves by stopping at this stage, rather than moving further with advanced products or by developing economies of scale. It would be risky, however, to see these developing countries replace the conventional division of labour across the Straits and in East Asia. The trend will definitely strike a blow to the market shares of the semi-products from Taiwan to China and to related regional states, and may eventually risk them being replaced by those from competitors along the OBOR route.

The above scenario is indicative of the gap between intention, however benign, and realities. Beijing seems interested in linking China, Hong Kong, Macau, Taiwan and overseas through OBOR to fulfil an ideal that is coded the *Chinese Economic Circle*. The political atmosphere across the Strait at present seems to involve an opposite trend. Legally speaking, Beijing does not consider businessmen from Taiwan as its citizens, which implies that Taiwanese do not enjoy equal status with the mainland Chinese when it comes to funding, taxation, environmental protection measures and government purchase. Fairly speaking, without partaking into the OBOR, it may be a problem to ask Beijing give Taiwanese businessmen a citizen status. In a nutshell, the issues related to OBOR's future development may create more troubles to Taiwan in political and economic areas.

OBOR vs New Southbound Policy

To cope with potential challenges from OBOR, Taiwan has come up with the *New Southbound Policy*. The *Policy* aims to weather the impact from the OBOR initiative, though it cannot compete with OBOR in terms of its financial basis and campaigning scale. As common sense would have it, when countries in Southeast Asia are increasingly industrialised, Taiwan's manufacturing sectors will get this good opportunity to increase their investment in a rational move. Whether Taiwan can detect the trend and seize the opportunity is key to the successful economic transformation in Taiwan. Take high-speed railways, the beacon of transportation infrastructure, for instance. Constructing a high-speed railway involves engineering, electro-mechanics, computer science, IT systems and electric power. Civil construction (engineering) requires raw materials like cement, steel and glass. Electro-mechanics involves generating systems. Computers and IT are associated with communications industry and optic fibre sector.

Storage and warehousing services have to be in place at all the stops along the railways, where tourist sector and town building may also thrive. Despite these potential prospects, there are in store threats and challenges as Taiwan's *New Southbound Policy* is bound to encounter Beijing's OBOR initiative. Potential threats from Beijing's high-profile foreign-policy activities including top-level visits and close contacts would certainly neutralise the campaign effort and dilute the attraction of Taiwan's *New Southbound Policy*. The neutralisation effect against Taiwan has affected some sub-regional programmes such as the Indo-China Economic Corridor and China, India, Myanmar and Bangladesh Economic Corridor that strengthen cooperation across Southeast Asia and South Asia by signing free trade agreements. Perhaps something worth saving a thought for are Beijing's economic initiatives that are often backed by political motivation. It has increasingly become a conventional practice that when signing agreements on deeper economic cooperation, the counterparts are often required to express their open support for *One-China Policy*.

A review of risks and challenges from the OBOR initiative shows that every silver lining has a dark cloud. *Co-opetition* (a combination of cooperation and competition) can be a balanced interpretation towards relations between OBOR and *New Southbound Policy*.[25] Despite the looming threats from OBOR, Taiwan enjoys a relative advantage in medical care, education, development of human resources, technological innovation, agriculture and disaster prevention. These help create windows of opportunity for cooperation between Taiwan and countries in Southeast Asia. The aim of the subsequent negotiations is to strike bilateral deals so that there are institutionalised modes in practice. On the other hand, there are spaces of shared interests in building infrastructure, capacity and economies and trades. Simply put, Taiwan is well experienced in transportation means, ports construction, electric power, communication network and waste disposal. That said, serious joint effort in the name of either OBOR or *New Southbound Policy* will offer prospects for a win-win result with shared interests through industrial cooperation across the Straits.

This paper illustrates the above ideal through an example, the China Technical Consultants, Inc. (CTCI). The CTCI was established in 1979 and has been well known for its rich experience in international projects dealing in engineering design and construction more than 20 years. The CTCI started from the work of engineering design and expanded in the oil refining and petro-chemical sector. Since then, the CTCI has been active in professional areas such as electric power, steel industry, public works, and environmental engineering.[26] Its annual income totalled NT$60 billion in

2015, nearly half of it comes from overseas contracts. The point worth noting is that the CTCI has already set its foot in countries related to the OBOR initiative.[27] Its other destinations include one of the movers and shakers that drafted the AIIB Charter, Singapore, where the CTCI is carrying out track construction. The CTCI is also currently one of the main actors in Singapore's rapid-transit expansion programme, in which the company has won three engineering contracts.

One of the reasons that the CTCI moved ahead with a successful layout lies in its long-term cooperation link to most companies in mainland China. The legacy of cooperation is threefold. First, based on the CTCI's rich experiences in dealing with international norms and green industry, it serves as a consultant for mainland Chinese companies. Second, the CTCI has succeeded in co-signing framework agreements with several mainland Chinese companies. When the framework agreements cover developing countries in the neighbourhood of OBOR, it helps build institutions that allow for further possibility of cooperation. Third, in contrast to those financing plans granted by the Asian Development Bank or the World Bank, Beijing in the OBOR initiative takes part in the game as an investor with a handsome financial support. The CTCI, to be a part of game, has only to demonstrate its engineering capabilities without too much concern about the source of financing. In short, the case of the CTCI is illustrative of both the strengths of a Taiwanese enterprise and OBOR. With geographic proximity, cultural resemblance, related industries like CTCI has rich experience in Chinese and neighbouring regions market, OBOR may also give Taiwan a potential chance to export the integration service of technology and labour, and help Taiwanese high-tech manufacturing become servitization.

The fruitful results of industrial cooperation across the Straits would be more meaningful because they are less prone to political suspicion and diplomatic intervention. For Taiwan, the cooperation may result in investments that are unique to Taiwan, or a market-based demand for specifically Taiwanese products. A final note here is that for Taiwan the OBOR initiative constitutes a two-pronged prospect that is mixed with gains and losses – a geopolitical entity combined with opportunities and risks. In order to prevent Taiwan businessmen from the political and diplomatic risks for China's outrageous business practices, it is important to do a good image management to differentiate between China and Taiwan businessmen and this will be an advisable agenda for future studies.

Conclusion

The main purpose of the OBOR initiative is to cope with issues of domestic overproduction in mainland China. While Beijing's emphasis of the OBOR initiative is on building infrastructure, some of Beijing's counterparts are not satisfied with investment proportions and operation rights in their deals. One of significant cases occurred between Islamabad and Beijing. The two sides signed a Memorandum of Understanding (MOU) in May 2017, when Beijing offered a fund that totalled US $14 billion to construct the Diamer Bhasha Dam in Pakistan. The deal is a part of the China-Pakistan Economic Corridor project. However, when Beijing expressed its intention to hold a mortgage on another dam in operation, and sought the ownership of the new dam in the contract, Pakistan, believing that Beijing's demands were farfetched, decided to reject the deal and walked away.[28]

The case between Pakistan and China is rather suggestive. It shows that the OBOR initiative is not a simply programme of economic aids. Rather, to address the problems of overproduction inside, Beijing is searching for opportunities outside, where diplomatic relations with those developing countries play an important role. This kind of stratagem creates a number of uncertainties for Taiwan, whose investors used to have relative advantages in language and culture compared with other competitors. That said, except in cases such as the CTCI, which has developed long-term relations with grass-roots enterprises in mainland China either in consultation or through cooperation in the field of infrastructure building, most Taiwanese-based enterprises still have a long way to go when it comes to the OBOR initiative. If Taiwan's *New Southbound Policy* want to compete with the OBOR initiative, then it is better that the Taiwanese side highlights it technical prowess and target countries with potential markets to accommodate these advanced technologies. The candidate countries on the suggested list may include, among others, India, Indonesia, Singapore, and the Philippines, which happen to be located on the sea map of the Silk Road.

It goes without saying that Taiwan has little space to manoeuvre its influence with those terrestrial countries along the economic zones mapped by the Belt. The space to manoeuvre could be even less due to limited extent of trade cooperation with countries in mid-Asia, the Middle East and East Europe. By contrast, countries on the sea route of the Silk Road indicate more opportunities for Taiwan to broaden trade and deepen cooperation on the international front. Given the constrained space in the international arena, Taiwan needs to make its best efforts to provide foreign investment and international aid and seize every possibility of signing economic agreements. Attention also has to be given to hard-won trade performance jointly achieved with the partner states in the Asia Pacific, which is the very cornerstone of economic prosperity that Taiwan is based upon.

NOTES

1. Prof. Zu-I Li argues that OBOR is China's grand strategy for its future development and long-term projects; but some scholars agree that OBOR is a national economic strategy.
2. Hsiung-Yang Li (李向陽), *OBOR's Positioning, Content and the Need to Prioritize the Relationship*, Social Science Literature Press, Beijing, 2015.
3. "Xi Jinping Says the Rejection of Protectionism Is Part of What 'One Belt, One Road' Is About", *Fortune*, May 15, 2017, at http://fortune.com/2017/05/15/china-xi-jinping-belt-road-summit-protectionism/. (Accessed February 8, 2018)
4. Cited from Xi Jinping's report at the 19th Party Congress, 2017; see Xi Jinping, "Secure a Decisive Victory in Building a Moderately Prosperous Society in All Respects and Strive for the Great Success of Socialism with Chinese Characteristics for a New Era", *Xinhuanet.com*, October 18, 2017,at http://www.xinhuanet.com/english/download/Xi_Jinping's_report_at_19th_CPC_National_Congress.pdf. (Accessed February 18, 2018)
5. "Our Bulldozers, Our Rules", *The Economist*, July 2, 2016, at https://www.economist.com/news/china/21701505-chinas-foreign-policy-could-reshape-good-part-world-economy-our-bulldozers-our-rules. (Accessed February 8, 2018)
6. I-Wei Wang (王義桅), *OBOR's Opportunity and Challenges*, People Press, Beijing, 2015, pp.85-185.
7. "The Vision and Announce Action of How to Promote the Economic Belt of Silk Road and 21st Century Maritime Silk Road", Hong Kong Trade Development Council (HKTDC) Research, March 31,2015, at http://china-trade-research.hktdc.com/business-news/article/The-Belt-and-Road-Initiative/Vision-and-Actions-on-Jointly-Building-the-Silk-Road-Economic-Belt-and-21st-Century-Maritime-Silk-Road/obor/en/1/1X000000/1X0A3JZG.htm (Accessed February 8, 2018)
8. "The Vision and Announce Action of How to Promote the Economic Belt of Silk Road and 21st Century Maritime Silk Road", *Xinhuanet.com*, March 28, 2015, at http://www.xinhuanet.com/english/china/2015-03/28/c_134105858. htm (Accessed February 8, 2018)
9. Sanjaya Baru, "China's One-Belt-One-Road Initiative Is Not Just About Economics", *Economic Times*, April 25, 2017, at https://blogs.economictimes.indiatimes.com/et-commentary/chinas-one-belt-one-road-initiative-is-not-just-about-economics/. (Accessed February 8, 2018)
10. Giorgio Cafiero and Daniel Wagner, "What the Gulf States Think of 'One Belt, One Road'", *The Diplomat*, May 24, 2017, at https://thediplomat.com/2017/05/what-the-gulf-states-think-of-one-belt-one-road/. (Accessed February 8, 2018)
11. Pete Baumgartner, "China's Massive 'One Road' Project Largely Bypasses Russia, But Moscow Still On Board", Radio Free Europe/Radio Liberty, June 26, 2017, at

https://www.rferl.org/a/russia-china-one-belt-one-road-project-putin-xi/28579849.html. (Accessed February 18, 2018)

12. I-Wei Wang (王義桅), No. 6, pp. 88-108.
13. Ibid., pp. 109-112.
14. Andrin Raj, "Terrorism Threat to China's OBOR Plan", *New Straits Times*, December 13, 2017, at https://www.nst.com.my/opinion/columnists/2017/06/245869/terrorism-threat-chinas-obor-plan.
15. Robin Lee, "What Might 'Globalization 2.0' Mean for The Environment? Why China's One Belt, One Road Is A Cause for Concern", Borderless Movement, July 24, 2017, at https://borderless-hk.com/2017/07/24/what-might-globalisation-2-0mean-for-the-environment-why-chinas-one-belt-one-road-is-a-cause-for-concern/. (Accessed February 28, 2018)
16. Liu Haiquan, "The Security Challenges of the 'One Belt, One Road' Initiative and China's Choices", *Croatian International Relations Review*, XXIII (78), 2017, pp.129-147.
17. Zhifei Li and Fengshih Wu, "China and Shared Water Resources: Geopolitics, Domestic Institutions and Global Governance", in Fengshi Wu and Hongzhou Zhang (ed.), *China's Global Quest for Resources: Energy, Food and Water*, Routledge, New York, 2017.
18. "China's New Silk Road Is Getting Muddy", OBOR Watch, January 9, 2017, at http://oborwatch.org/chinas-new-silk-road-is-getting-muddy/. (Accessed February 8, 2018)
19. I-Wei Wang (王義桅), No. 6, p. 136.
20. Ibid., pp.138-144.
21. Ibid., p.151.
22. "China and Sri Lankan Set to Finalize Agreements for Hambantota Port Phase 2", OBOR Watch, November 1,2016, at http://oborwatch.org/china-and-sri-lankan-set-to-finalize-agreements-for-hambantota-port-phase-2/. (Accessed February 8, 2018)
23. I-Wei Wang (王義桅), No. 6, p.156.
24. "Taiwan Look at the OBOR: Opportunities or Risk?", *The Storm Media* (Taipei), May 16, 2017, at http://www.storm.mg/article/266769.
25. "The New South Bound Policy", Ministry of Economic Affairs, at https://www.newsouthboundpolicy.tw/English/index.aspx.
26. I-Shion Chang, "CTCI Got the Big Opportunity of OBOR", *Apple Daily*, June 21, 2016, at http://home.appledaily.com.tw/article/index/20160621/37277243/news(Accessed February 8, 2018)
27. Man-Pen Diao (刁曼蓬), "Where's Opportunity of Taiwan Industries under China's OBOR", *Common Wealth* (Taipei), January 14, 2016, at http://www.cw.com.tw/article/article.action?id=5073890http://www.cw.com.tw/article/article.action?id=5073890. (Accessed February 8, 2018)
28. Shahbaz Rana, "Pakistan Stops Bid to Include Diamer-Bhasha Dam in CPEC", *The Express Tribune*, November 15, 2017, at https://tribune.com.pk/story/1558475/2-pakistan-stops-bid-include-diamer-bhasha-dam-cpec/. (Accessed February 18, 2018)

7

The Impact of China-Pakistan Economic Corridor (CPEC) on India-Pakistan Relations

Christian Wagner

The China-Pakistan Economic Corridor (CPEC) is one of the largest Chinese foreign investments in the context of Beijing's Belt and Road Initiative (BRI). In the coming years, China plans to invest more than US$ 60 billion in CPEC.[1] Hence, the completion of the corridor will further increase Pakistan's importance in China's foreign policy.

However, the economic and political consequences of the CPEC extend far beyond Pakistan. In addition to the economic attractiveness to neighbouring countries like Afghanistan and Iran, the corridor will also affect the relations between India and Pakistan. The CPEC runs through Kashmir over which India and Pakistan have already fought three out of four wars since their independence in 1947. The location of the corridor raises the question whether it will have positive or negative repercussions on the India-Pakistan relationship.

At first sight, a negative scenario seems to be most probable. The CPEC is intended to promote Pakistan's economic development. This could further intensify the existing rivalry with India, fuel the conventional and nuclear arms race and trigger new regional crises. But a positive scenario is also imaginable. Pakistan's better economic development can contribute to reduce extremist tendencies domestically. Moreover, the massive Chinese investment can be seen as a bet on the status between India and Pakistan. Hence, the Kashmir issue which so far has been a determining factor in Pakistan's foreign policy might lose its significance in the medium to long term perspective. These developments might pave the way for a new rapprochement between India and Pakistan.

In order to illustrate the opportunities and risks of these scenarios, the bilateral relations between China, India and Pakistan are briefly presented in the first part. The second part covers the discussion on the CPEC in Pakistan. But four years after its start in 2013, it is still too early to evaluate the impact both for Pakistan domestically and for its relations with India. The implementation is slowed down by political controversies and mismanagement leading to delays and cost increases. Therefore, the third part outlines a negative and a positive scenario that might conclude from the CPEC.

The Bilateral Relations: China, India, Pakistan

India and Pakistan: Kashmir

Since their independence in August 1947, the bilateral relationship between India and Pakistan has been determined by the dispute over Kashmir.[2] The princely state of Jammu & Kashmir (J&K), with its majority Muslim population, initially remained independent in August 1947. After the invasion of tribal warriors from Pakistan, Maharaja Hari Singh, the Hindu ruler of Kashmir, acceded to the Indian Union in October 1947. In return, India sent troops to support the Maharaja against the tribal invaders. The military action escalated into the first Indo-Pakistan War in 1947-48. The Indian Prime Minister Jawaharlal Nehru brought the conflict to the United Nations (UN) and encouraged the idea of a referendum for the Kashmiris to decide their future.

The UN adopted a series of resolutions. They included that after a truce, the Pakistani troops should withdraw from J&K. Subsequently, an Indian interim administration was to be established, which was entrusted to carry out the referendum on the question whether Kashmir should join India or Pakistan. The independence of the former princely state was not part of the UN resolutions.

The question of territoriality is overshadowed by the importance that Kashmir has for the national self-understanding of both Pakistan and India. For Pakistan, the majority Muslim state of Kashmir is the completion of the two-nation theory of its founder Muhammed Ali Jinnah. According to him, the Muslims of the Indian subcontinent formed a nation of their own which had the right to own a state in order not to live permanently under Hindu dominance after independence. For India, Kashmir as the only Muslim majority state symbolises the secular character of the Indian democracy that is open to all religious communities.

Despite numerous bilateral negotiations and international attempts for mediation, the conflict is lingering on and has repeatedly strained the bilateral relationship between the two nuclear-armed states. Kashmir was the cause of three (1947/48, 1965, 1999) of the four (1971) wars between India and Pakistan. With the Treaty of Shimla in 1972, India moved away from the UN resolutions, and has focused exclusively on bilateral talks with Pakistan since then.

Pakistan has always tried to internationalise the conflict with India. By not only citing and criticising human rights violations by Indian security forces in Kashmir but also provoking regional crises such as in 1999 or 2002, Pakistan had hoped for an intervention of the international community in its favour. However, this strategy was not successful. The Kargil War in 1999, which ended rapprochement between India and Pakistan, and the failed attack on the Indian Parliament in December 2001 triggered regional crises. But they did not cause an international intervention in favour of Pakistan's position on the Kashmir issue.

In Pakistan, the conflict with India has helped to strengthen the role of the military in domestic affairs and foreign policy. The alleged threat posed by India led to an expansion of military spending, which is hardly questioned or controlled by the parliament, as well as the buildup of the nuclear programme and the support of militant Islamic groups which have been used by the Inter-Services Intelligence (ISI) for its proxy wars in Afghanistan and Kashmir. In major foreign policy issues, which concern relations with the neighbouring states and the great powers like the US and China, no elected government in Pakistan is able to act against the interests of the armed forces.

The best phase of India-Pakistan relations so far was the composite dialogue between 2004 and 2008. In April 2003, Indian Prime Minister Vajpayee surprisingly launched the idea for new talks with Pakistan after the 2002 crisis. Pakistani President Musharraf, who was responsible for the Kargil War in 1999 and who had taken power with the coup in October that year, withdrew from the UN resolutions at the end of 2003.[3] At their meeting in January 2004, India and Pakistan agreed on a composite dialogue and Musharraf declared that the Pakistani territory would not be used for terrorist attacks against India.[4]

The dialogue brought an expansion of trade and people-to-people contacts. In April 2005, a bus service between the Indian and Pakistani parts of Kashmir was set up for the first time. After the earthquake in October that year, additional transitional crossings points were opened on the line of control for the local population. In secret negotiations, both countries reached a compromise on Kashmir in 2007, but this was never made public due to the domestic political turmoil in Pakistan at the time. However, the agreement was later confirmed by President Musharraf, Pakistani Foreign Minister Kasuri and Indian Prime Minister Manmohan Singh.[5] The Mumbai attack in November 2008, conducted by the terrorist group Lashkar-e-Toiba (LeT) and backed by the ISI, brought an end to the composite dialogue.[6]

Pakistan's strategy of internationalisation has turned out to be counterproductive in many ways. On the international level, not only Pakistan's closest allies, such as the US and China, but also the UN and European Union (EU) have made it clear that a settlement on Kashmir can only be reached through bilateral talks with India. Moreover, a number of militant groups that have been supported by the ISI have turned against their erstwhile supporters. The Tehrik-i-Taliban Pakistan (TTP) which was formed in 2007 established links with international terrorist organisations such as Al-Qaeda, involved the armed forces in a lengthy war in the Federally Administered Tribal Areas (FATA) on the border with Afghanistan and was responsible for attacks in Pakistan.

When Prime Minister Narendra Modi invited all the heads of states from the South Asian Association for Regional Cooperation (SAARC) for his inauguration in summer 2014, there were high hopes that relations with Pakistan would improve. There were positive approaches, such as Modi's surprise visit to Lahore to meet Nawaz Sharif in December 2015. However, the attacks in Pathankot and Uri in January and September 2016 attributed to Jaish-e-Mohammed (JeM), which operates from Pakistan, the protracted protests in the Indian part of Kashmir since summer 2016, the arrest of an Indian spy in Pakistan and numerous incidents at the Line of Control (LoC) in Kashmir have seriously strained the bilateral relations. Pakistan has offered new negotiations, but the Indian Government has stated that new talks can only start once the terror of militant attacks in India has ended.

India and China: Eternal Rivalry

The Indian Government under Prime Minister Jawaharlal Nehru wanted to develop closer relations with China in the 1950s, in order to strengthen Asia's importance in world politics. India supported the return of China to the international stage. Nehru even refused in view of India's relations with China, two offers to become a permanent member of the UN Security Council.[7] However, the dispute over the unsettled border strained the bilateral relationship since the mid-1950s. The military defeat in the 1962 border War became a trauma for India's foreign policy, which still affects contemporary debates about the relationship with China.

On the international level, the relationship between India and China has changed since the 1970s. Until then, many development experts regarded democratic India and not Communist China as a model for the new decolonised states in Africa and Asia. However, the Indian Union was not capable of achieving its great power ambitions on the international stage. The Non-Alignment Movement (NAM) founded in 1961 remained politically weak. The friendship treaty with the Soviet Union in 1971, which was a direct response to the previous rapprochement between the US and China, brought India closer to the Warsaw Pact countries. The first nuclear test in 1974 underlined India's technological capabilities, but the government refused to sign the Non-Proliferation Treaty (NPT). Its members responded with the creation of the Nuclear Suppliers Group (NSG), which imposed a series of trade sanctions against India. On the other hand, China gained significant international appreciation by becoming a permanent member in the UN Security Council in 1971 and a member of the NPT, which entered into force in 1970.

The visit of Prime Minister Rajiv Gandhi to Beijing in December 1988 paved the way for a significant improvement in bilateral relations. The unsettled boundary issue could be managed by a series of agreements (for instance, in 1993, 1996, 2013). But clashes like the Doklam stand-off in summer 2017 illustrate that the boundary is still the major bilateral problem. The liberalisation in India after 1991 fostered the economic relations between the two Asian giants. For many years, China has been India's biggest bilateral trading partner.

However, China's close political, economic and military relations with Pakistan continued to strain the India-Chinese relationship. In addition, both states are competing for power and influence in South and Southeast Asia[8], e.g. in Sri Lanka and Myanmar, and remain competitors in the global race for scarce resources. The Chinese infrastructure investments in India's neighbourhood and the littoral states of the Indian Ocean were regarded as a "String of Pearls" that aimed at encircling India.

Nonetheless, India and China have also developed new common ground on regional and international issues. Both states, together with Bangladesh and Myanmar, are working to establish an economic corridor linking the Bay of Bengal with the southern provinces of China.[9] Both are vehement supporters of the idea of national sovereignty and invariably refer to the principles of non-interference in internal affairs agreed upon by them already in 1954. Both countries share their critique of an international order which is dominated by Western powers, which is not consistent with their own status and power aspirations. It is not surprising that they are working together in the framework of new international clubs such as BRICS (Brazil, Russia, India, China, South Africa) and on global governance issues like trade and climate. In 2017, India became a member of the Shanghai Cooperation Organisation (SCO), which will deepen cooperation with China on security policy issues and in Central Asia.

The Indian discussion about China is oscillating between the poles of China Fear in the field of security and China Fever with regard to the economic opportunities. In China, too, there are different assessments of India. In summer 2016, for example, two controversial perspectives on India were published in the Chinese media. On the one hand, India was accused of blindly following the West; on the other hand, the Western media was seen as the main culprit for the tensions in the India-China relationship.[10] In its foreign policy strategy paper 2017, the Chinese leadership named India on the same level with the US, Russia and Japan, which can be seen as an appreciation of New Delhi's status.[11]

However, China's aggressive rhetoric, for instance, during the Doklam stand-off, may even overshadow Beijing's fears of a closer rapprochement between New Delhi and Washington. India's relations with the US have experienced a further upswing under the Modi government. President Obama and Prime Minister Modi met more than eight times after Modi took office in May 2014. The extensive military cooperation that began in the 1990s as part of the bilateral rapprochement led to the US overtaking Russia as India's largest arms supplier between 2011 and 2014.[12] In addition, India is now carrying out more military manoeuvres with the US than with any other country. In their joint strategic vision for the Asia Pacific region and the Indian Ocean, both heads of state explicitly voiced the right to freedom of navigation and overflying rights in the South China Sea, which was clearly directed against China.[13] Modi has also enhanced the bilateral ties with Japan and Vietnam, which is also directed against China. In 2015, India and Japan upgraded their relationship into a "Special Strategic and Global Partnership". In 2016, both sides agreed on the "Free and Open Indo-Pacific Strategy" which was the foundation for the "Asia Africa Growth Corridor" initiative in 2017. Both countries see these initiatives as a counterweight against China's BRI and its growing influence in the Indian

Ocean and Africa.[14] The different infrastructure initiatives underline that the bilateral relationship between India and China will continue to be characterised by a mixture of conflict, cooperation and competition, which can be described by concepts such as soft balancing or hedging.[15]

China and Pakistan: All-weather Friends

The rapprochement between China and Pakistan in the early 1960s was fostered by their common enmity with India.[16] In contrast to the US, China is consistently perceived as a reliable partner in Pakistan. The positive relationship is described by a series of metaphors, e.g. "all-weather friends", or "longer than Indus River, higher than K2, and deeper than the Arab Sea" or "deeper than the ocean and warmer than the sun".

Since the 1960s, China has contributed significantly to the build-up of Pakistan's conventional, missile and nuclear programme, and has expanded the economic and political relations with its neighbour. Since the early 2000s, China has been investing in the Gwadar Port and has improved the connection with its western provinces via the Karakorum Highway.[17]

China has always supported Pakistan in international organisations against India, for instance, in the UN during the 1965 and 1971 Wars. After the Indian-American agreement on civilian nuclear cooperation in 2005, China reached a similar bilateral agreement with Pakistan, but was able to circumvent the consent of the NSG. In 2016, China prevented India from being admitted to the NSG and blocked the UN sanctions against Masood Azhar, the founder of JeM, who is responsible for a series of attacks in India, e.g. the failed attack on the Parliament in 2001 and the attacks in Pathankot and Uri in 2016.[18]

But the changing international constellations after the end of the Cold War and the India Chinese rapprochement since 1989 (see above) have also impacted the parameters between the "all-weather friends".[19] Today, China is pursuing a more balanced policy towards both states, and is no longer fully supporting Islamabad in all aspects vis-à-vis India.[20] This is most evident in the Kashmir question where China has changed its stance on supporting Pakistan, a policy that started in the 1980s. Thus, the Chinese leadership was not willing to stand by Pakistan during the Kargil War in 1999. China propagates bilateral negotiations on the Kashmir conflict, which is not the position of Pakistan but of India.

The bilateral problems between China and Pakistan concern mainly security issues. The Chinese Government fears, in particular, the spread of radical Islamic ideas among the Muslim population in the province of Xinjiang.[21] The violent outbreaks of the Muslim Uighurs in Xinjiang in the summer of 2009 also impacted relations with Pakistan. The Chinese leadership held the East Turkestan Islamic Movement (ETIM) responsible for the unrest. China urged Pakistan to close down ETIM training camps in the tribal areas on the Afghanistan border.[22] Another aspect is the security of Chinese workers and experts in Pakistan. Due to their extensive economic cooperation, several thousand Chinese experts were already active in Pakistan before the launch of CPEC. They have repeatedly been the target of attacks and abductions by militant groups in Balochistan, Khyber Pakhtunkhwa and Kashmir.[23]

CPEC in Pakistan

The economic development of Pakistan has lagged behind expectations in recent years. The economic growth rate was only around 4.7 per cent in 2016, and thus below India and Bangladesh.[24] Due to the absence or inadequate economic reforms since the Nawaz Sharif government's mandate in 2013, the country's debt has risen further in recent years.[25] Against this background, it is not surprising that very high hopes combine with the implementation of the CPEC. Prime Minister Nawaz Sharif and other decision makers have named the project as a "game changer", "fate changer" or even "destiny changer" for Pakistan.[26]

On completion, the CPEC is intended to encompass a network of roads, railways and gas pipelines of about 3,000 kilometres. The infrastructure measures are expected to cost approximately US $ 11 billion.[27] On the other hand, by far the largest part of the funds of about US $ 33 billion is to be invested in energy projects. This is to remedy the chronic energy shortage of Pakistan and to set up new industrial parks for the settlement of foreign companies.[28]

The nature and extent of investment thus goes far beyond the current forms of economic cooperation with the US or the international community. On the Chinese side, there are also deliberations that these extensive infrastructure measures and the resulting local employment opportunities should contribute to de-radicalisation in Pakistan in the medium term.[29] There are also indications that China is going to invest heavily in Pakistan's agricultural sector in the context of the CPEC.[30]

The implementation of the corridor has sparked a series of domestic controversies in Pakistan. Firstly, there was initially a dispute between the provinces and the political parties over the itinerary of the roads and railroad routes between Gwadar in the south-west and China in the north-east. In the meantime there is consensus that there should be different routes, so that all the provinces benefit. However, the controversy continues over the issue as to whether the "Western" or "Eastern" route should be completed first. Part of this debate are concerns about the security situation in the different provinces and the dispute between the different ethnic groups in the provinces. The "western" route that is closer to Afghanistan is considered unsafe, as it runs through the two border provinces of Balochistan and Khyber Pakhtunkhwa. The "eastern" route runs through the provinces of Sindh and Punjab and is considered to be safer. However, the smaller provinces criticise the fact that Punjab would receive outsized benefits from this itinerary. This would further increase the economic and political dominance of Punjab vis-à-vis the other provinces.

Secondly, there are the long-term economic consequences of the CPEC for Pakistan. The criticism is directed above all against the growing debt against China. Energy projects are financed at higher interest rates than infrastructure projects. In addition, the Pakistani Government has granted Chinese energy companies a return on equity of between 27 and 31 per cent.[31] A further concern is that if Chinese companies are to produce in Pakistan on a large scale, this will have negative repercussions on the local industries.[32] For example, if the special economic zones would be open only for Chinese companies and their employees, there would be no significant employment effects for Pakistanis.[33] The advocates of the CPEC point out that by 2019 economic growth will increase by two percentage points. The resulting increases are intended to help Pakistan settle its debts.[34]

Thirdly, there is the issue of the security of the Chinese workers and professionals, whose number is likely to increase significantly in the course of the implementation of the CPEC. Since the Chinese have been victims of attacks or abductions, for example, in the past by separatist groups in Balochistan, the Pakistan Army has set up its own Special Security Division (SSD) with about 15,000 soldiers[35] for their protection.

The CPEC will deepen the bilateral relationship between China and Pakistan. However, new challenges will arise. The ambitious development projects will probably trigger a series of local resistance in Pakistan. The resettlement of population groups for industrial, agricultural, and transport projects will create new conflicts. The disputes over compensation and responsibilities between the centre, the provinces and the Chinese companies will not be achieved without friction losses. If economic expectations will not be met and if employment opportunities for Pakistanis will not improve significantly, then the local discontent with CPEC will increase. The main challenge for the Pakistani government will be to find compromises between the rising expectations of their people and the requirements of the Chinese investors.

Finally, the CPEC is also likely to restrict Pakistan's foreign policy room for manoeuvre. So far, Pakistan has often been successful in playing off the US against China or in cooperating with both of them. But relations with the US have deteriorated considerably over the years, not least because of the differences in the fight against terrorism. The government in Islamabad fears further sanctions by the new Trump administration[36], because of not only Pakistan's policy against Afghanistan, but also restrictions on the movement of Pakistani students and professionals to the US. The simultaneous growing financial dependency on China will thus restrict rather than enlarge Pakistan's foreign policy choices.

CPEC and India-Pakistan Relations: Scenarios

CPEC will also create new geopolitical realities that go beyond Pakistan. This is most evident in the case of the India-Pakistan relations, as the corridor runs through Gilgit-Baltistan which is part of Kashmir. The Indian Government has officially protested against the corridor because Gilgit-Baltistan is a part of the Indian Kashmir territory.[37] Pakistan, on the other hand, sees the whole of Kashmir as a disputed territory whose future status should be decided by a referendum as laid down in various UN resolutions.

According to the UN resolution, the conflict over Kashmir is between India and Pakistan. However, China is also part of the dispute. In the 1950s, China built an all-weather road to Tibet that ran through the Aksai Chin region of Kashmir. Since the border war with India in 1962, China controls the Aksai Chin. In 1963, Pakistan ceded parts of Kashmir to China.

Four years after its official launch in 2013, it seems still too early to give an assessment of the impact of the CPEC. In order to address the question of the impact of the CPEC on the India-Pakistan relationship, two scenarios – one negative and one positive – are described as follows:

The Negative Scenario: Endless Conflict of Kashmir

The negative scenario rests on the assumption that the positive economic effects from the CPEC will continue the negative cycle of India-Pakistan relations. The CPEC is intended to foster and improve Pakistan's long-term economic development. In recent years, economic growth has been lower than that of other countries in South Asia like India, Bangladesh and Sri Lanka.[38] Pakistan's gross domestic product (GDP) growth rate of nearly five per cent in 2016-17 may indicate a first positive effect of the massive Chinese investment. But this is still far away from the self-proclaimed goal of six to seven per cent GDP growth which is required over a longer period in order to create significant employment effects.[39]

One result of better economic development by the impact of CPEC would be higher tax revenues and a higher national budget. In view of the continuing tensions with India, this could also be used for additional military expenditures. A stronger Pakistan would have little interest in expanding its economic ties with India. So far, Pakistan has always made the economic collaboration with India dependent on the solution of the Kashmir issue. The already low trade with India will probably become even lower by the CPEC especially if India continues to refuse to participate in the BRI. Pakistan's new economic strength could stimulate its self-confidence towards India. The issue of Kashmir might therefore become even more prominent in Pakistan's foreign policy agenda. This could lead to new military adventures against India and give terrorist groups new impetus for further attacks in India. Pakistan has always used past crises and wars with India, although so far unsuccessfully, to achieve an internationalisation of the Kashmir conflict (see above).

However, the next India-Pakistan crisis or even another limited war like Kargil 1999 could have a new dimension. So far, China has generally supported Pakistan politically in its wars with India but has never intervened militarily. But if, for example, Chinese citizens would be killed in such a conflict, for example, in Gilgit-Baltistan or Balochistan, this could also lead to a crisis in the relationship between New Delhi and Beijing. Hence, another serious India-Pakistan conflict could then trigger a trilateral crisis including China. Such a constellation would then call for an intervention by other major powers such as the US and Russia.

The Positive Scenario: Phasing out of the Kashmir Conflict

However, a positive scenario is also conceivable, wherein the CPEC could have a moderating effect on the relations between India and Pakistan and the Kashmir conflict. The implications of the CPEC would impact firstly the future constitutional position of Gilgit-Baltistan, and secondly China's relations with Pakistan and India.

The parts of Kashmir which are controlled by India and Pakistan have very different positions in the respective constitutions of both the states. Through its accession to the Indian Union, J&K has a special position, which is laid down in Article 370 of the Indian Constitution. This has triggered a controversy over the degree of autonomy between New Delhi and successive state governments in Srinagar. The state elections in J&K in December 2014 had a voter turnout of about 65 per cent. This can be regarded as a strong consent of the Kashmiris to be part of the Indian Union. The pro-Pakistani Hurriyat Conference (HC) has always rejected any participation in state elections. There are also groups which demand the independence of Kashmir, like the Jammu & Kashmir Liberation Front (JKLF).

In Pakistan, Gilgit-Baltistan is formally a disputed territory.[40] Thus, this part of Kashmir has lesser rights than the other provinces of Pakistan. This has repeatedly led to protests by the local population, which demand more political participation and investment.[41] Pakistani governments have improved local self-government through a series of reforms, but without giving the region a full provincial status. The last major reform took place in 2009 when the former Northern Areas were renamed Gilgit-Baltistan. The region has a legislative assembly which has only limited powers compared to the other provincial assemblies in Pakistan. The last elections in the summer of 2015 brought a majority for the ruling Muslim League - Nawaz (PML-N). Because of its strategic importance, the region is de facto controlled by the armed forces. A number of militant organisations, such as the LeT, supported by the army and home services, have training camps in this area.[42]

If the CPEC improves economic development in Pakistan, this could further aggravate the discontent in Gilgit-Baltistan, as the gap between the other provinces would become even deeper.[43] The Pakistani Government will then be faced with a dilemma. It cannot transform the region constitutionally into a province, since this would undermine the government's official position that the region is a disputed territory. If Gilgit-Baltistan would become a normal province in Pakistan, then it would no longer be regarded as a disputed territory according to UN resolutions, which Pakistan maintains.

The legal integration of the two parts of Kashmir in the Indian and Pakistan constitutions would thus end the conflict. This could then pave the way for further confidence-building measures like the ones that were implemented during the composite dialogue between 2004 and 2008. Such a solution would probably be also in the interest of China because the CPEC would then have a stable constitutional status in India and Pakistan. A UN referendum that is favoured by Pakistan would also not be in China's interest. Given the better economic development and higher degree of democratic participation in the Indian part of Kashmir, there is always the probability that Kashmiris would vote for joining India. Then the Chinese investment in Gilgit-Baltistan would be scrapped overnight.

Another positive aspect of the CPEC is its impact on the relations between China, Pakistan and India. While Pakistan is one of the few strategic partners for China, it has been far from reliable in conflicts with

India. China does not share Pakistan's position on Kashmir. Pakistan is calling for an internationalisation of the conflict and a referendum, whereas India has emphasised bilateral talks between the two countries. The Chinese leadership has also signalled many times that only direct negotiations between the two sides can lead to a solution.[44] Above all, the Pakistani military has repeatedly prevented the expansion of economic relations with India. In 2010, the Chinese Prime Minister Wen Jiabao said during his visit to Pakistan that security problems should not hamper economic cooperation, which was also in line with India's position.[45] The CPEC can be seen as a continuation of this Chinese position, which holds that an improved economic development would have a moderating influence on bilateral relations between India and Pakistan. In its cooperation with Pakistan, China is more dependent on the military than on the political parties. One consequence of this close cooperation might be that military adventures such as the Kargil War would be less likely in 1999.[46]

The Regional Dimension: INSTC, SAARC

To the west of the CPEC, Iran, Russia and India have been driving the expansion of the International North South Transport Corridor (INSTC) to connect the Iranian port town of Chabahar with Central Asia and Russia. In May 2016, India committed to invest US $ 500 million in developing the Iranian port of Chabahar, which will improve its access to Afghanistan and Central Asia. In this way, India wants to achieve better access to Afghanistan, Russia and Central Asia.[47]

This has led to speculation whether and to what extent these two infrastructure projects may spur geopolitical rivalries between India, Iran, China and Pakistan. The two major port cities of Gwadar and Chabahar are only about 70 kilometres from each other. But the respective states seem to regard these projects as complementary rather than competing. China has already expressed its interest in the expansion of Chabahar.[48] Iran, on the other hand, has already expressed its interest in being included in the CPEC and proposed the construction of a railway line to connect the two port cities.[49]

The CPEC and BRI can also have positive and negative consequences for SAARC. South Asia is among the fastest growing regions in the global comparison, but the economic integration of the region is very weak. The intra-regional trade in SAARC is only about five per cent.

Besides the CPEC, China has also invested heavily in other South Asian countries in recent years. Between 2005 and 2015, China invested more than US$ 14 bn in Sri Lanka. In 2016, Beijing promised investments of

US$ 38 bn to Bangladesh. In 2017, the Chinese Government declared to invest US$ 8.3 bn in Nepal. These investments have raised concerns in New Delhi against China's growing political and economic influence in South Asia. So far, India and Bhutan are the only two South Asian countries that do not participate in the BRI. New Delhi did not participate in the BRI Summit in May 2017 in Beijing. The Indian Government has criticised that the CPEC violates its national sovereignty in Gilgit-Baltistan (see above). New Delhi also disapproves the high debts caused by Chinese investment because of the growing political dependencies of the recipient countries from China. Moreover, Indian security experts see the Chinese investments in port facilities in South Asia as potential military bases that could serve to encircle India (String of Pearls).

The long-term economic impact of the BRI and CPEC may therefore also change the face of regionalism in South Asia in either a positive or a negative way. In a positive scenario, the Chinese investment will stimulate economic development in the recipient countries. This could also have a positive impact on regional cooperation leading to higher intra-regional trade in South Asia. In a negative scenario, the BRI investments will strengthen the economic and trade links of the recipient countries with China and not with the neighbouring countries. This would create a reshaping of the region and would contribute to the decline of SAARC, which would economically become even less attractive for its member states.

The reshaping of South Asia is indirectly also promoted by India with its recent initiatives to isolate Pakistan within the region. India's decision to withdraw from the SAARC Summit in Islamabad in 2016 after the terrorist attacks in Uri was supported by many other SAARC members. Instead, New Delhi threw its weight behind the November 2016 Goa Summit of the Bay of Bengal Initiative for Multi-Sectoral Technical and Economic Cooperation (BIMSTEC), inviting two states – Afghanistan and the Maldives – that were members of SAARC but not of BIMSTEC. Given that Pakistan is not a member of BIMSTEC, the meeting could thus be viewed as a "SAARC minus one" summit. In their final declaration the participants underlined the importance of working together to combat terrorism – very obviously pointing a finger at Pakistan.

Conclusion

In Pakistan, there are high economic hopes connected with the CPEC. However, it is unclear how much of the promised investments will finally be implemented as there has always been a gap between official pledges and final implementation of large infrastructure projects. Despite all criticism in Pakistan,[50] the CPEC should make a positive contribution to the economic development of the country in the mid- to long-term perspective, for example, by improving the transportation infrastructure or the chronically deficient energy supply.

The CPEC will also further deepen the strategic alliance between Pakistan and China. Therefore, it seems consequent that it will contribute to fuel the India-Pakistan conflict. An economically powerful Pakistan could be more self-confident about India and further increase its military spending. On the Chinese side, however, the CPEC is also associated with the idea that its economic effects could make an important contribution to the transformation of Pakistani society and the strengthening of the moderate forces. Such a development could in turn also have positive repercussions on the regional environment, for instance, in Afghanistan.

In the Asian context, the CPEC remains China's single most important project in the context of the BRI. In reaction, India has started new initiatives, such as the Mausam project in the Indian Ocean and the Bangladesh, Bhutan, India, and Nepal (BBIN) cooperation. Moreover, India is trying to strengthen regional institutions like BIMSETC and the Indian Ocean Rim Association (IORA). However, Indian policymakers are aware that they cannot match the massive Chinese investment. So closer cooperation with like-minded countries like Japan in the context of the Asia-Africa Growth Corridor (AAGC) may be a new promising strategy for the future.

Nonetheless, the CPEC also seems to underline the Chinese interest in a continuation of the status quo in Kashmir. This would have several consequences for Pakistan. First, the constitutional integration of Gilgit-Baltistan into Pakistan could be pushed forward. The moment Gilgit-Baltistan becomes a full-fledged province in Pakistan, the chapter of the Kashmir conflict in world politics would close. Second, China may be aware that however small, there exists the possibility that India might one day advocate the internationalisation of the Kashmir conflict. The UN resolutions are more advantageous to India than to Pakistan. A referendum with an unclear outcome or a vote in favour of India would endanger the long-term CPEC investment. Finally, China's interest in trade could also weaken the traditional opposition of the Pakistani military against closer economic cooperation with India. This would truly be a real "game-changer" in India-Pakistan relations.

NOTES

1. Salman Siddiqui, "CPEC investment pushed from $55b to $62b", *The Express Tribune*, April 12, 2017 (Accessed April 12, 2017).
2. Sumit Ganguly, *Conflict Unending. India-Pakistan Tensions since 1947*, Oxford University Press, New Delhi and Oxford, 2002; Sumantra Bose, *Kashmir: Roots of Conflict, Paths to Peace*, Harvard University Press, Cambridge, 2003; Stephen P. Cohen, *Shooting for a Century: The India-Pakistan Conundrum*, Brookings Institution Press, Washington, 2013.
3. Syed Rifaat Hussain, "The India Factor", in Maleeha Lodhi (ed.), *Pakistan. Beyond the Crisis State*, Oxford University Press, Karachi, 2011, p. 329.
4. "Text of PM, Musharraf Statement", *The Hindu*, January 6, 2004, at http://www.thehindu.com/2004/01/07/stories/2004010706041100.htm (Accessed January 08, 2004)
5. "Governments of Both Countries Now Have to Decide on a Time to Disclose Solution ...", Interview with the Pakistani Foreign Secretary Khurshid Kasuri, *The Friday Times*, June 1-7, 2007, p. 6; "Pakistan and India Were Close to an Agreement", *The Daily Times*, May 2, 2009; "Musharraf: India, Pakistan Were Close to Agreement on 3 Issues", *The Hindu*, July 18, 2009.
6. "Pasha Admitted ISI Link to 26/11", *The Times of India*, September 29, 2010.
7. Anton Harder, "Not at the Cost of China: New Evidence Regarding US Proposals to Nehru for Joining the United Nations Security Council", Working Paper # 76, The Cold War International History Project, Woodrow Wilson International Center for Scholars, Washington, 2015, p. 12, at https://www.wilsoncenter.org/publication/not-the-cost-china-india-and-the-united-nations-security-council-1950.
8. Christian Wagner, "The Role of India and China in South Asia", *Strategic Analysis*, 40 (4), July-August 2016, pp. 307-320.
9. Atul Aneja, "China, India Fast-track BCIM Economic Corridor Project", *The Hindu*, June 26, 2015, at http://www.thehindu.com/news/national/china-india-fasttrack-bcim-economic-corridor-project/article7355496.ece (Accessed June 26, 2015).
10. Shailaja Neelakantan, "Indians Self-centered, Spoilt, Have Low Morals & Blindly Follow West: Chinese Paper", *The Economic Times*, June 28, 2016, at http://economictimes.indiatimes.com/news/politics-and-nation/indians-self-centered-spoilt-have-low-morals-blindly-follow-west-chinese-paper/articleshow/52952546.cms?prtpage=1 (Accessed June 28, 2016); Shailaja Neelakantan, "Now, China's State-run Newspaper Says Foreign Media to Blame for Tension with India", *The Economic Times*, July 07, 2016, at http://economictimes.indiatimes.com/news/politics-and-nation/now-chinas-state-run-newspaper-says-foreign-media-to-blame-for-tension-with-india/articleshow/53093701.cms?prtpage=1 (accessed July 07, 2016).
11. *China's Policies on Asia-Pacific Security Cooperation*, 1st ed., State Council Information Office of the People's Republic of China, Foreign Language Press, Beijing, 2017, p. 15.
12. Ramananda Sengupta, "How America Replaced Russia As India's Largest Arms Supplier", *Swarajya*, September 27, 2015, at http://swarajyamag.com/politics/how-america-replaced-russia-as-indias-largest-arms-supplier.

13. "U.S.-India Joint Strategic Vision for the Asia-Pacific and Indian Ocean Region", The White House, 2015, at https://www.whitehouse.gov/the-press-office/2015/01/25/us-india-joint-strategic-vision-asia-pacific-and-indian-ocean-region (Accessed January 26, 2015).
14. Amrita Jash, "India-Japan's Newton Logic to China's BRI", *China-India Brief*, 99, August 09-22, 2017, at http://lkyspp.nus.edu.sg/cag/publication/china-india-brief/china-india-brief-99#guest (Accessed September 01, 2017).
15. T.V. Paul, "Soft Balancing in the Age of U.S. Primacy", *International Security*, 30 (1), Summer 2005, pp. 46-71; Justin Kelley, "Strategic Non-cooperation as Soft Balancing: Why Iraq Was Not Just about Iraq", *International Politics*, 42, 2005, pp. 153-173.
16. Andrew Small, *The China Pakistan Axis. Asia's New Geopolitics*, Oxford University Press, London, 2015.
17. Fazal-ur Rahman, "Prospects of Pakistan becoming a Trade and Energy Corridor for China", *Strategic Studies*, 27 (23), 2007, pp. 52-89.
18. Suhasini Haidar, "Running into the Chinese Wall", *The Hindu*, January 5, 2017, at http://www.thehindu.com/opinion/op-ed/Running-into-the-Chinese-wall/article16988901.ece (Accessed January 05, 2017).
19. Ye Hailin, "China-Pakistan Relationship: All-Weathers, but maybe not All-Dimensional", in Kristina Zetterlund (ed.), *Pakistan – Consequences of Deteriorating Security in Afghanistan*, Swedish Defence Research Agency, Stockholm, 2009, pp. 122-124.
20. Zhang Li, "To Manage Conflict in South Asia: China's Stakes, Perceptions and Inputs", Institute for Security and Development Policy, Stockholm, 2009, p. 15.
21. M. Ehsan Ahrari, "China, Pakistan, and the 'Taliban Syndrome'", *Asian Survey*, 40 (4), 2000, pp. 658-671; Ziad Haider, "Sino-Pakistan Relations and Xinjiang Uighurs. Politics, Trade, and Islam along the Karakorum Highway", *Asian Survey*, 45 (4), July/August 2005, pp. 522-545.
22. Ananth Krishnan, "Stop Indulging Terror Groups, Says China", *The Hindu*, July 15, 2009.
23. Bhutta Zafar, "Chinese Govt Seeks Security for Its Nationals", *The Daily Times*, January 24, 2008.
24. "Pakistan Lags behind India, Bangladesh in Economic Growth: Report", *The Express Tribune*, October 10, 2016, at http://tribune.com.pk/story/1196602/pakistan-lags-behind-india-bangladesh-economic-growth-report/ (Accessed October 10, 2016).
25. Shahbaz Rana, "In Three Years, Pakistan Has Taken on $25b in Fresh Loans", *The Express Tribune*, October 20, 2016, at http://tribune.com.pk/story/1203863/external-debt-three-years-pakistan-taken-25b-fresh-loans/ (Accessed October 20, 2016).
26. "CPEC 'Game-changer' for Pakistan: PM", *Pakistan Today*, August 29, 2016, at http://www.pakistantoday.com.pk/2016/08/29/national/cpec-is-game-changer-for-pakistan-pm-nawaz/.
27. Muhammad Ali Ehsan, "Protectors of the CPEC", *The Express Tribune*, February 25, 2016, at http://tribune.com.pk/story/1054692/protectors-of-the-cpec (Accessed February 25, 2016).
28. Nasir Jamal, "CPEC-triggered Investment", *Dawn*, January 11, 2016, at http://www.dawn.com/news/1232178/cpec-triggered-investment; Niaz Murtaza,

"Tale of Two CPECs", *Dawn*, March 1, 2016, at http://www.dawn.com/news/1242804/tale-of-two-cpecs (Accessed March 01, 2016).

29. Andrew Small, No. 16, pp. 192-93.
30. Khurram Husain, "Setting the record straight", *Dawn*, May 18, 2017, at https://www.dawn.com/news/1333753/setting-the-record-straight (Accessed May 18, 2017); Zahoor Khan, "CPEC's Lesser Known Impacts", *The Daily Times*, May 23, 2017, at http://dailytimes.com.pk/opinion/23-May-17/cpecs-lesser-known-impacts (Accessed May 23, 2017).
31. Maqsood A. Butt, "CPEC – An Objective Analysis – I", *The Daily Times*, October 3, 2016, at http://dailytimes.com.pk/business/03-Oct-16/cpec-an-objective-analysis-i (Accessed October 03, 2016).
32. Maqsood A. Butt, "CPEC – An objective analysis – II", *The Daily Times*, October 4, 2016, at http://dailytimes.com.pk/business/04-Oct-16/cpec-an-objective-analysis-ii (Accessed October 04, 2016).
33. Khurram Husain, "CPEC Enclaves", *Dawn*, March 9, 2017, at https://www.dawn.com/news/1319301/cpec-enclaves/ (Accessed March 09, 2017).
34. Salman Siddiqui, "CPEC to Generate Returns for paying Back Foreign Debt", *The Express Tribune*, December 18, 2016, at http://tribune.com.pk/story/1267185/post-imf-scenario-cpec-generate-returns-paying-back-foreign-debt/ (Accessed December 18, 2016); Hasaan Khawar, "Local Industry and the CPEC Promise", *The Express Tribune*, March 2, 2017, at https://tribune.com.pk/story/1343274/local-industry-cpec-promise/ (Accessed March 02, 2017).
35. Zahid Gishkori, "Economic Corridor: 12,000-Strong Force to Guard Chinese Workers", *The Express Tribune*, March 30, 2015, at http://tribune.com.pk/story/861078/economic-corridor-12000-strong-force-to-guard-chinese-workers/.
36. "Trump's New Afghanistan Policy Leaves Pakistan Angry, Alarmed", *The Daily Times*, August, 31, 2017, at http://dailytimes.com.pk/pakistan/31-Aug-17/trumps-new-afghanistan-policy-leaves-pakistan-angry-alarmed (Accessed August 31, 2017)
37. Tanvi Madan, "What India Thinks about China's One Belt, One Road Initiative (but Doesn't Explicitly Say)", Brookings, March 14, 2016, at https://www.brookings.edu/blog/order-from-chaos/2016/03/14/what-india-thinks-about-chinas-one-belt-one-road-initiative-but-doesnt-explicitly-say/.
38. Nasir Jamal, No. 28.
39. Parvez Hasan, "State of Economy", *Dawn*, June 20, 2017, at https://www.dawn.com/news/1340544/state-of-economy (Accessed June 20, 2017).
40. In addition to Gilgit-Baltistan, Azad Jammu & Kashmir (AJK) belongs to the territory of the former princely state J&K, which has been controlled by Pakistan since 1947. Azad Kashmir is a formally independent state with President, Prime Minister and Parliament, but only recognised by Pakistan. In fact, AJK is governed by Pakistan. The government of AJK has also called for participation in CPEC projects. See "Azad Kashmir Seeks Share in CPEC", *Dawn*, November 18, 2016, at http://www.dawn.com/news/1297045 (Accessed January 24, 2017).
41. Aziz Ali Dad, "Discontents in Gilgit-Baltistan", *The Daily Times*, January 21, 2010; Ejaz Haider, "Terror in Gilgit-Baltistan Indicates More Trouble", *The Express Tribune*, June 26, 2013, at http://tribune.com.pk/story/568226/terror-in-gilgit-baltistan-indicates-more-trouble/.
42. Raza Rumi, "The Spectre of Islamist Infiltration", *The Friday Times*, May 27-June

2, 2011; Umer Farooq, "Islam in the Garrison", *Herald*, August 16, 2011.

43. Shabbir Mir, "Indian Interest in Gilgit", *The Express Tribune*, September 28, 2016, at http://tribune.com.pk/story/1190310/indian-interest-gilgit/.
44. Ananth Krishnan, "Pakistan Wants Third-party Role for China", *The Hindu*, February 24, 2010.
45. "Chinese PM's Visit", *Dawn*, December 20, 2010.
46. Andrew Small, No. 16, p. 193.
47. Meena Singh Roy, "International North-South Transport Corridor: Re-energising India's Gateway to Eurasia", *IDSA Issue Brief*, August 18, 2015.
48. "Projects in Iran, Pakistan Can Complement Each Other: China", *Dawn*, June 2, 2016, at http://www.dawn.com/news/1262242/projects-in-iran-pakistan-can-complement-each-other-china.
49. Saleem Shahid, "Rail Link Planned between Gwadar and Iranian Port", *Dawn*, January 12, 2016, at http://www.dawn.com/news/1232397/rail-link-planned-between-gwadar-and-iranian-port; "Iran Wants to be Part of CPEC, Says Consul General", *The Daily Times*, October 5, 2016, at http://dailytimes.com.pk/business/05-Oct-16/iran-wants-to-be-part-of-cpec-says-consul-general (Accessed October 05, 2016).
50. Syed Irfan Raza, "Questions Raised over Fate of Gwadar Port", *Dawn*, September 29, 2016, at http://www.dawn.com/news/1286840/questions-raised-over-fate-of-gwadar-port.

8

Xi Jinping's Chinese Dream in the Indian Ocean Region: Time to Move beyond Outdated Maritime Strategies

Sukjoon Yoon

Introduction

Chinese President Xi Jinping has declared his intention to transform China's perception and usage of the maritime domain: It is the medium through which most of the world's trade is transported, but it is also the platform upon which China aspires to become the regional or even global hegemon, such ambitions having been stated explicitly at the 19th National Congress. China has also announced its grand plan, the 'One Belt, One Road Initiative (BRI)' whereby as much as US$900 billion will be invested over 10 years in infrastructural development, across the whole of the Indian Ocean Region (IOR).

Beyond the economic significance of this Maritime Silk Road, there are potentially disruptive military implications for the IOR. Xi Jinping's primary current propaganda slogan exhorts the Chinese people to realise a 'Chinese Dream', which clearly references the BRI, but it also includes his declared aspiration for China to become a 'true maritime power'.[1] This in turn depends upon the strategic concept of 'absolute command of the sea', clearly implying a Chinese naval expansion into the IOR, and in fact China is already working towards this in various ways. By conflating military expansionism with the infrastructural development of the BRI, and justifying this approach, at least domestically, with putative historical entitlement, Xi Jinping risks being seen as neocolonialist, and is sure to provoke a strong reaction from China's regional rivals, most notably the US and India. Moreover, the sense that China is ignoring the established international order and playing by its own rules is likely to attract much wider censure.

Xi Jinping's idea of what constitutes a true maritime power conflicts with the reality of today's interconnected and interdependent world. China's national grand strategy needs to rely less upon history and more upon establishing China's bona fides as a capable and reliable maritime power contributing to shared efforts to maintain maritime peace and stability and to create prosperity.

Xi Jinping's Global Ambition, BRI and South Asia

General Secretary Xi Jinping was re-elected to lead the Communist Party of China (CPC) in the First Plenary Session of the 19th CPC Central Committee on October 25. He articulated his global ambition as part of "Xi Jinping Thought on Socialism with Chinese Characteristics for a New Era", reinforcing the "Two Centenary Goals" declared at the 19th National Congress of the CPC.[2] *China Daily* elaborated his vision:

> The Two Centenary Goals are not only significant for China's rejuvenation but also for the world to achieve common development of building a community of shared future for mankind.[3]

This is of great strategic importance for China's ambition to become a major country (大國) sustaining a 'New Type of International Relations' (新型國際關係) with the prevailing major power, the US. China is striving to achieve major country status to restore its historical prestige, not only through Xi Jinping's global initiative of The Two Centenary Goals, but also through the implementation of its BRI project, both components of which, the 'Silk Road Economic Belt' and the '21st Century Maritime Silk Road' indicate its direction and orientation toward China's West.[4]

The BRI clearly aims to integrate continental China with maritime South Asia, relying upon China's historical regional hegemony to project the contemporary Chinese worldview into Central Asia and Europe.[5] Thus, the 19th National Congress of the CPC enacted a Revised Constitution for the CPC, including this text:

> In international affairs, the Communist Party of China shall constantly work to develop good neighborly relations between China and its surrounding countries and work to strengthen unity and cooperation between China and other developing countries. It shall follow the

principle of achieving shared growth through discussion and collaboration, and pursue the Belt and Road Initiative.[6]

An enthusiastic academic supporter of Xi Jinping's BRI policies notes that China's outbound foreign direct investment has so far resulted in nearly 50 intergovernmental agreements for cooperation within the framework of BRI and over 70 major contracts for infrastructure projects, totalling an unprecedented US$ 50 billion. He concludes that the BRI as a strategy is closely linked with Xi's Chinese Dream concept:

> In a country like China, the Communist Party leads everything, everywhere and every decision. Once the BRI was enshrined in the Chinese Communist Party's Constitution, it has actually become one of the reliable and highest agenda in the China's foreign policy towards its neighbors. In this regard, no proposition by explaining better the outward ambition that is taking place in it today in the world than China's BRI.[7]

The BRI's rhetorical narrative, as well as strategic intention, can therefore be understood as a capacity- and trust-based device in the service of a more assertive Chinese national grand strategy.[8] The 19th National Congress of the CPC has clearly indicated that China will prioritise the BRI in its quest for regional reordering and dominance.[9]

By conflating the infrastructural development of the BRI with Chinese strategic expansionism, however, China lays itself open to criticism that it is neocolonialist, especially in Africa, leading to reluctance from some countries to become involved with the BRI.[10] Indeed, the wider world is concerned about Chinese intentions: Is the BRI just a kind of 'Marshall Plan', building trust and supplying mutually beneficial public goods to its neighbours; or is it more sinister, a disguised pursuit of Chinese foreign policy objectives and global ambitions aiming to restore the dominance of the Middle Kingdom?[11]

Although Xi Jinping has now acquired domestic power unrivalled in China since Mao Zedong, and is proclaiming a new role for China as a world-leading nation, he has made some policy blunders in the past regarding the IOR and South Asian countries and perhaps will do so again.[12] South Asia is now divided over how to respond to China's maritime ambitions in the IOR and the impact upon maritime security, especially over Xi Jinping's 21st Century Maritime Silk Road initiative. Since the early 2010s, India has argued against Chinese involvement in IOR maritime security, believing that China's naval presence and partnerships with IOR coastal states, under the auspices of the 21st Century Maritime Silk Road, are sowing disharmony and distrust between South Asian countries.[13]

On one side are countries, especially India, which worry about the reach of China's ambition, and which position themselves as regional or sub-regional rivals of China as guardians of the IOR; on the other side are smaller weaker countries, or rivals of India, including Sri Lanka, Bangladesh and Pakistan. The latter see economic opportunities in China's BRI, so long as it does not disrupt freedom and safety of navigation in the IOR. Both sides understand that as a result of fulfilling Xi Jinping's Chinese Dream and China's BRI projects, China will inevitably become a dominant naval power in the IOR with a permanent naval presence.

India's suspicions of the BRI, with its military and strategic implications, meant that they did not participate in the BRI summit in Beijing in May 2017, a decision which has placed its neighbours in an awkward position. Official Indian arguments, mostly from political and military leaders, emphasise the Chinese interest in the potential of the IOR's untapped markets, ignoring the value of building political trust, trade relationships, people-to-people bonds and infrastructural connectivity. India's preference for geopolitical vigilance over the trans-regional economic cooperation of the BRI has led it to perceive China purely in terms of the threat its domination of the IOR would represent. These divergent opinions of China's BRI are hotly debated in India, and have left very little room for bilateral BRI-based interactions between China and India.

Conversely, South Asian countries which have engaged with the BRI have seen an entirely different pattern.[14] Thus, the close cooperation between China and Pakistan has generated a trade volume of more than US$ 10 billion, and China is also cultivating links with Sri Lanka, Nepal, Afghanistan and the Maldives, where there is a rapidly growing demand for China's products, investment and technologies.[15] For these countries, the BRI has stimulated regional connectivity and trade, and there is massive scope for improved connectivity, sub-regional trade and economic cooperation.

The Maritime Ambitions Implicit in Xi Jinping's Chinese Dream

The dynamics of the relationship between the great powers in the Asia-Pacific region are in flux, and President Xi Jinping is leading China at a time of great historical significance, with a geopolitical shift away from the traditional Chinese continental emphasis towards much greater prominence for the maritime domain. Domestically, he is facing huge political and economic issues, though the 19th National Congress of the CPC has clearly consolidated his power.[16] The international situation is equally challenging, with China's national security now predicated upon a maritime expansion as China attempts to reclaim regional power from an unreliable and, to Chinese eyes, intrusive US. Together with its overt military maritime expansionism, China is also trying to bolster its geopolitical status through its intermodal infrastructure development programme, the BRI, which explicitly endorses an alternative 'Asian way'.[17]

Xi Jinping has articulated his strategic vision as the 'Chinese Dream', which clearly encompasses both continental and maritime affairs. Indeed, now that China has become the world's second largest power, both economically and militarily, Xi feels that it is time to leverage China's rich historical heritage. With the US unable to find an effective strategy to counter China's recent expansionism in the IOR, the Chinese Dream can be understood primarily as a rebalancing of China's continental power with its maritime power, restoring the historical situation in the region when China could access its maritime domain without suffering any rivals.[18]

To this end, China has coined a slogan referencing a situation which has not prevailed since the 19th century: "China dominates Asia with its rich history: as the Middle Kingdom, China controls the continent; by ruling the seas, China controls the world."[19] Since taking power in 2013, Xi Jinping has repeatedly spoken of China becoming a great power *again*. Thus, the decision to dispatcha People's Liberation Army (PLA) Navy (PLAN) task force to the Gulf of Aden in 2008, as part of the US-led anti-piracy force, should be seen from a historical perspective.[20] China wants to remind the Chinese people, as well as the wider world, of the remarkable expeditionary voyages of Admiral Zheng He in the early 15th century.[21] These diplomatic and trading missions through East Asian Seas and around the Indian Ocean were also intended to deter piracy in the Malacca Straits, and the scale of the vessels deployed dwarfed the ships of contemporary European powers.

Xi Jinping's ambition to restore China's economic dominance of Asia is being implemented through the BRI, whose two components, the Silk Road Economic Belt and the 21st Century Maritime Silk Road, are intended to integrate connections between the continental and maritime domains of the IOR.[22] Xi has also exploited US President Donald Trump's 'America First' policy to promote China as a viable alternative capable of replacing the US as the regional great power, since the US seems to be edging away from its established global role.[23] The current US administration has backed off from soft power diplomacy and apparently eschewed the controversial 'Rebalancing/Pivot to Asia' strategy. Washington seems to be disengaging from the Indo-Pacific region, replacing a full-throated support for free and open democracy with a more restrained assurance of freedom of navigation and international law in the IOR.[24] Xi Jinping's Chinese Dream has acquired a new and more explicit significance: it offers the region a common destiny, focusing on specifically Asian values, and the field has been left wide open for Xi Jinping to stamp Chinese maritime power upon the IOR.[25]

Xi Jinping's strategy of expanding China's infrastructural links to secure regional hegemony has clear geopolitical ramifications for the IOR, which connects the Pacific Ocean and East Asia to the Mediterranean Sea and Europe, and is therefore essential to China's Sea Lines of Communication (SLOC). At strategic choke points in the IOR, such as the Malacca Straits, the Gulf of Mannar, the Gulf of Aden and the Suez Canal, China currently lacks the ability to protect its maritime trade – a serious problem should China find itself in a major war at sea.[26]

It now seems quite plausible that Xi Jinping's Chinese Dream includes a Chinese naval expansion into the IOR. Recent articulations of China's stance on maritime strategy offer some support for this possibility: the aspiration to become a true maritime power surely implies amassing sufficient naval strength to control over the major sea routes between Europe and Asia. In this case, the maritime domains of the IOR are a key to the implementation of Xi Jinping's Chinese Dream, both nationally and internationally. China's national maritime strategy has certainly been clearly differentiated from earlier policies, with leaders of the government and the PLA committed to a naval strategy which defends and protects China's maritime trade and its economy by implementing a specifically Chinese approach to securing command of the sea. This strategy entails a huge and expensive naval presence capable of attacking of excluding potential adversaries; in Western terms, this involves a campaign of sea-line interdiction.[27]

A Reality Check for Xi Jinping's Chinese Dream in the IOR

Xi Jinping's Chinese Dream can be seen as the fulfilment of his 'Look West'[28] strategy first enunciated in 2013, and meanwhile Donald Trump is focusing on 'America First',[29] effectively undermining the superpower status of the US with his infamous speech to the United Nations General Assembly on September 19, 2017.[30] Nevertheless, Chinese aspirations for military and strategic control of the IOR, despite its geographical remoteness, will encounter a variety of difficult challenges. In addition, the cost and difficulty of building up its naval forces, establishing China as a true maritime power, could also threaten China's economy.

The first issue is historical: China's perception of its historical regional hegemony is simply inapplicable to the political and economic systems of the modern world. Of course, it is understandable that China is concerned about its dependence upon seaborne trade, whether imports or exports, but it can no longer be self-sufficient in the way that the Middle Kingdom once was. The Chinese leadership, including the military, should understand that Chinese security and prosperity rely upon China's interdependence and interconnectedness with the rest of the world.

The second issue concerns the strategic rivalry between China and India, with nationalist tendencies in both countries seeking to exert hegemony in their own spheres of Asia.[31] Although China has enjoyed double-digit economic growth since the late 1990s, the recent more business-friendly policies of the Indian Prime Minister Narendra Modi may allow India to catch up with and ultimately overtake China. The West would certainly prefer the ascendance of democratic India, which shares more of its values than authoritarian China.[32] Such a flourishing of India's economy could frustrate China's military expansion into the IOR. Pakistan is a wild card in this situation, as an entrenched adversary of India which helps to provoke competition between China and India. The US may also play an influential role in India as a potential supplier of military equipment to replace aging Russian kit.

The third issue is about whether China can in fact replace the forward-deployed military power of the US in the IOR. Since the 1980s, the US has published directives on maritime strategy, but a deep-rooted complacency prevails in its current approach to the IOR.[33] *A Cooperative Strategy for 21st Century Seapower* (CS21, 2007) and the revised iteration *A Cooperative Strategy for 21st Century Seapower: Forward, Engaged, Ready* (CS21-R, 2015) are too fixated on past scenarios, and do not adequately explain how the US will maintain its dominance of the IOR when facing the expansion of Chinese maritime power.[34] India is transitioning from its erstwhile military and security cooperation with the Soviet Union or Russia to a closer relationship with the US, and China is keen to step into the resulting power vacuum. Increasingly assertive Chinese naval operations have signalled their ambitions, and India has responded, for example, by acquiring from the US their newer C-130J transport aircraft and P-8I multi-mission maritime surveillance aircraft for the Indian Navy,[35] which is also trying to enhance the operational capabilities of its open-seas platforms and weapon systems.[36]

The fourth issue concerns China's requirement to maintain an uninterrupted flow of ships in and out of Chinese ports. Any disturbance would have serious consequences for the Chinese economy which is increasingly dependent on maritime trade. It has been reported that 60-70 per cent of China's economic activity is now directly or indirectly linked to trade with other nations, so its SLOC must be kept open, especially for importing oil and gas from Middle East and Africa, as well as for other raw materials.[37] China cannot afford to be sidelined in the IOR by the dominance of any other single naval power.

On the other hand, there are some factors conducive to China's shifting the focus of its military strategy from East Asian Seas to the IOR, and also Africa.[38] Foremost among these is the divided US command structure, as noted by *China's Military Strategy 2015:* there are three US Unified Commands in the Indian Ocean – Pacific Command, Central Command and Africa Command. The Pacific Command is busy dealing with North Korea and with US overseas bases in Japan and Guam; it also seems to be too remote, though it does control the Diego Garcia Islands in the middle of the Indian Ocean. The Central and Africa Commands are fighting against Islamic terrorists in Africa, South Asia and the Middle East, where their theatre military operations seem to be organised around land-based operational concepts, not sea control.[39] The story is similar with the major European powers: the UK, France and Germany have all reduced their presence and interests in the IOR. The balance of power in the IOR and Africa has become more fragile than it used to be, opening up a space for China to establish a naval presence.

Another factor in China's favour is that India currently lacks the ability to deter China's increasingly assertive naval presence in the IOR since the late 2000s, the so-called 'String of Pearls' strategy.[40] China has just opened its first overseas naval base on August 1, 2017, in Djibouti, to which the PLAN is preparing to dispatch its first-ever aircraft carrier expeditionary task force.[41] The PLAN will can also rely upon support from several international ports in the IOR which have benefited from Chinese lending, such as Gwadar in Pakistan and Hambantota in Sri Lanka, and will perhaps visit some ports in the Persian Gulf, in Iran or Yemen, having prepositioned nuclear-powered submarines.[42]

Two Views of China's 21st Century Maritime Silk Road to the IOR

History suggests that the most highly developed countries require a geopolitical dimension for their security and for their national economies to prosper, so that the maritime domain has always been the major medium upon which the great powers have depended: Spain, Portugal and the Netherlands, then Britain and France, later Germany, then the US.

According to one view of China's current situation, such a maritime dimension is still an essential requirement for any great power. Thus, China's expansion into the IOR and the construction of a 21st Century Maritime Silk Road with all the necessary infrastructural facilities, from the East and South China Seas through the Malacca Straits to the Indian Ocean, connecting China to the Middle East and Africa, can be justified by China's great economic strength alone. But China is surely also pursuing its historical maritime rights and interests in the IOR. As yet, China has declared no such explicit claim to the IOR, but there is a clear implication of a Chinese historical entitlement deriving from Zheng He's expeditionary voyages of the early 15th century.

In this light, China sees the IOR as an fitting and rightful avenue through which Xi Jinping's ambitious vision can be realised, restoring China's historical prestige following the traditional concepts of a maritime 'Ceramic Road' or 'Treasure Road'. Although China has deployed a relatively small-scale naval task force to the IOR, the most significant Chinese involvement is in joint investments to expand harbours and port facilities around the IOR, and in establishing leased naval bases, so far only in Djibouti.

In particular, Xi Jinping wants to build economic corridors to connect the sea routes of the IOR with land corridors linking port facilities and roads to western China, *without* passing through the narrow Malacca Straits which the US controls.[43] Xi Jinping's Chinese Dream clearly relies upon both pillars of the BRI initiative, a 21st Century Maritime Silk Road to the IOR and the Silk Road Economic Belt.[44] And it is also obvious how China plans to integrate the continental and maritime dimensions of its power in its national security strategy.

Unfortunately, this historical perspective is mostly interpreted in simplistically narrow terms, with the geopolitical value of sea-power justifying naval expansion into open seas to protect against a large-scale attack on Chinese merchant shipping.[45] In June 2013 the Chinese Academy of Social Science published a Blue Book denying any political and military implications of the BRI.[46] China's IOR strategy has been based on moderation and maintaining the status quo, but the changing dynamics of international relations require China to play a more proactive role in military affairs of the IOR and Africa. As the biggest investor into the IOR and Africa, Chinese policy in the IOR will not be driven purely by economic objectives, but will also take into account strategic and military interests.[47] Thus, *China's Military Strategy 2015* describes building combined, multi-functional and efficient marine combat forces to prepare for a military struggle over maritime trade.[48] According to this view, then, China must become a true maritime power by fully grasping sea control, by preparing for military struggle and for possible maritime trade wars in the IOR.

There is, however, a contrasting view held by many contemporary experts who believe that China is fundamentally unable to protect its SLOC against a maritime trade war, but that this matters much less now than in former centuries because of the degree of interconnectedness and interdependence of today's global trading system. Since the early 2000s, various studies of China's energy security and maritime interests in the IOR have questioned China's ability to establish absolute sea control in the open seas. They argue that the ever-growing size and sophistication of merchant fleets, ports and associated shore facilities mean that any Chinese attempts to unilaterally protect its SLOC by military means would be exposed in wartime as highly unrealistic.[49]

A strategy which prioritises military strength to ensure China's imports of oil, gas and raw materials would be fundamentally destabilising to the entire globalised system of maritime trade and would undermine China's efforts at infrastructure politics in the IOR.[50] China's economy is increasingly dependent upon the vast amounts of open-ocean transportation passing through the IOR, but hypothetical Chinese maritime trade war scenarios conjectured to occur in the IOR would have a devastating effect across the IOR itself and also in the surrounding areas.

At present, the Chinese Navy only has one aircraft carrier expeditionary group, and this is only capable of full combat readiness in Chinese coastal areas, such as the East and South China Seas and the Yellow Sea. Lacking fully operational naval bases in the IOR, to sustain long duration missions PLAN task forces still require logistical support escorts, such as the new Type 055 guided missile destroyers and the new Type 901 fast combat support ships, not to mention forward-deployed submarine forces to clear out any underwater threats.[51]

There is some speculation that the Hudong-Zhonghua shipyard has commenced building work on a Type 075 40,000 tonne landing helicopter dock amphibious assault ship, which would provide another major platform as the nucleus of a PLAN naval task force.[52] It has also been reported that a catamaran ocean surveillance ship (T-AGOS) similar in appearance to the USNS *Impeccable* is under construction. This vessel is designed for acoustic intelligence collection and equipped with acoustic arrays. If operated in the IOR, it could provide mapping support and clearance for underwater operations of the PLAN carrier-based naval task force.[53] Also, on September 8, 2017, a Type 815A 6,000 tonne intelligence collection vessel (AGI) was launched, the seventh in its class, tasked with national and regional intelligence collection activities to support the PLAN's far seas naval operation. Both these vessels are significant assets, either for a contingency-mission naval task force or for state intelligence agencies.[54]

Through its infrastructural development, China claims to be providing economic benefits to the IOR, which is all well and good, but there is a subtext of historical entitlement which is used in China's domestic politics to justify an ambitious military expansion, projecting powerful naval forces into the IOR. Xi Jinping's aspiration for China to become a true maritime power is portrayed as a great contribution to regional prosperity and peace, but a naval expansion into the IOR must be understood as an offensive military strategy.[55]

Lukewarm Reactions from India and the US

How have India and the US, as major stakeholders in the IOR, responded to Xi Jinping's Chinese dream as a justification for making China a true maritime power? So far, unfortunately, their response has been disappointing and disjointed. India has attempted to find other parties with interests in the IOR willing to cooperate to balance the Chinese expansion, and the US is supporting capacity-building measures for the nations of the IOR, but has done nothing directly to resist China's ambition to assert its military might in the IOR.[56] The most effective approach is surely for India and the US to work coherently together to deal with China's economic and political influence in the IOR and to counter the increasing presence of the PLAN.

India and the US share a common objective – to resist Chinese naval expansion in the IOR – but they disagree about the appropriate course of action, about who should take the lead role in any coalition formed for this purpose, and about how to implement the practical and operational aspects of such a strategy. India would like to lead a loose coalition against China, a non-binding partnership with like-minded nations, including some from outside the IOR, encompassing both navies and coast guards. Along these lines, a US-India-Australia-Japan quadrilateral security cooperation has been proposed which attempts to stitch together a narrative to counter the Chinese naval expansionism.[57]

India is indisputably the most important regional player in the IOR, with huge maritime and economic interests. India relies overwhelmingly upon the Indian Ocean for its external trade and for its energy supply. India has also been placed in a difficult position by China's BRI: it welcomes the Silk Road Economic Belt and the funding of the Asian Infrastructure Investment Bank, but is very concerned about the China-Pakistan Economic

Corridor.[58] In any case, India wants to take the leading role as guardian of the Indian Ocean, and prefers to ensure peace and stability by building bilateral and multilateral partnerships with other stakeholders.[59] This rather passive stance on the IOR underlies Indian actions in the recent China-India tensions, the worst for more than 30 years, over an unpaved road in a remote pass through the Himalayas in Bhutan, which is sandwiched between China and India, but has a great deal of leverage with both its neighbours.[60]

India also insists upon purely non-military alliances and pacts, still adhering to the non-aligned ideology it applied to resist US influence in the IOR during the Cold War; but this approach fails to address today's reality of India facing potential military threats from China. India participates in various bilateral and multilateral non-military coalitions and related maritime-oriented countermeasures: the India-US Framework for Maritime Strategy Cooperation, the Indian Ocean Rim Association for Regional Cooperation (IOR-ARC), the Bay of Bengal Initiative for Multi-Sectoral Technical and Economic Cooperation (BIMST-EC), the Indian Ocean Rim Business Forum (IORBF) and the Indian Ocean Rim Academic Group (IORAG).

In addition, there are some multilateral mechanisms concerned with countering non-traditional threats, including disruption of the peace and stability of the IOR: the Indian Ocean Naval Symposium (IONS); and Exercise Malabar, a naval drill coordinated with the US navy to which Japan was later invited as an observer.[61] It seems that India wants to formulate its own countermeasures against Chinese ambitions in the IOR, and these include trying to turn the tables on China by sponsoring economic development in the South China Sea (SCS): India's state-owned Oil and Natural Gas Corporation (ONGC) is collaborating with Vietnamese companies, such as PetroVietnam, to explore for oil and gas in the SCS, and this has provoked a strong reaction from China which opposes any third party involvement in energy exploration activities in disputed areas of the SCS.[62] In July 2017, Vietnam granted ONGC a two-year extension to explore oil block 128, a strong indication of Vietnamese resistance to China's territorial claims and its expanding military presence in the SCS.[63] Vietnam would clearly like India to play a bigger role in Southeast Asia, especially in the SCS. For India, its growing defence and commercial ties with Vietnam are part of its strategy of seeking many partnerships with stakeholders of the IOR and SCS while avoiding formal military alliances. China's reacted furiously to the Vietnamese decision on ONGC, referring to illegal oil and gas activities in waters within Chinese jurisdiction.

Despite the Indian reluctance to cooperate fully with the US against China's expansion into the IOR, the US continues to try to build useful partnerships with India. Some avenues of practical military cooperation have been established, such as the US-India Executive Steering Groups (ESGs) meetings, and other military cooperation at various levels has resulted in an impressive range of engagements between the two militaries and navies. Nevertheless, the US remains unhappy with the Indian stance and would prefer to move the US-Indian military interaction towards an alliance-like partnership. The US complains that Indian is too passive on the Chinese ambitions in the IOR with a wait-and-see policy about Chinese threats. A recent paper in *US Naval Institute Proceedings* argues that since India is not doing enough, the US should engage directly with Sri Lanka by offering capacity-building support. Sri Lanka has vital strategic importance, as it straddles the international sea routes of the IOR, with more than 30 per cent of global container traffic and 30 per cent of oil traffic (including 90 per cent of China's) passing the Sri Lankan coast, so this offers an opportunity for the US to fill the gap between India and China, even without Indian cooperation.[64]

How should China Approach the IOR?

Xi Jinping would like to exploit the IOR to establish China as the regional (if not yet global) hegemon, but what are the realistic prospects for his Chinese Dream, and what strategic approach would best serve China's maritime security?

The PLAN's current naval strategy is intended to be implemented in two stages.[65] First, conducting an Anti-Access/Area Denial (A2/AD) strategy to defend China's putative historical maritime rights to the so-called Nine-Dash Line which claims more than 80 per cent of the SCS, also pushing US forward-deployed naval forces back somewhat, beyond the 'first island chain', to establish a defensive posture. Second, pursuing a Look West strategy towards the IOR, adopting a more offensive posture by dispatching a naval task force escorted by submarines for underwater operations. Indeed, PLAN submarines have reportedly conducted annual underwater operations and made several port-call visits to Sri Lanka and Pakistan.[66]

Given the extent of global economic interdependence, there is considerable doubt whether any future major conflict at sea would involve targeting maritime trade, since this would disrupt the economy of the aggressors as much as that of their enemies. This contrasts with the traditional and historically supported understanding, but many contemporary experts believe that interrupting an opponent's SLOC would be counterproductive, so that this is highly unlikely in the foreseeable future.[67]

Xi Jinping's Chinese Dream conflates the infrastructural development of the BRI with military expansionism, and such an approach is readily interpreted as neocolonialist, which provokes strong resistance.[68] In today's interconnected world, with its vast and growing investment in infrastructure, and its global trading systems which secure the prosperity of all nations, it would be foolishly self-defeating for China to prioritise military control of the choke points upon which its economy depends, because all other economies also depend on these same international sea routes: it will not help China to become a major naval power in the IOR.[69]

So the PLAN must reach beyond its outdated view of the dangers that a major war at sea might pose to China's maritime trade, in particular in the SCS through which some 60,000 ships per year pass to the IOR, accounting for approximately 50 per cent of the world's maritime trade.[70] The PLAN's current strategy obliges them to prepare to attack their enemy's maritime trade and to simultaneously defend their own, and this is reflected in their naval modernisation programmes. And the details of the PLAN's unrealistic operational doctrine make it clear that their sea-line interdiction strategy is more of an offensive stance than a defensive one. Many Western experts now view a large-scale attack on merchant shipping as counterproductive, even as unthinkable, given the global nature of maritime transportation. The consequence of this understanding is that China cannot, and therefore should not try to, use its naval presence in the IOR to project China's status as a great power: this is a very different world from the one which the Western powers dominated during the 19th century.

Conclusions

The IOR appears to be among the most important theatres for Xi Jinping to pursue his Chinese Dream. Expanding China's naval presence in the IOR creates several new tasks for the PLAN: change China's military strategy from a defensive A2/AD to an offensive maritime control strategy; change the conceptual basis of how China uses the maritime domains, instead of using the land to control the sea, project naval power to achieve sea control; and integrate continental and maritime power so that both can be used simultaneously in the IOR. But these tasks will be difficult or impossible for China to accomplish, as has been argued above, and will not in any event secure China's position as a 'true maritime power' in the IOR.

This aspiration is incompatible with peace and stability in the IOR: instead of following outdated strategies which are no longer applicable to the modern interconnected and interdependent world, China would do better to base its actions upon its true economic interests, which are largely shared with other nations: it is wholly unrealistic for China to imagine that it can seize control of its SLOC. And unless China wishes to be condemned for neocolonialism, which would seriously affect its BRI infrastructural development programme and squander any goodwill it might obtain thereby, it should stop pretending any kind of entitlement in the IOR because of something that happened 600 years ago. Chinese policy to the IOR needs to be firmly grounded in reality, with a naval presence proportionate to need, as with their existing anti-piracy task force, and on good terms with other IOR stakeholders.

Chinese maritime trade is expected to continue to grow at a rapid pace in the future, but China's naval expansion appears designed to establish a maritime capacity which will overwhelm all other powers in the region. Instead of seeking to distinguish China as the sole regional hegemon, harking back to earlier centuries when European powers dominated the world by command of the seas, the Chinese leadership needs to recognise that the world has changed, and focus upon harmonising its grand national strategy with other powers, whether great or small, who share the same international sea routes, the same global supply chains, the same mutual prosperity, and the same requirements for peace at stability, not least in the IOR.

NOTES

1. Sukjoon Yoon, "Implications of Xi Jinping's 'True Maritime Power'", *U.S. Naval War College Review*, 68 (3), Summer 2015, pp. 40-63.
2. Baijie An, "Onward to Rejuvenation: Xi Jinping Re-elected General Secretary, Stresses Plan to Guide China through the 'Two Century Goals' and beyond", *China Daily*, November 3, 2017, p. 1.
3. "Editorial: Lineup Conveys Message of Cohesion and Resolve", *China Daily*, November 3, 2017, p. 11.
4. Xue Li (薛力), "One Belt One Road and China's Foreign Policy toward Its Neighbors (一帶一路戰略與中國外交調整)", a paper presented to China Workshop hosted by the Asiatic Research Institute, Korea University, on September 13, 2017 in Seoul, South Korea.
5. Janglin Xiao (趙江林) (ed.), *The 21st Century Maritime Silk Road: Target, Implementation and Policy Suggestions (中國社會科學院 一帶一路研究系列),* Social Science Academic Press, Beijing, May 2015, pp. 129-137.
6. "Full Text of Constitution of Communist Party of China", Xinhua, November 3, 2017, at http://news.xinhusnet.com/english/special/2017-11/03/c_136725945.html (Accessed December 11, 2017).

7. Yunsong Huang, "Appraisal of One Belt One Road", a paper presented to the 38th National Security Seminar 2017 entitled "From Contest to Cooperation: A Vision for Shared Prosperity in the Indo-Pacific Region", hosted by the United Service Institution of India (USI) and held in New Delhi, India, on November 2-3, 2017.
8. The author thanks Professor Jagannath Panda for his comments made at the workshop where a preliminary draft of this manuscript was delivered, which was held in the East Asia Centre at the Institute for Defence Studies and Analyses, New Delhi, India, on November 1, 2017.
9. Bates Gill, "China's Communist Party Congress an Opportunity for President Xi to Extend Power beyond his Five-year Term", *Strategic Capital*, Edition 5, December 13, 2017.
10. Xiaochen Su, "Why Chinese Infrastructure Loans in Africa Represent a Brand-New Type of Neocolonialism: How Will Africa Countries Repay Massive Debates to China?", *The Diplomat*, June 29, 2017, at http://thediplomat.com/2017/06/why-chinese-infrastruture-loans-in-africa-represent-a-brand-new-type-of-neocolonialism/ (Accessed December 12, 2017).
11. Jagannath Panda, *India-China Relations: Politics of Resources, Identify and Authority in a Multipolar World Order,* Routledge, London and New York, 2017, pp. 80 and 90-92; Jagannath Panda, "India's Current Perception of Indian Ocean Infrastructure: Search for New Partners", a paper presented at a workshop hosted by Korea Maritime Institute on July 14, 2017, in Busan, South Korea.
12. Ron Huisken, *CSCAP: Regional Security Outlook 2018,* Australian National University, Canberra, forthcoming (2018), at http://www.cscap.org/uploads/docs/crso/cscap2018web.pdf/ (Accessed December 12, 2017).
13. Rajesh Basrur, Kartik Bommakanti and Manjeet Pardesi, *India-China Dialogue: Report and Analysis, Report on a Closed-door Dialogue between Indian and Chinese Scholars,* S. Rajaratnam School of International Studies, Singapore, January 6-7,2011, pp. 6-7; Rajesh Basrur, Sam Bateman and Jane Chan, *Workshop on IORA and Strategic Stability in the Indian Ocean,* S. Rajaratnam School of International Studies, Singapore, March 4-5, 2014, p. 6; Major General Ravi Arora, "Modi in the United States: Expectations Fulfilled", *Indian Military Review*, 8 (7), July 2017, pp. 11-12.
14. Major General G.D. Bakshi, "Editorial: China's Aggressive Posture", *Indian Military Review*, 8(7), July 2017, p. 4.
15. Muhammad Azam Khan, "Pakistan's Port Is Pivotal", *US NI Proceedings*, March 2017, pp. 50-54.
16. Oki Nagai, and Tetsushi Takahashi, "Special Mention: China's Xi Aims to Join Mao and Deng in Having Namesake Philosophy Written into the Party Constitution", *Nikkei Asian Review*, October 23-29, 2017, pp. 44-45.
17. "Election Briefing: Foreign Policy", *The Economist*, November 5, 2016, p. 27; Sukjoon Yoon, "Asian Security and the True Asian Way", *MIMA Bulletin*, 23 (2), 2016, pp. 7-10.
18. Robert Haddick, "The Struggle for a Strategy", *US Naval Institute Proceedings*, January 2016, pp. 52-57; Sukjoon Yoon, "Decoding China's Maritime Aspirations", *U.S. Naval Institute Proceedings*, March 2017, pp. 44-49.
19. 2011-2017 Chinese-language maritime-related sources: 盖廠生, 大海國 (北京: 海軍出版社, 2011), 崔慶生, 海洋志 (北京: 海軍出版社, 2012), 楊文學 및 陳伯鏞, 海洋與近

代中國(北京: 海軍出版社, 2014), 張文穆, 論中國海權 (北京: 海軍出版社, 2014), 張劍鳳, 波起東海 (北京: 海軍出版社, 2015), 張文穆,中國地緣政治論 (北京: 海軍出版社, 2015) 및 董超鳳, 中國走向海洋 (北京: 海軍出版社, 2016) and 石家濤, 海權與中國 (上海: 上海三聯書店, 2017).

20. By late 2013, the PLAN naval task force had escorted more than 5,400 ships, including 2,760 foreign ones.
21. Gavin Menzies, *1434: The Year a Magnificent Chinese Fleet Sailed to Italy and Ignited the Renaissance,* Harper Perennial, New York, 2008.
22. Lee Willet, "US Strategy in the Pacific: Asia-Pacific Rebalance at Pivotal Point", *Jane's Defence Weekly,* May 17, 2017, pp. 28-31.
23. Thomas L. Friedman, "Folks, We're Home Alone", *The New York Times,* International Edition, September 28, 2017, p. 11; Thomas L. Friedman, "China Could Sell Trump a Bridge", *The New York Times,* International Edition, November 16, 2017, p. 13; Jane Perlez and Damien Cave, "Australia Questions Its Global Allegiances", *The New York Times,* International Edition, December 5, 2017, p. 7.
24. Ser Myo-Ja and Kang Tae-Hwa, "Moon Avoids 'Indo-Pacific Label", *Korea Joongang Daily,* November 11-12, 2017, pp. 1 and 2; Julie Hirschfeld Davis, "Trump's Charm Offensive", *The New York Times,* International Edition, November 16, 2017, p. 7; Thomas L. Friedman, No. 23.
25. Brahma Chellaney, "A New Emperor in China Is Bad News", *Hindustan Times,* November 1, 2017, p. 18; Susan Rice, "Trump Is Making China Great Again", *The New York Times,* International Edition, November 15, 2017, p. 13.
26. Milan Vego, "Chinese Shipping Could Be Risky Business", *U.S. Naval Institute Proceedings,* April 2014, pp. 38-43.
27. *China's Military Strategy,* The State Council Information Office of the People's Republic of China, Beijing, May 2015, *Chinadaily.com.cn,* May 26, 2015, at http://www.chinadaily.com.cn/china/2015-05/26/content_20820628.htm (Accessed October 1, 2017).
28. This slogan describes China's arduous efforts to expand its naval operations from the Pacific into the Indian Ocean. Also, see Eswar Prasad, "China Takes Aim at West's Global Clout", *The New York Times,* International Edition, September 2-3, 2017, pp. 1 and 11.
29. Some commentators who are reluctant to describe Donald Trump's flip-flop foreign policies as neo-isolationist prefer to characterise them as "America Home Alone", emphasising that US allies, partners and like-minded nations share an interest in working to strengthen US global power capabilities.
30. Mark Landler, "Trump Reshapes U.S. Role in world", *The New York Times,* International Edition, September 21, 2017, p. 4.
31. "China, India Eye Asian Century as Brexit Rattles Old Order", *The Korea Herald,* July 12, 2016, p. 2; Jagannath Panda, No. 11; Sukjoon Yoon, No. 18.
32. Nikhil Kumar, "India Rising", *TIME,* February 9, 2015, p. 10.
33. Sean Quirk and Maile Plan, "On the Maritime Superhighway: US-Sri Lanka Naval Cooperation", Pacific Forum CSIS, *PacNet,* 24, March 2017.
34. Craig Kafura, "Public Perceptions and US Alliance in the Asia-Pacific", Pacific Forum CSIS, *PacNet,* 52, July 20, 2017.
35. Mark Mazzetti and Salman Masood, "Trump Tilts the Political Balance in South Asia", *The New York Times,* International Edition, August 4, 2017, pp. 1 and 4.
36. Rahul Bedi, "Indian MoD Issues RFI for Navy Utility, Multi Helicopters", *Jane's*

Defence Weekly, August 30,2017, p. 14; Rahul Bedi, "India Issues RFI for Heavyweight Torpedoes", *Jane's Defence Weekly*, September 6, 2017, p. 23; Rahul Bedi, "India to Get Additional P-8Is from 2020", *Jane's Defence Weekly*, November 23, 2017, p. 18.

37. Ryan Clake, *Chinese Energy Security: The Myth of the PLAN's Frontline Status*, The Letort Papers, Strategic Studies Institute U.S. Army War College, Carlisle, August 2010, p. 1.
38. Jeremy Binnie, "China Opens Military Base in Djibouti", *Jane's Defence Weekly*, August 9,2017, p. 8; Erwan de Cherisey, "China Intensifies Training for African Armed Forces", *Jane's Defence Weekly*, August 30, 2017, p. 19.
39. Mosharraf Zaidi, "Is Pakistan Ready to Lose America", *The New York Times*, International Edition, August 30, 2017, pp. 1 and 11; Mujib Mashal, "Plan for Afghan Force Revives Fears of Abuses", *The New York Times*, International Edition, September 26, 2017, p. 3; Jagannath Panda, No. 11.
40. In fact, China has never declared any such policy, but China's coherent approach to its expansion into the Indian Ocean since the late 1990s is usually characterised in this way.
41. Gabriel Dominguez, "US says China Is Likely to Build More Overseas Bases", *Jane's Defence Weekly*, June 14,2017, p. 8; Gabriel Dominguez, Samuel Cranny Evans, Rahul Bedi and Richard Fisher, "India Withdraws Troops from Disputed Border Areas", *Jane's Defence Weekly*, September 6, 2017, p. 10.
42. "Gwadar Port Will Boost Pakistan's, Region's Economy: China", *The Economic Times*, May 4, 2017, at http://economictimes.indiatimes.com/news/defence/gwadar-port-will-boost-pakistans- regions-economy (Accessed August 2, 2017).
43. A Chinese publication about the BRI proposes six economic corridors linking China with the IOR through sea routes and ports where Chinese-owned companies have invested in building terrestrial roads and railways.
44. Sukjoon Yoon, No. 18; Robert C. Rubei, "Seeing the Maritime Forest for the Trees", *US Naval Institute Proceedings*, April 2017, pp. 68-73.
45. 2009-2017 Chinese-language sources: 孫科佳, 新中國成立60年 (北京: 國防大學出版社, 2009), 劉華淸, 劉華淸回顧錄 (北京: 解防軍出版社, 2011 再版), 邵永靈, 海洋全國策 (北京: 石油工業出版社, 2010), 左律玲, 中國海軍走向深藍 1980-2010 (上下卷) (北京: 解放軍出版社, 2011), 李烋, 大國: 由海權崛起 (北京: 求眞出版社, 2014), 消天亮, 戰略論 (北京: 國防大學出版社, 2015), 現代艦船, 中國航母編隊解析 (北京: 現代艦船編輯社, 2017) and 現代艦船, 中國海軍的弱點 (北京: 現代艦船編輯社, 2017).
46. Rana Divyank Chaudhary, "China: Reading Beijing's Blue Book on India", Institute of Peace and Conflict Studies (IPCS), May 28, 2013, at http://www.ipcs.org/article/india/china-reading-beijings-blue-book-on-india-395.html/ (Accessed December 8, 2017).
47. The author is grateful to Professor Jagannath Panda for discussions on this subject during the preparation of the manuscript.
48. *China's Military Strategy*, No. 27.
49. Ryan Clake, No. 37; Wood, 2012, Michael D, *Chinese Maritime Power – Is the Increase in China's maritime power internally consistent with China's national interests and foreign policy, or Cause for concern?* (Kingston, Ontario: Royal College of Defence Studies, July 2012).

Philippens, 2011, Henri, "Fueling China's Maritime Modernization: The Need to Guarantee Energy Security", *Journal of Energy Security*, 14 December 2011.

Lee, 2014, John and Charles Horner, "China faces barriers in the Indian Ocean", *Asia Times*, 10 January 2014; Milan Vego, No. 26.

50. Tangredi, 2017, Sam J, 'Fight Fire with Fire,' *US Naval Institute Proceedings*, August 2017, p. 43.
51. Andrew Tate, "China Expands Its Amphibious Force...", *Jane's Defence Weekly*, April 12,2017, p. 18. Andrew Tate, "China Launches Seventh Type 815A", *Jane's Defence Weekly*, September 20,2017, p. 15.
52. Andrew Tate, "China Expands Its Amphibious Force...", No. 51.
53. Andrew Tate, "China Building Possible Submarine Surveillance Ship", *Jane's Defence Weekly*, June 28, 2017, p. 17.
54. Andrew Tate, "China Launches Seventh Type 815A", No. 51.
55. Geoffrey Till, "China and Its Navy: Drifting towards Normality?", *RSIS Commentary*, 018, January 27,2016.
56. Vijay Sakhuja, *Asian Maritime Power in the 21st Century: Strategic Transactions China, India and Southeast Asia,* Institute of Southeast Asian Studies, Singapore, 2011, pp. 155-156; Geoffrey Till (ed.), *The Changing Maritime Scene in Asia: Rising Tensions and Future Strategic Stability,* Palgrave Macmillan, London, 2015; Jagannath Panda, *Indian Ocean and East Asia,* Stringer, New Delhi, 2016.
57. Indrani Bagchi, "Ghost Wars: China's Lengthening Shadow over Asia Can be Countered with an India-Japan-Australia-US Quadrilateral", *The Times of India,* November 4, 2017, p. 22.
58. Jagannath Panda, "India's Current Perception of Indian Ocean Infrastructure: Search for New Partners", No. 11.
59. Steven Lee Myers, Ellen Barry and Max Fisher, "China and India in Face-off at Border" *The New York Times,* International Edition, July 28, 2017, pp. 1 and 4; Steven Lee Myers, "Bhutan Holds Its Breath", *The New York Times,* International Edition, August 18, 2017, pp. 1 and 6.
60. Ibid.; Gabriel Dominguez, No. 41; Gabriel Dominguez et al., No. 41.
61. Srikanth Kondapalli, "Piracy Threats in the IOR and Implementation of Multilateral Naval Cooperation: The Contribution of the ROKN Chenghae Task Force", in Geoffrey Till and Sukjoon Yoon (eds.), *Korean Maritime Strategy: Issues and Challenges,* Korea Institute for Maritime Strategy, Seoul, 2011.
62. Vijay Sakhuja, No. 56; Benoit deTreglode, "Maritime Boundary Delimitation and Sino-Vietnam Cooperation in the Gulf of Tonkin (1994-2016)", *China Perspective,* 3, 2016, pp. 33-41; Raja C. Mohan, "Maritime Asia: An Indian Perspective", in Geoffrey Till (ed.), *The Changing Maritime Scene in Asia: Rising Tensions and Future Strategic Stability,* Palgrave Macmillan, London, 2015, pp. 49-58.
63. Mai Nguyen, Nidhi Verma and Sanjeev Miglani, "Vietnam Renews India Oil Deal in Tense South China Sea", *Reuters,* July 6, 2017, at http://www.reuters.com/article/us-southchinasea-vietnam/vietnam-renews-india-oil-deal-in-tense-south-china-sea-idUSKBN19R25P/ (Accessed December 10, 2017).
64. Nicholas R. Nappi, "Sri Lanka Is an Open Door to the Indian Ocean", *US Naval Institute Proceedings*, September 2017, p. 53.
65. Richard D. Fisher, "PLAN Plans: Former Navy Chief Details China's Upgrade Efforts", *Jane's Defence Weekly*, September 6, 2017, p. 30.
66. Ridzwan Rahmatand Lee Willett, "Near and Far: PLAN Maintains Global Presence despite Operational Pressures", *Jane's Navy International*, September 2017, pp. 10-11.

67. Milan Vego, No. 26.
68. James Kanter, "A chastised Greece Turns to China", *The New York Times,* International Edition, August 28, 2017, pp. 1 and 4; Barbara Surk, "As China Moves in, Serbia Reaps Benefits", *The New York Times,* International Edition, September 12, 2017, p. 4; "Chinese Industry Zone Launched, Sri Lanka Protests", *The Korea Herald*, January 9, 2017, p. 12.
69. "Chinese Industry Zone Launched, Sri Lanka Protests", No. 68.
70. Milan Vego, No. 26.

PART II

EVOLVING JAPANESE NARRATIVES

9

China's OBOR Initiative and Japan's Response: The Abe Doctrine, Free and Open Indo-Pacific Strategy and Japan-India Strategic Partnership

Yasuyuki Ishida

The interaction of geo-politics and geo-economics is a prevailing trend in contemporary Asian international relations. Asian major powers are pursuing diplomacy with competing regional visions, ideas and policies based on their own national interests and strategic objectives. After the terrorist attack on September 11, 2001, the US foreign policy focused on the war on terror and the Middle East, away from East Asia. By the early 2010s, however, in the context of China's rapid rise and expansion, the then US President Barack Obama pursued its pivot/rebalance policy to Asia as a comprehensive Asia-Pacific regional strategy to integrate various areas of diplomacy, security and economy. In response, the Chinese President Xi Jinping pursues proactive diplomacy concerning the Asia-Pacific, such as peripheral diplomacy, a new Asian security concept and the "One Belt, One Road (OBOR)" initiative. The OBOR initiative is Xi's pivot to Eurasia to create a Sino-centric Asia. In the context of China's assertive rise, the Japanese Prime Minister Shinzo Abe developed his proactive strategy, the so-called Abe Doctrine, based on the philosophy of Proactive Contribution to Peace and its strategic partnership with India, Australia and the Association of Southeast Asian Nations (ASEAN). In response to China's OBOR initiative, Japan has pursued the Partnership for Quality Infrastructure (PQI) and Free and Open Indo-Pacific Strategy. Japan's Indo-Pacific Strategy places India, the US and Australia as key partners for a free, open and rules-based international order. Japan's Indo-Pacific policy is meeting with India's Look/Act East policy and compliments the Japan-India Strategic Partnership with the Indo-Pacific 2025 Vision.

In November 2017, the US President Donald Trump's first trip to Asia gained attention given the absence of a clearly articulated Asia policy. During his visit to Japan, the first stopover on his Asia tour, the US President repeatedly used the term "Indo-Pacific region". At the Japan-US Summit, Abe and Trump agreed to cooperate on Japan's Free and Open Indo-Pacific Strategy. In Manila, the Japanese initiative of Indo-Pacific Strategy was also supported by Japan, India, the US and Australia Quadrilateral.

Initially, when asked about Trump's remarks on the "Indo-Pacific", the Director General of the Department of International Economic Affairs of China's Foreign Ministry Zhang Jun kept a cautious attitude, saying that "there had not been a lot of discussion on the topic, but China needed to understand the idea of the 'Indo-Pacific' better".[1] However, a day after the four democracies met on the sidelines of the ASEAN Summit in Manila, the Chinese Foreign Ministry Spokesperson Geng Shuang warned, "The US, Japan, India and Australia should not target Beijing. Indo-Pacific... should avoid politicising or excluding some relevant parties."[2] The Hong Kong media commented, "Obviously, the group will have a China-centric security agenda. The Quad's rebirth highlights the growing suspicion and unease diplomats in Washington, Tokyo, Canberra and New Delhi feel about China's meteoric military and economic rise... The aegis these democracies create has the potential to develop into an Asian Nato."[3] Following these reactions, the Japanese media reported, "Japan's Indo-Pacific Strategy aims not to check China, and Prime Minister Abe seems to decide to foster Japan-China cooperation for Japan's security and economic interests according to several official sources."[4]

Considering reports and analyses on Japanese foreign policy towards China, it is necessary to analyse how Japanese diplomacy under Prime Minister Shinzo Abe copes with President Xi Jinping's proactive initiatives.[5] This chapter argues that Japan's Indo-Pacific Strategy aims to realise peace, stability and prosperity on a rules-based order in Asia and the Pacific. Abe's Indo-Pacific Strategy aims to embrace China's OBOR initiative, not to confront it, and to constrain China's hegemonic maritime expansion. Japan's Indo-Pacific Strategy strengthens the US alliance network and

Japan-India partnership as a hard balancing in order to encourage China to play a more responsible and constructive role in the region. Tokyo and New Delhi aim to strengthen the ASEAN-centred regional architecture as a soft-balancing and management of major-powers' relations. The Japan-India strategic partnership as an Asian maritime democratic pivot is the critical foundation of the Asian and Indo-Pacific regional order in order to manage uncertain US-China relations and to strengthen stable major-powers relations and ASEAN-centred regional architecture.

Emerging regional geo-political and geo-economic trends are remaking Asia. The Asian indeterminate regional trends of rising nationalism and remarkable economic development are fundamentally reshaping Asian geo-politics. "Geo-politics" aims to analyse national policies in terms of its geographical environment and conditions. "Geo-economics" means the politico-diplomatic strategy to gain geo-political national interests by economic means and measures. In the context of a waning American leadership under President Donald Trump, major Asian powers – Japan, India and China – are developing a strategic triangularity in Asia. The geo-economics of infrastructure development has geo-political implications for Asia and the Indo-Pacific order in the future.[6]

This chapter looks at the competing strategies, foreign policies and national objectives of China, Japan and India with respect to their regional visions in Asia and the Indo-Pacific, particularly concerning their geo-economic initiatives on infrastructure building and connectivity projects across Asia. The first part of this chapter outlines the strategic trends and challenges to the US liberal international order in view of the US-China rivalry. The second part contextualises Chinese strategy and foreign policies, Asia-Pacific policy and the geo-economic OBOR initiative under Xi Jinping. The third part explores Japan's strategy and foreign policies such as the PQI initiative, Indo-Pacific Strategy and Japan-India strategic partnership under Shinzo Abe. This chapter also examines the implications and challenges of emerging Japan-India-China strategic triangularity on infrastructure development in Asia. China's OBOR is a geo-economic initiative to foster Chinese influence in order to create a China-driven order.

Strategic Trends and Challenges: A Japanese View

The current liberal international order has largely been shaped by the US. After the World War II, the US as a superpower promoted a liberal international order with its military, economic and cultural power. During the Cold War, the US played a leading role in creating and maintaining international regimes and institutions in the areas of security, trade, economy and finance. During the post-Cold War era, in the 1990s, America enjoyed its "uni-polar moment" as the sole global superpower. Backed by its unrivalled politico-military and economic power, the so-called Washington Consensus enhanced liberal globalisation. The underlying premises were wide expectations of economic benefits under the liberal economic order as well as the trust of liberal values, the rule of law and the respect of human rights.

Currently, the US-led liberal international order has been challenged in various ways: (1) global shift in the balance of power; (2) rise of state capitalism; (3) competition for resources and energy; and (4) return of geo-politics and geo-economics. With the globalisation, international competition is increasingly getting severe in search of energy and resources. For example, the US model of Washington Consensus has been challenged by state capitalism, such as China's state-owned company and Russian and the Gulf states' companies dealing with oil and natural gas. President Trump's invocation of an "America first" agenda has been regarded as a threat or a risk factor of retreat from the world by its allies and partners.[7]

Asia's remarkable economic development has significantly changed its regional characteristics and position in the region. Asia was once characterised by "war, conflict, and poverty", but it has transformed itself into a region of "remarkable economic growth and development". While 21st century Asia progresses as a growth centre for world economy, this region is taking centre stage in the "new power game".[8]

In the 21st century, the Asian regional powers have been increasingly facing the dilemma of choosing between the US-led regional security system without China and the regional economic integration led by China. Despite this, the East Asian system has remained relatively stable, so long as China's policy has focused on its economic development without challenging the US-led regional security system. The US-led regional security system has been reinforced by the US-Japan security alliance. This East Asian regional system was constructed as a multi-layered functional and network system with flexibility. China's rise did not mean rebuilding China-centred hierarchical regional order. Asian leaders embraced China's rise in the existing regional system in East Asia. The East Asian economic crisis in 1997-98 enhanced the East Asian regional cooperation without the US, as a hedge against US intervention. Many Asian countries perceived the US policy intervention as a risk to their economic recovery. Asian leaders created East Asian regional frameworks for an East Asian Community.[9] In the 2010s, however, China has showed more assertive and proactive expansionism in the East and South China Seas. Many Asian countries perceive China's military and political expansion and assertive behaviour as a threat to the region. Former US President Obama's rebalance strategy aimed to check China's expansionism. The US and China are competing not only for military and geo-political interests, but also for taking initiatives of setting equitable principles, rules and norms in the regional order making.[10]

The structural tensions between the "US-led Asian security system" and the "China-driven Asian economic system" are gradually and steadily increasing. Asia is becoming a "dichotomous" region that comprises an "economic order" led by China and a "security order" centred on the US network of alliances that conspicuously exclude China. Miyagi questions, "How can the latent tension between these two versions of Asia be managed in order to maintain a stable regional order? This is a critical question on which the future of 21st century Asia hinges." Asian countries need to develop the future direction and strategies base on a rules-based international order.[11]

China's Strategic Initiative under Xi Jinping

China's Resurgence to Great Power

In modern times, China has been seeking to recover the lost greatness of its ancient civilisation. Michel Oksenberg notes,

> China has the most ancient and continuous civilization among today's major powers, but it was the only one among them suffer a total eclipse of the official ideology and institutions that had sustained that continuity. Chinese foreign policy in the twentieth century involves a quest to redress national grievances and to restore the lost greatness. This search for wealth and power defined the tasks facing China's political leaders: how to reconstitute the Chinese state: on what system of beliefs to root that state: what its territorial and political domain should be; and how to attain wealth, power, and security for their country.

China's often-stated objectives, such as "unity and stability", "independence", "strength and security", "wealth and prosperity", "respect, dignity and a voice in the councils of nations", are rooted in its bitter historical experience of modern history .[12]

Since Deng Xiaoping's reform and open policy, leaders continue China's comprehensive security strategy based on following components: (1) maintaining "internal political stability"; (2) building China's "comprehensive national strength"; and (3) advancing China's international status and influence by skilful diplomatic manoeuvres.[13] Jiang Zemin's diplomacy continued Deng's approach of "conceal your strength, bide your time", and prophesied that the first 20 years of the 21st century would be strategically important for China's prospects. Hu Jintao's foreign policy was about striking a balance between "conceal your strength, bide your time" and "accomplishing a little", showing autonomous development in foreign activities. Currently, Xi Jinping's major-power diplomacy is about pursuing action-oriented autonomous diplomatic activity with China's neighbours. Towards China's neighbouring nations, Xi's external policy mixes actions producing harmony with a hard stance, while developing a proactive position of doing pragmatic things.[14]

Chinese leaders' top domestic priority is maintaining political stability and the rule of the Chinese Communist Party (CCP). Xi Jinping stresses that the "Communist Party's leadership" is for "China's independence, the people's liberation, national unification, and social stability". The CCP takes the responsibility of political and social stability, national integrity and security, pursuing the "Chinese Dream" for the revival of the Chinese nation. The Party maintains its political integrity to "protect against potential danger" and to safeguard "China's sovereignty, security, and development interests" by "pursuing a holistic approach to national security". The CCP leadership is anxious about threats both in domestic and external areas, particularly the threat of "encirclement of China" by foreign powers. The CCP leaders need their political legitimacy to raise the living standards through economic growth in a stable international environment. The CCP needs to create a strong political leadership to deal with the top three agendas simultaneously: reform, development and stability. It is not a democratic decision-making system, but a model of concentrated decision-making that deals with the top agendas.[15]

Xi Jinping's "Chinese Dream" for a China-centric Order

In response to Obama's pivot/rebalance to Asia, Xi Jinping prioritised strengthening China's regional strategy. China's peripheral diplomacy aims to stabilise its neighbours via economic integration and security cooperation. In October 2013, Beijing convened the Peripheral Diplomacy Work Conference. President Xi Jinping stressed that China's neighbours had "extremely significant strategic value", and emphasised the need to improve relations, strengthen economic ties and deepen security cooperation between China and its neighbours:

> Maintaining stability in China's neighbourhood is the key objective of peripheral diplomacy. We must encourage and participate in the process of regional economic integration, speed up the process of

> building up infrastructure and connectivity. We must build the Silk Road Economic Belt and 21st Century Maritime Silk Road, creating a new regional economic order.

President Xi reiterated the value the country places on the Asia-Pacific region in his first Southeast Asia tour of October 2013. He stated that China has long pursued a "comprehensive foreign policy, viewing great powers as the key to its foreign policy, its periphery is principal, the developing countries as the foundation, and multilateral diplomacy as an important arena".[16]

China's White Paper on Policies on Asia-Pacific Security Cooperation, issued in January 2017, is its road map for regional security framework. China has ambitions to take "greater responsibilities for regional and global security", "provide more public security services" for the Asia-Pacific region and the world and create "international rules" for regional and global security. The policy package includes "the promotion of common development; the building of partnerships; improvement of existing multilateral frameworks; rule-setting; military exchanges; and proper settlement of differences". Beijing proposes idealistic security concepts of "common, comprehensive, cooperative and sustainable security" for regional security while maintaining good relations with major powers: the US, Russia, India and Japan. At the same time, China claims to "build a strong national defence force" as the "military is at the centre of security", and "increase its exchanges and cooperation".[17]

China is making a China-centric world order by geo-economic and geo-political means. Leonard argues,

> If the big China story of the past few decades was about growth, exports and investments, the story of the next decade will be about the creation of a Chinese economic and political order. China is becoming part of the fabric of the economic life of most countries around the world. Rather than trying to overthrow existing institutions as many had feared, Beijing is instead using this economic might to link up to the rest of the world and develop a series of relationships and institutions which result in a more China-centric world order.

It should be noted that China's new economic and political order is structured differently from Western-led multilateral institutions which are underpinned by "treaties, international law and the pooling of sovereignty". In the making of a new Sino-centric order, Beijing's preferred style is "to craft a series of bilateral relationships" that link it to different capitals.[18]

OBOR Initiative as a Geo-economic Strategy

China's OBOR initiative stemmed from proposals by President Xi Jinping and Premier Li Keqiang,[19] and was originally drafted as a proposal by China's Foreign Ministry. After the establishment of the Shanghai Cooperation Organisation (SCO) in 2001, China's diplomatic community discussed the formation of various regional cooperation ideas proposed by regional countries. During this process, various ideas were formulated such as "China-ASEAN Community", "21st century Maritime Silk Road" and "Silk Road Economic Belt". The blueprint of the OBOR initiative, "Vision and Actions on Jointly Building Silk Road Economic Belt and 21st-Century Maritime Silk Road", was issued in March 2015, which unveiled the principles, framework and cooperation priorities and mechanisms in its Belt and Road Initiative in a bid to enhance regional connectivity. The initiative aims to promote orderly and free flow of economic factors, highly efficient allocation of resources and deep integration of markets by enhancing connectivity. China tries to build consensus with neighbouring countries on the OBOR initiative by putting emphasis on "mutually beneficial connectivity" and a "form of network of equal relations, which can develop to a win-win system for coexistence". China established the Asian Infrastructure Investment Bank (AIIB) in October 2013, the Silk Road Fund in November 2014 and the China-Central and Eastern Europe Fund in November 2016.

China's gigantic infrastructure initiative has geo-political and geo-economic objectives. First, OBOR is China's economic development strategy both within China's domestic regions as well as across Asia and Europe. The concept is a further development of China's earlier Great Western Development Strategy for China's central and western regions towards a more balanced and inclusive economic development. The "Belt and Road" concept explores the possibility of driving Chinese economic expansion west through Eurasia over both land-based and maritime routes. China aims to deal with its economic slowdown by sustaining economic development based on directing domestic industries' current excess production capacity outside its borders, and by expanding foreign investment and having greater influence over the international community. The immediate goal of the OBOR initiative is to boost China's influence in Central Asia, a resource-rich region that used to be within the Russian orbit. As a growing number of countries become dependent on Chinese transport and energy infrastructure, stronger economic ties will make it increasingly costly for Central Asian governments to oppose China.[20]

Second, OBOR is a geo-strategy heading west from China to avoid conflicting with the US rebalance policy to Asia. The strategy combines China's historical position as a "continental power" with the new and aspiring "maritime power". OBOR provides for a Chinese advance into the South Pacific and the Indian Ocean, reflecting China's intention to expand its presence in those waters. Stressing peripheral diplomacy and China's deepening involvement in Central Asia may be a crucial factor behind OBOR. While China is not a participant in the Trans Pacific Partnership (TPP), it has not openly opposed the TPP. Chinese diplomacy has put its strategic emphasis on the Eurasian continent.[21]

Third, OBOR is a geo-economic strategy to build infrastructure by providing financial assistance in order to expand trade and human exchanges, and eventually to lead to economic development and stable foreign and security environment. It is an instrument to enhance collaboration with major powers and to accommodate neighbouring countries. China puts emphasis on collaboration with major powers like the US, Europe and Russia. It aims to play a leading role in setting international rules of trade and security in the Asian region. China intends to expand its dominant influence on Asia. It introduced its new Asian security concept at the meeting of the Conference on Interaction and Confidence-Building Measures in Asia (CICA), of which the US and Japan are not members. China wants to be the foremost leader in Asia by free-riding on the American-formed international order. China's remarkable expansion towards the west, north and south suggests the Chinese expansion of its sphere in Asia. The only exception is Japan, whom China considers a regional rival and an ally of the US within the Asian region.[22] China will involve its neighbours in a series of institutional setups – such as the AIIB, CICA security architecture and corridors through Pakistan and Myanmar to the Indian Ocean. Chinese diplomacy will expand into Eurasia by constructing its "connectivity network" on political and economic areas, and combining various economic development strategy via bilateral and multilateral diplomacy in Eurasia.[23]

According to the Chinese Government, its promising objective is to construct a "community of shared interests, common destiny and responsibility", in order to lead its reform of global governance and develop a more equal international order. Chinese diplomacy seeks to expand its geographic concept of its "periphery diplomacy". China has been taking initiatives to develop and deepen economic cooperation, in order to construct a community of common destiny. China will construct a more concrete security cooperation framework, expand and deepen this security cooperation to a broader region. Beijing stresses on international institution building and rules-making for reforming global governance. China has been expanding its influence on developing countries and emerging powers through institution-building and multilateral mechanisms such as the SCO, CICA, East Asia Summit (EAS), and ASEAN Regional Forum (ARF). It aims to create a China-driven region of economic cooperation through OBOR and the AIIB. Beijing's strategic ambition is to become a global power, leading an equitable and rational international order.

Japan's Strategic Initiative under Shinzo Abe

Japan's Evolving Strategy in Response to the Global Power Shift and China's Rise

Japan has its national style and distinctive characteristics of foreign policy such as "Sino-centrism versus Japanese independence" and "the legacy of prolonged Japanese experience of feudalism". Japan's diplomacy shows the recurrent characteristics of realism. Japanese leaders have always sought to read the direction of the flow of events, the so-called "trend of the times", and to act in accordance with it. Japan seeks not to "change" it, but rather to "move with" it, so long as it is to the nation's advantage.[24]

Japan achieved its goals of security and prosperity by the 1980s, but it failed to respond promptly to new challenges after the Cold War. Since the 1990s, after the Cold War was over, Japan's search for a new presence and role in the transforming international system has been in flux. In the 2000s, Japan's foreign policy showed the inclination towards "reluctant realism": a greater focus on balance of power, growing realism and frayed idealism, higher sensitivity to security and a more determined push for an independent foreign policy. In the 2010s, Japan's strategic culture has been shifting from "traditional pacifism and passivity" towards a "more pronounced balance of power behaviour" in response to pressing external threats: China and North Korea.[25] Facing pressing security threats, Japan ended Yoshida Doctrine's prohibition against overseas dispatch of Japanese forces. Japanese governments have gradually eased a narrow interpretation of the Constitution banning participation in collective self-defence to accommodate a greater role and cooperation within the US-Japan alliance. Japan is set to acquire power-projection capability beyond strict self-defence policy. Japanese security community and media threw away its taboo to discuss the issue of nuclear weapons (although the self-prohibition on nuclear weapons since 1967 remains in place). Japan has also loosened the self-binding prohibition on the sharing of military technology and the export of arms since 1976, and removed its self-restriction of the defence budget at less than 1 percent of gross domestic product (GDP) as well as the 1969 Diet Resolution proscribing the military use of space. Japan's security reform has been prompted by the North Korean provocative nuclear/missile threats and China's military development and provocation.[26]

Japan's first National Security Strategy (NSS) of 2013 clearly explains the fundamentals of Japan's security. The NSS defines Japan's national interests and objectives, demonstrates the security environment surrounding Japan and challenges to the national security and explains the strategic approaches that Japan should take to address those challenges. Japan is a country with a "rich culture and tradition", one that upholds "universal values, such as freedom, democracy, respect for fundamental human rights and the rule of law". Japan has a wealth of "highly educated human capital and high cultural standards, and is an economic power with strong economic capacity and high technological capabilities". Japan's development is benefiting from an "open international economic system". As a "maritime state", Japan needs to play a leading role in maintaining and developing "Open and Stable Seas", under a maritime order that is based on such "fundamental principles as the rule of law, ensuring the freedom and safety of navigation and overflight and peaceful settlement of disputes". Japan's national interests are maintaining its own peace and security and ensuring its survival in order to achieve prosperity for the country and its people, as well as maintaining and protecting the international order based on universal values and rules.[27]

In the long term, Japan seeks three strategic goals: closer US-Japan alliance, closer relations with its neighbours in Asia and the development of a new Asia. Japan's role in greater Asia is bridging the gap between geo-economic Asia and geo-political Asia. First, Japan can maintain the US military presence as a stabiliser in Asia by reinforcing the Japan-US alliance. Second, Japan can foster economic cooperation and integration in Asia including China. Third, under the military-economic framework, mentioned above, Japan can continue its efforts towards long-term democratisation in Asia. The US military presence will remain crucially important to prevent an arms race and accidental conflict, while economic integration enhances multilateral regional cooperation framework in the long term.[28]

The Japan-US alliance as a foundation for Japan's security has played the role of a stabiliser and a pillar of the Asia-Pacific region since the 1970s. The alliance as a maritime alliance has also helped in the maintenance of the current regional order, the progress of free trade, and the creation of the "Asia-Pacific" region by interaction and trade. Japan in the periphery of Eurasia must deal with the increase of the Eurasian continental violence, and the alliance remains an ultimate guarantor. In the context of power shifts and transitions, Japan's role and responsibility to maintain peace and stability in Asia and the Indo-Pacific region are increasing. Facing a power shift and transition, the Japan-US alliance needs to find common policies towards China's assent. Japan pursues its careful policy in the oscillating US-China relations fearing the Nixon Shock again. Japan is more likely to adjust its strategy in increments depending on how these two powers conduct themselves, avoiding either the hardline China policy or the China-US strategic deal bypassing Japan.[29]

Since around 2005, after China clearly laid bare its anti-Japanese stance, the three post-Koizumi Liberal Democratic Party (LDP) cabinets of Shinzo Abe, Yasuo Fukuda and Taro Aso faced the persistent question of what kinds of bilateral relations Japan should build with the rise of China. Prime Ministers Shinzo Abe and Taro Aso chose to respond to the expanding China by increasing Japan's assertiveness. Prime Minister Yasuo Fukuda sought to emphasise "partnership" and "harmonisation of interests" with China. Since the Koizumi cabinet, there was a clear vision at play in bringing India and Australia into the mainstream of Japanese diplomatic initiatives as a counterweight to the rise of China. However, diplomatic strategies and policies cannot be properly implemented without a firm political ground and stability of government at home. From September 2009 to December 2011, the three Democratic Party of Japan (DPJ) cabinets tried to change the style of governance from the conventional LDP approach: Prime Minister Yukio Hotoyama's "East Asian Community", Prime Minister Naoto Kan's "TPP" and the nationalisation of the Senkaku Islands under Prime Minister Yoshihiko Noda. But their alternative policies could not bear fruits.[30]

The Abe Doctrine and Japan's Proactive Security Strategy[31]

Japan's proactive diplomacy under Abe has been gradually evolving with the so-called "Abe Doctrine". According to Shotaro Yachi, a former foreign secretary in Abe's cabinet, in his first term, "Mr. Abe has [had] a clear axis in politics. Mr. Abe aimed to bring strategy in Japanese diplomacy, and put emphasis on geo-political viewpoints as well as universal values. Mr. Abe worked on national security as a national foundation and practiced his assertive diplomacy." In his first term, the Abe cabinet proposed value-based diplomacy. Mr. Abe and Mr. Aso undertook steps towards proactive and strategic diplomacy. At the beginning of his first term, then Foreign Minister Taro Aso proposed the "Arc of Freedom and Prosperity: Japan's Expanding Diplomatic Horizons" in November 2006. This new pillar of

Japanese diplomacy put emphasis on universal values such as freedom, democracy, fundamental human rights and the rule of law, as well as market economy. Prime Minister Abe also visited India to deliver his memorable speech on the "Confluence of Two Oceans" on August 22, 2007. Abe's speech pointed out the geographic importance of a "broader Asia", now called the "Indo-Pacific" region, with regard to maritime security and of the potential and responsibility of Japan-India partnership as a maritime democratic alliance.[32] However, Abe resigned in less than a year, and this new and creative strategic vision has not properly succeeded.[33]

Abe resumed his second term in December 2012. The second Abe cabinet undertook several proactive security strategy and diplomatic initiatives. First, it aimed at security reform under the principles of "proactive contribution to peace" with international cooperation. Japan's proactive security policies are based on its place and role with its recognition of the current trend of globalisation, interdependence and a rapid change in global power balance. The Abe cabinet has been making various efforts on its security policy: the establishment of the National Security Council (NSC), the adoption of the NSS and National Defence Programme Guidelines (NDPG) in 2013, adoption of Three Principles on Transfer of Defence Equipment and Technology in 2014 and development of Security Legislation and Japan's Legislation for Peace and Security in 2015. As mentioned earlier, Japan's first NSS was adopted in 2013, and it is planned to be revised in 2018 to include Japan's effective response to North Korean missile threat and China's military expansion and Japan's Indo-Pacific Strategy in cooperation with the US, Australia and India.

Second, Prime Minister Abe outlined the "Five Principles of Japan's ASEAN Diplomacy" during his visit to Southeast Asia, his first trip abroad, in January 2013:

(1) Protect and promote universal values, such as freedom, democracy and basic human rights;
(2) Ensure that the free and open seas, as the most vital common asset, are governed by laws and rules and not by force, and to welcome the US rebalancing to the Asia-Pacific region;
(3) Further promote trade and investment, including flows of goods, money, people and services, through various economic partnership networks;
(4) Protect and nurture Asia's diverse cultural heritages and traditions;
(5) Promote exchanges among the younger generation to further foster mutual understanding.

Third, Abe advocated three principles on maritime security in his keynote address, "Peace and prosperity in Asia, forevermore", at the 13th Institute for International and Strategic Studies (IISS) Asian Security Summit (the Shangri-La Dialogue) in May 2014: making and clarifying claims based on international law; not using force or coercion in trying to drive claims; and seeking to settle disputes by peaceful means.

Lastly, Abe has proactively pursued the "Diplomacy Taking a Panoramic Perspective of the World Map". By the end of 2017, Abe had visited about 70 nations and regions attending more than 540 summit talks. In the context of China's expansionism, Abe has developed closer relationship with the US, India, Australia, ASEAN and Europe. Abe also manages the difficult diplomacy with China, Russia and the two Koreas. Compared to the yearly changing prime ministers of Japan, after Prime Minister Koizumi, Abe has provided a stable government and enhanced Japan's diplomatic relations in Asia and within the international community.

Japan's Free and Open Indo-Pacific Strategy in Response to China's OBOR

The Abe cabinet took a series of geo-economic initiatives to deal with the Chinese geo-economic strategies such as OBOR and periphery diplomacy. First, the Abe cabinet adopted the Development Cooperation Charter in February 2015. It changed the name of the Official Development Assistance (ODA) Charter adopted in 1992 and revised in 2003. The new Charter aims to promote Japan's development cooperation to contribute more proactively to peace, stability and prosperity of the international community. The ODA contributes to development and serves as a catalyst for mobilising a wide range of resources in cooperation with various funds and actors, and as an engine for various activities aimed at securing peace, stability and prosperity of the international community. Utilising Japan's experience of ODA in Asia, such as assisting infrastructure and human resource development with the spirit of self-help, the new Charter emphasises the concept of human security and quality infrastructure.[34]

Second, Abe announced the PQI at the 21st International Conference on the Future of Asia held in Tokyo in May 2015. From Southeast and Southwest Asia to Central Asia, the Asian region needs an immense amount of infrastructure development and financial resources as a leading growth centre for the world economy. In meeting this challenge, it is important to ensure the quality of infrastructure in order for a government to achieve sustainable development and to bring well-being and benefits to its people.

Japan promotes quality infrastructure investment in collaboration with other countries and international organisations. In collaboration with the Asian Development Bank (ADB), Japan is committed to providing approximately US$110 billion (about a 30 per cent increase) for quality infrastructure investment in Asia over the next five years. Japan's infrastructure initiative plays a catalytic role in further mobilising financial resources and the know-how of the private sector across the globe into Asia.[35]

Above all, the "Free and Open Indo-Pacific Strategy" was announced by Abe at the Sixth Tokyo International Conference on African Development (TICAD VI) held in Kenya in August 2016. The Indo-Pacific Strategy aims to create the synergy between the "two continents" and "two free and open seas" (see Figure 1). A key for stability and prosperity of the international community is the dynamism that is created by combining two continents and two oceans. Asia is rapidly growing and Africa has huge potential for growth. The strategy emphasises on improving the "connectivity" between Asia, the Middle East and Africa through Free and Open Indo-Pacific, and on promoting peace and prosperity in the region as a whole. Concerning Asia, Japan will expand infrastructure development, trade and investment, and enhance business environment and human development from East Asia as a starting-point, to the Middle East and Africa. Concerning Africa, Japan will provide nation-building support in the area of development as well as politics and governance. The Japanese way respects the ownership of African countries, and does not believe in either coercion or intervention against the will of any country. Japan has also been strengthening its strategic cooperation with India, the US and Australia.[36]

Japan's Indo-Pacific Strategy was originally formulated in response to China's OBOR by the Japanese Ministry of Foreign Affairs (MOFA) around Spring 2016. According to a Japanese journalist, Koji Sugimoto, this geo-political and geo-economic strategy pursues the following objectives: First, the Indo-Pacific strategy embraces China's proactive maritime expansion. It aims to constrain China's hegemonic maritime expansion, but neither excludes nor confronts the OBOR initiative. The Strategy encourages China's constructive role as a responsible player in the rules-based Indo-Pacific region. Second, the Strategy ensures US presence and commitment to Asia and the Indo-Pacific region. However, irrespective of Obama's pivot/rebalance policy towards Asia, the Trump administration's Asia policy remains uncertain. Third, the Indo-Pacific Strategy aims to strengthen India's critical role and the Japan-India strategic partnership through the Indo-Pacific Vision 2025.

Figure 1: Japan's New Foreign Policy Strategy

Source: MOFA, Japan, 2017

Japan-India Strategic Partnership and Its Indo-Pacific Vision

Japan and India have enjoyed an accelerated rapprochement since the 2000s. This Japan-India rapprochement is the result of growing convergence between the two countries' world views, interests and goals in regional and global issues. During their tenures, Prime Ministers Koizumi and Manmohan Singh emphasised the "strategic" partnership in the "region", and allowed Tokyo and New Delhi to become reliable partners in terms of strategic, security and economic issues and their China policies, to the extent described as mutually indispensable. The Japan-India bilateral partnership is now experiencing "a second honeymoon period". Japan and India have developed their strategic cooperation as a form of mini-lateral network in the Indo-Pacific region: the Japan-India-US trilateral partnership and the Japan-India-Australia trilateral partnership. The trilateral cooperation is virtually functioning as an alternative form of a Japan-US-India-Australia quadrilateral cooperation.[37]

Prime Ministers Shinzo Abe and Narendra Modi share a good personal relationship and aim to broaden and deepen the Japan-India partnership further. Between Abe and Modi, Japan and India have rapidly developed their comprehensive and multilayered partnership particularly on strategic and security terms, terming it a "special" strategic partnership in the Indo-Pacific region. In December 2015, the two leaders resolved to transform the Japan-India Special Strategic and Global Partnership into a "deep, broad-based and action-oriented partnership" and issued a joint statement, "Japan and India Vision 2025 Special Strategic and Global Partnership Working Together for Peace and Prosperity of the Indo-Pacific Region and the World". In September 2017, the two leaders held strategic discussions on a wide range of issues, and issued another Japan-India Joint Statement, "Toward a Free, Open and Prosperous Indo-Pacific". In response to Beijing's proactive expansionism, Tokyo and New Delhi, in collaboration with other partners, have reconfirmed their commitment to a peaceful, open, equitable, stable and rules-based Indo-Pacific region and beyond.

The two Asian maritime democracies seek the synergy between Japan's PQI and "Free and Open Indo-Pacific Strategy" and India's "Act East" Policy. Tokyo and New Delhi aim to "develop and strengthen reliable, sustainable and resilient infrastructures that augment connectivity within India and between India and other countries in the region", and to "advance industrial networks and regional value chains with open, fair and transparent business environment in the region". The Japan-India strategic partnership on infrastructure development and connectivity has geo-economic and geo-political implications for China's proactive expansionism.

Japan-India-China Strategic Triangularity in Asia and the Indo-Pacific

During this current period of global power shifts and transitions, international and regional security remains unstable and uncertain. China, Japan and India are actively pursuing their strategies, policies and initiatives based on their national interests and objectives. Beijing has its Asia-Pacific Vision in place while pursuing its geo-economic OBOR initiative. Tokyo and New Delhi issued the Japan-India Indo-Pacific Vision 2025 while pursuing their geo-strategic and geo-economic Indo-Pacific Strategy and Act East Policy. What is the geo-strategic and geo-economic confluence or difference in the two visions? It is possible to find both confluence and contrast between the two competing visions: China's Asia-Pacific Vision and Japan and India's Indo-Pacific Vision.

The Promise of Japan-India-China Triangularity

An idealist view promises peace, harmony and prosperity for everyone. The three Asian countries of China, Japan and India claim to maintain stable major-powers' relations and peaceful regional environment for economic development and prosperity in general. Both China's Asia-Pacific Vision and the Japan-India Indo-Pacific Vision 2025 emphasise peace and stability for economic prosperity, maintaining major-powers' relations, solving disputes by peaceful means, consultations and negotiations and the respect of the law. Both China's OBOR initiative and the Japan-India Vision 2025 stress on enhancing connectivity and infrastructure building for sustainable economic development and prosperity in the region. Both infrastructure initiatives put emphasis on openness, coordination, consultation and cooperation within and among countries. There is some idealistic confluence of these two visions, at least in their promising plans and general principles.

The Geo-economics of Competing Infrastructure Initiatives in Asia

A realist perspective focuses on competition and conflicts in international politics. States pursue power and influence via strategies and policies guided by their own national interests and objectives. A closer comparison of competing visions and policies in detail indicates considerable contrast and contradiction in the geo-economics of infrastructure initiatives of the Asian powers.

First, the two aforementioned visions show differences in geography and routes. On the one hand, China's OBOR initiative is "enhancing connectivity of Asian, European and African continents and their adjacent seas". In the Eurasian continent, it covers the Chinese periphery of Central Asia and Southeast Asia. OBOR in effect encircles India via its on-going connectivity projects of two corridors in India's strategic sphere of Jammu and Kashmir (J&K) and Myanmar. China's Maritime Silk Road encircles India via the so-called "Strings of Pearls" around the Indian Ocean. India has repeated its firm reservation to China's OBOR initiative. China's OBOR is its pivot to Eurasia to exclude the US and Japan.

On the other hand, the Japan-India Vision 2025 aims to "augment connectivity within India and between India and other countries in the Indo-Pacific region". It will enhance "connectivity in India and with other countries in the Indo-Pacific region including Africa". India is at the central position of connectivity in and between the Indo-Pacific region. The Japan-India ongoing connectivity project in India's Northeast Region connects India and Southeast Asia via China's strategic sphere of Myanmar. Japan-India cooperation on Southeast Asian connectivity would deter China's ambition to dominate Southeast Asia. In the Indo-Pacific Ocean, China's maritime expansion has faced strong opposition by neighbouring maritime countries, including maritime Southeast Asia, Japan, and India backed by the US. The Mekong region already has many international projects on infrastructure and connectivity involving various regional stakeholders including Japan, India and China.

Particularly, the contradictions and conflicts among major powers are concentrated on the expanding Chinese strategic periphery, including disputed maritime and territorial domains, which China claims are its "core national interests" and a matter of "sovereign rights": the militarisation of artificial islands in the South China Sea, stepping up of military activity in the Senkaku (Diaoyu) islands in the East China Sea, pressure on Taiwan as a democratic polity and aggravating of tension on the China-India border. China's strategic periphery remains the potential zone of conflicts with its increasing penetration and influence. The Indo-China region needs stability without the domination by external powers.

Second, the two broad regional visions put contrasting emphases on the role and place of China in terms of economic development and geo-economics. Analysts point out underlying strategies with national objectives under the competing regional visions. On the one hand, Beijing's Asia-Pacific Vision aims to expand China's greater role and influence to develop a China-centred regional order excluding the US influence. "China is prepared to take on greater responsibilities for regional and global security, and provide more public security services to the Asia-Pacific region and the world at large." China's greater responsibilities are to be pursued through its policy package including "the promotion of common development; the building of partnerships; improvement of existing multilateral frameworks; rule-setting; military exchanges; and proper settlement of differences". China's strategy is to rise and expand as a global power while maintaining stable relations with the US. In the Eurasian continent, China is developing a China-led economic and political international order.

On the other hand, Japan-India Indo-Pacific Vision 2025 will enhance cooperation with major regional partners like the US and Australia to enhance China's constructive role as a responsible major power. Japan and India "promote trilateral dialogues and cooperation with major partners in the region" through "the Japan-India-US Trilateral dialogue among the Foreign Ministers" and "the inaugural Japan-India-Australia Trilateral dialogue". Japan and India support the US rebalance policy to the Asia-Pacific to engage China as a "responsible major power" to play a "constructive role" in the region. In response, Beijing opposes Japan-India Strategic Partnership, Trump's cooperation to Japan's Indo-Pacific Strategy and cooperation among Japan, India, the US and Australia.

Third, China's Asia-Pacific Vision and the Japan-India Indo-Pacific Vision 2025 are different from each other in their guiding principles, values, norms and rules. On the one hand, Beijing's Asia-Pacific Vision claims to justify its "historical rights" as its "core interests", such as the Spratly Islands and the South China Sea:

> China supports the creation of international and regional rules set through discussion with all countries concerned rather than being dictated by any particular country. Rules of individual countries should not automatically become "international rules," and countries should not be allowed to violate the lawful rights and interests of others under the pretext of rule of law.

On the other hand, the Japan-India Indo-Pacific Vision 2025 stresses the underpinned principles and values for the two partners' "unwavering commitment to realise a peaceful, open, equitable, stable and rule-based order in the Indo-Pacific region and beyond. Japan and India uphold the principles of sovereignty and territorial integrity; peaceful settlement of disputes; democracy, human rights and the rule of law; open global trade regime; and freedom of navigation and overflight". Japan and India aim to enhance "regional efforts to evolve an open, inclusive, stable and transparent economic, political and security architecture in the Indo-Pacific region".

Fourth, the contrast between the two regional visions also emerges in the business code of conduct and practice on the ways of governance, lending practices and transparency. On the one hand, many studies point out the China-created government-funded bank is not transparent in its governance and lending practices and the OBOR infrastructure initiatives are governed by Chinese governmental influence and interests without considering the concerns of local people and stakeholders. Some observers argue that China has neo-colonial ambitions, in that Chinese business proposals and other projects are often neither sustainable nor profitable for the economy and interests of the local people and countries. The Chinese model of infrastructure development has led to debt traps, for example, in Sri Lanka and Cambodia. Such debt traps are not seen in the Japanese ODA-funded infrastructure development models, emphasising the virtues of transparency, sustainability and self-help. On the other hand, Japan-India Indo-Pacific Vision 2025 details Japan's accumulated experience and know-how of development cooperation suggested in its ODA Charter and its revised Development Cooperation Charter emphasising the "human security" concept. The Japan-India vision encourages the self-help model and local development plans of the countries being financed, considering the aspects of human security, environment and sustainability.

China's geo-economic policy utilizesits economic power and influence to seek an international environment more suitable for China. China's long-term strategic ambition seems to be the expansion of Chinese spheres of influence. China has proposed to working with the US to build a "new model of major-country relations" featuring non-conflict, non-confrontation, mutual respect and mutually beneficial cooperation. China's "peripheral diplomacy" rejects the US rebalance policy to Asia concerning China's "core national interests". China's increasing influence makes South Korea dependent on China as a "buffer state" and "neutralisation", leading it away from the US in the long term. China seeks for Japan's isolation. It seeks to increase its presence and capabilities in the South China Sea, and to construct its sea lane defence capability in the maritime domain (from the East and South China Seas via the Strait of Malacca to the Indian Ocean and the Middle East). Behind China's proposal to assist in the infrastructure building in Asia, the Middle East and Africa, OBOR in effect aims to expand China's hegemony and the encirclement of India by building military bases at strategic points in countries around the Indian Ocean. Further, China pursues its peripheral policy to Central Asia and Southeast Asia as a "buffer region". Beijing aims to build its energy route covering the Eurasian continent, from China to Central Asia to the Middle East and Europe, to control China-Russia relations, and to enhance politico-economic cooperation. In the long term, China seems to be constructing a "Eurasian partnership" for expanding China's sphere of influence to counter the US-led alliance network of North Atlantic Treaty Organisation (NATO) and the Asia-Pacific.[38]

Strategic Competition between Japan and China

Japan-China relations remain at the heart of geo-politics and geo-economics in East Asia. Japan and China have had an uneasy relationship for nearly 2000 years, with difficult modern and contemporary historical experience. Japanese and Chinese people are geographically so close and yet psychologically quite remote. Despite their common cultural roots, the two peoples have developed a sense of "commonality and disparity, interdependence and autonomy, mutual respect and suspicion, attraction and repulsion, and admiration and condescension" towards one another. Japan and China talk of their shared heritage and their identity as Asians, but they seek outside assistance to fight against one another. Despite their contribution to each other's cultural and modern transformation, their patterns of development have been vastly dissimilar. The fact and patterns of Japan-China relations have been among the most enduring features of East Asia.[39]

Table 1: Comparison of Key Strategies and Policies

	Japan	*China*
Regional strategy	Japan's Free and Open Indo-Pacific Strategy	China's Policies on Asia-Pacific Security Cooperation
National model	Japan as a beautiful country A maritime and trading nation	Chinese dream A traditional continental power and an ascending maritime power
Strategic concepts and objectives	Japan-India-US-Australia Quad Strengthening ASEAN integrity and India's role Enhancing China's responsibility	Expanding China's influence Managing and excluding the US influence Checking India, Japan, Russia Integrating China's peripheral regions
Main policies and security concepts	Proactive Contribution to Peace National Security Strategy Diplomacy Taking a Panoramic Perspective of the World Map Three Maritime Rules of Law Five Principles of ASEAN diplomacy Development Cooperation Charter	The reform and leadership of global governance Major-power diplomacy Periphery diplomacy New Security Concept in Asia China-ASEAN Community
Regional vision	A Free, Open, and Rules-based Asia and the Indo-Pacific (The concert of maritime powers with China as a responsible player)	A Community of Common Destiny (China-driven region in periphery countries)
Convergence	• Prosperity and sustainable economic development of Asia • Enhancing connectivity and infrastructure of Asia and Africa • Peace, stability, security, stable major power relations • Solving territorial and maritime disputes by peaceful means	
Competition	• Disputes on Senkaku (Diaoyu) islands and the East China Sea • Understanding and role of UNCLOS in maritime and territorial issues • Influence and leadership in rules-making and multilateralism • Values of human rights, liberty, freedom and democracy • Ways of economic integration and connectivity • Ways of governance, lending practice and transparency • China-centred economic integration and TPP regime • China's reach to the South and West and US rebalance to Asia • Influence in Southeast Asia and Central Asia • India-Pakistan-China in South Asia and the Indian Ocean	

China is seeking for a Sino-centric order, whereas Japan intends to maintain the liberal international order based on US leadership. Xi's China and Abe's Japan pursue proactive strategy and diplomacy in Asia and the world. The Chinese President Xi Jinping appeals to the nationalistic Chinese dream. Beijing's top priorities include China's domestic stability under CCP's leadership based on economic development, China-centred regional integration and order-building in Asia and China's leadership in global governance and reform. In the Asia-Pacific region, China seeks for China-US coordination and China-led economic and security order building. For these purposes, President Xi emphasises periphery diplomacy, new security concept in Asia and China's OBOR initiative as a strategic and geo-economic means. As a result, China's strategic expansion is of grave concern to Japan.

In contrast, the Japanese Prime Minister Shinzo Abe emphasises Japan's economic recovery by "Abenomics" with the ideal of Japan as a beautiful country. Abe's top priorities include Japan's economic recovery, global strategic diplomacy, Free and Open Indo-Pacific Strategy and proactive contribution to peace. In Asia and the Indo-Pacific region, Japan aims to maintain the current regional order based on the Japan-US alliance and its security network with partners like India, Australia, ASEAN and South Korea. Japan's PQI and Indo-Pacific Strategy are based on the Development Cooperation Charter as the strategic and geo-economic means. Japan's initiatives pose challenges to China's proactive expansionism.

Japan and China share some common objectives, but also have vastly divergent worldviews. The two countries share general objectives, such as prosperity and sustainable economic development in Asia; enhanced connectivity and infrastructure building in Asia and Africa; peace, stability, security and cooperation between major-powers; and solving territorial and maritime disputes by peaceful means. However, Tokyo and Beijing do not see eye to eye on various geo-strategic issues: territorial disputes on the Senkaku (Diaoyu) islands; leadership in rules-making and multilateralism; values of human rights, liberty, freedom, and democracy; understanding of United Nations Convention on the Law of the Sea (UNCLOS) in maritime and territorial issues; influence in Southeast Asia and Central Asia; and issues involving India-Pakistan-China in South Asia and the Indian Ocean. Furthermore, Japan and China have competing opinions on geo-economic initiatives: ways of economic integration and connectivity; ways of governance, lending practice and transparency; and China-centred economic integration and TPP regime. Despite various conflicts and competition, Tokyo and Beijing seek to develop and revise the Japan-China Strategic Partnership.

Developing Japan-India Strategic Partnership and China

India is a rising power that can compete with China. India's approach in geopolitics is guided by a balance between engagement and autonomy. New Delhi's strategy pursues its quest for multi-polarity and great power identity in world politics. New Delhi pragmatically engages with all the important players to ensure regional peace and stability, which is salient for further economic development. India's top priorities are to continue its economic development and modernisation, by seeking resources and technology from major partners.[40] From a Japanese perspective,

> India is becoming increasingly influential, due to what is projected to become the world's largest population, and to high economic growth and potential. India is also geo-politically important for Japan, as it is positioned in the center of sea lanes of communication. Japan will strengthen bilateral relations in a broad range of areas, including maritime security, based on the bilateral Strategic and Global Partnership.[41]

The Japan-India partnership is based on the two countries' common cultural traditions and their commitment to the ideals of liberal democracy. The two Asian democracies share commitment to the "ideals of democracy, tolerance, pluralism and open society". Furthermore, the development of Japan-India partnership has been facilitated by international and geo-political factors. First, Tokyo and New Delhi share concerns regarding China, especially its assertive rise and maritime expansion. Second, both Japan and India develop their cooperation with the US. Developments in the India-US relations facilitated India-Japan relations. Tokyo and New Delhi are now concerned about the uncertainty in US Asia policy, particularly under the Trump administration. Third, the two Asian democracies as reliable partners share a high degree of political, economic and strategic interests responding to regional and global challenges. Japan is the biggest donor for India and India is the biggest receiver of Japan's ODA. Tokyo and New Delhi are willing to cooperate to reform the United Nations Security Council. Japan and India have the bi-partisan domestic support to develop their overall Japan-India strategic partnership further.[42]

Policy debates on Japan-India partnership show both convergence and divergence regarding the international order and China policy. The leadership in both countries has sounded positive about forming a rule-based international order to check China's rise, for it to play a more constructive role as a responsible stakeholder. In particular, China's expansion has been a "decisive security and strategic factor" in Japan-India rapprochement. Since the mid-2000s, Tokyo and New Delhi have shared common strategic/security concerns to deal with a rising China and its maritime expansion. Chinese Navy's activities near Japan have aggravated Japan's concerns of Chinese provocative activities on the Senkaku Islands and the East China Sea. China's so-called "String of pearls" strategy around the Indian Ocean rim is perceived as its encirclement of India. India is also seriously concerned about the growing China-Pakistan coalition. China's rapid military development and its active naval activities are perceived as a threat both in Japan and India. Above all, China's militarisation of the South China Sea poses serious security challenges to Japan, India and other stakeholders in the Indo-Pacific region.[43]

Tokyo and New Delhi do not hesitate to embrace Beijing wherever their national interests converge with Beijing's. While Japan denounces China's aggressive behaviour, it has been amenable to the idea that China should play an influential role in the Six-party Talks to restrain Pyongyang. While Japan as an advanced country, so far finds itself comfortable with the Western-led economic order, India as a new rising power is uncomfortable with this existing Western-led economic order. Though India allies with Japan on security issues, it has aligned with China to forge a new alternative economic order that includes the China-led AIIB. China and India as new rising powers are cooperating together to reform the existing economic order. While Japan and India hedge against China's military development and expansion, Japan and India are at the same time committed to economic relations with China.[44]

Facing the uncertainty of global power shift, Japan and India are working together for peace, stability and prosperity of the Indo-Pacific region and beyond. The two Asian maritime pivots need to strengthen a "peaceful, open, equitable, stable and rules-based order" in the Indo-Pacific region and beyond. On security and geo-strategic side, Japan-India as key Asian maritime pivots need to encourage China's peaceful rise, coexistence, and its constructive role as a responsible major power in the region. The two Asian democracies need to strengthen ASEAN's leading role and centrality in ASEAN-centred regionalism, especially the EAS as a premier regional forum, to deal with geo-political and strategic issues. On economic and geo-economic side, Tokyo and New Delhi must also strengthen their broad support of ASEAN, particularly its integration through capacity-building and connectivity. Japan-India cooperation on infrastructure development on Northeast India will enhance the connectivity between South Asia and Southeast Asia, contributing to the prosperity and stability in the Asian region as a whole. Japan-India cooperation on "Asia-Africa Growth Corridor" project will enhance India's critical role in connectivity and linkage between East Asia, South Asia, the Middle East, and Africa. Japan and India may cooperate with China's OBOR on conditions of international standards of transparency, accountability and responsible governance. Through consultation and cooperation, Japan's Indo-Pacific Strategy and India's Look East Policy seek to synergise with China's OBOR for peace, stability and prosperity in Asia and the Indo-Pacific region.

Conclusion

Major-powers' relations and their strategies in Asia are competing with each other. The US liberal international order has been challenged by

China's rise and expansionism. In response to China's assertive and proactive expansion in the East and South China Seas, former US President Obama pursued a rebalance/pivot policy towards Asia. In response, President Xi pursued his action-oriented proactive external policy and OBOR initiative. China's ambitious OBOR initiative aims to expand China's influence in Eurasian continent from Asia toEurope, Africa and the Indo-Pacific Ocean. In turn, Abe pursued various proactive strategies, including the so-called Abe Doctrine based on Proactive Contribution to Peace. Japan's Indo-Pacific Strategy is a geo-economic tool that aims to embrace China's ambitious maritime expansion, ensure US pivot/rebalance to Asia and enhance India's role and Japan-India partnership in Asia and the Indo-Pacific regional order building.

India's role is crucial for both China's OBOR initiative and Japan's Indo-Pacific Strategy. Japan-India Special Global Partnership gains more importance in the context of changing dynamics of major powers in Asia and the Indo-Pacific region. The Japan-India partnership is pivotal for these two Asian maritime democracies to work together as responsible partners for stability in Asia and the Indo-Pacific regional order building. It can do so by encouraging China's constructive role as a major power, managing the China-US rivalry, strengthening stable major-powers' relations and developing an ASEAN-centred regional architecture in Asia and the Indo-Pacific region. Japan and India need closer cooperation to hedge against China's hegemonic maritime expansionism in the maritime domain. Thus, Japan and India are closely working together to foster a stable, peaceful and prosperous Asia based on a free, open, and equitable rules-based regional order building.

As the world is facing a global power shift, it is imperative to realise that a peaceful change, without disastrous and direct military confrontation, is the need of the times. The three Asian major powers – Japan, India and China – need to share responsibilities towards establishing peace, stability and prosperity in Asia, the Indo-Pacific region and the international community as a whole. Geo-strategically speaking, China's proactive maritime expansionism seeks to change the existing international status quo by coercion in the East and South China Seas. In response, Japan's Indo-Pacific Strategy aims to strengthen a free, open and rules-based international order together with its partners, the US, Australia and India. On the geo-economic side, Japan and India need a deeper and broader partnership to enhance economic cooperation on infrastructure building in India, and South Asia in general, and its connectivity with Southeast Asia and Africa. The Japan-India partnership needs to work towards ASEAN integration and enhancing ASEAN's role in the region. Otherwise,

ASEAN might disintegrate into a weak, unstable and troubled coalition because of hegemonic rivalries and excessive interference. Due to its increasing power and influence, China's responsible and constructive role is also critical for ensuring peace, stability and prosperity in China's peripheral region.

Japan, India and China need to work together to seek for synergy between China's OBOR Initiative and the Japan-India Indo-Pacific Vision 2025. To look into the reservations and concerns of geo-strategic issues of these three nations, India, for example, may host a dialogue on India-Japan-China strategic triangularity focusing on geo-economics, economic development assistance, infrastructure and connectivity development at the Track II level. Japan-India-China strategic triangular cooperation could benefit from the Japan-China-South Korea Summit and ASEAN Plus Three Summit. The three Asian nations can certainly work together to cope with salient common agendas and issues in the region, such as sustainable development, environmental issues, resource management, disaster prevention and confidence-building mechanism. The Japan-India-China strategic triangularity needs proper management of geo-political and geo-economic competition on infrastructure and connectivity network building. Competing geo-economic initiatives across Asia will have critical geo-political implications on Asia and the Indo-Pacific regional order.

NOTES

1. "China Says Doesn't Feel 'Targeted' by Trump's Indo-Pacific Concept", *Reuters*, November 12, 2017, at http://www.asahi.com/ajw/articles/AJ201711120016.html.
2. "India, US, Japan and Australia Must Not Target Us: China", *The Economic Times*, November 13, 2017, at https://economictimes.indiatimes.com/news/defence/india-us-japan-and-australia-must-not-target-us-china/articleshow/61628031.cms.
3. "China This Week: The "Indo Pacific": A New American Strategy for Asia?", *China-US Focus*, November 20, 2017, at https://www.chinausfocus.com/foreign-policy/china-this-week-the-indo-pacific-a-new-american-strategy-for-asia; Cary Huang, "US, Japan, India, Australia ... Is Quad the First Step to an Asian Nato?", *South-China Morning Post*, November 25, 2017, at http://www.scmp.com/week-asia/opinion/article/2121474/us-japan-india-australia-quad-first-step-asian-nato.
4. "Prime Minister Abe Decides to Cooperate with China's OBOR: Policy Shift from Anti-China Policy" (in Japanese), Kyodo, December 18, 2017, at https://this.kiji.is/315172162732819553.
5. For recent works on Japanese diplomacy and Asia, see, for example, Akio Watanabe (ed.), *The Asia-Pacific Region and the Development of New Regionalism* (in Japanese), Chikura Shobo, Tokyo, 2010; Mie Oba (ed.), *The Making of East Asia:*

Order, Integration and Stakeholders (in Japanese), Chikura-Shobo, Tokyo, 2016.

6. William H. Overholt, *Asia, America, and the Transformation of Geopolitics*, Cambridge University Press, New York, 2008; Yoichi Kato, "Why Do Geo-politics and Geo-economics Matter Now" and "Geo-political and Geo-economic Risks for Japan", in Rebuild Japan Initiative Foundation (ed.), *Japan's Geopolitics – 13 Risks and the Age of Geo-Economics* (in Japanese), Chuokoron-Shinsha, Tokyo, 2017.
7. For a path-breaking geo-economic analysis in Japanese, see Ken Jimbo, "Japan's Role in Emerging Geo-economic Trends", in Rebuild Japan Initiative Foundation (ed.), *Japan's Geopolitics - 13 Risks and the Age of Geo-Economics* (in Japanese), Chuokoron-Shinsha, Tokyo, 2017.
8. Taizo Miyagi (ed.), *Asia and Japan in the 21st Century – The Decade of the 2000s* (in Japanese), Minerva-Shobo, Kyoto, 2015.
9. As for Japanese literature on Japan and East Asia, see Akihiko Tanaka, *Japanese Diplomacy in Asia* (in Japanese), NTT Publishing, Tokyo, 2007; Takashi Shiraishi, *Maritime Asia vs. Continental Asia* (in Japanese), Minerva-Shobo, Tokyo, 2016.
10. Phillip C. Saunders, "China's Role in Asia: Alternative or Assertive?", in David Shambaugh and Michael Yahuda (eds.), *International Relations of Asia*, 2nd Edition, Rowman & Littlefield, Lanham, 2014.
11. Taizo Miyagi, No. 8.
12. For a review of Chinese diplomatic characteristics and history, see, for example, Michael Oksenberg, "China", in Robert A. Pastor (ed.), *A Century's Journey – How the Great Powers Shape the World*, Basic Books, New York, 1990.
13. Wu Xinbo, "China: Security Practice of a Modernizing and Ascending Power", in Muthiah Alagappa (ed.), *Asian Security Practice*, Stanford University Press, Stanford, 1998.
14. *East Asian Strategic Review 2017*, Japan's National Institute for Defense Studies, Tokyo, 2017.
15. For recent Japanese analyses of contemporary Chinese diplomacy, see Tomoki Kamo, "Chinese Diplomacy with its Confidence as Great Power", in Rebuild Japan Initiative Foundation (ed.), *Japan's Geopolitics – 13 Risks and the Age of Geo-Economics* (in Japanese), Chuokoron-Shinsha, Tokyo, 2017; Masayuki Masuda, "China's Strategy of One Belt, One Road", in Rebuild Japan Initiative Foundation (ed.), *Japan's Geopolitics – 13 Risks and the Age of Geo-Economics* (in Japanese), Chuokoron-Shinsha, Tokyo, 2017.
16. "Xi Jinping: Let the Sense of Community of Common Destiny Take Deep Root in Neighbouring Countries", October 25, 2013, Ministry of Foreign Affairs of the People's Republic of China, at http://www.fmprc.gov.cn/mfa_eng/wjb_663304/wjbz_663308/activities_663312/t1093870.shtml.
17. "China Issues White Paper on Asia-Pacific Security Cooperation", *Xinhua*, January 11, 2017, at http://english.cri.cn/12394/2017/01/11/4261s949427.htm.
18. Mark Leonard, "Geo-economics with Chinese Characteristics: How China's Economic Might Is Reshaping World Politics", World Economic Forum, January 2016.
19. "Vision and Actions on Jointly Building Silk Road Economic Belt and 21st-Century Maritime Silk Road", National Development and Reform Commission, People's Republic of China, March 2015, at http://en.ndrc.gov.cn/newsrelease/201503/t20150330_669367.html.

20. *East Asian Strategic Review 2017*, No. 14; Oliver Stuenkel, "OBOR: China's Pivot to Eurasia", *Post-Western World*, March 10, 2015, at http://www.postwesternworld.com/2015/03/10/chinas-pivot-eurasia/.
21. *East Asian Strategic Review 2017*, No. 14; Masayuki Masuda, No. 15.
22. Keiko Yoshioka, "Truth and Myth on China's 'Silkroad Economic Belt'" (in Japanese), *Gaiko*, 32, July 2015.
23. Oliver Stuenkel, No. 20; Masayuki Masuda, No. 15.
24. For a comprehensive review and analysis of Japanese diplomacy, see Kenneth Pyle, *Japan Rising – The Resurgence of Japanese Power and Purpose*, Public Affairs TM, New York, 2007.
25. Michael Green, "Japan's Role in Asia: Searching for Certainty", in David Shambaugh and Michael Yahuda (eds.), *International Relations of Asia*, 2nd Edition, Rowman & Littlefield, Lanham, 2014.
26. Kenneth Pyle, No. 24.
27. *National Security Strategy of Japan 2013*, Government of Japan, 2013, at www.kantei.go.jp.
28. Taizo Miyagi, *Japan's Post-war Diplomatic History as a Maritime Nation – Understanding the Path of Asian Evolution* (in Japanese), *Expanded Edition*, Chhikuma-Shobo, Tokyo, 2017. .
29. Yoichiro Sato, "Transition in Japan's Strategic Landscape", in Yoichiro Sato and Satu Limaye (eds.), *Japan in a Dynamic Asia*, Lexington Books, Oxford, 2006; Michael Green No. 25.
30. Taizo Miyagi, No. 8.
31. Makiko Takita, "The Abe Doctrine and Japanese Strategy" (in Japanese), *Sankei Shinbun*, November 3, 2017.
32. "'Confluence of the Two Seas': Speech by H.E. Mr. Shinzo Abe, Prime Minister of Japan at the Parliament of the Republic of India", Ministry of Foreign Affairs of Japan, August 22, 2007, at http://www.mofa.go.jp/region/asia-paci/pmv0708/speech-2.html.
33. Shotaro Yachi, *Japan's Strategy and Idealism* (in Japanese), Sankei Shinbun Shuppansha, Tokyo, 2009.
34. "Cabinet Decision on the Development Cooperation Charter", Government of Japan, February 10, 2015, at http://www.mofa.go.jp/files/000067701.pdf.
35. "'The Future of Asia: Be Innovative'" – Speech by Prime Minister Shinzo Abe at the Banquet of the 21st International Conference on the Future of Asia", Prime Minister of Japan and His Cabinet, Cabinet Public Relations Office, Cabinet Secretariat, May 21, 2015, at http://japan.kantei.go.jp/97_abe/statement/201505/0521foaspeech.html.
36. "Chapter 1: International Situation and Japan's Diplomacy in 2016", *Diplomatic Bluebook 2017*, Ministry of Foreign Affairs, Japan, at http://www.mofa.go.jp/policy/other/bluebook/2017/html/chapter1/c0102.html.
37. For comprehensive analyses of contemporary Japan-India relations, see Takenori Horimoto (ed.), *Introduction to Contemporary Japan-India Relations* (in Japanese), University of Tokyo Press, Tokyo, 2017.
38. Takashi Shiraishi, No. 9.
39. Kenneth Pyle, No. 24.
40. Tilti Basu, "India's Approach towards Indo-Pacific Triangularity", *IDSA News*,

May 27, 2016, at https://idsa.in/idsanews/indias-approach-towards-indo-pacific-triangularity (Accessed December 1, 2017).

41. *National Security Strategy of Japan 2013*, No. 27.
42. Takenori Horimoto, No. 37.
43. For Japan-India cooperation and China, see Shamshad A. Khan, "India-Japan Cooperation towards a Rule-Based Order in the Asia-Pacific: Mapping Indian and Japanese Strategic Thinking", Research Paper, Japan Institute of International Affairs (JIIA), 2015, at https://www2.jiia.or.jp/pdf/fellow_report/151218_Shamshad_Khan_JIIA_paper_Final.pdf (Accessed December 1, 2017); Emi Mifune, "Rising China and Japan-India Relations", in Takenori Horimoto (ed.), *Introduction to Contemporary Japan-India Relations* (in Japanese), University of Tokyo Press, Tokyo, 2017.
44. Shamshad A. Khan, No. 43; for contemporary India-China relations, see Jagannath P. Panda, *India-China Relations: Politics of Resources, Identity and Authority in a Multipolar World Order*, Routledge, London and New York, 2017.

10

Japan's Struggle in China-led Asian Economic Order: Reactive Initiatives in Asian Infrastructure

*Takashi Terada**

Introduction

According to the Asian Development Bank (ADB), there is a huge potential demand in the infrastructure development in Asia, amounting to US$26 trillion in 2016-30, or US$1.7 trillion per year, doubled from the previous version of its estimate.[1] Japan, as the largest "developed economy" in the region, has consistently considered initiatives towards regional economic cooperation as one of the main strategic fields in its regional diplomacy over decades. It has served as a primary source of capital, technology and foreign aid in the regional development. Yet, Japan's predominant position in Asian infrastructure and development has been challenged by China, which has formulated and promoted the Belt and Road Initiative (BRI) and established the Asian Infrastructure Investment Bank (AIIB). In November 2013, the Chinese Communist Party leadership announced that China seeks to build regional infrastructure and to enhance trade and financial links between its economy and those of Central and Southeast Asia, the Middle East and eventually Europe. To those ends, China has allocated US$40 billion to a Silk Road Fund and established the AIIB, funded with US$100 billion, to promote infrastructure projects and investment

*The author appreciates Yuma Osaki for his research assistance.

opportunities. China also became a key player in building other financial institutions such as the New Development Bank (NDB) in Shanghai and the New Silk Road Fund, smaller and equipped with less capital than the AIIB. With these initiatives on development and infrastructure, China has rapidly emerged as a challenger in the international economic stage to the existing western institutions such as the International Monetary Fund (IMF) and the World Bank. In May 2017, President Xi Jinping hosted the Belt and Road Forum (BRF) in Beijing which drew delegates from more than 130 countries and 70 institutions, including 29 foreign heads of state and government representatives, and positioned China as a champion of globalisation and free trade, as stated in the joint communique, demonstrating China's capacity and willingness to act as the global leader for infrastructure development.

This chapter intends to explore Japan's reactive commitment to quantitative and qualitative improvement in its government-led infrastructure export projects and to identify China's infrastructure initiatives as a key factor behind the promotion of Japan's infrastructure strategy. China's rapid rise as a global infrastructure leader with its proposal of new "silk roads", including transport links such as roads, railroads, ports and airports, is designed to establish a foundation for robust growth across the Eurasian Continent. Japan, however, has criticised China's approach as lacking any firm commitment to set high standards regarding environmental and social safeguards, influencing Japan's non-commitment to the AIIB. Symbolically, Japan came to seek and deepen its infrastructure investment strategy only after facing China's active engagement in this field. China's interest in quantity rather than quality in its infrastructure development approach urged Japan to re-emphasise the significance of high standards with a special attention to environment and human health, for instance. Japan's Finance Minister Taro Aso repeatedly raised his concerns about what the AIIB's governance would look like and stressed the need of the transparency. The chapter then illustrates Japan's growing interest in a partnership with India, which also finds China's economic rise a military threat, and argues the growth of the bilateral relations, partly sustained by their shared perception of China's economic and military rise. Given Japan's potential but partial acceptance of China's infrastructure strategy as a way of improving strained bilateral relations, it can be concluded that Japan is inclined to take a balancing stance in the face of China's growing regional and global influence and America's decreased interest in Asian infrastructure and multilateralism.

Japan's Suspicious Views towards AIIB

As the second biggest economy in Asia, Japan is China's most direct competitor in the region. The countries are often at odds – including over territorial issues – and the strategic rivalry for influence in the region between them is intensifying. As long as the US does not join the AIIB and remains uncommitted to it, Abe being loyal to the US-Japan alliance will not consider Japan's participation. Japan thus chose to confront the AIIB, rather than welcome the move. Indeed, the AIIB has been viewed as part of China's potential institutional weaponry against the ADB, in which Japan and the US serve as the two leading shareholders, a 15.6 per cent each. A cause for their shared concern is the belief that the AIIB would effectively give Beijing veto power and strong leverage, and thereby accelerate the internationalisation of the renminbi and encourage its use as a reserve currency, sustaining China's "geopolitical influence and regional leadership in Asia, while eroding US regional primacy".[2] China's possession of over 26 per cent of the voting rights, which affords it a de facto veto over important decisions, created doubts over the real purpose behind the AIIB's establishment. Japanese key political leaders, in addition to Prime Minister Abe, accordingly did not conceal their distrust arising from China's institutional ambitions and remarked upon Japan's negative view regarding the AIIB. Chief Cabinet Secretary Yoshihide Suga commented that "participation is impossible to the extent that these problems are not resolved"; and Minister of Finance Taro Aso has also repeatedly raised similar concerns about what the AIIB's governance will look like and reiterated a call for transparency.[3]

The US and Japan also share the same basic stance on the AIIB, at least according to their stated reasons for not joining. For one, while the AIIB is co-financing several projects with ADB and WB, the way of finance by the China-led institution is perceived to undercut existing institutions and could loosen lending standards. Furthermore, given the requirement for "fair governance", some infrastructural projects may be unsustainable, particularly in posing too much of a burden on the environment. Lastly, the AIIB may not prevent taxpayers' money from being used without restriction due to the lack of transparency.[4] The often-highlighted US$ 8 trillion demand for infrastructure projects in Asia can be questionable as China dominates the figure (nearly US$ 4.5 trillion) as seen in Figure 1. China can theoretically manipulate the AIIB to help its own infrastructure demands with the money coming from other more experienced nations and financial institutions with skilful expertise, possibly causing a moral hazard problem. In sum, since the AIIB will not mitigate these undesired effects that contradict current US and Japanese rules and norms concerning foreign aid and infrastructure investment, neither country has sought participation in the organisation. This assessment seemed to be sustained by Chinese Minister of Finance Lou Jiwei, who indicated that China has little appetite for rules that the US and Japan have cherished, given his claim that "the West puts forward some rules that we don't think are optimal".[5]

Figure 1: Demand for Infrastructure in Asia[6]
(2008 US$ billion)

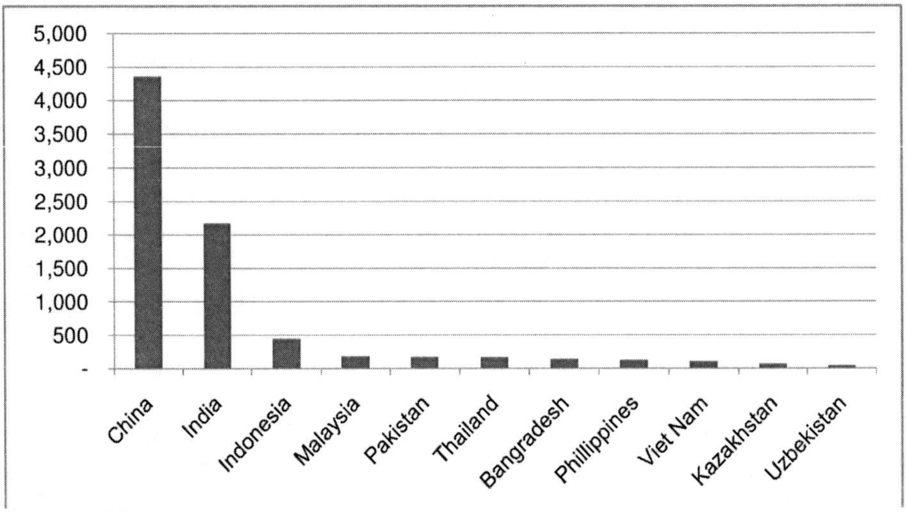

Source: ADBI 2010.

Prime Minister Abe sceptically described the Bank in the following manner: "A company that borrows money from a so-called bad loan shark may overcome immediate problems, but will end up losing its future. The [AIIB] should not turn into something like that."[7] More profoundly, AIIB's status as the first multilateral lender where China can play a dominant role through its 26 percent of the voting rights – giving it a de facto veto over important decisions – is another reason why Japan found it difficult to support the Bank. Japan's negative approach to the AIIB was partly based on the lingering view within Japanese policy circles that China could use the new bank to increase its economic influence in both regional and global settings. Yet, the AIIB's ascendance with the participation of major European Union (EU) member states surprised Abe, who reportedly condemned his policy aides, blaming the Finance and Foreign Ministries for misleading him by stating that the UK and Germany would not join the AIIB.[8] For its part, the US condemned the UK's decision to join the AIIB, saying that there had been virtually no consultation with the US and that it is "wary about a trend toward constant accommodation of China, which is not the best way to engage a rising power".[9]

Japan's Reforms in the Face of AIIB's Growing Influence

China's AIIB venture also forced Japan to push for reforms in the domestic system for its overseas infrastructure investment projects to challenge the Chinese ambition. In May 2015, Prime Minister Abe quickly responded by announcing a plan to increase investment in infrastructure in Asia by 30 per cent to US $110 billion during 2016–2020, and he also decided to expand the financial basis of domestic agencies, including the Japan Bank of International Cooperation (JBIC) and the Japan International Cooperation Agency (JICA), by supplying funds from the private sector. – US$ 2,204 million and US$ 569 million, respectively in 2018. In terms of fiscal investment and loan programmes in FY 2018, JICA will take additional US$ 5.5 billion and JBIC US$ 11 billion.[10] The total of updated budgets for Japan's foreign aid and infrastructure agencies went slightly beyond the capital of the AIIB ($ 100 billion).[11]

Before conceptualising the Partnership for Quality Infrastructure (PQI) in Asia, the Infrastructure System Export Strategy was already formulated in May 2013 under the Ministerial Meeting on Strategy relating Infrastructure Export and Economic Cooperation; and the June 2013 Japan Revitalising Strategy has aimed to stress the importance of creating new frontiers for growth by grappling with the international infrastructure market, which stipulated tripling infrastructure sales, from US$ 102 billion to 306 billion by 2020.[12] However, "in order to make innovations extend to every corner of Asia, we no longer want a 'cheap, but shoddy' approach", as announced by Prime Minister Abe;[13] the core idea is to support the "innovative" Asian infrastructure projects such as high-speed railway, advanced water treatment, energy-saving technology and efficient power plant with the high-standard Japanese finance. Thus, while the PQI aims to consolidate Japan's regional clout among the emerging Asian economies, it is also viewed as a competing formulation vis-à-vis China's infrastructure ambition.

Another incentive to beef up Japan's Asian infrastructure-oriented policy also came from China, but this time more directly when Indonesia decided to offer China the Jakarta–Bandung high-speed rail project contract in September 2015, despite Japan having been involved in the project since 2008 and China for hardly more than half a year. Key components of the Chinese proposal include funding that does not require the Indonesian

Government to provide any guarantee or state budget and a completion timeframe of only three years, which means the project will conclude while President Joko Widodo is still in office. Moreover, China has agreed to jointly produce train cars for not only high-speed trains, but also electric and light rail, all of which would be used in the local train system. To support the programme, China has even agreed to build an aluminium plant to provide raw materials to manufacture train cars. Overall, China's offer – perhaps only to win the bid – seems to be an overkill for only 150 km of railway. From one angle, China's generous approach to Indonesia's high-speed railway contract is a reflection of its eagerness to realise its BRI initiative, a strategy in which Indonesia forms the eastern edge. Yet, the land acquisition cost is expected to rise US $ 227 million, a huge financial burden already causing the delay in the construction.[14]

Japan's loss to China's bid was a blow to the Abe government's policy aims to attain economic growth by expanding infrastructural projects overseas, and Japan responded swiftly by shortening the application process from three years to one and by simplifying the implementation process by aligning paperwork needed for multiple steps, for infrastructure projects, especially those involving high-speed rail, which focused on improving quality. Japan has also become more expeditious in executing infrastructural projects in Asia by reducing funding guarantees by the recipient government from 100 per cent to 50 per cent in the case of yen loans, as well as by reforming the JBIC law to make risky infrastructure investments possible.

Importantly, changes in quantity and quality in its aid policy, all in pursuit of Asian infrastructure, were decided without any clear decision on potential participation in the China-led AIIB. In 2015, Hiroshi Watanabe, the then Governor of the JBIC, welcomed the AIIB for its ability to bring more funds to finance regional infrastructure projects, but he did not expect JBIC to cooperate with the AIIB on loans and investment because of the latter's looser governance criteria.[15] Japan also became more committed to the partnership with the ADB by establishing a trust fund within it financed by the JICA with a view to supporting the infrastructure projects led by the private sector including the public-private partnerships (PPPs).[16] This approach is also designed to help JICA provide its funds towards more risky projects beyond its traditional sphere.

Furthermore, the Japanese Government reinterpreted its Official Development Assistance (ODA) Charter with the Development Cooperation Charter, which explicitly focuses on relevant projects that fit Japan's strategic goals. Japan's choice of the Mekong region to offer US

$6.2 billion of new ODA in 2015, where China's economic and political presence is dominant, was designed to respond to China's predominant economic and political presence in the region, as seen in its substantial level of aid flows to Laos and Cambodia. For instance, China, especially Yunnan Province and the Guangxi Zhuang Autonomous Region, engaged in the "Greater Mekong Sub-region Economic Cooperation Programme" with four Indochina countries and Thailand, and actively delivered aid to the advancement of infrastructure and transportation sectors in the region. Consequently, the deepening economic interdependence between China and the region (e.g. the trade volumes of the two provinces of China soared five-fold with Myanmar, 11-fold with Laos, and six-and-a-half-fold with Thailand) enabled China to increase its influence in these countries.[17] Those states heavily dependent on China's economic aid, when it served as the Association of Southeast Asian Nations (ASEAN) chair, worked for China by making it difficult for ASEAN to take a united approach, resulting in it not acting as an effective shield to protect the interests of some other member states involved in the South China Sea disputes. In fact, when a Japan-Cambodia summit was held in November 2015, Abe used the occasion to deliver his concern over the South China Sea, saying he was "deeply concerned about unilateral changes to the status quo such as large-scale land reclamation, the building of outposts, and its use for military purposes" in the South China Sea, and that "Japan is focusing on a peaceful resolution to the situation based on the principle of the rule of law at sea".[18] This represents Japan's challenge to China's strategic economic diplomacy.

Strengthened Partnership with India

Symbolically, while Japan (as well as the US) has refused to accept China's economic sphere of influence, India has followed suit, creating a larger scope for the bilateral partnership. For instance, India's Prime Minister did not attend the BRF in May 2017, nor did India send any other official representative to the meeting, despite the fact that India is the second-largest financial contributor to the AIIB. India's rejection of Chinese infrastructure initiatives stemmed from its long-term territorial confrontation with China. Earlier that month, the AIIB approved its first-ever loan for a project in India, US $160 million to back a power project in the Indian state of Andhra Pradesh.[19] India sent an official letter expressing concerns about China's way of promoting the connectivity initiative. The primary reason is that India could not endorse development of the China-Pakistan Economic Corridor (CPEC), the flagship project of the BRI, which runs through parts of Pakistan-administered Kashmir that India considers its territory.[20] A former senior Indian Government official commented that

"China not only seeks to besiege India but is also sticking its nose into the territorial issue".[21] In fact, China has routinely threatened India; Chinese troops have conducted joint patrols with Pakistan's border police in the region since 2014.

Another issue over the border in terms of India's growing uncomfortable relations with China is the Doklam stand-off. In mid-June 2017, Chinese troops commenced the expansion of the existing road in Doklam, a narrow plateau at the disputed China-Bhutan-India tri-junction in the Sikkim Himalayas. Indian troops saw this as a challenge to the status quo, and it led to months of stand-off. With important security interests in this area, India has been supportive of Bhutan – Prime Minister Modi's first foreign destination since he took over.[22] The tensions eventually calmed as pressures resolved a week before President Xi hosted Prime Minister Modi in Xiamen for the BRICS (Brazil, Russia, India, China and South Africa) summit, but India symbolically decided to rely on Japan to prepare for the potential escalation of the border problem with China. As part of supporting Prime Minister Modi's priority policy of economic development, dubbed the "Act-East" policy, and reinstating the confidence of investors and good governance, which require a resilient infrastructure that facilitates industrial networks and regional value chains, Japan and India established the India-Japan Act East Forum. This is designed to advance road, electricity and other projects in the northeast part of India, close to the Doklam plateau, with Japan's US$ 345 million loan. Prime Minister Abe stated: "We will promote comprehensive support of India's northeastern states, and the two sides will further drive prosperity throughout the entire region."[23] The strengthened connectivity would serve to hamper China from encroaching on India's strategically significant territory.

Faced with these complicated bilateral relationships with China, India seeks to establish its own regional policy by strengthening comprehensive ties with Japan, as evinced by the announcement of the Asia-Africa Growth Corridor (AAGC), an India-Japan joint plan to support development in Africa. This project is part of Japan's "free and open Indo-Pacific" strategy, as the AAGC is part of the India-Japan Vision 2025 for the Indo-Pacific Region.[24] Correspondingly, Prime Minister Abe's visit to Ahmadabad in September 2017 included his and Prime Minister Modi's participation in the opening ceremony of India's first high-speed rail project, from Mumbai to Ahmadabad. The contract reassured Japan, particularly after its well-planned high-speed railway project in Indonesia was defeated by a much inferior Chinese one in 2015, and which cast a cloud on Japan's relations with Indonesia. Symbolically, the loss of the high-speed railway project to

China in Indonesia urged Japan to offer an even more attractive loan timeframe and Shinkansen technology for the high-speed rail project during Abe's previous visit to India in December 2015. Japan will offer a highly concessional loan of about US$ 13.5 billion at an interest rate as low as 0.1 percent, with the repayment duration of over 50 years, starting 15 years after the loan is provided.[25] This concession from Japan reduced the negative view in India about the need for such a high-cost project between two already well-connected cities in a developing economy.

While Japan and India have strengthened their economic ties, a key motive behind them has originated from their shared strategic interest in dealing with China's expanding sphere of influence in Asia through the AIIB and BRI. Symbolically, the Japan-India partnership likely develops within a broader regional strategic concept, the Indo-Pacific; and the concept was founded upon a speech given by Prime Minister Abe who proposed a strategic dialogue among Japan, the US, India and Australia. In his speech at the Indian Parliament on August 22, 2007, Abe introduced a new regional concept, a "broader Asia", by stating, "The Pacific and the Indian Oceans are now bringing about a dynamic coupling as seas of freedom and prosperity." A key message Abe wanted to carry to India and the region was to promote cooperation within this regional framework further by incorporating the US and Australia – four democratic nations located at opposite edges of these seas, based on their shared values such as democracy. The purpose behind this assertion was to discuss the ways of making East Asian countries, including China, accept these values.[26] This was a basis of the Indo-Pacific concept, officially announced in 2016 by Abe. Unlike the case in 2007, India has become supportive of the concept, a move which the US officially backed as seen in President Trump's frequent utterances of the concept during his Asia tour in October-November 2017. Australian Foreign Minister Julie Bishop also agreed to support it, as she mentioned in her meeting with her Japanese counterpart.[27] In fact, the 2013 Australian Defence White Paper has already identified the 'Indo-Pacific strategic arc' as a key framework of Australia's foreign and defence policy, followed by the 2017 Foreign Policy White Paper which used the Indo-Pacific term more than 70 times. As a result, a basic framework which may develop into a democratic quadrangle or strategic diamond was formed through the first quadrilateral meeting at the senior official level on the sidelines of the Association of Southeast Asian Nations (ASEAN)-sponsored summit meeting in Manila in November 2017. China's growing economic influence, potentially rewriting existing economic rules and norms, is a crucial factor behind the four nations coming closer, as the US Secretary of State Rex Tillerson suggested.[28] A remaining question is whether "India will have both the power and the motive to intervene decisively to support America against China to prevent it dominating East Asia"; Hugh White is however doubtful of the scenario and comments that it is "most unlikely".[29]

In short, sharing thorny experiences with China over territorial disputes, India and Japan are commonly responding to China's regional initiatives cautiously, considering the risk of the "unsustainable debt burden" the BRI would bring to the relevant countries, which highly rely upon China's investment. A major example is the US$1.4 billion Colombo Port City project in Sri Lanka, which left the country with a total of US$8 billion national debt burden only to China, and Tillerson criticised China's approach thorough the BRI by calling it "predatory economics", meaning that it offers "fledgling democracies and emerging economies financing mechanisms that saddled them with enormous levels of debt". Aiming to "improve inter- and intra- region connectivity, and to promote fundamental values such as freedom, openness and rule of law",[30] the free and open Indo-Pacific concept can serve as a convenient platform for Japan and India to flourish their bilateral partnership.

Japan's Possible Changing Stance towards BRI

While Prime Minister Abe has been active in his diplomacy, his attempt to ameliorate Japan-China relations has not succeeded, symbolised by the fact that Chinese leaders, President Xi Jinping and Premier Li Keqiang, have never visited Tokyo since they came into power in 2010. An approach Abe and his aides employed to break this diplomatic impasse was to show, not so palpably or enthusiastically, Japan's potential interest in China's grand strategy of BRI. In June 2017, Abe officially expressed his conditional support for his cooperative stance on the BRI for the first time. While noting that "it is critical for infrastructure to be open to use by all, and to be developed through procurement that is transparent and fair", he stated that "Japan is ready to extend cooperation" on the "One Belt, One Road" initiative.[31] It was quite a symbolic statement because it marked a clear shift from his conventional reluctant – rather challenging – stance on China's infrastructure initiative, after two years of proposing his own infrastructure initiative of PQI at the same international conference banquet. However, Abe still has not referred to the possibility of joining the AIIB, thus keeping Japan isolated, together with the US, from other G7 members. Abe still maintains scepticism, like his key cabinet members such as Aso and Suga, over concerns of fair governance, the sustainability of debt servicing on the part of the borrowing countries and whether the societal and environmental impacts are duly considered under the China-led international lending institution.[32]

It was Toshihiro Nikai, the Secretary General of the ruling Liberal Democratic Party and Takaya Imai, an Executive Secretary to the Prime Minister, who became pivotal in persuading Abe to take a softer turn on China's infrastructure initiatives. Nikai, a well-known pro-China politician, attended the BRF in May 2017 as the Japanese representative and, on the sidelines, delivered a letter from Prime Minister Abe to President Xi, which called for more visits to Tokyo by key Chinese figures.[33] Serving as Abe's right-hand man and formerly working as a senior official at the Ministry of Economy, Trade and Industry (METI), responsible for the formulation of Japan's economic growth strategy, Imai was also dispatched to Beijing to attend the forum without his boss. Imai met with Yang Jiechi, then China's top diplomat who recently got promoted to the Politburo, to convey Tokyo's wish to improve ties with Beijing.[34] Imai's meeting with Yang was unusual since Yang normally sees his Japanese counterpart, Shotaro Yachi, the Director-General of the Secretariat for the National Security Council (NSC). More surprisingly, Imai was reported to rewrite the content of the letter from Abe to Xi, including the passage concerning the government's conditional support for the BRI. Consequently, Abe unusually met with two top Chinese leaders in a single overseas visit: Xi in the Asia-Pacific Economic Cooperation (APEC) Summit in Danang, Vietnam, and Li in the East Asian Summit in Manila, Philippines. The Nikai-Imai faction with the priority of economic ties with China seemed to gain more prominence in Abe's foreign policy structure, while the US under President Trump had no interest in regional economic cooperation. This group will gain more significance when Japan and China start to coordinate Abe's visit to Beijing, a pre-condition of Li's and then Xi's visit to Tokyo.

It should be noted that China also wanted to improve relations with Japan since its neighbourhood diplomacy is in trouble: limited influence on North Korea's long-ranged missile and nuclear development; South Korea's deployment of a Terminal High Altitude Area Defence (THAAD) missile system which can survey all of mainland China; a Taiwanese President who advocates Taiwan's independence; South China Sea disputes with Vietnam, inviting criticism from non-claimants such as Australia and Singapore; and the aforementioned border disputes with India. Finally, with regard to Japan, Prime Minister Abe and his party won a landslide victory in the Lower House election held in October 2017, ensuring Abe's retention of power for more years. Xi Jinping found a good opportunity to make the relations with Japan better and change these diplomatic impasses surrounding China. As mentioned earlier, Japan's burgeoning interest and possible engagement in the BRI would be a welcome move for China, another factor for China's growing positive view on the relations with Japan.

Conclusion

This chapter attributes an upsurge of Japan's interest in and approach to Asian infrastructure vis-à-vis China's initiatives in the field through the launch of the BRI and the establishment of the AIIB. While giving cold shoulder to the BRI and AIIB, Japan has increased the amount of its infrastructure budgets as well as the amount of ODA by stressing the significance of quality, including health and environmental considerations. The fact that two adjectives, free and open, are linked with the Indo-Pacific is important as these two words symbolise the Japanese intention to distinguish its approach to economic diplomacy from that of China which exceeds in terms of the scale and quantity. Japan thus tends to stress, for instance, that the procurement should be transparent and fair, and that any infrastructure project should also be "economically viable and to be financed by debt that can be repaid, and not to harm the soundness of the debtor nation's finances".[35] Japan has worked together with the US, which also decided not to join the AIIB, and increasingly uses the phrase "free and open Indo-Pacific". If this concept were developed as a counterbalancing mechanism against the BRI with a different set of economic rules, based on freedom, openness, transparency and fairness, China would feel uncomfortable, resulting in harsher competition over regional economic hegemony. Yet, no concrete policy or institutional body has emerged within the Indo-Pacific concept, (for instance, President Trump decided to withdraw from the Trans-Pacific Partnership [TPP] and displayed his strong preference to bilateral approach to trade promotion ahead of regional integration), while more than 50 Chinese state-owned enterprises have invested in 1,700 BRI projects. Therefore, Hugh White views the 'Indo-Pacific' concept as "much more an expression of hope than of geo-strategic reality".[36] However, the BRI has been viewed in the Chinese military circle as instrumental in supporting Chinese military strategy through the provision of easy access to foreign ports, management of which is relegated to Chinese state-owned enterprises (SOEs) by the local governments due to a much higher return rate than ones offered by multilateral banks such as the ADB. China's courtship with Pakistan and Sri Lanka, located in key geographical areas covered by the BRI, through the provision of funds for the development of their ports enables Chinese military vessels and submarines to operate in the Indian Ocean, despite Chinese Foreign Minister Wang Yi's rejection of the view that the BRI is a

Chinese Marshall Plan, and that the initiative was "the product of inclusive cooperation, not a tool of geopolitics, and must not be viewed with an outdated Cold War mentality".[37] Therefore, the possibility exists that the Indo-Pacific concept will develop with more strategic elements by strengthening defence and security cooperation among the four nations (Japan, Australia, India and the US); and the success partly depends on India's determination to defy China's regional ambition.

NOTES

1. *Meeting Asia's Infrastructure Needs,* Asian Development Bank, 2017.
2. "China's Ambitious Silk Road Vision", *Strategic Comments*, 21 (6), 2015.
3. Bloomberg, April 14, 2015.
4. "Remarks by President Obama and Prime Minister Abe of Japan in Joint Press Conference", White House, April 28, 2015.
5. *Nikkei*, March 22,2015.
6. *Estimating Demand for Infrastructure in Energy, Transport, Telecommunications, Water and Sanitation in Asia and the Pacific: 2010-2020*, Asian Development Bank Institute (ADBI) Working Paper Series, 2010.
7. *Asahi Shimbun*, April 21, 2015.
8. Takao Toshikawa, "AIIB-wa Chugoku Gaiko-no Shori" [Triumph of Chinese Diplomacy over the AIIB], *Gendai Business*, April 4, 2015.
9. G. Dyer and G. Parker, "US Attacks UK's 'Constant Accommodation' with China", *Financial Times*, March 12, 2015.
10. Ministry of Finance, January 22, 2018.
11. Jiji Press, May 21, 2015.
12. *Japan Revitalization Strategy - Japan Is Back*, Prime Minister's Office, Japan, 2013.
13. *Nikkei*, May 21, 2015.
14. *Nikkei Asia Review*, March 18, 2016.
15. Bloomberg, April 3, 2015.
16. "ADB and Japan Partner to Support $16 Billion Infrastructure Investment", Asian Development Bank News Release, November 21, 2015.
17. Xiaobo Su, "Rescaling the Chinese State and Regionalization in the Great Mekong Subregion", *Review of International Political Economy*, 19 (3), 2012.
18. "Japan-Cambodia Summit Meeting", Ministry of Foreign Affairs, Japan, November 2, 2015.
19. Ankit Panda, "AIIB Makes Its First Loan to India, the Bank's Second-Largest Shareholder", *The Diplomat*, May 17, 2017.
20. "Official Spokesperson's Response to a Query on Participation of India in OBOR/ BRI Forum", Ministry of Foreign Affairs, India, May 13, 2017.
21. *Nikkei*, November 17, 2017.
22. *Asahi Shimbun*, September 20, 2017.
23. *Nikkei*, September 14, 2017.
24. Titli Basu, "Thinking Africa: India, Japan, and the Asia-Africa Growth Corridor", *The Diplomat*, June 3, 2017.
25. *Nikkei*, September 14, 2017.

26. Takashi Terada, "The Origins of ASEAN+6 and Japan's Initiatives: China's Rise and the Agent–structure Analysis", *The Pacific Review*, 23 (1), 2010, pp. 71-92.
27. "Japan-Australia Foreign Ministers' Working Dinner", Ministry of Foreign Affairs, Japan, November 7, 2017.
28. Rex Tillerson, "Defining Our Relationship with India for the Next Century", speech addressed at the Center for Strategic & International Studies, Washington D.C., October 17, 2017.
29. Hugh White, "Canberra Voices Fears but Who Will Contain The Dragon?", *The Straits Times*, November 25, 2017.
30. Kenji Hiramatsu, "Challenges and Prospects in the Indo-Pacific Region in the Context of India-Japan Relationship", speech given at the United Service Institution of India, November 2, 2017.
31. Shinzo Abe, "Asia's Dream: Linking the Pacific and Eurasia", speech by Prime Minister Shinzo Abe at the Banquet of the 23rd International Conference on "The Future of Asia", June 5, 2017.
32. "Transcript: Japanese Prime Minister, Shinzo Abe", *CNBC*, May 16, 2017.
33. *Japan Times*, May 16, 2017.
34. *Nikkei Asia Review*, July 8, 2017.
35. *New Straits Times*, December 19, 2017.
36. Hugh White, No. 30.
37. *China Daily*, March 8, 2015.

11

Infrastructure Development in Asia: Japan's New Initiatives and Its Cooperation with India

Ryohei Kasai

Infrastructure development has become one of the key issues in Asia, a vast region with some 60 per cent of the world population and rapid economic growth, in recent years. According to an estimate made by the Asian Development Bank (ADB) in February 2017, developing countries in Asia and the Pacific need more than US $22.6 trillion from 2016 to 2030, or US $1.7 trillion per year for infrastructure.[1]

While the purpose of infrastructure development is in the economic domain, it has been increasingly seen from strategic, diplomatic and political perspectives. Whether it is highway, pipeline or economic corridor, any decision by a certain country or a group of countries to develop such infrastructure is made based not only on thorough economic and social necessity considerations but also on its relations with neighbouring countries and strategic implications. That is to say, infrastructure development reflects their international and regional preferences and calculations, along with economic interests, and Asia is no exception.

This chapter aims to analyse Japan's infrastructure development strategy in Asia, with a particular emphasis on its collaboration and cooperation with India. The largest donor in many Asian countries for decades, Japan has contributed to the economic development in various fields including infrastructure building. However, the geostrategic landscape in the region is rapidly changing with the rise of China, which is also advancing its own development initiatives. What kinds of projects are Japan and India working on and what are the motivations and intentions? Are Japan-India partnership and Chinese initiatives compatible with each other, or are confrontations more likely? These are the questions to be discussed in this chapter. It first overviews how infrastructure development has become an important and vital component in the bilateral relations between Japan and India. It next examines specific infrastructure cooperation projects between the two countries, which now expands beyond South Asia, including the port development project in Iran and the "Asia Africa Growth Corridor" in comparison with the China-led "Belt and Road Initiative". It also makes an assessment on "Expanded Partnership for Quality Infrastructure", a new initiative by Japan. Finally, the conclusion is presented with references to several relevant issues.

Emergence of Infrastructure as a Significant Agenda in Japan-India Relations

Japan and India established diplomatic relations in 1952. While the two countries maintained cordial amity in the following decades, development of the bilateral relationship remained more or less limited, despite the historical and cultural ties for centuries. This was largely due to the Cold War, under which it was not a viable option for Japan, a staunch US ally, to unilaterally proceed to build a strong partnership with India, a non-aligned power but with strong ties with the USSR. Although there were positive trends in early 1990s, including Japan's financial aid to India in the wake of the economic crisis, India's nuclear test in May 1998 made Tokyo more cautious on its approach towards New Delhi.

It is since the visit to India by Japanese Prime Minister Yoshiro Mori in August 2000 that the two countries have forged a robust partnership in wide-ranging areas including trade and investment, security, development, energy, the United Nations Security Council reform, science and technology and cultural exchanges. During Mori's India visit, the first by a Japanese Prime Minister since 1990, he and Atal Behari Vajpayee, his counterpart, decided to establish "Global Partnership", which was later elevated to "Strategic and Global Partnership" on the visit to Tokyo by former Indian Prime Minister Dr Manmohan Singh in December 2006, reflecting the deepened and expanded cooperation and convergence of their interests.

Cooperation in infrastructure development has been one of the major drivers to advance the bilateral relations. The construction of Delhi Metro, started in 1998, was funded by Japanese Official Development Assistance

(ODA) and inaugurated four years later. Japan has also been involved in some of the major infrastructure projects in India such as the Delhi-Mumbai Industrial Corridor (DMIC) and the western part of the Dedicated Freight Corridor (DFC). India became the largest recipient of Japanese ODA in 2004, and has remained so since then.

2014 might be remembered as one of the landmark years in Japan-India relations with the visit to Japan by Indian Prime Minister Narendra Modi in August-September. Prime Ministers Modi and Shinzo Abe of Japan agreed to upgrade the bilateral ties to "Special Strategic Global Partnership."[2]

In the "Tokyo Declaration" issued after the summit meeting, Japanese commitment to support infrastructure development in India was reconfirmed. Prime Minister Abe unveiled Japan's "intention to realize US$33.2 billion of public and private investment and financing" in five years.[3] There have been numerous newly added projects such as the Chennai-Bangalore Industrial Corridor (CBIC), metro projects in Ahmedabad and Chennai, the construction of a new state capital in Andhra Pradesh and Smart City, among others. However, no other project attracted bigger attention than the Mumbai-Ahmedabad High Speed Rail (MAHSR). The Memorandum of Cooperation on introducing the *Shinkansen* (bullet train) system to the route connecting two commercially important cities was signed during Prime Minister Abe's India visit in December 2015. It was hailed as a major achievement for Japan's infrastructure diplomacy and brought much confidence to its team as it failed to win a similar bid in a high-speed rail construction in Indonesia just a few months earlier. Construction of the MAHSR started in September 2017 and is expected to be operational in 2023.

The upward trend in Japan-India relations has continued, bringing the two powers much closer than ever before. Prime Minister Abe became the first Japanese dignitary as the Chief Guest of India's Republic Day Parade in January 2014. At the end of the following year, he visited Delhi again and, together with Prime Minister Modi, set the vision and agenda for 2025. Japan and India advanced cooperation in security, among others. They institutionalized meetings, exercises and exchanges at different levels, such as the so-called "2+2" (Foreign and Defence) dialogue, annual defence ministerial dialogue and joint exercises between Japan Maritime Self-Defence (JMSDF) and Indian Navy as well as between Coast Guards of both countries. However, the fact that there are several limitations between the two countries should also be noted. Cooperation in defence procurement is one such area. For instance, both governments agreed to establish a Joint Working Group (JWG) to discuss cooperation in US-2, an amphibian aircraft manufactured by a Japanese company in May 2013, but no significant progress has been achieved yet, indicating that they have not addressed major bottlenecks including price and technology transfer.

Japan-India Cooperation Goes Regional, and Further

While the projects mentioned above are designed to improve transport and connectivity within India, a new trend has been seen in recent years. Japan and India are increasingly engaged in infrastructure projects aimed at connecting South Asia with Southeast Asia, West and Central Asia and even Africa.

Development Projects in North East Region and Andaman & Nicobar Islands

India's North East, sometimes referred as the "final frontier"[4] in the country, is a remote and landlocked region comprising seven small states, bordering China in the north, Myanmar in the east, Bangladesh in the south and Bhutan in the west. Insurgencies and poor connectivity with the other parts of India kept the level of economic development in the North East Region (NER) low. However, NER is rapidly becoming a destination for Japan's economic assistance while India itself is also working on the region's development more than before, as NER is now regarded as a vital land gateway to Southeast Asia by India as it implements the "Act East Policy." The reason why Japan attaches special importance to NER is mainly its strategic location, but a sense of familiarity based on the historical background during the Second World War[5] could be one of the other factors. Prime Minister Abe expressed Japan's "intention to provide ODA loans for the improvement of road network connectivity in northeastern states of India"[6] during his visit to New Delhi in December 2015. Improved connectivity between South and Southeast Asia through NER is expected to benefit the Mekong region countries,[7] where Japan has attached great importance and strengthened partnership by holding eight rounds of the Mekong-Japan Summit Meeting. It will certainly be beneficial for India too, as it will make initiatives such as the Mekong-Ganga Cooperation (MGC) and more recently, the Mekong-India Economic Corridor (MIEC). There is, therefore, a mutual interest for both Japan and India in developing infrastructure in NER.

In March 2017, the Japan International Cooperation Agency (JICA) signed an agreement with India for providing an ODA loan of ¥ 67,170 million (approximately US$740 million) for the improvement of National

Highways 51 (Meghalaya) and 54 (Mizoram).[8] In a meeting with the Union Minister of State for Development of North Eastern Region (DoNER) Dr Jitendra Singh in May 2017, Japanese Ambassador to India Kenji Hiramatsu said that Assam, Manipur and Nagaland are the preferred states in NER where the Japanese Government looks forward to invest, citing a "historic and emotional link".[9] His remarks indicate the future cooperation in infrastructure projects in the region. Meanwhile, the Indian Government also gave its nod for the widening of Imphal-Moreh route in Manipur by allocating US $250 million in July 2017.[10] These are interesting developments as Moreh, a town bordering Myanmar, is an Indian part of the proposed India-Myanmar-Thailand Trilateral Highway, expected to connect South Asia with Southeast Asia and boost trade, commerce and tourism. Furthermore, the Japan-India Coordination Forum for Development of North-Eastern Region was set up by the two governments in August 2017, in order to discuss and expand cooperation in NER.[11]

Another development project Japan is considering in India is to offer assistance for a power generation facility in Andaman & Nicobar Islands, remote islands designated as a Union Territory in the Indian Ocean. A Japanese Government proposal for the project states that it will overhaul and replace related facilities including three 5 MW diesel power generators in Chatham Power House in South Andaman island through Grant-in-Aid.[12] According to a news report, JICA will visit the site for the project in January 2018.[13] While the project is aimed at improving power generation capacity for a civilian purpose, the fact that India invited only Japan for an infrastructure project in the strategically significant islands located in the south of Bay of Bengal and between the Indian subcontinent and Southeast Asia shows how strong and deep the mutual trust is between the two countries. It may pave the way for larger projects in the islands in the future.

Chabahar Port Development

Japan and India have also articulated their intention to develop Chabahar, a port in the southeastern part of Iran facing the Gulf of Oman. Chabahar has strategic significance as it is located near Gwadar port in southwestern Pakistan, one of the strongholds in the China-Pakistan Economic Corridor (CPEC). An idea to jointly develop infrastructure and connectivity for Chabahar first appeared in Japan-India Joint Statement when Prime Minister Modi visited Tokyo in November 2016 in the context of "promoting peace and prosperity in South Asia and neighboring region".

New Delhi showed its interest in the Iranian port as early as 2003 when it agreed to develop the port and build a railway connecting Chabahar and Zaranj, a city in southwestern Afghanistan, with Tehran and Kabul. It also invested US $135 million to construct the Delaram-Zaranj Highway (Route 606) in Afghanistan, which became operational in 2009, as one of the efforts to improve road connectivity in the landlocked country. Chabahar can even be connected to Central Asian countries through the Afghan Garland Highway, thus enabling India's "Connect Central Asia" policy work. Its possible integration with the North-South Transport Corridor, a grand freight network project connecting India, Iran, Azerbaijan and Russia, is also being discussed.[14] These projects were expected to give New Delhi a strategic alternative to Afghanistan by bypassing Pakistan. Development of the Chabahar port, however, did not proceed swiftly as there were international pressures and economic sanctions on Iran over the nuclear weapons development programme.

The nuclear deal signed between Iran and the P5+1 (China, France, Russia, the UK and US; plus Germany) in Vienna in July 2015 gave a fresh momentum to the relevant countries including New Delhi and Kabul to engage with Tehran. In May 2016, within a year of the deal, a trilateral agreement to establish an international transport and transit corridor was signed by India, Iran and Afghanistan when Prime Minister Modi visited Tehran. The first phase of the port was inaugurated by Iranian President Hassan Rouhani in early December.[15] In addition, according to some news reports, India Ports Global Private Limited, a joint venture between Jawaharlal Nehru Port Trust and Kandla Port Trust, set up in January 2015, will invest US $85 million to build two more container berths and three multi-cargo berths for the port.[16]

Tokyo also became more positive towards Tehran after the Iran nuclear deal. Iran is one of the most important partners in the Middle East for Japan as it is not only the third largest crude oil exporter but also seen as an influential player in the rebuilding and reconciliation in Afghanistan. Prime Minister Abe, in deliberations at Lower House Budget Committee in February 2016, stated that he would "like to positively consider a visit (to Iran) at an appropriate time".[17] He reiterated his willingness to realise the visit when he had a meeting with President Rouhani at the sidelines of the United Nations General Assembly in New York in September 2016. It would have been a landmark event for Japan-Iran relations as no Japanese prime minister has visited Iran since 1978.

However, the result of the US Presidential election in November 2016 changed the course of these developments. The new President Donald Trump maintains his hard-line attitude towards Iran, indicating more than once a possibility to suspend or even scrap the nuclear deal, which would re-impose the economic sanctions lifted earlier. Interestingly, the Japan-India Joint Statement in September 2017 made no reference to Chabahar despite the growing cooperation in the bilateral relations. While the reason is not made public, Tokyo may have changed its attitude on this agenda from "positive engagement" to a "wait-and-see" mode. Nevertheless, it does not mean Tokyo's strengthening of ties with Tehran was given a pause. Masahiko Komura, the Vice President of the ruling Liberal Democratic Party and former Foreign Minister, visited Tehran as Prime Minister Abe's special envoy in September 2017. Japanese Ambassador to India Hiramatsu, in an exclusive interview with *The Hindu* in May 2017, pointed out the Tokyo's continued interest, saying "an important port like Chabahar is good for regional connectivity".[18]

Asia Africa Growth Corridor

In further advancing their bilateral cooperation, Japan and India have started looking outward. Their destination is Africa, a huge continent with more than 1.2 billion people living in 54 countries. The two countries expressed to "work jointly and cooperatively with the international community to promote the development of industrial corridors and industrial network in Asia and Africa" thorough "realising a free, open and prosperous Indo-Pacific"[19] during the visit to Tokyo by Prime Minister Modi in November 2016. Commonly known as the "Asia Africa Growth Corridor" (AAGC), the idea to develop such corridors was stressed again in the bilateral Joint Statement in September 2017.

It was not the first time that Africa was taken up as an agenda in the context of Japan-India cooperation. Tokyo and New Delhi began a director general/additional secretary level dialogue on Africa as early as 2010, and five rounds of talks were already held by 2016. Both the capitals have also been engaged in establishing a long-term partnership with African countries: Tokyo International Conference on African Development (TICAD) since 1993 and India-Africa Forum Summit (IAFS) since 2008.

Efforts to conceptualise the idea and identify issues are already being undertaken by think tanks in Japan, India and Southeast Asia. "A Vision Document" was released at African Development Bank meeting in Ahmedabad, India, in May 2017. Prepared by Research and Information System for Developing Countries (RIS), Economic Research Institute for ASEAN and East Asia (ERIA) and Institute of Developing Economies (IDE-JETRO), the document states that the AAGC has the following four components: development and cooperation projects, quality infrastructure and institutional connectivity, capacity and skill enhancement and people-to-people partnerships.[20] It also stresses that India and Japan have a complementary role in realising the AAGC.[21] RIS, ERIA and IDE-JETRO continue to work on this ambitious project including "organizing a joint study team with other think tanks and organizations in Asia and Africa" as the next step.

While details are to be worked out, the AAGC is also expected to facilitate economic activities between the two greater regions. Automobile industry could become such an example. While the commencement of construction for the MAHSR may have been the highlight of Prime Minister Abe's visit to India in September 2017, there was another important event from the perspective of wider regional connectivity: the inauguration ceremony of Suzuki's new plant in Gujarat in the presence of Prime Ministers Abe and Modi, along with Chairman Osamu Suzuki. Both the prime ministers attended the ceremony not only because the new plant is a symbol of "Make in India" but also because it has the potential to become a hub for exporting its automobiles overseas, including Africa. The AAGC will benefit not only Japan and India but also African countries, providing a new route for exporting their products. Furthermore, this corridor may connect Southeast Asia (MIEC) and parts of East and Southern Africa (Kenya-Tanzania-Mozambique growth zone) via India's Jawaharlal Nehru and Kochi ports.

Since its inception, the AAGC has been compared with "One Belt, One Road", or the "Belt and Road Initiative" (BRI) as it is now called. It is often seen as a joint strategy by Japan and India to "counter" the BRI, a China-led grand development and connectivity strategy stretching from Asia to Europe and even Africa.[22] It could be said that the BRI was one of the major catalysts for Tokyo and New Delhi to propose their own connectivity strategy, as both governments kept a distance from it. When the Belt & Road Forum for International Cooperation was held in Beijing in May 2017, attended by as many as 130 countries from Asia, Europe, Africa, and South America and 70 international organisations, Japan did not send any ministerial-level official delegation[23] amid the deteriorating bilateral relations over the disputed islands. India also decided not to be a part of the forum on the grounds that the CPEC, one of the crucial components of the BRI, passes through Pakistan-controlled Kashmir where India claims its sovereignty, coupled with its growing concern over the 21st Maritime Silk Route crossing the Indian Ocean.

However, more positive remarks and moves are being seen in both the capitals at the same time. In June 2017, Prime Minister Abe stated that the BRI held "the potential to connect East and West as well as the diverse regions found in between" and Tokyo was ready to extend cooperation as far as it would "come into harmony with the free and fair Trans Pacific economic zone, and contribute to the peace and prosperity of the region and the world" during a banquet of "The Future of Asia", an annual international conference organised by *Nikkei*, one of the leading Japanese newspapers.[24] This remark was interpreted as a "cautious turn"[25] towards the BRI, reversing the earlier impression that Tokyo was highly leery of the Beijing's grand development strategy. New Delhi, too, seems to go by a "case-by-case" approach towards China-led initiatives. While keeping away from the BRI, it became one of the founding members in the Asia Infrastructure Investment Bank (AIIB) when it signed the Articles of Agreement in June 2015. Prof. Srikanth Kondapalli of Jawaharlal Nehru University points out that India is the second largest contributor and secures more than 8 per cent voting rights at the bank.[26]

Furthermore, New Delhi is also involved in the Bangladesh-China-India-Myanmar Economic Corridor (BCIM-EC), another infrastructure and connectivity project in the BRI.

Quality Matters: Japan's New Initiatives in Infrastructure Strategy

As observed above, Japan has proposed and started working on various infrastructure and connectivity projects in Asia and beyond with India as an indispensable, reliable partner. But it should be noted that Japan has not only launched the specific projects but also unveiled its guiding principles recently: "Partnership for Quality Infrastructure (PQI)". First proposed by Prime Minister Abe in his speech at *Nikkei*'s "The Future of Asia" International Conference in May 2015, Japan, through PQI, aims to "spread high-quality and innovative infrastructure throughout Asia", providing US $110 billion in collaboration with the ADB over the next five years.[27]

An emphasis on "quality" is the central concept in PQI; Prime Minister Abe used the term seven times in his speech. However, it does not necessarily mean that Tokyo attaches significance to "quality" over "quantity". According to a document jointly issued by the relevant ministries including Ministry of Foreign Affairs and Ministry of Finance, what Japan pursues is "quality *as well as* quantity", referring to not only depending on ODA by JICA but also developing and utilising private funding including Public-Private Partnership (PPP) through the Japan Bank for International Cooperation (JBIC) and Japan Overseas Infrastructure Investment Corporation for Transport & Urban Development (JOIN).[28] In an effort to allay concerns that PQI may be costly, the document stresses that it is "indeed cost-effective in the long run", citing that it is "easy to use and durable, as well as environmentally friendly and disaster resilient".[29] It also mentions several successful examples of "Quality Infrastructure Investment" such as Delhi Metro in India, Ulan Bator Railway Fly-over in Mongolia and Vietnam-Japan Friendship Bridge in Vietnam, inter alia.

The introduction of the *Shinkansen* system in the MAHSR project could be the next hallmark of PQI. Its safe, effective and speedy construction is crucial as Japan aspires to win more bids in the other routes of high-speed rails within India in the coming years. PQI could also serve as the core policy principle in planning and implementing specific projects, such as the AAGC, in the future. Moreover, Japan expressed its intention to apply PQI worldwide as "Expanded Partnership for Quality Infrastructure" at the G-7 Ise-Shima summit meeting in May 2016.

Conclusion

Collaboration and cooperation in infrastructure and connectivity areas has become an integral part in Japan-India relations. Both countries have been engaged in such projects not only in India but also in the extended neighbourhood and even in Africa across the Indian Ocean. While these initiatives are manifestations of the improved and expanding bilateral relations based on mutual trust and interests, they are also being brought about, in part, as an answer to the BRI. Certainly, concerns on the China-led initiative exist, such as it would eventually turn out to be China-ruled, encircle India and undermine Japan's position in the region. On the other hand, Beijing also sees the AAGC with caution, and even suspicion, saying it would mean "division", not "connectivity", for Asia and Africa.[30] In order to allay such concerns on both sides, dialogue and coordination on a regular basis should be sought after in one way or another. It should be recalled that the ADB and AIIB co-financed development projects including building highway in Pakistan and the green energy corridor in India.[31] Furthermore, in order to make the Japan-India cooperation more viable and effective, consultation and possible involvement with related regional organisations including the Indian Ocean Rim Association (IORA), African Union (AU) and Bay of Bengal Initiative for Multi-Sectoral Technical and Economic Cooperation (BIMSTEC) could also help. While competition may be likely in infrastructure and connectivity initiatives, synergy between Japan-India and China would benefit the region. After all, neither Japan-India nor China can satisfy the huge infrastructure needs in Asia single-handedly.

NOTES

1. "Asia Infrastructure Needs Exceed $1.7 Trillion Per Year, Double Previous Estimates", Asian Development Bank, February 17, 2017, at https://www.adb.org/news/asia-infrastructure-needs-exceed-17-trillion-year-double-previous-estimates (Accessed September 1, 2017).
2. In India's partnership with foreign countries, the term "special" is used only for Japan, Russia (Special and Privileged Strategic Partnership) and South Korea (Special Strategic Partnership).
3. "Tokyo Declaration for Japan-India Special Strategic Partnership", Ministry of Foreign Affairs (Japan), 2014, at http://www.mofa.go.jp/files/000050532.pdf (Accessed September 10, 2017).
4. Jonathan Glancey, "Finding Nagaland: India's Final Frontier", *The Guardian*, December 11,2010, at https://www.theguardian.com/travel/2010/dec/11/india-nagaland-jonathan-glancey (Accessed September 10, 2017).
5. In 1944, Japanese Imperial Army attacked Imphal and Kohima, both in the current state of Manipur, though it was defeated by British Army. Indian National Army (INA) of Subhas Chandra Bose, in alliance with Japan, also joined the battle.
6. "Japan and India Vision 2025 Special Strategic Partnership: Working Together for Peace and Prosperity of the Indo-Pacific Region and the World", Ministry of Foreign Affairs (Japan), at http://www.mofa.go.jp/s_sa/sw/in/page3e_000432.html (Accessed September 10, 2017).
7. Thailand, Myanmar, Vietnam, Cambodia and Laos.
8. "JICA Extends ODA Loan of approximately INR 4,000 Crores for the North-East Road Network Connectivity Improvement Project (Phase I)", Japan International Cooperation Agency, 2017, at https://www.jica.go.jp/india/english/office/topics/press170331_01.html (Accessed September 10, 2017).
9. Dr Singh appreciated Japan's engagement with NER and identified development of inland waterways transport along Brahmaputra River down to Bay of Bengal and supplementing the Venture Fund as possible areas of cooperation in the future. See "Japan Offers Support for Northeast Projects", Press Information Bureau (India), 2017, at http://pib.nic.in/newsite/PrintRelease.aspx?relid = 161902 (Accessed September 10, 2017).
10. "Imphal-Moreh Highway in Manipur to be Widened", *The Hindu Business Line*, July 12, 2017, at http://www.thehindubusinessline.com/economy/policy/imphalmoreh-highway-in-manipur-to-be-widened/article9763332.ece (Accessed September 10, 2017).
11. "Inauguration of Japan-India Coordination Forum for Development of North Eastern Region", Embassy of Japan in India, 2017, at http://www.in.emb-japan.go.jp/itpr_en/00_000394.html (Accessed September 10, 2017).
12. Anken gaiyosho (Outline for the Project Proposal), Ministry of Foreign Affairs (Japan), February 23, 2016, at http://www.mofa.go.jp/mofaj/gaiko/oda/files/000132459.pdf (Accessed January 10, 2018).
13. Roopa Lall, "Efforts on to Achieve 24x7 Power Supply Soon: Sanjeev Khirwar", *The Echo of India*, December 19, 2017, at http://echoofindia.com/port-blair-efforts-achieve-24x7-power-supply-soon-sanjeev-khirwar-136526 (Accessed January 10, 2018).
14. Meena Singh Roy, "International North-South Corridor: Re-energising India's

Gateway to Eurasia", *IDSA Issue Brief*, August 18, 2015, at http://www.idsa.in/system/files/issuebrief/IB_msroy_180815.pdf (Accessed September 25, 2017).

15. "The First Phase of Chabahar Port Inaugurated", *Business Standard*, December 4, 2017, at http://www.business-standard.com/article/economy-policy/first-phase-of-chabahar-port-inaugurated-117120300540_1.html (Accessed January 11, 2018).
16. "India, Iran and Afghanistan Sign Chabahar Port Agreement", *Hindustan Times*, May 24, 2016, at http://www.hindustantimes.com/india/india-iran-afghanistan-sign-chabahar-port-agreement/story-2EytbKZeo6ze ClpR8WSuAO.html (Accessed September 11, 2017).
17. "Abe shushou Iran houmon 'sekkyokuteki ni kentou'" (PM Abe Positively Considers an Iran Visit), *Sankei News*, February 3, 2016, at http://www.sankei.com/politics/news/160203/plt1602030022-n1.html (Accessed September 10, 2017).
18. Suhasini Haidar, "Japan Pitches for Chabahar Port", *The Hindu*. May 8, 2017, at http://www.thehindu.com/todays-paper/tp-national/japan-pitches-for-chabahar-port/article18405900.ece (Accessed September 10, 2017).
19. Japan-India Joint Statement, Ministry of Foreign Affairs (Japan), at http://www.mofa.go.jp/files/000202950.pdf (Accessed September 11, 2017).
20. *Asia Africa Growth Corridor Partnership for Sustainable and Innovative Development: A Vision Document*, Research and Information System for Developing Countries, Economic Research Institute for ASEAN and East Asia, and Institute of Developing Economies, 2017, at http://www.eria.org/Asia-Africa-Growth-Corridor-Document.pdf (Accessed September 10, 2017).
21. Ibid.
22. Dipanjan Roy Chaudhury, "India, Japan Come up with AAGC to Counter China's OBOR", *The Economic Times*, May 26, 2017, at http://economictimes. indiatimes.com/news/economy/policy/india-japan-come-up-with-aagc-to-counter-chinas-obor/articleshow/58846673.cms (Accessed September 11, 2017); Avinash Nair, "To Counter OBOR, India and Japan Propose Asia-Africa Sea Corridor", *The Indian Express*, May 31, 2017, at http://indianexpress.com/article/explained/to-counter-obor-india-and-japan-propose-asia-africa-sea-corridor-4681749 (Accessed September 11, 2017).
23. A quasi-official delegation led by Toshihiro Nikai, Secretary-general of the ruling Liberal Democratic Party and one of the Japanese politicians who have strong ties with China, participated in the BRI forum. Nikai also met Chinese President Xi Jinping and handed a personal letter from Prime Minister Abe. See "Xi Tells LDP's Nikai He Wants to Move Bilateral Relations 'in Right Direction'", *The Japan Times*, May 16, 2017, at https://www.japantimes.co.jp/news/2017/05/16/national/politics-diplomacy/xi-tells-ldps-nikai-wants-move-bilateral-relations-right-direction/#.WdX1oxO0OA8 (Accessed September 12, 2017).
24. "Asia's Dream: Linking the Pacific and Eurasia (Speech by Prime Minister Shinzo Abe at the Banquet of the 23rd International Conference on the Future of Asia)", Prime Minister of Japan and His Cabinet, June 5, 2017, at http://japan.kantei.go.jp/97_abe/statement/201706/1222768_11579.html (Accessed September 12, 2017).
25. "Japan Takes Cautious Turn toward China's 'Belt and Road'", *Nikkei Asian Review*, June 6, 2017, at https://asia.nikkei.com/Spotlight/The-Future-of-Asia-2017/

Japan-takes-cautious-turn-toward-China-s-Belt-and-Road?page=1 (Accessed September 12, 2017).

26. Srikanth Kondapalli, "Why India Is Not Part of the Belt and Road Initiative Summit", *The Indian Express*, May 15, 2017, at http://indianexpress.com/article/opinion/why-india-is-not-part-of-the-belt-and-road-initiative-summit-4656150/ (Accessed September 12, 2017).
27. "The Future of Asia: Be Innovative", Speech by Prime Minister Shinzo Abe at the Banquet of the 21st International Conference on the Future of Asia, Prime Minister of Japan and His Cabinet, May 21, 2017, at http://japan.kantei.go.jp/97_abe/statement/201505/0521foaspeech.html (Accessed September 20, 2017).
28. "Partnership for Quality Infrastructure: Investment for Asia's Future", Ministry of Foreign Affairs, Ministry of Finance, Ministry of Economy, Trade and Industry and Ministry of Land, Infrastructure and Transport (Japan), May 21, 2015, at http://www.meti.go.jp/english/press/2015/pdf/0521_01a.pdf (Accessed September 25, 2017).
29. Ibid.
30. Xin Xiao, "India-Japan Growth Corridor May Mean Division, Not Connectivity, for Asia, Africa", *The Global Times*, August 1, 2017, at http://www.globaltimes.cn/content/1059129.shtml (Accessed October 1, 2017).
31. "ADB Expands Clean Energy Project in India with AIIB cofinancing", Asian Development Bank, September 28, 2017, at https://www.adb.org/news/adb-expands-clean-energy-project-india-aiib-cofinancing (Accessed October 5, 2017).

12

China in Japan-India Security Ties: Infrastructure as a Factor

Satoru Nagao

Today, furthering cooperation in military relations between Japan and India has become increasingly plausible. It is an important point to bear in mind with regards to infrastructure projects. For example, Japan is building roads in northeast India. One must also note that India has not accepted any foreign aid in its northeastern region, except from Japan. Furthermore, in the Andaman and Nicobar Islands in India, Japan is planning to support infrastructure developments, for example, various port projects. It is also investing to build ports in the coastal area of the Bay of Bengal, including the Trincomalee port in Sri Lanka. Moreover, Japan and India are collaborating to improve the Chabahar port in Iran.[1] In addition, Japan, India and the US are collaborating to aid countries in the African continent. The Asia-Africa Growth Corridor (AAGC) is an apt example of Japan-India cooperation in Africa. So, what is the reason behind Japanese and Indian collaborations on these projects lately?

The most salient feature of these projects is that they were developed after China launched similar infrastructure projects in the same area. For example, China is improving infrastructure projects in the India-China border area near northeast India. It had started building the Hambantota port project before the initiation of the Japan-India Trincomalee port project in Sri Lanka. China is also building the Gwadar port near Chabahar. Moreover, it is investing vast sums in Africa. Therefore, Japan-India investments in infrastructure projects there have a competitive edge with the Chinese projects.

Thereby, this chapter attempts to address two key questions: Why are Japan and India expressing concern over China's infrastructure projects? How are China's development schemes and the Japan-India collaboration related?

Figure 1: Location

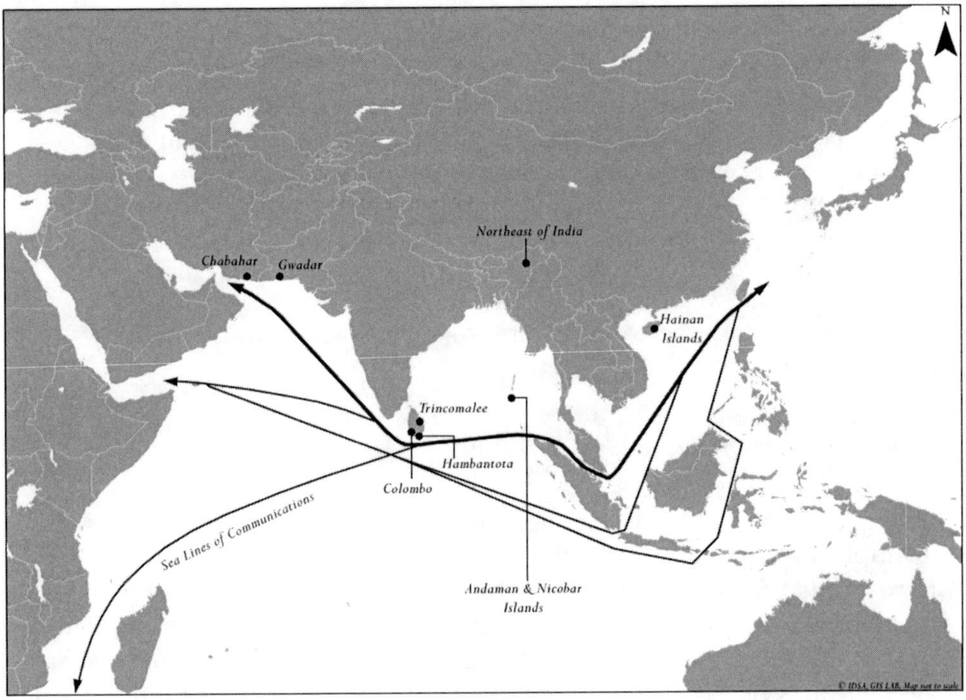

Source: Prepared by the author.

Why Are Japan and India Concerned about China's Infrastructure Projects?

What are the difficulties presented by China's infrastructure projects? Currently, China has reorganised its infrastructure projects under the framework of "One Belt and One Road" (OBOR), renamed the Belt and Road Initiative (BRI). One can understand the Japanese and Indian perceptions of OBOR just by looking at their stances. In a speech delivered in June 2017, Japanese Prime Minister Shinzo Abe expressed Japan's will to support the BRI if certain conditions were met, which are "essential for projects to be economically viable and to be financed by debt that can be repaid, and not to harm the soundness of the debtor nation's finances". He also emphasised that the projects must maintain "harmony with a free and fair Trans-Pacific economic zone", and that it was "critical for infrastructure to be open to use by all, and to be developed through procurement that is transparent and fair".[2] This "conditional cooperation" approach of Japan indicates that it has some relation to certain Chinese projects which did not meet these conditions.

India's stance is even stronger. When China invited India to the OBOR Forum, India refused to join and issued a statement which pointed out at least two problems concerning OBOR. This statement read,

> Connectivity initiatives must follow principles of financial responsibility to avoid projects that would create unsustainable debt burden for communities ...Connectivity projects must be pursued in a manner that respects sovereignty and territorial integrity ... Regarding the so-called 'China–Pakistan Economic Corridor', which is being projected as the flagship project of the BRI/OBOR, the international community is well aware of India's position. No country can accept a project that ignores its core concerns on sovereignty and territorial integrity.[3]

China's Loan System as a "Trap" for Recipients, Putting Them under Chinese Influence

China's projects are not economically viable for the host nations. For example, in the case of Sri Lanka, 400 years of operation will be necessary to repay its US$ 5 billion debt to China. Consequently, to compensate for the debt, Sri Lanka decided to give China the right to use the Hambantota port for 99 years.[4] Even so, the interest rate for China's loan is 6.3 percent. This figure is very high when compared with the interest rate for the Japan-led Asia Development Bank or World Bank: 0.25-0.3 percent.[5] Thus, from the perspective of Japan and India, China's loan system is a "trap" for host countries, placing them under China's influence.

Indeed, this practice presents severe difficulties to both Japan and India. For a long time, Japan was the foremost donor to Northeast Asian and Southeast Asian countries; China itself was the top recipient of its Official Development Assistance (ODA) during the 1990s. Moreover, throughout those years, Japan never pressured or influenced the ODA recipient countries. However, ever since China started providing greater assistance to build infrastructure in those regions, Japan has faced strong pressure. As a symbolic case, in 2015, Indonesia chose China's bullet train system over Japan's. Because China obtained the bullet train technological know-how from Japan, the experience has served as a warning to Japan to prepare for a tough competition with China in Asia.

The case of India – the largest country of South Asia – represents a similar situation because China's influence has eclipsed India's in South Asia. India's influence there has been largely based on geography.[6] For example, India has spent about 80 percent of the total defence budget of all South Asian countries, including India, Pakistan, Maldives, Sri Lanka, Bangladesh, Bhutan and Nepal. India also shares ethnic similarities with all other South Asian countries, such as Punjabis with Pakistan, Tamils with Sri Lanka and Bengalis with Bangladesh. Thus, India's influence has penetrated deeply. Consequently, an important concern for India is growing intervention in South Asia from outside. In fact, it is the same reason why it sent troops to Sri Lanka when the US set up a naval communication facility there in the 1980s.[7]

China's intervention in countries around India, except for Pakistan, started at the end of the 1980s, when India was actually confronting a difficult situation in Sri Lanka. Chinese influence was growing through the export of weapons to countries like Sri Lanka, Bangladesh and Myanmar (Figure 2). Furthermore, since the 2000s, China also started developing infrastructure projects in Pakistan, Sri Lanka, Bangladesh and

Figure 2: China's Weapons Exports to Sri Lanka, Bangladesh and Myanmar[10]

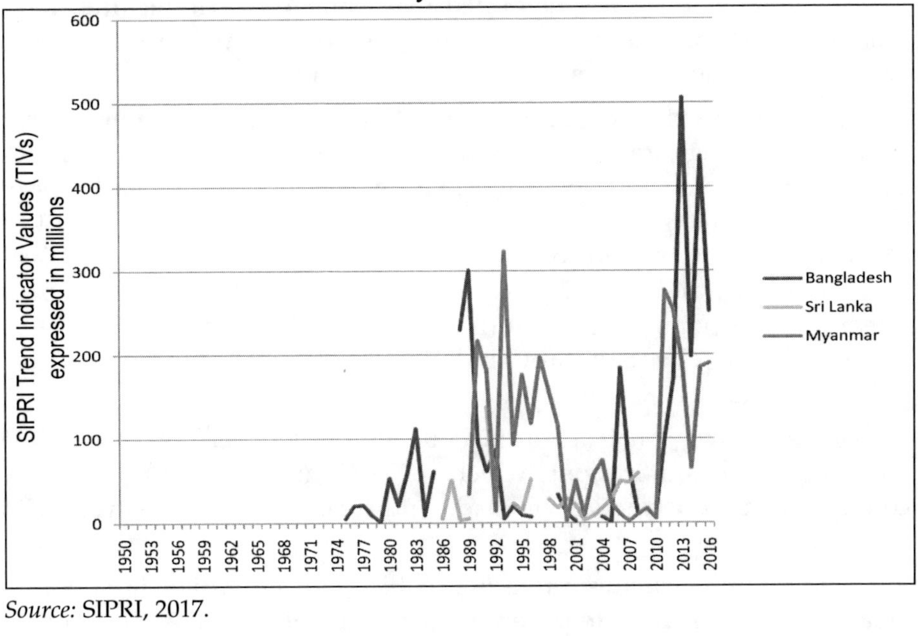

Source: SIPRI, 2017.

Myanmar for its "String of Pearls Strategy".[8] Apparently, Pakistan and Sri Lanka are unable to repay their debts to China,[9] thus increasing China's leverage on them.

China Ignores Core Concerns Related to Sovereignty

It is claimed that while pursuing development projects, China tends to disregard the host country's sovereignty issues. For example, although the Permanent Court of Arbitration rejected China's ownership claim of 90 percent of the South China Sea in 2016, it is still ignoring the verdict and building new airports on the artificial islands in the South China Sea.[11] Although these facilities have a clear military purpose, the Ministry of Foreign Affairs of the People's Republic of China Hua Chunying claimed in 2016 that these facilities are civil.[12] This indicates that China's ostensibly civil infrastructure development projects are indistinguishable from Chinese military infrastructure.

In fact, China can deploy ballistic missile submarines under the protection of fighter jets launched from these artificial islands and then exclude all foreign ships and airplanes that might identify their submarines.[13] A report issued by the Japanese Prime Minister Shinzo Abe pointed out, "If Japan were to yield, the South China Sea would become even more fortified."[14]

Along similar lines, China is developing natural gas in the East China Sea unilaterally. Japan has identified that China's gas rig facilities have radar systems. If China wants to deploy more forces in the East China Sea, China can use these radar systems to guide their military forces.[15]

China's infrastructure projects in South Asia are another example. First, China is building strategic roads in Pakistan-occupied Kashmir (PoK). Because it is concerned about its total dependence on its Sea Lines of Communication (SLOCs) from the Middle East through the Strait of Malacca, it has attempted to build an alternative route via Middle East-Pakistan-China and Middle East-Myanmar-China through the Indian Ocean. China's ports project countries around India provide an alternative route for China. The road through PoK is a vital part of the Middle East-Pakistan-China route.

However, any construction in PoK without the permission of India has sovereignty implications, which so far China has been ignoring by continuing its construction of roads and holding of joint patrols with Pakistan.

Chinese infrastructure projects in Tibet near the India-China border area also have security implications for India. Not only is the Chinese military infrastructure modernisation (such as roads and airports to deploy armed forces) progressing very rapidly, but there are other conditions in favour of China as well. China's armed forces can be deployed in two days if needed in border areas, whereas India needs one week for preparation because roads on its side are insufficient.[16] Therefore, chances of them being in a more dangerous situation are three times larger than Chinese forces in the border area.[17]

Along with such rapid military modernisation, the scope of Chinese military activities has also been expanding. Since 2011, India has recorded more than 300-500 incursions every year. The frequency of their air force incursion has also increased in the Tibet region.[18] In 2017, when China tried to build roads in Doklam, where both Bhutan and China have staked their claim, as a security provider of Bhutan, India had to deploy forces to stop China's construction. If the road were to be built, it could support 40 tonne loads, enabling Chinese tanks to run smoothly.[19] In addition, the location of Doklam presents a weak case for India as it gives way to the so-called "Chicken's neck". This narrow area connects the mainland and northeast regions of India by a very narrow strip. Consequently, there are doubts that the main purpose of this road was to quench China's military concerns.

In the Indian Ocean, China is building ports in countries circumjacent to India: Gwadar in Pakistan, Hambantota in Sri Lanka, Chittagong in Bangladesh and Kyaoukpyu in Myanmar. Although on surface these port projects are meant for civil use, there are doubts expressed by Japan and India that China is going to use these ports to deploy its naval forces to safeguard its SLOCs. In fact, China started to increase its military activities in the Indian Ocean region (IOR) since the mid-2000s. In 2012, at least 22 contacts were recorded with vessels suspected to be Chinese submarines patrolling in the IOR.[20] In 2014, at least two Chinese submarines and one submarine support-ship were docked at a port in Sri Lanka. In 2015, one Chinese submarine was called at the port of Karachi in Pakistan. By May 2017, the Indian Navy tracked at least seven Chinese submarines in the IOR.[21] Chinese activities indicate that China has a desire to expand its area of influence in the region, thereby putting at risk India's nuclear ballistic missile submarines and SLOCs.

So, whether it is the South China Sea or PoK, China's tendency to expand in areas not ventured before has accelerated. Through its aid policies, it creates a huge debt on the recipient country, thereby drawing them under its influence. Furthermore, under the pretext of building infrastructure, China has deployed more and more forces in different countries, hence strengthening its presence in a self-reinforcing manner.

The smaller countries have caved in, feeding China's quest to expand its military influence. In this current geopolitical scenario, Japan and India are undoubtedly together in abating this concern in their neighbourhood and halting its progress.

How Are China's Infrastructure Projects and Japan-India Collaboration Projects Related?

Recently, Japan and India have started collaborating on infrastructure projects in areas like northeastern India, Andaman and Nicobar islands, Trincomalee in Sri Lanka, Chabahar in Iran and the African continent. How are these projects related to China's projects?

Northeast India

Japan and India have negotiated quite a few strategic road projects in northeast India. The main purpose of these projects is the promotion of economic development in northeastern Asia. Moreover, it will ease India's access to Southeast Asia by giving it access to a land route. Most importantly, these constructions offer two countering tactics against Chinese influence. First, if India succeeds in developing the northeast like mainstream India, it might help to subside insurgencies there and have a better defence in the India-China border area. In the past, there have been several rebellions against the Indian Government such as those in Nagaland, Mizoram, Manipur and Assam. India has even suspected China's support to these rebels for a long time. In 1978, however, China told the then External Affairs Minister of India Atal Bihari Vajpayee that supporting rebels was a thing of the past.[22] Nonetheless, stabilising the region by developing its infrastructure is important for India's security. In addition, Arunachal Pradesh in northeast India is being claimed by China as "South Tibet". If Japan were to support India's infrastructure project in northeast India, it would be much easier for India to complete it faster and defend its borders more competently.

Second, if India and Southeast Asia are well connected through trade and investments, it could mitigate China's influence in the region. Although the Chinese stance and attitude in the South China Sea has not really been benign to the claims of various Southeast Asian countries, they still have not taken any firm stand against China's activities. One reason is that these countries are economically heavily dependent on trade with China. In this scenario, there is an even greater need for them to reach out to other trade partners and neutralise China's influence on them. Consequently, road connections between India and Southeast Asia, and Japan's East-West

Economic Corridor from Vietnam to Myanmar can play a major role in helping these countries.

Andaman and Nicobar Islands in India

The Andaman and Nicobar Islands are strategically important because they are situated near the Malacca Strait and SLOCs. In 2001, India set up the Andaman-Nicobar Command, with an integrated Army, Navy and Air Force headquarters. Furthermore, it is modernising its infrastructure to deploy larger warships, patrol planes and transport planes to other locations. When contact was lost with a Malaysian airplane in the Indian Ocean, India had dispatched warships to search for the plane from these islands.

While no detailed official report has been published, some media reports have indicated that Japan has decided to support radar facilities and power plants in these islands.[23] It is also planning to build a fibre cable connection with mainland India. While on paper these are civil projects aimed to resolve electric power shortage difficulties, there is a high probability that these projects have a strategic purpose against China's maritime expansion.

As described above, Chinese submarines supported by their support vessels have found their way into the Indian Ocean. Though there have always been infiltrations – from a weak flotilla to a few warships and destroyers – in recent years, seven nuclear and conventional submarines have also been tracked in the IOR, sailing from the Hainan Island of China though the South China Sea and Malacca Strait. However, the strategic location of Andaman and Nicobar Islands gives India the leverage to track China's submarine activities in the Ocean. Since 1993, India has been engaging with Singapore in joint naval exercises. Since 2002, it has also started coordinated patrols with Indonesia, and with Thailand since 2005. It is also set to join the Malacca Strait Patrol Group, comprising Singapore, Indonesia, Thailand and Malaysia.[24] According to recent media reports, Japan, India and the US are planning to install a submarine detecting sensor system along the coastline of the Bay of Bengal.[25] Furthermore, India and the US are also negotiating to share information on Chinese manoeuvring of its submarines from Hainan to the Indian Ocean. In this regard, Japanese investments in the region have come at the most opportune time for India if it wants to enhance its naval capacities and deflect Chinese submarines.

Trincomalee Port in Sri Lanka

While China is busy developing the Hambantota port project in Sri Lanka,

Japan and India too are seeking to build the Trincomalee port in the region and neutralise China's influence. Although Hambantota is located rather strategically for China's BRI, it has certain deficits which must be overcome for it to be completely functional. Firstly, because there are no large cities near the port, the use of commercial ships there is rare. Only Colombo has sufficient capacity, but it is located far away from Hambantota.

Secondly, even if China wanted to move ships from the port to Colombo, the connecting road does not have the required capacity to carry the load. Hence, most ships refrain from using this particular port and use Colombo port instead.

Thirdly, Hambantota port does not meet the criteria to be used as a hub. Though it is strategically placed near the SLOCs and has an opportune location, for example, ships coming from Europe unload their cargoes there and ships going to Bangladesh, Myanmar, etc. reload their cargo, it does not have certain facilities. Hambantota is a small town with only a big international airport and a five-star hotel, offering no facilities to ships' crews for a stopover before moving on to the next destination. Therefore, most ships are redirected to use the Colombo port as a hub.

Notwithstanding these issues, this particular port can be most fittingly used as a naval port due to its location near the SLOCs. Therefore, when the Sri Lankan Government decided to lease the Hambantota port to China for 99 years, both Japan and India (and US, too) expressed strong concerns. As a result, the Sri Lankan Government decided to maintain the security right to inspect ships entering the port and restrict any if it feels any threat to its sovereignty.[26]

Compared with the Hambantota port, the Japan-India Trincomalee port project is better situated. It already boasts of certain merits and facilities because it is a former naval base of the British Empire. Firstly, it is surrounded by natural "walls" to protect ships from natural disasters such as tsunami or cyclones, as seen during the 2004 tsunami. Secondly, its sea depth is greater than 25 metres, sufficient for all conventional and naval ships including US nuclear aircraft carrier. In fact, during the World War II, a Japanese aircraft carrier battle group bombed the port because of its location which was strategically important even then. In the 1980s, US naval ships called at Trincomalee port and were seen there from time to time. Therefore, India saw no point in wasting time and concluded an India-Sri Lanka Agreement with an Annexure which included, "Trincomalee or any other ports in Sri Lanka will not be made available for military use by any country in a manner prejudicial to India's interest."[27] Under the agreement,

India also sent 60,000 troops as part of the Indian Peace Keeping Force during 1987-1990, which is often called India's "Vietnam War".

Like the Hambantota port, Trincomalee, too, has no connection with Colombo but because of the Japanese Trincomalee-Colombo Economic Corridor project the distance of 255 km can be covered in six hours by car, or eight hours by train. However, Trincomalee is not located near any of the main SLOCs. It is situated on the east side of Sri Lanka where most ships do not ply. Nonetheless, to go to Bangladesh, Myanmar or other coastal countries around the Bay of Bengal, Trincomalee is a better location. Consequently, a ship can use this port as a hub, to unload and reload the cargo to go to the other coastal countries in the Bay of Bengal.

In addition, the Trincomalee project will promote the economy of the eastern part of Sri Lanka, which was destroyed during the civil war of 1983-2009. From this perspective, building of this port is beneficial to maintain the internal stability of the country. For the reasons cited above, this particular port is more beneficial than the Hambantota port for Sri Lanka, and if it succeeds in its operations, it will help to reduce the importance of Hambantota. In April 2017, when the Prime Minister of Sri Lanka Ranil Wickremesinghe visited Japan, Tokyo granted an aid of US$9 million aimed at providing facilities for improved management of the port of Trincomalee.[28] Furthermore, in May 2017, when the Indian Prime Minister Narendra Modi visited Sri Lanka, the two countries agreed that at least 73 of the 99 oil storage tanks in Trincomalee should be managed jointly.[29] Because oil storage management identifies how the port is used, this agreement is an important step.

Chabahar Port in Iran

Japan and India are also collaborating to modernise the Chabahar port project in Iran because there is a possibility that its construction will negate the prominence of China's Gwadar port in Pakistan. Both the ports have important competitive locations. When Central Asian countries need to find a route to export their energy resources through the Indian Ocean, the Afghanistan-Pakistan route is an option. As a core project of OBOR, China has started the China-Pakistan Economic Corridor (CPEC) project connecting Afghanistan to the Indian Ocean. Therefore, this route is the most important route currently.

Moreover, the CPEC has a strong military aspect – China has deployed military forces to construct the road in PoK – and for the protection of this route, Pakistan has established a Security Division of 9,000 army and 6,000 paramilitary soldiers. They are thus crucial for internal security issues.

Gwadar port located in Balochistan, Pakistan, is also used as a site to crack down rebellions in Pakistan.

Increasingly, Central Asian countries and Afghanistan are becoming more dependent on China and the amenities presented by the CPEC. Again, the Chabahar project can act as a neutraliser in this scenario because it is located just about 100 km west from Gwadar, and is connected with Mashhad, the second largest city of Iran, through a well-built road. The road also connects Mashhad to Turkmenistan and Afghanistan. To ease connection, there are talks of building a railway network as well.

This Turkmenistan-Iran, Afghanistan-Iran route will be a good choice for Central Asian countries. Once the Chabahar port project is ready and operating, these countries need not depend on the Pakistan route. When the Indian Prime Minister Narendra Modi visited Iran in May 2016, India promised US$ 20 billion for port facility construction.[30] Furthermore, Japan is planning to pitch in and build other infrastructure facilities to connect ports to cities.[31]

Africa

In May 2017, Modi initiated a new concept: the Asia-Africa Growth Corridor (AAGC).[32] Many scholars are seeing this initiative as a firm retort to China's growing influence in Africa through the BRI,[33] which is of grave concern to both India and Japan for three reasons. Firstly, Africa has plenty of resources for developing economies but China might be getting the best bargain of them all. Secondly, to be permanent members of the United Nations Security Council, Japan and India require support from African countries, which might get affected adversely because of China's influence in the region. Thirdly, China's infrastructure projects have a military aspect as well. In the coastal countries of the Indian Ocean in Africa, China's infrastructure projects can facilitate its deployment of troops. Though currently China deploys troops in Africa for anti-piracy missions, United Nations Peace Keeping Operations (UNPKO) and weapons exports, there are doubts that these troops might also be engaging in collecting information, safeguarding mining facilities, protecting pro-China politicians in African countries, etc. China has already set up naval bases in Djibouti for that matter.

Therefore, to offset China's influence, during 2010-2016, the Japan-India Dialogue on Africa was held five times. India also negotiates African policy with the US. In Africa, Japan has few human connection, but there is a large Indian diaspora in Africa. As India has insufficient funding to counter China, Japan can cooperate with India in this regard. To address military aspects, the role of the US is vital as it has already established the Africa Command. India and the US will jointly train troops of African countries for UNPKO.[34] As a result, Japan, India and the US can make several gains if they collaborate.

In addition, the AAGC will achieve many objectives. Such cooperation will present a model case to promote Japan-India cooperation in other areas, such as in Arctic, Antarctic and space policies.

Conclusion

China's infrastructure projects are intrinsically related to its foreign and military policies. In many cases, it is seen that its loan system is a "trap" for the recipient country – by claiming to set up development projects, China gives them loans at a very high interest rate, thus putting them in a 'debt trap'. Furthermore, core issues concerning sovereignty are disregarded, especially when it is regarding countries such as Japan and India. As a result, Japan and India have teamed up and are starting to negotiate with the recipient countries from Asia and Africa along similar lines. However, apart from negating Chinese influence, such cooperation can also enhance the scope and depth of Japan-India relations. For these countries, the advent of a bright future will depend on the strength of the Japan-India collaboration achievements.

NOTES

1. Author's own interactions with officials
2. "'Asia's Dream: Linking the Pacific and Eurasia' – Speech by Prime Minister Shinzo Abe at the Banquet of the 23rd International Conference on The Future of Asia", Prime Minister of Japan and His Cabinet, June 5,2017, at https://japan.kantei.go.jp/97_abe/statement/201706/1222768_11579.html.
3. "Official Spokesperson's Response to a Query on Participation of India in OBOR/BRI Forum", Ministry of External Affairs, Government of India, May 13,2017, at http://mea.gov.in/media-briefings.htm?dtl%2F28463%2FOfficial_Spokespersons _ response_to_a_query_on_participation_of_India_in_OBORBRI_Forum.
4. Yogita Limaye, "Sri Lanka: A country Trapped in Debt", *BBC*, May 26, 2017, at http://www.bbc.com/news/business-40044113.
5. Dipanjan Roy Chaudhury, "China May Put South Asia on Road to Debt Trap", *The Economic Times*, May 02, 2017, at http://economictimes.indiatimes.com/news/politics-and-nation/china-may-put-south-asia-on-road-to-debt-trap/articleshow/58467309.cms
6. *The Military Balance 2017*, International Institute for Strategic Studies (IISS), 2017.
7. P.A. Ghosh, *Ethnic Conflict in Sri Lanka and Role of Indian Peace Keeping Force (I.P.K.F.)*, A.P.H. Publishing, New Delhi, 1999.

8. Virginia Marantidou, "Revisiting China's 'String of Pearls' Strategy", *Issues & Insights*, 14 (7), June 24, 2014, at https://www.csis.org/analysis/issues-insights-vol-14-no-7-revisiting-chinas-string-pearls-strategy.
9. Yogita Limaye, No. 3.
10. "SIPRI Arms Transfer Database", Stockholm International Peace Research Institute (SIPRI), 2017, at https://www.sipri.org/databases/armstransfers.
11. Swaran Singh and Lilian Yamamoto, "Spectre of China's Artificial Islands", *Indian Defence Review*, July-September 2015, pp.78-82.
12. Shannon Tiezzi, "China Defends Airstrip Construction in the South China Sea", *The Diplomat*, January 06, 2016, at http://thediplomat.com/2016/01/china-defends-airstrip-construction-in-the-south-china-sea/.
13. Reiji Yoshida, "Beijing's Senkaku Goal: Sub 'Safe Haven' in South China Sea", *The Japan Times*, November 07, 2012, at http://www.japantimes.co.jp/news/2012/11/07/national/beijings-senkaku-goal-sub-safe-haven-in-south-china-sea/#.WDQ774VOKUk.
14. Shinzo Abe, "Asia's Democratic Security Diamond", *Project Syndicate*, December 27,2012, at https://www.project-syndicate.org/commentary/a-strategic-alliance-for-japan-and-india-by-shinzo-abe?barrier=accessreg# Vd6yyt DokZJ Ciwtv.01.
15. Ankit Panda, "East China Sea: Japan Spots Chinese Radar on Gas Exploration Platform", *The Diplomat*, August 09, 2016, at http://thediplomat.com/2016/08/east-china-sea-japan-spots-chinese-radar-on-gas-exploration-platform/.
16. Deeptiman Tiwary, "Chinese Clearing Forest Cover to Grab Border Land", *The Times of India*, August 26, 2013, at http://articles.timesofindia.indiatimes.com/2013-08-26/india/41453967_1_chinese-troops-incursion-sino-indian-border.
17. Rajat Pandit, "India Boring Border Tunnels to Take on China, Pakistan", *The Times of India*, August 16, 2012, at http://articles.timesofindia.indiatimes.com/2012-08-16/india/33232484_1_tunnels-rangpo-sikkim.
18. M. Matheswaran, "China's Tibet Build up", *Deccan Herald*, May 05, 2015, at http://www.deccanherald.com/content/475657/chinas-tibet-build-up.html.
19. Rajat Pandit, "Border Face-off: China and India Each Deploy 3,000 Troops", *The Times of India*, June 30, 2017, at http://timesofindia.indiatimes.com/india/border-face-off-china-india-each-deploy-3000-troops/articleshow/59377716.cms.
20. Singh Rahul, "China's Submarines in Indian Ocean Worry Indian Navy", *Hindustan Times*, April 07, 2013, at http://www.hindustantimes.com/delhi/china-s-submarines-in-indian-ocean-worry-indian-navy/story-0Fjcrc7s9jlHwg1ybpiTsL.html.
21. Rajat Pandit, "After Sri Lanka Snub, Chinese Submarine May Head to Karachi", *The Times of India*, May 13, 2017, at http://timesofindia.indiatimes.com/india/india-closely-tracking-chinese-submarine-which-is-likely-to-head-for-karachi-after-colombo-snub/articleshow/58649191.cms.
22. V. N. Khanna, *Foreign Policy of India*, 6th Edition, Vikas Publishing, 2007, p.127.
23. Ellen Barry, "As India Collaborates with Japan on Islands, It Looks to Check China", *The New York Times*, March 11,2016, at https://www.nytimes.com/2016/03/12/world/asia/india-japan-china-andaman-nicobar-islands.html.
24. Ajay Banerjee, "India Set to Join Malacca Patrol Group", *The Tribune*, April 10,2017, at http://www.tribuneindia.com/news/nation/india-set-to-join-malacca-

patrol-group/389602.html.

25. Abhijit Singh, "India's 'Undersea Wall' in the Eastern Indian Ocean", Asia Maritime Transparency Initiative, June 15,2016, at http://amti.csis.org/indias-undersea-wall-eastern-indian-ocean/.
26. Shihar Aneez, "Exclusive: Sri Lanka's Cabinet 'Clears Port Deal' with China Firm after Concerns Addressed", *Reuters*, July 25, 2017, at https://www.reuters.com/article/us-sri-lanka-china-port/exclusive-sri-lankas-cabinet-clears-port-deal-with-china-firm-after-concerns-addressed-idUSKBN1AA0PI.
27. P.A. Ghosh, No. 6, p.181.
28. "Japan-Sri Lanka Summit Meeting Joint Statement – Deepening and Expansion of the Comprehensive Partnership between Japan and Sri Lanka", Ministry of Foreign Affairs of Japan (MOFA), April 12, 2017, at http://www.mofa.go.jp/files/000249616.pdf.
29. "PM Narendra Modi's Visit a Grand Success, Says Sri Lanka Minister", *Hindustan Times*, May 17, 2017, at http://www.hindustantimes.com/india-news/pm-narendra-modi-s-visit-a-grand-success-says-sri-lanka-minister/story-4rair1RfTsAkocLVPeAG8N.html.
30. "India to Invest $20 Billion in Iran's Chabahar Port Development", *NDTV*, April 11, 2016, at http://www.ndtv.com/india-news/india-to-invest-20-billion-in-irans-chabahar-port-development-1381864.
31. Nikkei Asia Review 2016 "Japan eyes Iran infrastructure development", Nikkei Asia Review, May 8 https://asia.nikkei.com/Politics-Economy/International-Relations/Japan-eyes-Iran-infrastructure-development
32. Purnendra Jain, "Japan and India Challenging China in Africa", East Asia Forum, June 16, 2017, at http://www.eastasiaforum.org/2017/06/16/japan-and-india-challenging-china-in-africa/.
33. Saibal Dasgupta, "China Wants India to Go Slow on Asia-Africa Corridor", *The Times of India*, September 3, 2017, at http://timesofindia.indiatimes.com/world/china/china-tries-to-dilute-africa-growth-initiative-crafted-by-india-japan/articleshow/60341683.cms.
34. Dinakar Peri, "India, U.S. to Train African Troops for U.N. Peacekeeping", *The Hindu*, July 24, 2017, at http://www.thehindu.com/news/national/India-U.S.-to-train-African-troops-for-U.N.-peacekeeping/article14504907.ece.

13

Asia's Democratic Security Diamond in the Indo-Pacific Region: A Maritime Perspective

Takuya Shimodaira

Why Indo-Pacific?

Maps matter. Robert D. Kaplan emphasises that the right map can stimulate foresight by providing a spatial view of critical trends in world politics.[1] The map of Asia is being changed as the main actors express their own initiative. Japan and the US have promulgated the "Indo-Pacific strategy" to bear the responsibility of fostering the confluence of the Pacific and Indian Oceans and of Asia and Africa into a place that values freedom, the rule of law and market economy, free from force or coercion, and making it prosperous.[2] India is implementing the "Act East" policy, replacing the previous "Look East" policy to more actively engage its neighbours.[3] China's "One Belt, One Road" concept which combined the Silk Road Economic Belt with the 21st Century Maritime Silk Road influences the entire region.[4] The Indian Ocean is now taking centre stage in the world, which has far-reaching consequences.

The common posture of these initiatives is outward looking for economic, geopolitical and security connectivity. It is crucial for the international society to ensure that the common objective of each initiative works for regional and international development rather than the countries' own gains.

Why in the US is the new term Indo-Pacific used instead of the more commonly used term Asia-Pacific? Admiral Harry B. Harris Jr, the commander of US Pacific Command (USPACOM), defines simply that the Indo-Asia-Pacific more accurately captures the fact that Indian and Pacific Oceans are the economic lifeblood linking the Indian Subcontinent, Southeast Asia, Australia, Northeast Asia, Oceania and the US together.[5] This concurs with the Prime Minister of Japan Shinzo Abe's "Confluence of the Two Seas" notion of the Indian and Pacific Oceans to bring about their dynamic coupling as seas of freedom and prosperity.[6]

However, there is still the unavoidable and non-negligible challenge of creating new ties in the Indo-Pacific region: It is the unfolding Chinese assertiveness, as China expands its military footprint, alarming its neighbours. China has always protested the US Navy's Freedom of Navigation Operations (USN FONOPS) in accordance with their proclaimed interpretation of jurisdiction rights. In March 2009, USN *Impeccable* and *Victorious* were harassed by Chinese oceanographic vessels in international waters off Hainan Island. In June 2009, a Chinese submarine fouled the towed array sonar of USN Aegis destroyer *John S. McCain* off Subic Bay of the Philippines. USN Aegis destroyer *Cowpens* nearly collided with one of the escorts of the Chinese aircraft carrier *Liaoning* in December 2013. China had justified its action against USN assets in accordance with the United Nations Convention on the Law of the Sea (UNCLOS) provisions.[7]

How should Japan manage and incorporate China in close cooperation with the US in the rules-based regional order? Which framework is appropriate in the Indo-Pacific region, cooperative or competitive?

Maritime issues matter. The idea of Indo-Pacific emphasises the sea as the main conduit for trade and commerce. Focusing on the maritime perspectives in the Indo-Pacific region will be a good driver for the rules-based world order.

Japan-US Initiative and India's Way

Japan-US alliance has been an anchor of peace, stability and prosperity in the Indo-Pacific region for over 50 years. Japan and the US have been arguably the quintessential Pacific nation and Pacific power binding closely through a strong Japan-US alliance. Prime Minister Abe called it the "Alliance of Hope", towards a future-oriented, more prosperous world, at the Joint Meeting of the US Congress in April 29, 2015.[8] The alliance has benefited both nations and is critical to the future of both nations and the Indo-Pacific region. Japan upholds the banner of "proactive contribution to peace" based on the principle of international cooperation. The time has come for the Japan-US alliance to jointly tackle the impending challenges.

Japan and the US are important drivers of regional and global growth. From Africa to East Asia, Japan and the US could build on the enhanced partnership to support sustainable, inclusive development and increased regional connectivity by collaborating with the other interested partners.

As Michael J. Green, senior vice president for Asia and Japan Chair at the Center for Strategic and International Studies (CSIS), mentioned that the Indian Ocean is a highway for international commerce, particularly between the oil-rich Gulf States and an economically dynamic East Asia.[9] The Indian Ocean has replaced the Atlantic as the globe's busiest and most strategically significant trade and commerce corridor, carrying two-thirds of global oil shipments.[10] 84 percent of China's oil imports and up to 90 percent of Japan's are shipped from the Middle East and Africa through the Indian Ocean.[11] The potential benefits of deeper engagement with the Indo-Pacific region are immense. The Indo-Pacific region is emerging as the epicentre of economic growth.

The *Quadrennial Defense Review Report*, 2010, emphasised, "...As its military capabilities grow, India will contribute to Asia as a net provider of security in the Indian Ocean and beyond."[12] The *National Security Strategy* report, released on May 2010, stated that: "The United States and India are building a strategic partnership that is underpinned by our shared interests."[13] The US Department of Defence declared in the document released on January 2012: "The United States is also investing in a long-term strategic partnership with India to support its ability to serve as a regional economic anchor and provider of security in the broader Indian Ocean region."[14] Admiral Harry B. Harris Jr described India as a beacon on a hill, not on castles of sand, to take a leading role in the region.[15] Robert D. Kaplan describes India as a politically stable, manifestly democratic great pivot power with great possibilities in the 21st century politics.[16]

The resolution of the India-Bangladesh maritime dispute is a remarkable and praiseworthy example of India's stance towards world politics. The Hague's Arbitration Tribunal on the India-Bangladesh maritime delimitation delivered its final verdict on the maritime dispute between India and Bangladesh in the Bay of Bengal, over New Moore Island, on July 2014.[17] India and Bangladesh resolved the 40-year-old maritime dispute because of India's willingness to resolve the conflict through peaceful means and international law, and by upholding the tribunal's verdict India showed its respect for arbitration.

Not assertiveness, but peaceful means and respect for the law are required in the Indo-Pacific region. Shinzo Abe expressed his respect for India's spirit of tolerance by quoting its great spiritual leader Vivekananda at the Indian Parliament in 2007: "Help and not fight", "assimilation and not destruction", "harmony and peace and not dissension".[18] There are several possibilities for deepening security and economic cooperation in a peaceful manner through the Japan-US initiative and incorporating India's way in the maritime arena of the Indo-Pacific region.

Prime Minister of India Narendra Modi and Prime Minister of Japan Shinzo Abe had a summit meeting on December 2015, and declared Japan and India Joint Vision 2025 as Special Strategic and Global Partnership for advancing peace, stability and prosperity in the Indo-Pacific region and shared an abiding commitment to peace and stability, international rule of law and open global trade regime.[19] In this document, Abe and Modi agreed on expanding bilateral cooperation on a wide range of issues such as investment, disaster risk management and people-to-people exchange. They also acknowledged that the stability of the region was "indispensable" to their respective national security and prosperity, calling for a more robust cooperation on security issues. Japan and India are two great democracies and have a pivotal role to play in the Indo-Pacific region's emerging power structure.

New Formulation for Evolving Maritime Connectivity

The Indo-Pacific region remains the most consequential area for the security and economy of the world. The era of maritime Indo-Pacific will be a new phase to rejuvenate ties with the nations in the region for intensifying diplomatic, economic and security engagement.

There is a unique framework, what Admiral Harry B. Harris Jr calls the regional democracies multilateral alliance – Japan, the US, Australia and India – for creating a model of strategic partnership for the rest of the world to emulate.[20] On November 2017, the 'Quad' was back for the first time since 2007.[21] Admiral Harris is mainly concerned about North Korea's nuclear and missile programme, Chinese assertiveness and the potential for the spread of Islamic State of Iraq and the Levant or other violent extremists to the Indo-Pacific region, and has often emphasised the importance and necessity of multilateralism in the Indo-Pacific region. With allies and partners, the USPACOM enhances stability in the Indo-Pacific region by promoting security cooperation, encouraging peaceful development, responding to contingencies, deterring aggression and, when necessary, fighting to win. This approach is based on military preparedness, partnership and presence.[22]

This completely concurs with Shinzo Abe's "Asia's Democratic Security Diamond (ADSD)" to expand allies and partners' strategic horizons.[23] He has also emphasised multilateralism through connectivity and mentioned,

> Peace, stability, and freedom of navigation in the Pacific Ocean are inseparable from peace, stability, and freedom of navigation in the Indian Ocean. Developments affecting each are more closely connected than ever. Japan, as one of the oldest sea-faring democracies in Asia, should play a greater role in preserving the common good in both regions.[24]

As the next step, Japan and the US should invite the Philippines to the regional democracies multilateral alliance and the ADSD. One of the most important reasons to include the Philippines is its geopolitical position in the Indo-Pacific region, located at the centre of the ADSD and middle of the 3,700-km-long sea lane from Okinawa to Singapore, where there are no US bases. The alliance between the US and Philippines has been important for more than 65 years. The US and Philippines updated the Enhanced Defense Cooperation Agreement (EDCA) to strengthen cooperative capacities and efforts such as promoting the interoperability, capability building and maritime domain awareness on April 28, 2014.[25] US P-3s and P-8s have already operated from Clark Air Base on a rotational basis, and in a crisis, the EDCA will increase the US access to the Philippine facilities that are important strategic locations.[26]

Based on Admiral Harris's regional democracies multilateral alliance and Prime Minister Abe's ADSD concept, the proposed Quintuple partnership of Japan, the US, Australia, India and the Philippines could restructure new regional formulations through enhancing the mixture of economic, geopolitical and security connectivity and accomplishments in the Indo-Pacific region as a maritime super region. It will be the most realistic measure for these five sides to expand the scope of cooperation on Humanitarian Assistance and Disaster Relief (HA/DR) with the other partner nations.

Through its ambitious "One Belt, One Road" strategy, China is set to promote its national interests and project its influence in the Indo-Pacific region more aggressively than ever before. The convergence of the updated "Indo-Pacific strategy" of Japan and the US and India's "Act East" might well be a good start for developing a comprehensive strategy against growing Chinese influence in the Indo-Pacific region. It should be noted that there have already been some new developments in the Indo-Pacific region. The most significant is the rise in Chinese power and influence.

The security and economic relationship in the region should be recognised from common, comprehensive, cooperative and sustainable perspectives.

The Japan-US alliance can be a strong springboard for the quintuple partnership for better security cooperation. In the aftermath of the devastating Great East Japan Earthquake on March 2011 and the consequent tsunami, the US forces conducted operation "TOMODACHI", the largest bilateral mission in the history of the alliance, and demonstrated the resilience and interoperability of the alliance.[27] Australia and India were also quick to respond to the situation as friends and partners.[28] The quintuple partnership has many opportunities to work with the Association of Southeast Asian Nations (ASEAN) in the non- traditional security fields such as HA/DR in the Indo-Pacific region.

The quintuple partnership will be the unique security and economic formulation to deepen the bonds and spread maritime connectivity from economic, geopolitical and security perspectives for maintaining peace and stability in the Indo-Pacific region.

Role of Naval Engagements

It is crucial to deepen and expand the network of the quintuple partnership to meet global challenges and support an open and inclusive rules-based global order based on international law. It is important to note that Abe formulated three principles for the rule of law at sea:

> The first principle is that states shall make and clarify their claims based on international law.
>
> The second is that states shall not use force or coercion in trying to drive their claims.
>
> The third principle is that states shall seek to settle disputes by peaceful means.[29]

An excellent case for truly embodying the rule of law to resolve the disputes was Indonesia and the Philippines peacefully reaching an agreement on the delimitation of overlapping exclusive economic zone (EEZ) on May 2014.[30] The Philippines Department of Foreign Affairs (DFA) explained, "The agreement is a milestone for Philippine-Indonesia relations as the EEZ boundary will open opportunities for closer cooperation in the preservation and protection of the rich marine environment in the area, increased trade, and enhanced maritime security."[31]

It is certain that the rules-based order is crucial. However, it is also true that the rules-based order is getting weak. There are several challenges; for instance, a great power like China does not respect the rules and violates the law in the Indo-Pacific region albeit having partnership at the strategic level.

Thinking operationally will be the key driver for evolving maritime connectivity to increase the naval engagements. Admiral Harry B. Harris Jr emphasises that presence matters and military-to-military contacts are the heartbeat of growing multilateral relationships in the region.[32]

Japan and India in cooperation with the US will be the new key enablers to increase the naval engagements for evolving maritime connectivity in the Indo-Pacific region from the perspective of operational level engagements. India has made unique military-to-military efforts recently by providing support to the armed forces of Southeast Asian countries. India has trained the crew of Thailand's aircraft carrier, the crew of submarine and fighter pilots in Vietnam and fighter pilots and crew in Malaysia. Furthermore, India has agreed to train pilots and provide maintenance for fighter planes of the Indonesian Airforce.[33]

A strong and prosperous Japan is essential to a strong and prosperous Indo-Pacific. Deepening US-Japan security cooperation is the starting point for defending universal values including rules-based international order.

The G7 Foreign Ministers at Hiroshima on April 2016 expressed very strongly that "recognizing the importance of maintaining the sea as governed by the rule of law, which is indispensable for the peace and prosperity of the international community, we, as G7, are committed to further action on maritime security".[34] They shared the determination to cooperate through capacity building assistance for maritime security and safety in such areas as maritime governance, coast guard, disaster relief, maritime search and rescue and maritime information sharing and integration, as well as legislative, judicial, prosecutorial and correctional assistance in order to help coastal states to deal with their own vulnerabilities.[35]

Japan should seek to play the leading role as regional security provider by recalibrating its "Free and Open Indo-Pacific Strategy", with the quintuple partnership members, especially the US and India. The G7 Ministers further stressed that improving connectivity in the Indo-Pacific region, through the realisation of a free and open region, is vital to achieving peace, stability and prosperity in the entire region. The synergy between Abe's "Free and Open Indo-Pacific Strategy" and Modi's "Act East" is welcome. The proposed new proactive approach called Training, Exercise and Operation for Non-Traditional Security (TEON) which focuses on HA/DR such as international search for missing flights MH370, 2004-2005 Indian Ocean tsunami relief and 2013 Typhoon Haiyan relief effort will be needed as a good start for enhancing naval engagements and more cooperation in the Indo-Pacific region.

TEON should aim to be a proactive and concrete measure and a strong first step to spread maritime connectivity for peace and stability in the Indo-Pacific region.

Training and Exercise

Training and Exercise will be the first enabler of the TEON approach. Following a step-by-step approach is important. Security dialogues, seminars and mutual assistance are welcome. One of the related powerful and characteristic initiatives the Japan Ministry of Defence proposed is the "Vientiane Vision", which seeks to advance defence cooperation with its neighbours through cooperation, support and assistance focused on promoting the rule of law and strengthening maritime security.[36]

Practical defence cooperation is conducted by effectively combining the following measures:

1. Sharing understanding and experience regarding international law
2. Conducting capacity building cooperation, such as HA/DR and Peacekeeping Operations
3. Transferring equipment and technology
4. Continued participation in multilateral joint training and exercises
5. Inviting Opinion Leaders[37]

TEON would be the new wave and a strong incentive to proceed with the "Vientiane Vision" for creating a future-oriented cooperative relationship.

In November 2016, Prime Minister Modi and Prime Minister Abe welcomed the holding of a trilateral dialogue among Japan, India and the US, and strengthened coordination and cooperation in areas such as HA/DR, regional connectivity and maritime security and safety. The two Prime Ministers also welcomed continued and deepened trilateral dialogues among Japan, India and Australia.[38]

The Indian Navy has already launched a golden opportunity to leverage the enormous potential of a regional HA/DR maritime mission within the Indian Ocean under the Indian Ocean Naval Symposium (IONS) framework and presented a guidance on HA/DR in 2016.[39]

The annual Malabar naval exercise shows possibilities for further action on maritime security in the Indo-Pacific region. The Malabar exercise, which commenced in 1992, marked a turning point in the relationship between the navies of India and the US. Japan joined the other two as a permanent participant in 2015.[40] Previously, Malabar 2007 conveyed a powerful message for regional maritime security. It was designed to increase the ability of five nations' maritime forces – Australia, India, Japan, Singapore and the US – to respond to maritime threats such as terrorism, proliferation of weapons of mass destruction and transnational challenges such as pandemic disease and natural disaster.[41] A more upgraded version of the Malabar exercise which invites multilateral partner nations will be expected within the TEON framework shaping the future of the Indo-Pacific region.

There is another good practical example, the Indo-Thai Coordinated Patrol, CORPAT for short. CORPAT has been a bilateral exercise to clearly focus on search and rescue at sea and preventing unlawful activities since 2005.[42] Such bilateral cooperation besides multilateral exercises is important in the Indo-Pacific region.

Japan, the US and India can double down on expanding opportunities for joint and combined training and exercises. Training and exercises are just the beginning; however, exercising together will lead to operating together.

Furthermore, naval connectivity forms a crucial part of the multilateral cooperation in the Indo-Pacific region. Working with regional partners to ensure that global commons like ocean, space and cyberspace remain avenues of shared prosperity is very important. Championing unfettered access to shared domains matter.

Another important aspect is capability building at the joint and combined training and exercises. Japan and India are coordinating the deal for US-2 amphibious aircraft. If India were to possess US-2, it could project a stronger presence in the Indo-Pacific region and extend tangible support to regional search and rescue.[43] The transfer of US-2 from Japan to India will be emblematic of a close relationship.

The development of naval presence through training and exercises and capability building is a clear sign of strategic priorities in the Indo-Pacific region. The allies and partners for Japan and the US have had a long record of basing, surveillance and patrolling in many places of the Indo-Pacific region.

The quintuple partnership members could work together across the full spectrum of military operations. But how would a powerful China respond to the quintuple partnership security efforts? The quintuple partnership members are open to inviting China as the sixth member, because China has contributed in the international anti-piracy operations in the Gulf of Aden/Horn of Africa region since December 2008 and sent its naval forces to participate in the US-led largest-scale exercise, Rim of the Pacific Exercise (RIMPAC), since 2014. Such operations and exercises help the participants foster and sustain the cooperative relationships that are critical for ensuring the safety of sea lanes and security across the world's oceans.

Chinese Participation

China is accelerating military modernisation to firmly protect its national defence, security and development interests for realising the "Chinese dream". It is becoming a great regional power by providing more and more public goods and strengthening its security role in the Indo-Pacific region. As China rises, it will more aggressively promote its national interests and project its influence in its neighbourhood.

The nature of the military threat environment has changed as adversaries and potential adversaries increasingly use non-military and paramilitary means to achieve strategic and operational objectives that were previously considered a purely military task.[44] More recently, China used its maritime militia personnel, disguised as fishermen, to conduct landing on Japan's Senkaku islands.

The cooperation between the People's Liberation Army Navy (PLAN) and the China Coast Guard (CCG) has also become remarkable in recent training exercises. The first large-scale joint exercise, East China Sea Cooperation, was held in October 2012, where scenarios included Chinese fishing vessels being harassed. A subsequent joint exercise was held near the Spratly Islands in May 2013 and in Guangdong Province in November 2013, in which participants included local military and customs units.[45]

While China's actions are causing concern among neighbours in the region, there are potential opportunities. Its small but growing number of bilateral and multinational exercises suggest Beijing's greater willingness to interact with partners. Support for the UN Peacekeeping missions is an encouraging sign of Chinese willingness to play a more active and constructive role in international affairs.[46]

Any significant shift in the tempo of military operations or presence can invite instability. Quintuple partnership members should encourage China to participate in TEON, especially the HA/DR operations. Peaceful engagement through the TEON approach will usher in peaceful and stable order. Quintuple partnership members intend to check and deter assertive behaviours and highlight their own role as a credible regional security guarantor in the Indo-Pacific region.

Another important point for proceeding with the TEON approach is the participants. The military is critical in TEON to lead and coordinate with the other members, and military-to-military contacts are key to successful friendly cooperation in the Indo-Pacific region. But not only the military, the non-military and/or paramilitary member should also join TEON.

Conclusion

China's military build-up in the artificial islands of the South China Sea is now a fact. China's rise is not a real problem, but the way it is exercising its military power can be.

Cooperation focused on operational engagement through training and exercises stimulates the gradual emergence of understanding and amelioration of mistrust among the participating nations. Cooperation focused on operational engagement breaks down the boundaries between economic, geopolitical and security competitions.

Geopolitical competition is not a positive-sum relationship, whereas economic engagements can be. Attention to security is a minimum requirement to safeguard economic interests and vulnerabilities. Thus, strengthening of economic, geopolitical and security interactions among the quintuple partnership is a major part of Indo-Pacific regional power game.

The quintuple partnership will determine how the Indo-Pacific region is managed. The issues at play here are manageable from the perspective of operational naval engagements through training and exercises. It is an incremental security step, but it will deliver a steady output. The security issues of the East China Sea and South China Sea in the Indo-Pacific region should not be considered separately. It is required to cope with them as regional and global agenda. In the Indo-Pacific region, the operative phrase should be "Asia first", not "America first" or "China first". It is not only economy, but also security issues that are important, through the strengthening of economic, geopolitical and security interactions, for peace, stability and prosperity in the Indo-Pacific region. It is time to deepen and expand the network of ADSD through naval engagements to meet global challenges and support an open and inclusive rules-based global order based on international law.

NOTES

1. Robert D. Kaplan, "Center Stage for the 21st Century: Power Plays in the Indian Ocean", *Foreign Affairs*, 88 (2), March/April 2009.
2. "Remarks by President Trump and Prime Minister Abe of Japan in Joint Press Conference Tokyo, Japan", White House, November 6, 2017, at https://www.whitehouse.gov/briefings-statements/remarks-president-trump-prime-minister-abe-japan-joint-press-conference-tokyo-japan/; the original idea comes from Address by Prime Minister of Japan Shinzo Abe at the Opening Session of the Sixth Tokyo International Conference on African Development (TICAD VI), August 27, 2016, at http://www.mofa.go.jp/afr/af2/page4e_000496.html/.
3. Anil Sasi, "'Look East' Has Become 'Act East Policy,' Says PM Modi at ASEAN Summit", *The Indian Express*, November 13, 2014.
4. Xi Jinping announced the initiative to build the Silk Road Economic Belt on September 7, 2013, during his visit to Kazakhstan, and called for the building of the 21st Century Maritime Silk Road during his visit to Indonesia on October 3, 2013. See "President Xi Jinping Delivers Important Speech and Proposes to Build a Silk Road Economic Belt with Central Asian Countries", Ministry of Foreign Affairs, People's Republic of China, September 7, 2013, at http://www.fmprc.gov.cn/mfa_eng/topics_665678/xjpfwzysiesgjtfhshzzfh_665686/t1076334.shtml; Wu Jiao and Zhang Yunbi, "Xi in Call for Building of New 'Maritime Silk Road'", *China Daily*, October 4, 2013, at http://usa.chinadaily.com.cn/china/2013-10/04/content_17008940.htm.
5. Admiral Harry Harris' Address to the Lowy Institute for International Policy, December 14, 2016, at http://www.pacom.mil/Media/Speeches-Testimony/Article/1029173/address-to-the-lowy-institute-for-international-policy/.
6. Shinzo Abe, "Confluence of the Two Seas", Address at the Parliament of the Republic of India, August 22, 2007, at http://www.mofa.go.jp/region/asia-paci/pmv0708/speech-2.html.
7. Peter Dutton, *Military Activities in the EEZ: A US-China Dialogue on Security and International Law in the Maritime Common*, China Maritime Studies Institute, US Naval War College, 2010, pp. 20-21.
8. Shinzo Abe, "Toward an Alliance of Hope", Address to a Joint Meeting of the US Congress, April 29, 2015, at http://www.mofa.go.jp/na/na1/us/page4e_000241.html.
9. Michael J. Green and Andrew Shearer, "Defining U.S. Indian Ocean Strategy", *The Washington Quarterly*, 35 (2), Spring 2012, p. 177.
10. "Defense White Paper 2013", Department of Defence, Australian Government, p. 74.
11. "Annual Report to Congress: Military and Security Developments Involving the People's Republic of China, 2014", Office of the Secretary of Defence, US Department of Defence, p. 18.
12. *Quadrennial Defense Review Report*, US Department of Defence, February 2010, p. 60.
13. *National Security Strategy*, The White House, May 2010, p. 43.
14. *Sustaining US Global Leadership: Priorities for 21st Century Defense*, US Department of Defence, January 2012, p. 2.
15. Admiral Harry Harris, "Let's Be Ambitious Together", Raisina Dialogue Remarks,

March 2, 2016, at http://www.pacom.mil/Media/Speeches-Testimony/Article/683842/raisina-dialogue-remarks-lets-be-ambitious-together/.

16. Robert D. Kaplan, *Earning the Rockies: How Geography Shapes America's Role in the World,* Random House, New York, 2017.
17. Bay of Bengal Maritime Boundary Arbitration between Bangladesh and India, July 8, 2014, at https://www.pcacases.com/web/sendAttach/410/.
18. Shinzo Abe, No. 6.
19. "Japan and India Vision 2025 Special Strategic Partnership: Working Together for Peace and Prosperity of the Indo-Pacific Region and the World", Ministry of Foreign Affairs of Japan, December 12, 2015, at http://www.mofa.go.jp/s_sa/sw/in/page3e_000432.html.
20. Admiral Harry Harris, No. 15.
21. Ankit Panda, "US, Japan, India, and Australia Hold Working-Level Quadrilateral Meeting on Regional Cooperation", *The Diplomat,* November 13, 2017, at https://thediplomat.com/2017/11/us-japan-india-and-australia-hold-working-level-quadrilateral-meeting-on-regional-cooperation/
22. Statement of Admiral Harry B. Harris Jr, US Navy Commander, US Pacific Command before the House Armed Services Committee on US Pacific Command Posture, February 24, 2016, p. 1, at https://www.armed-services.senate.gov/imo/media/doc/Harris_02-23-16.pdf.
23. Shinzo Abe, "Asia's Democratic Security Diamond", *Project Syndicate,* December 27, 2012, at https://www.project-syndicate.org/commentary/a-strategic-alliance-for-japan-and-india-by-shinzo-abe?barrier=accessreg http://www.mofa.go.jp/region/asia-paci/pmv0708/speech-2.html.
24. Ibid.
25. Agreement between the United States of America and the Philippines, April 28, 2014, at https://www.state.gov/documents/organization/244799.pdf# search =%27Agreement+between+ the+ Government+of+the+Republic+ of+the+ Philippines +and+the+ Government+of+the+United+States+of+America+on+ Enhanced+ Defense+Cooperation%27
26. Statement of Admiral Harry B. Harris Jr, No. 22, p. 12.
27. Takuya Shimodaira, "The JMSDF's Resilient Power for Civil Society: Lessons from the Great East Japan Earthquake", *Naval War College Review,* 68 (3), Summer 2015, pp. 64-75.
28. "Arrival of India's Aid Team", Ministry of Foreign Affairs of Japan, March 25, 2011, at www.mofa.go.jp/announce/announce/2011/3/0325_12.html; "Australia Stands with Tohoku", Australian Embassy, Tokyo, at http://japan.embassy.gov.au/tkyo/tohoku.html.
29. Shinzo Abe, "Peace and Prosperity in Asia, Forevermore: Japan for the Rule of Law, Asia for the Rule of Law, and the Rule of Law for All of Us", 13th IISS Asian Security Summit-The Shangri-La Dialogue-Keynote Address, May 30, 2014, at http://www.mofa.go.jp/fp/nsp/page4e_000086.html.
30. Arif Havas Oegroseno, "How Indonesia and the Philippines Solved Their Maritime Dispute", *The Diplomat,* June 14, 2014, at http://thediplomat.com/2014/06/how-indonesia-and-the-philippines-solved-their-maritime-dispute/.
31. Paterno Esmaquel II, "Philippines, Indonesia Seal Historic Maritime Deal", *Rappler,* May 23, 2014, at http://www.rappler.com/nation/58737-philippines-indonesia-eez-boundary-agreement/.

32. Jim Garamone, "Indo-Asia-Pacific Region Remains 'Most Consequential' to America, Pacom Chief Says", *DoD News*, November 15, 2016.
33. Satoru Nagao, "Japan & India Should Collaborate to Support Countries around the South China Sea", *cogit ASIA*, CSIS Asia Policy Blog, March 31, 2015, at https://www.cogitasia.com/japan-india-should-collaborate-to-support-countries-around-the-south-china-sea/
34. "G7 Foreign Ministers' Statement on Maritime Security", G7 Hiroshima Foreign Ministers' Meeting, April 11, 2016, at http://www.mofa.go.jp/mofaj/files/000147444.pdf.
35. Ibid.
36. *Vientiane Vision: Japan's Defense Cooperation Initiative with ASEAN*, Ministry of Defence, at http://www.mod.go.jp/e/d_act/exc/vientianevision/index.html.
37. Ibid.
38. "Japan-India Joint Statement", Japan-India Summit Meeting, November 11, 2016, at http://www.mofa.go.jp/files/000202950.pdf#search=%27japan+india + joint + statement%27/.
39. Pradeep Chauhan, "The Criticality of the INOS Maritime Security Construct", Center for International Maritime Security, May 25, 2016.
40. Vivek Raghuvanshi, "Japan to Join Malabar as Permanent Participant", *Defense News*, October 13, 2015.
41. "Five Nations in Exercise Malabar off India", *Stars and Stripes*, September 7, 2007.
42. Vivek Mishra, "Revealed: India's Ambitious New Naval Strategy", *The National Interest*, June 2, 2016, at http://nationalinterest.org/feature/revealed-indias-ambitious-new-naval-strategy-16438/.
43. Satoru Nagao, "The Importance of a Japan-India Amphibious Aircraft Deal", *The Diplomat*, December 12, 2016, at http://thediplomat.com/2016/12/the-importance-of-a-japan-india-amphibious-aircraft-deal/.
44. Arthur N. Tulak, "Hybrid Warfare: New Challenges in the Information Environment", *Indo-Asia-Pacific Defense Forum*, 41 (3), 2016, p. 19.
45. Lyle J. Morris, "Blunt Defenders of Sovereignty: The Rise of Coast Guards in East and Southeast Asia", *Naval War College Review*, 70 (2), Spring 2017, pp. 87-88.
46. Statement of Admiral Harry B. Harris Jr, No. 22, p. 4.

PART III

REFLECTIONS ON INDIA AND THE INDO-PACIFIC

14

The Strategic Implications of Maritime Infrastructure Developments in the Indo-Pacific

Lee Cordner

The maritime context of the Indian and western Pacific oceanic and littoral regions, collectively known as the Indo-Pacific, is dynamic and rapidly evolving. As China looks south and west, and states like India and Indonesia emerge, the need for deeper understanding of the global and regional strategic implications grows. Capability analyses supported by data are important to understanding the means available for strategic change and for estimating probable intent: the likely strategic ends being pursued by various actors. One evolving element that aids calculation is maritime infrastructure developments: existing and forecast. In assessing the strategic consequences, this chapter explores which maritime infrastructure developments are happening, who is involved and what are the likely objectives. A primary question to be addressed is 'so what?' for regional maritime security – how are prospects for sustainable peace and prosperity in the region likely to be affected – and what are the risks?

Tangible infrastructure developments in the maritime domain are important indicators of progress and intent. They go beyond rhetoric and demonstrate actual commitment of energy and resources to pursuing political, economic and other objectives. Importantly, infrastructure in the maritime context offers shared and communal aspects that can be to the benefit, or indeed to the detriment, of many actors. Those directly involved in developing and supporting the infrastructure are affected along with all users of the maritime domain. The maritime domain remains very much a common, although increasingly contested, space.

Maritime Infrastructure Defined

What is encompassed by the term 'maritime infrastructure' requires explanation. Maritime strategic perspectives recognise the systemic nature of global and regional maritime contexts – and maritime infrastructure is an essential component. Understanding the interconnected, integrated and systemic nature of the world's oceans, of factors like trade and the environment, is fundamental to considering the place of infrastructure and its relationship with maritime security. There is an abiding need for security of the whole global maritime system to enable it to function effectively.[1] A general systems approach to geopolitics is useful for understanding relationships between political structures and geographical environments,[2] and this has particular relevance in the Indo-Pacific maritime context.

The sea lanes are highways for world commerce. They pass between states and through maritime areas under national jurisdiction and the high seas for the mutual benefit of internal Indo-Pacific and external actors. The western and north-western Indian Ocean extremities of the Indo-Pacific confluence, choke points and connections to the Mediterranean Sea and the Atlantic Ocean, along with the central maritime trading routes, need to be considered in equal measure to those on the eastern and north-eastern side that connect with and flow into the Pacific Ocean. A maritime security problem, for example piracy, that impacts maritime trade in the Gulf of Aden or the Malacca Straits effects the whole Indo-Pacific (and global) trading system and therefore presents systemic maritime security risks.

Maritime infrastructure needs to be understood as an essential component of the regional and global maritime system. Ports and port facilities, including shore side connections via rail, road or perhaps inland waterways are important elements of maritime infrastructure vital to conveying goods and people to and from the sea. Offshore facilities, like oil and gas fields and other man-made features, like wind farms along with aids to maritime navigation, can also be included as part of infrastructure. Less clearly included in the frame of maritime infrastructure is shipping, and the international shipping industry as a whole. For the purposes of this analysis, shipping and associated facilities, along with the people and organisations that operate and sustain them, are included under a broad banner of maritime infrastructure; they are vital elements of the maritime system.

The regional and global sea lines of communication (SLOCs) can also be acknowledged as being part of maritime infrastructure. Although this proposition may be arguable, the sea highways need to be considered as vital features of regional and global maritime systems and therefore central elements of maritime infrastructure. The SLOCs are generally not precisely geographically defined. They are mostly open waterways and largely available for use by all comers, unlike roads on land that are clearly delineated with access closely controlled within sovereign territory. Coastal and maritime geography combines to determine where shipping can safely navigate. Inevitably, strategic choke points arise where large volumes of shipping traffic converge, for example the Malacca Straits, Strait of Hormuz and Bab el-Mendeb Strait, along with the approaches to key regional ports.

How the SLOCs are to be used is broadly addressed by the United Nations Convention on the Law of the Sea (UNCLOS). UNCLOS establishes a comprehensive framework for regulation of oceanic domains including a broad concept of freedom of navigation. There are, of course, varying levels of sovereign control in the maritime and littoral domains ranging from ports established in sovereign territory through territorial seas and exclusive economic zones (EEZs) to the high seas, also known as areas beyond national jurisdiction (ABNJ). Freedom to navigate is moderated within areas under national jurisdictions by the traditional right of innocent passage through territorial seas, transit passage through international straits, and archipelagic sea-lanes passage. Traditional freedoms of the high seas (or ABNJ) are intended to apply in EEZs.[3] In practice, differing interpretations by nation-states and attempts by various nation-states to impose levels of sovereign control increasingly complicate notions of navigational freedom, particularly in EEZs.[4]

The oceans and seas provide a common strategic and economic medium for regional and extra-regional actors. The major maritime trade routes of the Indo-Pacific are central to extra and intra-regional trade that is vital to the global economy. They provide the essential means for facilitating the transport of vast volumes of energy resources and other bulk cargoes, and increasingly manufactured goods between West Asia,[5] Europe, East Africa, South Asia, East Asia, the Americas and Australia. The definition of maritime infrastructure needs to accommodate all of the key elements that contribute to the maritime system: ports, port infrastructure and shore connections; offshore facilities and structures; SLOCs – including maritime choke points; and shipping.

Maritime Security Defined

The other key concept in this analysis is 'maritime security' – a distinct and pervasive subset of global, regional and national security that is important to all actors who seek to use the maritime domain. There is no single, universal, internationally accepted definition of maritime security. Bateman characterised the inability for regional countries in the Asia-Pacific to agree on a definition of maritime security as a "basic wicked problem". He noted that the lack of definition presents enormous difficulties for endeavours to develop regional cooperative approaches.[6]

In Northeast Asia, the larger maritime powers like China, Japan and South Korea tend to prefer a narrow, traditional state on state concept of maritime security based around potential conflict and ongoing competition between maritime security forces. In Southeast Asia, the smaller states are generally amenable to a more holistic concept of maritime security. This notion encompasses traditional (state on state) security and also non-traditional security that overlaps with broader security concerns, including economic, energy, environmental, human and food security, as they intersect with the maritime domain. In South Asia, the Indian Navy also favours a more inclusive concept of maritime security.[7] The concept of maritime security should be based upon the recognition of a common need among multiple actors for "good order at sea".[8] This includes dealing with multifarious non-traditional security problems at sea for example "piracy and armed robbery against ships, maritime terrorism, illicit trafficking in drugs and arms, people smuggling, pollution, illegal fishing and marine natural hazards".[9]

Maritime security needs to embrace communal objectives among maritime users for unfettered maritime trade and a healthy marine environment combined with respecting and supporting the sovereign rights and obligations of littoral states. This requires recognition of shared risks and common vulnerabilities that may impact the achievement of mutual objectives. Providing security in the vast and interconnected maritime domain lies beyond the rights and responsibilities, and capacities, of any single actor or group of actors; the requirement is comprehensive and the responsibilities are collective.

Understanding commonly held objectives for the maritime system, and the uncertainties that may impact their achievement, is central to devising a universal concept of maritime security. The notion of shared risks and common vulnerabilities that may impact the achievement of mutual objectives forms an important coalescing factor. There are collective security needs that require cooperative approaches to implement.[10] In contributing to a workable and relevant concept of maritime security the internationally accepted description of 'risk', simply defined as the "effect of uncertainty on objectives",[11] is adequate. There are numerous definitions of 'vulnerability' in international literature. For the purposes of this analysis, the following definition is applied:

> Vulnerability is the state of susceptibility to harm from exposure to risks posing unquantifiable uncertainty combined with insufficient capacities to prevent, prepare, respond or adapt.

Drawing these ideas together, and cognisant that concepts of maritime security should reflect the profoundly international, interconnected and systemic realities of the oceans, a broad characterisation is necessary. Developed and defined for the Indo-Pacific context[12] the proposition employed here is:

> Maritime security is an inclusive concept that derives from the systemic nature of the maritime domain presenting multiple and inter-related requirements for security cooperation between state and non-state actors; it addresses traditional and non-traditional security challenges. Maritime security involves coordinating collective and cooperative risk mitigation and vulnerability reduction efforts in order to protect and promote national, regional and global vital interests, objectives and core values including those relating to state sovereignty, freedom of navigation, economic development, environment and ocean resources, human and social development, and political stability.

Maritime Infrastructure Trends in the Indo-Pacific

Analysis of maritime infrastructure developments and the maritime security strategic implications needs to take account of numerous contextual factors and related trends. Specific contemporary activities and initiatives perpetrated by key Indo-Pacific states – China, India and Japan along with the US and Indonesia – are analysed in the following sections.

China – Maritime Infrastructure Trendsetter

China has rapidly become the major contributor to maritime infrastructure development in the Indo-Pacific through its 'One Belt, One Road (OBOR)' programme also known as the 'Belt and Road Initiative (BRI)'. China held a grand forum in Beijing to engage the international community with the BRI on May 14-15, 2017. It was attended by 130 countries and 70 international organisations; notably, India chose not to be represented. The forum reportedly produced 32 trade and financial agreements, and President Xi Jinping announced US$8.7 billion worth of aid and assistance to participating countries and entities.[13]

This ambitious undertaking aims to connect China with 65 Asian, African and European countries covering approximately two-thirds of the world's population at an estimated investment cost of US$ 4-8 trillion.[14] The massive proposal includes the integral '21st Century Maritime Silk Road (MSR)', which according to the official People's Republic of China (PRC) Government vision statement,[15] aims to:

> deepen ocean cooperation by fostering closer ties with countries along the Road, supported by the coastal economic belt in China. Ocean cooperation will focus on building the China-Indian Ocean-Africa-Mediterranean Sea Blue Economic Passage, by linking the China-Indochina Peninsula Economic Corridor, running westward from the South China Sea to the Indian Ocean, and connecting the China-Pakistan Economic Corridor (CPEC) and the Bangladesh-China-India-Myanmar Economic Corridor (BCIM-EC). Efforts will also be made to jointly build the blue economic passage of China-Oceania-South Pacific, travelling southward from the South China Sea into the Pacific Ocean.

The Chinese MSR vision includes expansive aspirations. These are intended to enhance "marine industry cooperation"; include upgraded "maritime connectivity" that will involve Chinese participation in the "construction and operation" of ports; facilitate improvements to maritime transport; and improve "connectivity of information infrastructure and networks". The vision statement includes a section on maritime security recognising that it "is a key assurance for developing the blue economy". Across the maritime routes, China proposes to cooperate in providing "common maritime security for mutual benefits" that would encompass "maritime navigation security", marine search and rescue, "prevention and mitigation" of marine disasters and "maritime law enforcement".[16]

The MSR vision statement cites numerous projects already being implemented across the length and breadth of the Indo-Pacific maritime domain. These include the Malacca Seaside Industrial Park in Malaysia, the Gwadar port in Pakistan, the Kyaukpyu port in Myanmar, the Colombo Port City and the Phase II Hambantota Port Project in Sri Lanka, the railway linking Ethiopia and Djibouti and the railway between Mombasa and Nairobi in Kenya. In addition, China claims "collaboration with the Netherlands in developing offshore wind power generation and with Indonesia, Kazakhstan and Iran in implementing seawater desalination projects" and improved submarine cable communication connectivity through the Asia-Pacific Gateway (APG) submarine optical fibre cable. Industrial parks are under construction in "China's Qinzhou and Malaysia's Kuantan, the Sihanoukville Special Economic Zone in Cambodia, and the Suez Economic and Trade Cooperative Zone in Egypt".[17]

When the MSR vision is viewed in conjunction with China's Military Strategy, publicly released in 2015, a powerful strategic shift towards China's intent to become a major global maritime power is clearly apparent. The Military Strategy states, inter alia, that "the PLA Navy (PLAN) will gradually shift its focus from 'offshore waters defense' to the combination of 'offshore waters defense' with 'open seas protection'". The need is identified to "develop a modern maritime military force structure commensurate with its national security and development interests ... protect the security of strategic SLOCs and overseas interests, and participate in international maritime cooperation, so as to provide strategic support for building itself into a maritime power".[18]

Traditionally a land-focused country with strategic geography that has logically dictated a primarily continental strategic outlook, China is now clearly pursuing more comprehensive national and military strategies that have strong maritime emphases. Further, it has become apparent that China seeks to supplant the US as the global guardian of the oceans, at least in the areas encompassed by the MSR.

Whether China's objectives are geo-strategic, geo-economic or a combination of the two is an important question. China's support for MSR infrastructure development is consistent with both strategic and economic aspirations. China's strategic centre of gravity is the Chinese Communist Party (CCP), whose survival is central to the survival of the PRC. Continued economic growth is necessary for the CCP to keep the vast Chinese population and potentially fractious polity under control. There is also a very distinct mercantilist aspect to China's activities. Geopolitical goals are served by binding BRI countries economically closer to China. Chinese objectives include gaining unfettered access to the resources necessary to maintain economic progress while also building markets for high-end manufactured goods, and absorbing excess Chinese industrial capacity and growing technical expertise.[19]

China is hugely strategically vulnerable. It is heavily reliant upon the extended SLOCs that navigate strategic choke points in the northwest and northeast corners of the Indian Ocean and pass close by India as they traverse the 4,000 nautical mile oceanic expanse. In addition to potential longer-term economic benefits, China is endeavouring to reduce its strategic risks, particularly in accessing vital energy supplies, by developing alternative entree points through new ports at Gwadar, Pakistan, and Kyaukpyu, Myanmar. Observing these developments, particularly with Gwadar, India is deeply apprehensive that China will be afforded enhanced opportunities to spread economic and political influence throughout West and South Asia.[20]

Progress with the MSR has not been all smooth sailing for China and its partners. China has reportedly funded port developments in Sri Lanka 98 percent through loans and only 2 percent through grants under provisos that projects must be awarded to Chinese companies and at least 50 percent of associated procurements (equipment and personnel) must be sourced from China.[21] This imposes a heavy burden upon the developing Sri Lankan economy and is hardly in keeping with an alleged BRI spirit of equality and mutual benefit. Hambantota and Colombo are designed principally as hub ports for the regional transhipment of containers from large to smaller vessels. Profitability is dependent upon a critical mass of throughput, which will be hard to achieve.[22]

Balancing Chinese strategic aspirations with support for economic development is proving to be problematic for recipient states and for China. India has become increasingly concerned about Chinese submarine forays into the Indian Ocean, allegedly to support anti-piracy operations, when submarines are demonstrably unsuitable for such tasks. Submarines are essentially strategic, stealth weapons systems designed for covert surveillance and maritime warfare. At least seven Chinese submarine deployments have been reported since 2013; these have included three by nuclear powered submarines.[23] Sri Lanka has been keen to assuage India's concerns about providing support for Chinese navy activities in the Indian Ocean. It reportedly refused to give the PLAN permission to dock a submarine in Colombo in May 2017, despite having permitted a Chinese submarine to use the port in October 2014.[24]

The Gwadar port development in the Balochistan province, Pakistan, is the gateway to the aspirational CPEC, which is intended to connect yet to be constructed road and rail links through Pakistan, Afghanistan and Central Asia with new overland transport corridors to western China. Gwadar potentially offers significant economic and strategic advantages for both Pakistan and China, with its location close to the Strait of Hormuz.

Chinese companies are reported to be negotiating with the Government of Myanmar for construction and operation of the other proposed Indian Ocean gateway deep sea port at Kyaukpyu. The port would provide an entry point for an overland oil and gas pipeline to southern China that would enable the Malacca Strait to be avoided. The so-called 'Malacca Strait dilemma' remains a major strategic concern for China with its heavy reliance upon bulk imports via that extensive maritime choke point, particularly oil from West Asia. The port proposal includes an industrial park intended to support development of a special economic zone in Myanmar's western Rakhine State. A Chinese company is reported to be looking at funding up to 85 percent of the projects, which means that China would hold a strong controlling interest in the port.[25]

An important strategic and economic addition to Chinese maritime infrastructure development began operation in May 2017 when the Doraleh Multi-purpose Port project in Djibouti officially opened. Doraleh is one of four new ports in Djibouti that have been co-financed and equipped by China. The Chinese naval base in Djibouti, China's first overseas military installation, is also due to open soon. China will ostensibly use its new military base in Djibouti to support anti-piracy operations off the Horn of Africa, although support for other Chinese activities in the western Indian Ocean, West Asia and Africa appears likely.

Djibouti is strategically located on the Bab el-Mandeb chokepoint, entry point to the Red Sea and the Suez Canal. It already hosts permanent US, French and Japanese military installations.[26] Apart from the close proximity to naval and military forces from several other nations, Chinese operations and investments may be put at risk due to instability in the immediate region. There is an ongoing border dispute between Djibouti and Eritrea; the Saudi-Qatari spat in early 2017 has impacted because Qatari peacekeepers on the border have been withdrawn.[27]

In 2017, Chinese companies completed a 750 kilometre electric railway line between Addis Ababa, Ethiopia, and Djibouti. A 550 kilometre refined petroleum pipeline and a natural gas liquefaction plant, with a 770 kilometre pipeline between Ethiopia and an export terminal in Djibouti, are also reported to be slated for development. Major strategic risks are presented for Chinese investments because of rising instability in Ethiopia, including along the border with Djibouti and potential conflict spilling over from South Sudan.[28]

China's aggressive infrastructure developments in the South China Sea, particularly in the Spratly Islands but also in the Paracel Islands, have major regional security implications. A July 2016 award by an arbitration tribunal, constituted under Annex VII of UNCLOS, ruled against Chinese claims in the South China Sea.[29] The tribunal determined China's claimed historic rights to the area to be invalid. It also held that Scarborough Shoal and five of the features occupied by China in the Spratly Islands are "rocks that cannot sustain human habitation or economic life of their own". These features can generate a 12 nautical mile territorial sea but are not entitled to an EEZ or continental shelf in their own right. Despite these rulings, and noting that China chose not to participate in the tribunal case that was brought by the Philippines, China continues massive reclamation and construction activities that have converted seven features[30] into large artificial islands. Airstrips, port facilities and other structures have rapidly been constructed on these artificial islands. There are allegations that China is militarising these features to support naval and air warfare operations in the South China Sea.[31]

China's actions in the South China Sea continue to be the cause of major strategic disquiet in the region, including rising maritime security concerns. Littoral states and extra-regional actors are apprehensive about Chinese actions and intentions. Concerns include potential Chinese disruptions to freedom of navigation of important sea routes, ongoing Chinese sponsored oil and gas exploration activities in areas subject to overlapping territorial claims, damage to highly sensitive marine environments from reclamation activities and the possibility that China may declare an aerial defence identification zone (ADIZ) when the airfields on artificial islands are completed (as it has already done in the East China Sea).

Responses by the South China Sea littoral states vary. The Philippines has adopted an appeasement strategy towards its large and powerful neighbour, despite the arbitration tribunal ruling in its favour. Vietnam continues to aggressively assert its territorial claims in the South China Sea,[32] while Malaysia has adopted a more conciliatory approach to China. In 2017, Indonesia, not a direct claimant in the South China Sea territorial dispute, newly declared the 'North Natuna Sea'.[33] It is investing in enhanced military capabilities on its South China Sea islands in order to hedge against rising Chinese assertiveness. While efforts to find peaceful ways forward are pursued, the prospects of regional conflict at sea involving at least low-level clashes are high and continue to rise.[34] Chinese infrastructure developments in the South China Sea, while having some economic aspects, must be seen as fundamentally intended to support China's strategic aspirations of becoming a regional and global great power; the situation is unstable and becoming increasingly dangerous.

China's very active and expanding maritime infrastructure programmes across the Indo-Pacific are having significant maritime security implications. Many of the developments can be attributed to mercantilist ambitions intended to support China's hunger for raw materials and search for new markets for its manufactured goods and technical expertise.

However, growing Chinese assertiveness in the western Pacific and the spread of Chinese influence across the Indian Ocean has major strategic and security implications. China has embarked upon a declared policy of expanding its maritime security capabilities and presence. This can be viewed as a positive contribution to regional maritime security; it is also seen as threatening by many regional states, particularly India. China is inexorably realising its aspirations of becoming a major regional and global power.

India's Emergence

India continues to experience strong economic growth and, under prime minister Narendra Modi, has become more confident and strategically assertive. India is the major regional power in the Indian Ocean and has been developing its maritime security forces to support its aspirations of regional pre-eminence. India has the largest regional maritime security forces and occupies a central geostrategic position. Modi has led an increasingly proactive approach with strong attention to maritime affairs. Modi declared, in November 2014, that India's former 'Look East' policy had become an 'Act East' policy.[35] Much greater strategic importance has been placed upon the Bay of Bengal[36] and soft power engagement with South Asian states, particularly the members of the Association of Southeast Asian Nations (ASEAN).[37]

India is reported to be following a five-pronged strategy towards its Maritime South Asian neighbours. This involves targeting the Seychelles, Mauritius, Sri Lanka, the Maldives, Bangladesh and Myanmar. Specific programmes are aimed at strengthening their maritime security capacities and developing "blue economy" partnerships.[38] With regard to the latter programme, economic assistance for maritime infrastructure developments is part of the agenda, with India seeking to compete with Chinese influence among its near neighbours.

India is also seeking to hedge against Pakistan and China with a recently announced Chabahar Agreement with Iran and Afghanistan. Chabahar is an Iranian port city on the coast of the Gulf of Oman, near the border with Pakistan. This development will give India access to Afghanistan and eventually energy resources from Central Asia while bypassing Pakistan. The agreement has the potential to impact the regional strategic dynamic as it provides Afghanistan with port access to the Indian Ocean and will enable India to access oil and gas without having to rely on vulnerable pipelines passing through Pakistan. India is reported to be making significant government and private industry investments in developing the port of Chabahar and related shore-side connections, including investing in Iranian oil and gas developments.[39]

Japan and India – Working Together

Another important development with both maritime infrastructure and maritime security consequences is India's growing strategic and economic partnership with Japan in Africa and Asia. Prime Minister Modi and Prime Minister Shinzo Abe announced the concept of an Asia Africa Growth Corridor (AAGC) in a joint declaration in November 2016. In what can be seen as a direct challenge to China's BRI, the AAGC is to be based upon "four pillars of Development and Cooperation Projects, Quality Infrastructure and Institutional Connectivity, Enhancing Capacities and Skills and People-to-People partnership".[40]

The AAGC focus is on development of countries and sub-regions in Africa, seeking synergies where possible. The priority is economic growth, and while not specifically targeted towards maritime infrastructure, the interconnectedness aspects would likely have significant maritime components. The concept aspires to build bridges between Asia and Africa toward realising a "free and open Indo-Pacific region", as advocated by Japan in an initiative that resonates with India's Act East policy. A joint India-Japan research project has been initiated to flesh out the concept.[41]

Japanese financial support is integral to achievement of India's Act East policy. For example, work is reported to have commenced on a highway from Meghalaya in northeast India to Myanmar as part of the India-Myanmar-Thailand trilateral pact to build a 1,400 km highway that will link India with Southeast Asia. Related to this is Japan's Official Development Loan Assistance (ODA) commitment to India that reached an all-time high of US$1 billion in 2015, with future commitments of US$2 billion. US$30 billion of Japanese public and private financing has already gone to India over five years.[42] Further, Japan committed ODA loans of more than US$2 billion to infrastructure developments in Bangladesh. In 2014, Bangladesh accepted a Japanese proposal which, along with a deep-sea port, included four coal fired power plants in Chittagong. This was seen as directly related to Bangladesh's decision not to proceed with a Chinese proposal to fund a deep-sea port.[43] When combined with growing India-Japan security ties, ODA commitments represent tangible evidence of the strengthening relationship designed to hedge against Chinese expansionism, while promoting mutually beneficial regional infrastructure and economic development.[44]

US – Period of Strategic Uncertainty

With the advent of President Trump's 'America First' rhetoric and associated isolationist tendencies, the US is perceived, to a significant degree, to have withdrawn from the Indo-Pacific fuelling a period of uncertainty and therefore rising strategic risk. In cancelling US involvement in the Obama administration's Trans Pacific Partnership (TPP) initiative, the US ceded economic influence to the major Asian powers – and China is taking full advantage of the opportunity this presents. A forecast conflict of choices for regional states between supporting OBOR or TPP has been removed.[45]

The US appears to be in strategic disarray while China is rapidly implementing clearly articulated and ambitious plans. The US, however, maintains far and away the largest maritime security capabilities in the world and remains the world's largest economy. Indo-Pacific formal US security alliance partners like Japan, Australia and South Korea, along with other countries that have cooperative security arrangements with the US, like India and Singapore, are endeavouring to keep the US engaged. However, mixed messages continue to emanate from the White House and other parts of the US administration that contribute to the uncertainty. The overall outcome for Indo-Pacific maritime security and related infrastructure developments is that regional states are adopting hedging strategies. This involves looking to diversify away from dependence upon the US for security assurance while enhancing national maritime security forces.

Indonesia – Global Maritime Hub?

Indonesia holds an important position in the Indo-Pacific strategic maritime context. It is the most populous state in Southeast Asia, the world's largest archipelagic state, and it occupies a central geographical location at the confluence of the Indian and Pacific Oceans. It sits astride four maritime choke points, including the vital Malacca Strait.

Maritime issues are beginning to feature more prominently in Indonesia's strategic thinking. In 2014, President Joko 'Jokowi' Widodo announced a vision for Indonesia to become a 'Global Maritime Nexus' and this raised national and regional expectations.[46] However, there has been little real progress toward Indonesia becoming a regional and global maritime hub.[47] Indonesia's capacity and political will to contribute to regional maritime security risk reduction efforts remain modest. Indonesia has limited capacity to control its immediate maritime domain and respond to humanitarian and natural disaster crises. There has been little real progress with Indonesian maritime infrastructure developments.

Other Maritime Infrastructure and Security Factors

Offshore Oil and Gas

The offshore oil and gas industry is an important and rapidly expanding area of maritime infrastructure in the Indo-Pacific. There have been massive increases in offshore oil and gas exploration and exploitation activity, and investment, driven by economic growth and the rising demand for energy in Asia. China is forecast to be the largest energy consumer in the world by 2035, with consumption increasing to more than 70 percent higher than the US. Energy consumption rates in developing Indo-Pacific economies, including India and Indonesia, are forecast to grow even faster than China.[48]

In addition to highly significant oil and gas supplies from West Asia, several new offshore areas are producing oil and gas while others have potential. They range from the Mumbai High Basin off India's west coast, and the Bay of Bengal; the northwest shelf and Timor Basin areas off north-western Australia; the South China Sea where Malaysia, Brunei, China, Taiwan, Vietnam and the Philippines are active in the Spratly and Paracel Island areas,[49] Indonesian offshore developments that are progressing in the Makassar Strait; the Gulf of Thailand; and the East China Sea that includes disputed areas, for example, around the Senkaku/Diaoyu/Tiaoyutai Islands. Offshore oil and gas exploration activities are also increasing off parts of the east African coast, although most commercial fields discovered so far lie off Africa's west coast. Competition for access to new offshore oil and gas fields is expected to intensify over the next two decades.[50]

Pressures to increase production are compelling the offshore oil and gas sector into deeper and more remote waters at the edge of human experience and technological capacity. Multinational companies operate across multiple regulatory regimes and sometimes disputed national jurisdictions; they will exploit any perceived weaknesses to their advantage. Political and commercial pressures combine to promote risk-taking and to undermine regulatory regimes that are inadequately constituted, resourced and experienced.[51]

Competition for access to undersea resources is intense, as exemplified in the South China Sea. Overlapping maritime territorial claims and maritime boundary delimitation concerns have contributed to rising tensions. For example, bilateral relations between Vietnam and China took a negative turn in May 2014 when a large Chinese exploratory drilling ship commenced operations in waters also claimed by Vietnam. This action fuelled profound anti-Chinese sentiment in Vietnam. It resulted in Vietnam increasing its investment in maritime security capabilities and broadening its foreign engagement to include seeking improved relations with and support from the US and India.[52]

There are also significant tensions in the East China Sea arising from numerous sovereignty disputes primarily involving China, Japan and South Korea[53] with the prospect of access to hydrocarbons a key factor. Conversely, India and Bangladesh set a very positive example of resolving a sensitive maritime boundary dispute where offshore oil and gas prospects loomed when, on July 7, 2014, they accepted a determination by the UN Permanent Court of Arbitration on the delimitation of shared boundaries in the Bay of Bengal.[54]

The majority of oil and gas sector security incidents involve petty theft primarily against small, slow local oil tankers and vessels at anchor. Large fixed oil and gas installations are difficult targets for pirates and sea robbers. The likelihood of terrorist attacks on the global energy sector, although low, continues to be of concern. Large fixed offshore oil and gas installations present difficult targets for terrorists, although the risks must be viewed as credible as major damage can be inflicted that will have global security and economic consequences.[55]

Shipping Developments

Merchant shipping comprises an essential element of the global and regional maritime infrastructure. Developments with shipping are integral to systemic maritime security considerations. Over 90 percent of goods worldwide are transported by sea; the maritime trading system provides the core of the increasingly interconnected global economic network.

Ship ownership in the Indo-Pacific is increasing, with 18 of the top 35 ship-owning economies to be found in Asia. Japan, China (plus Hong Kong), Singapore, South Korea, Taiwan, India and Indonesia rank highly.[56] However, ship ownership only tells part of the story; in many respects, the shipping industry epitomises globalisation. Typically, a merchant ship exemplifies an internationalised enterprise: the ship owner, ship manager, operating company and crew will likely be drawn from multiple nationalities. The cargo is likely to be from another nation or multiple nations; the Flag State will likely be different again. Ships are often registered with 'flags of convenience' states that have little direct dealings with the ship, its operation or its crew. There remain instances of nationalised merchant shipping, for example, those under US or Chinese Flag, but these are more the exception than the rule. Conversely, the countries of beneficial ownership, as opposed to the Flag State, are mainly rich industrialised countries.[57]

Global economic factors have driven massive restructuring of the commercial shipping industry. Oil crises and rising fuel costs have required the industry to become highly efficient, employing rapidly evolving technology and innovative crewing models in order to cut costs and improve competitiveness. The shipping industry has undergone major changes in organisational structures to improve efficiency. This has involved ship owners separating from ship management by engaging highly specialised ship management companies, consolidation of individual shipping companies into massive multinational conglomerates that often specialise in a particular global shipping industry sector (i.e. liner [container] ships, tankers, bulk carriers, etc.), and shipping companies diversifying into logistics and other forms of transport.[58]

The 'just in time', high and large volume logistics nature of the international shipping sector make it highly sensitive to disruptions. Over 40,000 ships navigate the strategic waterways of the Indo-Pacific annually and contribute to an estimated 40 percent of global sea trade.[59] Maintaining traffic flows through the Indo-Pacific SLOCs, particularly the regional choke points, is vital to the interests of the shipping user nations. From a maritime security perspective, any interference or impedance of shipping will have significant impacts on global, regional and national economies.

Strategic Risk Assessment

In this analysis, maritime infrastructure and maritime security have been defined as holistic concepts. They overlap with and impact other aspects of development and security: economic, energy, human, food, and environmental. The synergies and interrelationships need to be understood and accommodated because the integrity of the interconnected regional and global maritime system is vital to the security and prosperity of all participants. There is a powerful proposition that attaining mutual objectives in the maritime domain, and dealing with the shared risks and common vulnerabilities that impact their realisation, require ever greater collective and cooperative approaches. There is a communal need to address traditional and non-traditional threats to maritime security. Against this notion must be balanced the realities of strategic competition between states, with risks arising from great power rivalries.

What are the overall strategic implications of maritime infrastructure investments around the vast Indo-Pacific rim? The situation is dynamic, and it presents both opportunities and threats. Increasing Indian, Japanese and Chinese investments in infrastructure development are likely to provide systemic maritime infrastructure improvements. Many developing countries in the Indo-Pacific sorely need investment in infrastructure; they are being given opportunities to boost their domestic capacity. In many respects they are beneficiaries of the growing strategic competition between the Asian great powers. However, there will be expectations of strategic support for one or other of the donor nations from states that are increasingly obligated, and are often economically, socially, politically and militarily weak.

An expansionist and increasingly assertive China that is also strategically and economically vulnerable is clearly evident. When considered in the context of growing India-Japan economic and security ties and military capabilities, designed primarily to hedge against Chinese expansionism, a potentially dangerous prospect is emerging. Regional great power rivalry has both positive and negative implications. A dearth of effective regional dialogue mechanisms to help manage differences and reduce the likelihood of conflict is of concern. Growing uncertainty surrounding the US willingness and capacity to continue providing a balancing mechanism in the Indo-Pacific adds to strategic risks.

Chinese agendas can be seen as both mercantilist and strategic. The Chinese hunger for raw materials and search for markets for manufactured goods and Chinese expertise, being pursued through the BRI and other initiatives, can be seen as fundamentally about Chinese economic security. Diversifying port opportunities in the Indian Ocean to connect with land routes to China, along with protecting the integrity of the extended SLOCs, are consistent with a mercantilist agenda. However, massive Chinese investment in claiming, developing and militarising isolated features in the South China Sea must principally be viewed as driven by strategic aspirations.

Added to the emerging Indo-Pacific strategic context are displays of hubris emanating from both China and India. Both countries have very large populations, large geography and growing economies overshadowed by histories of colonial subjugation and disadvantage. They are each pursuing what they perceive as their rightful places in the world: China as a global power and the major Indo-Pacific power, and India as the major power in the Indian Ocean. Inevitably, the spheres of influence of the two emerging Asian great powers will overlap, bringing prospects of conflict. Maritime infrastructure investment represents an important aspect of China-India strategic competition because it supports both economic and security aspirations. As the weaker of the two Asian giants, India's alignment with Japan clearly has economic and strategic consequences as they both endeavour to offset growing Chinese power and influence.

Medium and small Indo-Pacific regional states, both developed and developing, are being presented with difficult choices that have strategic and economic implications. Maritime infrastructure improvements offer benefits to the maritime system while concomitantly creating security challenges. Increasingly, littoral states are adopting hedging strategies that include enhancing their military capabilities, particularly forces designed to contribute to maritime security.

Freedom to navigate the Indo-Pacific SLOCs remains central to globalised economic well-being. The SLOCs are vital maritime infrastructure components: maintaining SLOC integrity is a fundamental collective maritime security requirement. Similarly, supporting the rights of coastal states to explore and exploit their offshore resources, particularly oil and gas, is growing in importance across the region. Recognising that rights bring obligations to provide for safety, security and environmental health is important. The inherently internationalised nature of the global maritime sectors – ports, shipping, and oil and gas industries – must be recognised and accommodated by all involved.

Maritime infrastructure developments in the Indo-Pacific, when viewed through a maritime security strategic lens, offer both benefits and challenges. Improved infrastructure adds to the efficacy of the regional maritime system, which serves the entire maritime community. Increasing investments from China, India and Japan in ports and other maritime assets, along with greater commitment to security of the SLOCs and offshore industries, have positive strategic implications. Against this, rising strategic competition and the potential for conflict between the Asian great powers, probably implicating and involving medium and small powers, must be considered. All participants in the Indo-Pacific maritime system need certainty and stability, they are essential to economic progress; uncertainty gives rise to increasing security risks.

This analysis underscores the need for deeper understanding of mutual objectives in the Indo-Pacific maritime domain, and the need to address shared risks and common vulnerabilities. Concurrent with the emerging Asian great power competition, there is a growing need to create and enhance mechanisms for collective and cooperative approaches to maritime security essential to protecting the regional maritime system, including its infrastructure.

NOTES

1. Lee Cordner, "Maritime Cooperation in the Indian Ocean Region", in Sam Bateman, Rajni Gamage and Jane Chan (eds.), *ASEAN and the Indian Ocean: The*

Key Maritime Links, RSIS Monograph No. 33, S. Rajaratnam School of International Studies, Singapore, 2017, p. 34.

2. Saul Bernard Cohen, *Geopolitics of the World System*, Rowman & Littlefield Publishers, Lanham, 2003, pp. 3 and 58.
3. *The United Nations Convention on the Law of the Sea (UNCLOS)*, United Nations, New York, 1983, pp. xxiv-xxvi.
4. Stuart Kaye, "Indian Ocean Maritime Claims", *Journal of the Indian Ocean Region*, 6 (1), 2010, pp. 122-124.
5. The term West Asia is used in preference to Middle East. The latter term has European/British colonial connotations and is therefore increasingly redundant in the modern context. West Asia more accurately and appropriately describes the geographic area between South and Central Asia, Europe and North Africa.
6. Sam Bateman, "Solving the 'Wicked Problems' of Maritime Security: Are Regional Forums up to the Task?", *Contemporary Southeast Asia*, 33 (1), 2011, pp. 2-3.
7. *Freedom to Use the Seas: India's Maritime Military Strategy*, Indian Navy, Integrated Headquarters Ministry of Defence (Navy), New Delhi, 2007, pp. iii-iv.
8. Sam Bateman, Joshua Ho and Jane Chan, *Good Order at Sea*, RSIS Policy Paper, Nanyang Technological University, Singapore, 2009, p. 4; Geoffrey Till, *Seapower: A Guide for the Twenty-First Century*, 3rd ed., Routledge, London and New York, 2013, pp. 282-317.
9. Sam Bateman, Joshua Ho and Jane Chan, No. 8, p. 4.
10. Lee Cordner, "Risk Managing Maritime Security in the Indian Ocean Region", *Journal of the Indian Ocean Region*, 10 (1), 2014, pp. 46-66; Lee Cordner, "Exploring Risks and Vulnerabilities: An Alternate Approach to Maritime Security Cooperation in the Indian Ocean Region", *Journal of Defence Studies*, 8 (2), 2014, pp. 21-43.
11. The meanings of the words in the definition of *risk* are explained as follows: "Effect is a deviation from the expected – positive and/or negative"; "Objectives can have different aspects (such as financial, health and safety, and environmental goals) and can apply at different levels (such as strategic, organization-wide, project, product and process)"; and "Uncertainty is the state, even partial, of deficiency of information related to, understanding or knowledge of, an event, its consequence, or likelihood". The definition Notes state that "Risk is often characterized by reference to potential *events*... and *consequences* or a combination of these" and is "often expressed in terms of a combination of the consequence of an event...and the associated *likelihood*... of occurrence". The associated term "risk management" is defined as "coordination activities to direct and control an organization with regard to *risk*". See *ISO Guide 73: Risk Management – Vocabulary*, 1st ed., International Organisation for Standardisation (ISO), Switzerland, 2009, pp. 1-2.
12. Lee Cordner, "Risk Managing Maritime Security in the Indian Ocean Region", No. 10, pp. 47-48; Lee Cordner, "Exploring Risks and Vulnerabilities", No. 10, pp. 22-26.
13. Xue Gong, "Belt & Road Initiative: China's Belt and Road Forum: What Now?", *RSIS Commentary*, 096, 2017.
14. Bipul Chatterjee and Saurabh Kumar, "Promises and Pitfalls of the Belt and Road Initiative", *Asia Pacific Bulletin*, 388, 2017.

15. *Vision for Maritime Cooperation under the Belt and Road Initiative*, Government of the People's Republic of China, Beijing, 2017.
16. Ibid.
17. Ibid.
18. *China's Military Strategy*, Information Office of the State Council, People's Republic of China, Beijing, 2015.
19. Peter Cai, *Understanding China's Belt and Road Initiative*, Lowy Institute, Sydney, 2017, p. 17.
20. Rajeev Ranjan Chaturvedy, "China's Strategic Access to Gwadar Port: Pivotal Position in Belt and Road", *RSIS Commentary*, 005, 2017.
21. Shiyana Gunasekara, "Sri Lanka Suffers from China's Indian Ocean Strategy", *Asia Pacific Bulletin*, 372, 2017.
22. David Brewster, "Silk Roads and Strings of Pearls: The Strategic Geography of China's New Pathways in the Indian Ocean", *Geopolitics*, August 30, 2016, pp. 8-9, at http://dx.doi.org/10.1080/14650045.2016.1223631 (Accessed September 20, 2016).
23. Abhijit Singh, "Countering China's Submarine Operations in South Asia", *The Interpreter* (Lowy Institute), May 23. 2017, https://www.lowyinstitute.org/the-interpreter/countering-china-s-submarine-operations-south-asia (Accessed July 20, 2017).
24. Shihar Aneez and Ranga Sirilal, "Sri Lanka Rejects Chinese Request for Submarine Visit: Sources", *Reuters*, May 13, 2017, at http://www.reuters.com/article/us-sri-lanka-china-submarine-idUSKBN1871P9 (Accessed July 20, 2017).
25. Yimou Lee and Shwe Yee Saw Myint, "China Seeks up to 85 Percent Stake in Strategic Port in Myanmar", *Reuters*, May 5, 2017, at http://mobile.reuters.com/article/idUSKBN1811DF (Accessed May 20, 2017).
26. Michael Wieteska, "China and Djibouti: A Strategic Paradise?", Future Directions International, June 7, 2017.
27. Laura Fatovich, "Spectre of Larger Conflict Looms above Djibouti-Eritrea Disagreement", Future Directions International, July 5, 2017, at http://www.futuredirections.org.au/publication/spectre-larger-conflict-looms-djibouti-eritrea-disagreement/(Accessed July 20, 2017).
28. Alessandro Arduino, "Belt & Road Initiative: China's Energy Security: Reality Roadblock in Ethiopia", *RSIS Commentary*, 097, 2017.
29. "Press Release: The South China Sea Arbitration (The Republic of the Philippines V. The People's Republic of China)", Permanent Court of Arbitration, The Hague, the Netherlands, July 12, 2016.
30. The seven Spratly Island area features converted into artificial islands by China are Mischief Reef, Cuarteron Reef, Fiery Cross Reef, Gaven Reef (North), Johnson Reef, Hughes Reef, and Subi Reef.
31. Robert Beckman, "China's 'Island-Building' in the South China Sea: Implications for Regional Security", in Ron Huisken (ed.), *CSCAP Regional Security Outlook 2017*, Council for Security Cooperation in the Asia Pacific, Canberra, 2017, pp. 40-42.
32. Ha Anh Tuan, "Vietnam's Regional Security Challenges", in Abhijit Singh (ed.), *Line in the Waters: The South China Sea Dispute and its Implications for Asia*, Observer Research Foundation, New Delhi, 2017, pp. 47-54.

33. Aaron Connelly, "Indonesia's New North Natuna Sea: What's in a Name?", *The Interpreter* July 23. 2017, at https://www.lowyinstitute.org/the-interpreter/indonesia-s-new-north-natuna-sea-what-s-name (Accessed July 23, 2017).
34. Ristian Atriandi Supriyanto, "Indonesia's South China Sea Problem", in Abhijit Singh (ed.), *Line in the Waters: The South China Sea Dispute and its Implications for Asia*, Observer Research Foundation, New Delhi, 2017, pp. 38-46.
35. Isabelle Saint-Mézard, "India's Act East Policy: Strategic Implications for the Indian Ocean", *Journal of the Indian Ocean Region*, 12 (2), 2016, p. 178.
36. David Brewster, "The Rise of the Bengal Tigers: The Growing Strategic Importance of the Bay of Bengal", *Journal of Defence Studies*, 9 (2), 2015, pp. 81-104.
37. Lee Cordner, "Indian Ocean Conference 2016 in Singapore: India's Soft Power on Display", *RSIS Commentary*, 231, 2016.
38. Smruti S. Pattanaik, "Indian Ocean in the Emerging Geo-strategic Context: Examining India's Relations with Its Maritime South Asian Neighbours", *Journal of the Indian Ocean Region*, 12 (2),2016, pp. 134-138.
39. Lindsay Hughes, "Bypassing Pakistan: Afghanistan, India, Iran and Chabahar", Future Directions International Strategic Analysis Paper, April 26, 2016.
40. *Asia Africa Development Corridor: Partnership for Sustainable and Innovative Development: A Vision Document*, Research and Information System for Developing Countries, Africa Development Bank, New Delhi, 2017.
41. Ibid.
42. Monika Chansoria, "Japanese Investments Are Instrumental to India's Act East Policy", *Asia Pacific Bulletin*, 385, 2017.
43. Tanya Matthews, "Japanese Infrastructure Deal with Bangladesh May Disrupt 'Belt and Road' Initiative", Future Directions International, July 19,2017, at http://www.futuredirections.org.au/publication/japanese-infrastructure-deal-bangladesh-may-disrupt-belt-road-initiative/(Accessed July 23, 2017).
44. Dhruva Jaishankar, "India and Japan: Emerging Indo-Pacific Security Partnership", *RSIS Commentary*, 130, 2016.
45. Alice D. Ba, "TPP, OBOR and ASEAN: Where Will They Lead To?", *RSIS Commentary*, 108, 2016.
46. Adelle Neary, "Jokowi Spells out Vision for Indonesia's 'Global Maritime Nexus'", *Southeast Asia from Scott Circle*, Centre for Strategic & International Studies, v (24), November 26,2014.
47. Natalie Sambhi, "Jokowi's 'Global Maritime Axis': Smooth Sailing or Rocky Seas Ahead?", *Security Challenges*, 11 (2), 2015, pp. 39-55.
48. Lee Cordner, *Offshore Oil and Gas Safety and Security in the Asia Pacific: The Need for Regional Approaches to Managing Risks*, RSIS Monograph No. 26, S. Rajaratnam School of International Studies, Singapore, 2013, at http://www.rsis.edu.sg/publications/monographs/Monograph26.pdf (Accessed March 6, 2017).
49. Lee Cordner, "The Spratly Islands Dispute and the Law of the Sea", *Ocean Development and International Law*, 25, 1994, pp. 61-74.
50. Lee Cordner, No. 48.
51. Ibid.
52. Ha Hoang Hop, "The Oil Rig Incident: A Line Has Been Crossed in Vietnam's Relations with China", *ISEAS Perspective*, 61, 2014.
53. K. Hyun-kyungand C. Min-uck, "Lee's Dokdo Trip Presses Japan", *Korea Times*,

August 11,2012, at http://www.koreatimes.co.kr/www/news/nation/2012/08/116_117130.html (Accessed August 20, 2012).

54. "Bay of Bengal Maritime Boundary Arbitration between Bangladesh and India", Permanent Court of Arbitration, 2014, at http://www.pca-cpa.org/showpage.asp?pag_id=1376 (Accessed July 22, 2014).
55. S. Bajpai and J.P. Gupta, "Securing Oil and Gas Infrastructure", *Journal of Petroleum Science and Engineering*, 55, 2007, pp. 174-186.
56. *Review of Maritime Transport 2016*, United Nations Convention on Trade Development (UNCTAD) Secretariat, Geneva, 2016, pp. 36-42.
57. Shaun Ruggunan, *Waves of Change: Globalisation and Seafaring Labour Markets*, HSRC Press, Cape Town, 2016, p. 83.
58. Ibid., pp. 77-95.
59. *Review of Maritime Transport 2016*, No. 56.

15

Soft Balancing: Asia-Africa Growth Corridor (AAGC), India-Japan Arch in contrast to the Belt and Road Initiative (BRI) and China's Rising Influence

Jagannath P. Panda

Soft balancing is an integral aspect of balance of power strategy in international politics. State(s) rely on soft balancing to not only maximise their national interests but also enhance domestic capabilities in bringing out growth and development.[1] States engaging in this form of balancing primarily aim to protect their respective national security interests ahead of other competing powers while adapting to the rapidly changing international distribution of power system.[2] Balancing comes as a protective measure for less competent entities by forming an "alliance against the principal threat(s) or concern(s)".[3] The Asia-Africa Growth Corridor (AAGC), co-envisioned by India and Japan in consultation with Africa, replicates a fine interface of soft balancing and balance of power that aims to not only enhance the Indian and Japanese domestic growth and development but also protect and enrich their national interests and presence in Africa and Asia, factoring the Indian Ocean Region (IOR) as a core interest and balancing China's rising influence in the region.

The AAGC is aimed more at enhancing India's and Japan's national interests while promoting a "liberal and value-based order" in the Indo-Pacific that would possibly challenge emerging unilateral and non-democratic measures. As K.S. Bajpai has rightly argued: "India and Japan can honestly say that they are not building relations in hostility against China; but it is right for them to plan for the eventuality of Chinese hostility."[4] The AAGC proposition draws from the two countries' increasing geopolitical convergence of economic and strategic interests, wherein concerns over China's growing strategic influence in the Indian Ocean, Africa and the Indo-Pacific in general remain a strong factor.

This chapter examines how the AAGC is the genesis of growing India-Japan strategic convergence to promote a "liberal value-based order" and a strategic response to the growing Chinese influence in Asia, Africa and the IOR. It contends that the AAGC proposition combines both overt and covert strategic interests to promote a liberal and value-based order in the Indo-Pacific by establishing strategic linkages between the continents of Asia and Africa while balancing the rapid growth of Chinese influence in these two continents.[5] The AAGC overlaps China's Belt and Road Initiative (BRI) in terms of its core objectives, particularly in focusing on infrastructural investments, connectivity and growth corridors, among other things. In a comparative perspective, the BRI through its geographical coverage of Asia, Africa and Europe surpasses the AAGC in terms of its continental outreach. But the AAGC transcends the scope and scale of the BRI in terms of its universal approach of addressing human resource development in Asia and Africa. Unlike a single-country initiative that is based more on unilateral interests, the AAGC brings an intercontinental consultative mechanism to the core while aiming to promote infrastructural investments, connectivity and growth corridors, including human resource development that is based on universal values and norms. The AAGC is therefore more of a soft-balancing strategy of India and Japan to contest the rising Chinese influence, both within and outside the purview of the BRI, in Asia, Africa and the IOR.

AAGC's Genesis: Between Concept and Conception

Many in India and Japan contend that the AAGC is an old proposition in the making, much before China's BRI was proposed by Xi Jinping in 2013.[6] A credible reference, including an official one, to this contention is however missing.[7] The AAGC proposition was formally discussed between Prime Ministers Narendra Modi and Shinzo Abe at the India-Japan Annual Summit Meeting held in Tokyo in 2016.[8] The main thrust of this meeting was that both India and Japan must take advantage of their growing strategic convergence in the Indo-Pacific region by establishing a chain of industrial corridors and industrial networks in and between Asia and

Africa. The joint statement, released on November 11, 2016, emphasised the need to "promote cooperation and collaboration in Africa" by focusing on joint projects in areas such as training and capacity building, infrastructure, connectivity and health.[9] Aiming to improve connectivity between the two continents, the two leaders stressed the need to promote a "free and open Indo-Pacific region" where a strategic synergy between India's "Act East" and Japan's "Expanded Partnership for Quality Infrastructure" (EPQI; earlier known as PQI) was made clear.[10]

Formally, the idea of the AAGC was announced at the 52nd Annual Summit Meeting of the African Development Bank (AfDB) in Gandhinagar, India, during May 22-26, 2017, where Prime Minister Narendra Modi emphatically stated that both India and Japan would aim to achieve closer developmental cooperation in Africa.[11] The announcement came against the backdrop of China's much-highlighted BRI meeting that was held from May 14-15, 2017 in Beijing. The Chinese strategic circles commented that the AAGC was a "duplication of the freedom corridor" that was originally proposed by Prime Minister Shinzo Abe in 2016 in Tokyo while meeting with Prime Minister Modi.[12] Many comparisons are being drawn between the AAGC and BRI since the compass of both the initiatives overlaps to some degree, particularly in factoring connectivity and infrastructure as two main constituents in the Indo-Pacific/Asia-Pacific region.[13]

Since its official conception in 2016, premier think tanks in India, Japan and Indonesia have worked together to enrich the AAGC's vision. A vision document was released in May 2017 at the AfDB Summit in Gandhinagar which was jointly prepared by the Research and Information System for Developing Countries (RIS) in India, the Economic Research Institute for ASEAN and East Asia (ERIA) in Jakarta, and the Institute of Developing Economies-Japan External Trade Organisation (IDE-JETRO), in consultation with their respective governments.[14] Focusing on Africa and the Indian Ocean, the vision document stresses on building capacity in the Indo-Pacific region with four target areas: (a) development and cooperation; (b) "quality infrastructure" and digital and institutional connectivity; (c) enhancing capabilities and skills; and (d) establishing people-to-people partnerships. The AAGC promotes an intercontinental framework of cooperation based on a "people-centric" proposition with the goal to enhance "growth and interconnectedness between and within Asia and Africa".[15] Based on a consultative mechanism, it aims to promote quality infrastructure and digital and regulatory connectivity in the Indo-Pacific region with the collaboration of Asia and Africa. In this strategic formulation, Africa remain the focal point.[16]

The target is to integrate Africa by establishing strategic linkages with other regions South Asia, including India, Southeast Asia, East Asia and Oceania (see Map 1). Though an official map of the AAGC is as yet unavailable, depicting the AAGC's geographical parameters points to the global ambitions that both India and Japan hold in the Indo-Pacific (see Map I). The *AAGC Vision Document* lists a number of objectives: *First*, an intercontinental framework where India and Japan can play leadership roles in attaining the infrastructural investment needs of both Asia and Africa. Asia's total infrastructural investment needs are themselves more than half of the world requirement, with China, India and Japan having the greatest infrastructural needs in Asia.[17] Likewise, Africa needs around US$100 billion in new infrastructure every year to remain competitive in the developing world.[18] The AAGC aims to address these infrastructural needs through various multilateral banks, wherein India and Japan could possibly play a leading role. Though a concrete charter and work plan on how to generate funds to meet these infrastructural needs is missing at present in the *AAGC Vision Document*, still, it is expected that the AAGC maybe able to address these current infrastructural needs of both Asia and Africa by taking advantage of Japan's influencing position in the Asian

Map 1: Asia-Africa Growth Corridor

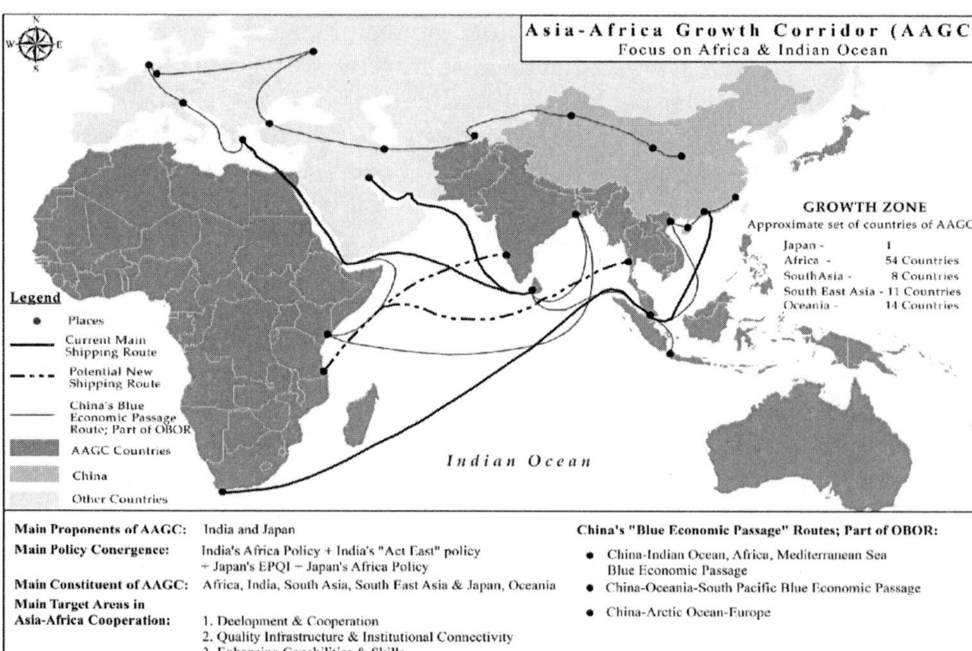

Development Bank (ADB) and in the AfDB where both India and Japan can cooperate.

Second, promoting quality infrastructure and establishing digital and institutional connectivity in and between Asia and Africa are AAGC's two main targets. These two issues are complementary in many respects. The United Nations Industrial Development Organisation (UNIDO) states that "quality infrastructure" brings together different "initiatives, institutions, organisations, activities and people" to promote or implement a particular policy or a combination of different national-quality policies within a regulatory framework.[19] Quality infrastructure is generally promoted through a public-private mode of participation involving a consultative process between local, national and regional or international actors. The AAGC aims to promote it by focusing on digital and institutional connectivity. Though these objectives look quite ambitious at present, they are the prime national policy focus of India and Japan currently and linked to their foreign policy outreach. Japan has long been aiming to promote quality infrastructure, in order to position its own influence in the world by highlighting the deficiencies in the Chinese non-qualitative infrastructural investment across the world, mainly in Africa.

Third, the AAGC aims to promote a liberal and value-based Indo-Pacific order, coinciding with the co-envisioned India-Japan *Vision 2025*.[20] Conceptualised between India and Japan in 2015 as part of their "Special Strategic and Global Partnership", *Vision 2025* has the thrust to develop a "deep, broad-based and action-oriented partnership" in the Indo-Pacific. The demand is more for principles of sovereignty and territorial integrity, where the emphasis is on promoting an "open global trade regime" along with "freedom of navigation and overflight", among other things. It stresses the focus on "reliable, sustainable and resilient infrastructures" aimed at enhancing connectivity in the IOR, which not only complements India's Act East policy and Japan's EPQI initiative but also forms a strategic convergence between India's and Japan's security interests in the Indo-Pacific. Most importantly, the AAGC facilitates the "Free and Open Indo-Pacific Strategy" that Japan aims to promote in the IOR in order to deal with the rising unilateral Chinese presence and influence in the region. The idea is to establish a strategic synergy between the "two oceans" – Indian and Pacific– and two continents – Asia and Africa[21] – where both India and Japan can cooperate to balance China's influence in the region.

These objectives indicate that the AAGC proposition is more aspirational. Indeed, a further reading of the *AAGC Vision Document* indicates that the India-Japan soft-balancing strategy is an effective and advanced tool to balance China's rising influence. It exhibits elements of soft balancing while involving a tactical, informal and adhoc security understanding between India and Japan in the Indo-Pacific. Besides, it complements the spirit of the US-India-Japan trilateralism that supports the idea of strengthening "regional connectivity" in the Indo-Pacific.[22] In other words, the AAGC concept is based on foreign policy strategic consonance between India and Japan by taking a panoramic view of the evolving Indo-Pacific security order to prepare to meet the challenges emanating from a futuristic China. The US' retreat from Asia under President Donald Trump would make the AAGC proposition even more relevant in the times to come for both India and Japan, and importantly, to think for an alternative futuristic security calculus even though both embrace the idea of a "quadrilateral" initiative along with the US and Australia. Besides, the AAGC exhibits the changing calculus of both Indian and Japanese strategic thinking on the Indo-Pacific, which is set to emerge stronger than earlier, showing that both India and Japan are no longer reluctant to show leadership visions in Asia. The intent to establish a liberal order, in an envisioned "free and open" Indo-Pacific, explains the strategic nuances that India and Japan attach to the AAGC.

AAGC: Competing with China's BRI?

Fundamentally, the AAGC and BRI have some overlap in their objectives. The BRI's major goals, as per China's vision and action plan document released in March 2015, are to promote policy coordination, facilitate connectivity, enhance trade and investment cooperation, achieve financial integration and enhance people-to-people contacts.[23] Its main focus has been more on connectivity and infrastructural investment, which have been the two main aspects of China's external engagement strategy. That draws a parallel to the AAGC, which equally emphasises on connectivity and promotion of infrastructural investment, among other issues, including the promotion of people-to-people contacts. Nevertheless, the AAGC is not really a direct response to the BRI since the policy character and connotations of both these initiatives differ, which make the AAGC more a soft initiative to balance China's presence and influence in Africa and Asia than completely negating the BRI itself.

In particular, the AAGC embraces universal values concerning human resource development while prioritising infrastructure investments, connectivity and growth corridors. On the other hand, the BRI prioritises China's national interests in promoting infrastructure investments and connectivity across different continents. The funding for BRI projects comes essentially from Chinese banks, or from Chinese Government sources like the Silk Road Fund (SRF) or through collaborative international measures where Beijing holds a dominant say in project financing. The scope of the BRI is promoted within Beijing's national perspective to position China as the centre of regional and global development. In fact, the BRI compliments greatly China's international vision of emerging as a "leader of globalisation". In his speech at the 19th National Congress of the Communist Party of China (CPC), the Chinese President Xi Jinping stressed the promotion of economic globalisation to increase "China's economic power and composite strength".[24] The AAGC, on the other hand, intends to generate private, government and also international funding, possibly from the AfDB and ADB.

By stressing on the Sustainable Developmental Goals (SDGs), the AAGC aims to priorities areas such as health, agriculture, agro-processing, skill development, pharmaceuticals and tackling disaster management issues, apart from infrastructure development and connectivity. Though the BRI equally stresses on some of these issues, still, a more 'people-friendly' approach is envisioned in the AAGC proposed framework, which is based on a universal consultative approach that China's BRI does not employ. Essentially, the AAGC embraces more the international democratic norms and values that the BRI essentially overlooks. Differences notwithstanding, both the initiatives exhibit a certain degree of overlap and competing intentions. The BRI's success depends upon Chinese diplomacy, whereas the AAGC's success depends on the extent to which India and Japan push forward this idea with Africa. The success of the AAGC will depend upon the consultative execution of policies that India, Japan and Africa undertake collectively. If anything, the AAGC's primary vision is not to compete with any other propositions per se, but to engage in more meaningful developmental partnerships, both within and outside of Africa, within an intercontinental framework with Asia.

A Shared Perspective on BRI

New Delhi's and Tokyo's stances on the BRI are both state-centric and governance-centric, linked to China's rise and influence in the world. Their problematic relationship with China comes as an additional factor. This shared perspective might encourage them further to promote the AAGC more prudently. India's primary reservation over the BRI is attached to the connectivity issues, which is aptly reflected in India's official position on the BRI.[25]

Three things are clearly reflected in India's stance on the BRI. *First*, in principle, India does not concede the grandeur to China on being the leading regional connectivity promoter. New Delhi firmly argues that the BRI is a unilateral initiative of China that ignores "universally recognized international norms, good governance, rule of law, openness, transparency and equality".[26] This is a strong stance even though India is linked with China in the sub-regional Bangladesh-China-India-Myanmar (BCIM) Economic Corridor. India's growing seriousness to pursue the India-Thailand-Myanmar Trilateral Highway and Bangladesh-Bhutan-India-Nepal (BBIN) initiative, promote the North-South Transport Corridor (NSTC) and accede to the Convention on International Transport of Goods under Cover of TIR Carnets (TIR Convention)[27] explains that New Delhi has its own regional ambition of emerging as a leading connectivity promoter. New Delhi's "Act East", "Link West" and "neighbourhood first" policies also figure connectivity as a core agenda.

Second, New Delhi emphasises how India aims to enhance connectivity based on universal values and norms, contrary to China's unilateral and authoritarian approach. India places equal importance on physical and digital connectivity, whereas China gives prime importance to promoting physical connectivity and economic corridors that will benefit primarily the Chinese economy.

Third, in opposing the China-Pakistan Economic Corridor (CPEC), India brings the question of sovereignty and territorial integrity to the forefront, which the BRI undermines. In Beijing's strategic foreign policy setting, the logic of sovereignty and history are employed selectively. This is clear in the context of China's reservation on India's oil exploration in the South China Sea vis-à-vis its unilateral engagement with Pakistan to implement the CPEC project in Pakistan-occupied Kashmir (PoK).[28] The Chinese and Indian approaches, reactions and pursuit of national interests in these matters highlight their different state-centric approaches.

Japan's stance on the BRI is not identical to that of India. Japan sent political representation to attend the May 2017 BRI Summit in Beijing. Abe has even publicly acknowledged the BRI as a grand initiative that offers scope for connecting the East and the West.[29] Taro Kono, Japan's Foreign Minister, has even stated that the BRI "will be highly conducive to global economy" if pursued in an open and transparent manner.[30] Hiroshige Seko, Japan's Minister of Economy, Trade and Industry, has expressed support to Beijing's Silk Road projects and has signed a few cooperative projects which are seen as part of the BRI.[31] Still, Japan shares a state-centric and governance-centric opposition to the BRI, regionally and globally, that is similar to the Indian stance. Abe had earlier stated that "it is necessary for infrastructure to be open to use by all, and to be developed through procurement that should be transparent and fair".[32] Calling for the BRI to adhere to a "common frame of thinking" in the region, Japan has maintained that projects must be "economically viable" and must take into account the interests of parties holding debts to return.[33] A similar concern is also noticeable on Japan's part where Tokyo decided not to join the Chinese-led Asian Infrastructure Investment Bank (AIIB), noting that the AIIB falls short on "fair governance", "mainly relating to offering clarity on debt repayment and loan sanctions".[34] The principal Japanese position has been not only to highlight the flaws in the BRI but also equally to draw the attention of the global community towards how the Chinese state approach on infrastructure investment overlooks transparency and international norms.

The Japanese opposition to the BRI is more infrastructure investment oriented while India's prime opposition is based on connectivity that involves sovereignty and territorial integrity. Given India's neighbourhood proximity to China, New Delhi perceives the BRI as a strategy in expanding China's neighbourhood connectivity projects and sees it in terms of a security concern regionally, while Japan views the BRI more in the context of competition, for its own regional and global investment plan. The AAGC, that boards connectivity and infrastructure as two core objectives, combines these Indian and Japanese perspectives together, both regionally and globally. From a holistic perspective, the AAGC objectives – intercontinental cooperation, quality infrastructural promotion, connectivity and Indo-Pacific liberal order – are important strategic necessities for India and Japan in a rapidly evolving security order where China's rising influence and unilateral initiatives are common concerns for both.

Soft Balancing the Chinese Presence in Africa and Indian Ocean

Africa as a strategic geographic location has attracted many countries which have prioritised the continent in their foreign policies. Accessing raw materials and energy resources and undertaking investments in the continent top many countries' policy agendas. Sectors such as manufacturing, services, infrastructure and telecommunications are equally attractive ends that offer massive opportunities. Aiming to have a longer-term impact in creating human development conditionality and forging ahead institutional capabilities are also among the foreign policy priorities for many countries, particularly India and China,[35] and including Japan today. At present, the West is less concerned about Africa politically. Earlier, the Western presence in Africa was more focused on checking the communist expansion.[36] Since, in its view, the threat of communism has evaporated in Africa, the West currently prefers to engage with the continent by means of trade, aid, assistance and economic contacts.[37] Asian powers such as China, India and Japan equally see the African continent not only as an opportunity but also as an effective international continental partner for global partnership and for advancing their respective foreign policy objectives. Over the last one decade, the Chinese economic and infrastructural investment initiatives have emerged as an attractive model for many African countries ahead of the Indian and Japanese economic outreach programmes. China's trade and economic contact with Africa is still higher in order than other major countries, making it the most influential power in the making in this strategic continent (see Figure 1). The relationship between China and the rest of the developing world, including the Sino-African engagement, is becoming increasingly pragmatic, secularised and commercialised.[38] The African response to this Chinese developmental discourse initially was somewhat welcoming.[39] A subtle change has however been noticed in this African approach, with a number of Chinese projects and initiatives being questioned for their non-qualitative measures and low-cost offers. Many African countries are increasingly searching for alternative modes of cooperation without completely abandoning the option to cooperate with China. Both India

Figure 1: Bilateral Trade with Africa, 2015

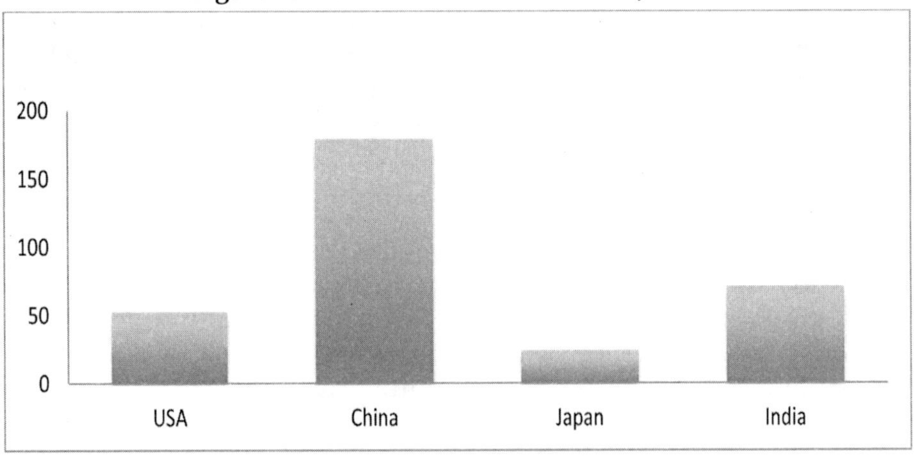

Source: Data collected from various open sources: https://www.census.gov/foreign-trade/balance/c0013.html; http://www.thisdaylive.com/index.php/2016/03/15/india-africa-bilateral-trade-hits-72-billion/; http://www.japantimes.co.jp/news/2016/08/28/national/politics-diplomacy/abe-pledges-japan-will-invest-30-billion-in-africa-by-2018/#.WUbHSd6FUux.

and Japan aim to capitalise on this critical change of mood in Africa. This serves Africa's interests, too, since the continent has been searching for alternative modes of interactions and networking for long.[40]

The year 1993 witnessed a new and meaningful attention in Japan's Africa outreach through the introduction of the Tokyo International Conference on African Development (TICAD). With the gradual decline of the official assistance from the developed countries to Africa, Tokyo saw an opportunity for itself in the early 1990s by offering more assistance through a more serious policy focus. The introduction of the TICAD (see Table 1), aiming to focus more on improving the socio-economic conditions, was a fine effort in this context.[41] Since then, Japan's economic interests in Africa have been growing continuously, with TICAD playing an instrumental role. The recent visits of Japanese Prime Ministers to Africa testify to this phenomenon (see Table 2). But though Tokyo's overall presence has increased in Africa and the relationship has become more institutionalised, Japan's engagement with Africa also faces a number of limitations. Through TICAD, Japan might have emerged as a key investor in Africa, but the Japanese official development assistance (ODA) to Africa has not increased significantly[42] (see Figures 2 and 3). Africa has hitherto not been a pivotal focus in Japanese policymaking. Nor has Japan tried to implement a "comprehensive" strategy towards Africa which would have allowed it to allocate more ODA. Rather, Japan's approach has been to concentrate on key countries in North Africa and sub-Saharan Africa. Meanwhile, the Chinese presence has expanded in Africa through a "continental" strategy. The rapid emergence of China as a strong economic actor in Africa has discouraged Japan from offering higher amounts of ODA to the continent as it previously did in 2006-07.[43]

Shinzo Abe has shown a renewed commitment to Africa in the recent past (Table 2), and has tried to further institutionalise and strengthen Japan's outreach in Africa by attending the 6th TICAD in August, 2016, in Nairobi. This was the first time when TICAD was held outside Japan. With the theme "Quality and Empowerment", the 6th TICAD focused on quality infrastructure and development. Abe stressed on building "quality Africa" centred on infrastructure, human resources, and "Kaizen" (business efficiency).[44] Building on grass-roots governance outreach, Japan outlined an Africa policy, stressing on "resilient Africa", emphasising on health and social stability.[45] Tokyo's main intent is to promote investment-oriented high-quality infrastructure-specific outreach that will subdue the Chinese substandard and quantitative infrastructural development initiative in Africa. Japan has always alleged that Beijing's outreach in Africa is

Table1: Japan in Africa –Tokyo International Conference on African Development (TICAD)

Year/TICAD	*Japan's Major Focus/Policy*	*Comments/Outcome*
October 5-6, 1993: TICAD I	**Theme:** ***Tokyo Declaration on African Development "Towards the 21st Century"*** Focus on sustainable, broad-based economic growth; improving quality of governance, transparency and accountability; sustainable development, stressing on regional economic cooperation and development; preparing a platform to share Asian developmental experiences with Africa; promoting international cooperation.	Inaugural conference where the focus was on political and economic reforms of Africa. Japan advocated for economic development of Africa through private sector engagement, regional cooperation and integration process, and sharing of Asian and African experiences with each other.
October 19-21, 1998: TICAD II	**Theme:** ***African Development Towards the 21st Century: The Tokyo Agenda for Action*** Poverty Reduction and Integration into Global Economy: focus on coordination, regional cooperation & integration; South-South cooperation; capacity building; gender mainstreaming; environmental management; social development and poverty reduction; promoting human development, education.	Japanese focus was on sub-Saharan countries of Africa. Japan aimed to extend approximately ¥ 90 billion of grant aid over the next five years, including educational facilities and improving living conditions.
September 29–October 1, 2003; TICAD III	**Theme:** ***African Development*** Overcoming poverty, low levels of agricultural and industrial and political insecurity and social strife; need for a more supportive international environment; promotion of "market access and fair trade to support the efforts of African countries to gain a meaningful foothold in the global market place".	10th anniversary declaration was released. Emphasis was more on developmental partnership, "ownership and partnership" and raising awareness aboutAfrica.
May28-30, 2008; TICAD IV	**Theme:** ***Towards a Vibrant Africa*** **(Yokohama Declaration)** Focus on infrastructure, trade, investment cooperation, including tourism and rural development; ensuring human security while focusing on education, health, governance; stress on climate change and environmental upgrade; enhancing Asia-African Intra-Africa cooperation, public-private partnership; development of African frontiers; dialogue with civil society, etc.	Boosting economic growth through Human resources development, industrial, agricultural & rural development. Focus on millennium development goals (MDGs); pledged to double ODA without debt relief including bilateral grants by 2012. Concentrating in the areas of infrastructure, agriculture, trade and investment, education, health and water.

Table1 Contd.

Year/TICAD	*Japan's Major Focus/Policy*	*Comments/Outcome*
June 1-3, 2013; TICAD V	**Theme:** ***Hand in Hand with a More Dynamic Africa*** In February 2015, Japan revised the Official Developmental Charter; focus on Japan's assistance through joint efforts of both public and private sector through TICAD; stress on peace building and assistance to human security.	Aiming for inclusive and dynamic development of Africa. US$ 32 billion in the next five years to boost economic growth including trade and investment, private sector development and natural resources. Also supported infrastructure, tourism, science and technology and human resource development.
27-28 August 2016; TICAD VI	**Theme:** ***Advancing Africa's Sustainable Development Agenda: TICAD Partnership for Shared Prosperity*** Promotion of structural economic transformation through economic diversification and industrialisation; quality of life and health, social stability; Nairobi Declaration and Nairobi Implementation Plan.	Nairobi Declaration: focused on the challenges faced by Africa, such as decline of global commodity prices, Ebola outbreak and other issues including terrorism, radicalisation and climate change. US$30 billion to support implementation of the three priority areas of the Nairobi Declaration and Implementation Plan, namely: (1) Promoting structural economic transformation through economic diversification and industrialisation. (2) Promoting resilient health systems for quality of life. (3) Promoting social stability for shared prosperity.

Source: Ministry of Foreign Affairs of Japan, at http://www.mofa.go.jp/region/africa/ticad/index.html. Prepared by the author.

Table 2: Japanese Prime Ministers' Visits to Africa in Recent Years

Date Visited	*Countries Visited*	*Dignitaries Visiting*	*Important Joint Statements/MOUs*
April 28-30, 2006	Ethiopia	Prime Minister Junichiro Koizumi	The visit witnessed the announcement of the Yokohama Action Plan and the TICAD follow-up mechanism
August 27, 2013	Djibouti	Prime Minister Shinzo Abe	The Prime Minister announced support for continued economic cooperation and ODA up to $14 billion, electricity infrastructure and maritime security
January 10–14, 2014	Mozambique, Côte d'Ivoire and Ethiopia	Prime Minister Shinzo Abe	14 governmental and private agreements were signed, including the diplomatic notes amending the Annex of Japan-Ethiopia air services agreement as well as documents on economic or academic cooperation in Mozambique. Japan agreed to provide financial support of approximately $320 million, aiming to respond to conflicts and disasters, peace and stability, including contributions to improve the situation in South Sudan, the Sahel region and Central African Republic.
January 18, 2015	Egypt	Prime Minister Shinzo Abe	Dialogue to strengthen bilateral, economic relations and tourism.
28 August, 2016	Kenya	Prime Minister Shinzo Abe	73 MOUs were signed between 20 African countries and Japan.

Sources: Ministry of Foreign Affairs of Japan; *The Japan Times*; *Asahi Shimbun*.

Figure 2: Net ODA, % of Gross National Income (GNI), 2000-2016

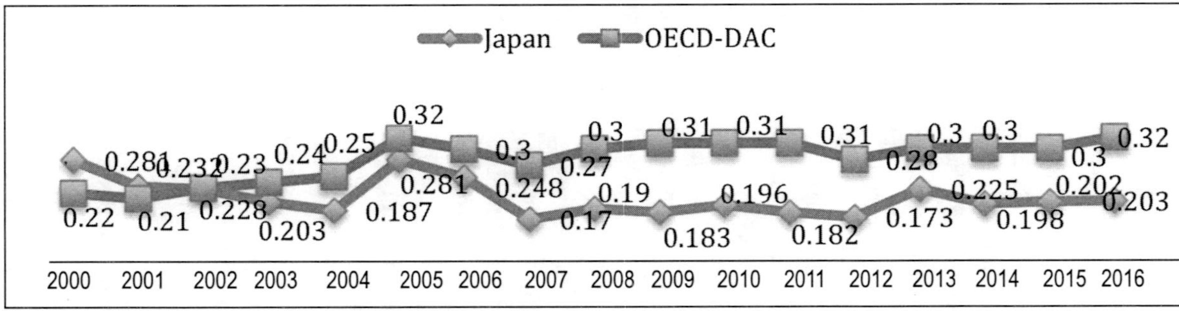

Source: OECD Data, at https://data.oecd.org.

Figure 3: Japan's Allocation of ODA to Africa (in million US$)

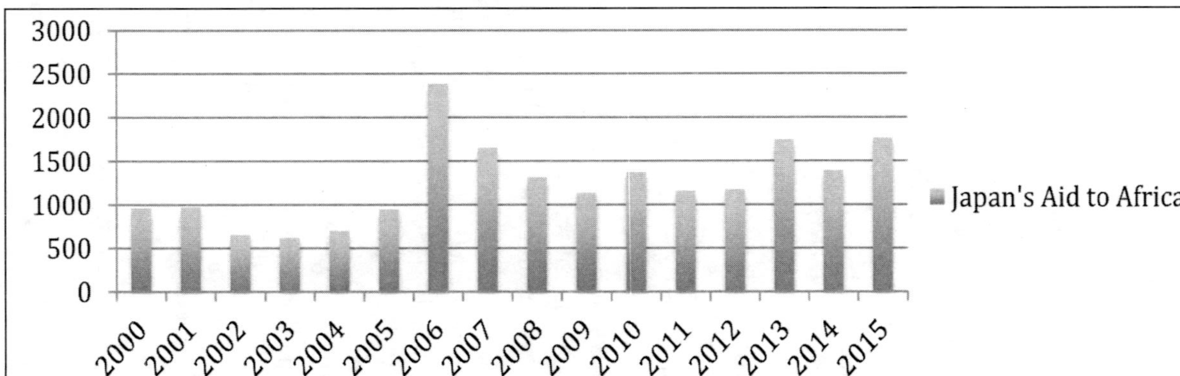

Source: OECD Data, at https://data.oecd.org.

unethical, where China floods cheap goods and offers attractive ODA that is unaccountable to take advantage of the African resources.[46]

Japan's rising international ambition to gather Africa's support on multilateral forums, especially for the United Nations Security Council (UNSC) permanent berth, is an additional factor which the AAGC may facilitate. Japan's strong advocacy to reform the UN and UNSC factors African support as a crucial component. Germany, India, Japan and Brazil, clubbed as G-4 countries, have a credible case for demanding a permanent berth at the UNSC. To side-line the G-4 demand, China advocates for African representation in the UNSC, bringing the logic of continental representation to the UNSC reform debate. Keeping this background in perspective, Japan equally advocates African representation in the UNSC. Offering "complete support" to Africa and its "Agenda 2063",[47] Shinzo Abe in his TICAD VI speech stated that Japan supports the idea of Africa having a representation in the permanent membership at the UNSC by 2023.[48]

This Japanese perspective conveniently establishes a strategic congruence with India's Africa policy. Stressing the need to establish a "model of cooperation" between India and Africa that will be "demand-driven and free of conditions", Prime Minister Narendra Modi has labelled engagement with Africa as a "top priority" in Indian foreign and economic engagement policy.[49] While announcing the AAGC, Modi had announced both the US and Japan as India's partners for developmental work in Africa. The year 2000 witnessed India introducing a "Focus Africa" programme,[50] aiming to design a "developmental partnership". Gradually, over the last two decades, India-Africa relations have become more institutionalised through a range of bilateral and multilateral mechanisms. Prime Minister Narendra Modi seems to be offering a newness to this engagement, showing a greater level of engagement in the field of energy security, greater market access, co-development of infrastructure and maritime security cooperation.[51] The third India-Africa Summit held in New Delhi in October 2015 renewed India's outreach in Africa and strengthened India-Africa relations.

Newness has certainly been noticed in India's current Africa outreach. *First*, in contrast to India's earlier "Focus Africa" programme, India's current approach towards Africa is based on a continental framework. For example, almost 40 African representatives attended the Third India-Africa Summit. India earlier used to invite only 15 countries under the Banjul formula, where the choice of countries was always decided by the African Union.[52]

Second, Africa is seen as a multilateral partner in a range of areas such as climate change, trade regimes and UN/UNSC reforms. For instance, centred on a "common, but differentiated, negotiation framework" in multilateral forums, India advocates for a unified policy position with Africa on a range of issues including climate change.[53] India has invited Africa to join hands not only in dealing with the global climate change, but also in a collaborative effort to forge an "alliance of solar-rich countries". Focusing on the Doha Development agenda, India foresees Africa as a partner in global trading regimes in the field of agriculture and food security.

Third, rejecting a "donor-recipient" archetype of engagement, India has advocated developmental challenges as an "international responsibility" and has tried to forge a more credible India-Africa partnership. Three principles – no conditionality, no policy prescriptions and no questioning of the sovereignty of the partnering country – have been the basis of the India-Africa partnership.[54]

Fourth, India sees the African littoral countries as strategically important to its Indian Ocean policy. Aiming to have stronger India-Africa maritime relations, India has been trying to solidify its maritime linkages with many African littoral and inland countries. Prime Minister Modi's visits to Mozambique, South Africa, Tanzania and Kenya in 2016 and to Mauritius and Seychelles in 2015 strengthen this assertion. Offering greater military aid, training assistance and capacity-building exercises has been the main thrust of India's maritime diplomacy especially with regard to the African littoral countries. Crafting stronger maritime and shipping contacts has been one of the focuses in India's Africa policy. Prime Minister Modi stressed the same in his second Raisina Dialogue speech in New Delhi on January 17, 2017, where he stated that India wants to build its own developmental partnership that "... extends from the islands of the Indian Ocean and Pacific to the islands of the Caribbean and from the great continent of Africa to the Americas".[55]

These efforts, complementing the AAGC, certainly explain India's increasing seriousness towards Africa. In recent years, Beijing has invested heavily in diplomatic, economic and political ties with Africa, resulting in substantial China-Africa engagement. Beijing's naval outreach has increased in the East African coast where China focuses on key maritime zones, capacity-building exercises, building infrastructure and promoting investment for the protection of maritime zones in the IOR. Specifically, the East African countries are factored importantly in China's 21st century Maritime Silk Road (MSR). The *Vision for Maritime Cooperation under the Belt and Road Initiative*, an official document released by China on June 20, 2017, stresses on ocean cooperation and highlights how China aims to build on the China-Indian Ocean-Africa-Mediterranean Sea blue economic passage.[56]

The Chinese intent is to establish new initiatives and maritime routes to promote maritime connectivity in the IOR, stressing on the Indian Ocean.

In fact, China's aim to emerge as a stronger maritime power is gaining momentum. In his speech at the 19th National Congress of the CPC, Xi Jinping stated that "China will pursue a coordinated land and marine development, and step up efforts to build China into a strong maritime country".[57] Hu Jintao, too, in his 18th National Congress report had emphasised on the Chinese intent to enhance capacity for exploring marine resources, increase marine economy and safeguard China's marine interests and rights to eventually establish China as a maritime power.[58] A reflection of this Chinese interest has been clearly visible in the last few years when the Chinese focus has been on the IOR to invest in strategic ports, construct marine commercial points and naval bases. Given this rising Chinese presence, many countries' foreign policies have witnessed changes, if not in reaction, then in retrospection, including that of India and Japan. The arrival of the AAGC is a clear reflection of this India-Japanese retrospection.

Summing Up: AAGC is a Product of India-Japan Globalism

In response to China's growing ambitions in the Indian Ocean and Africa, Japan and India agreed in 2015 to increase industrial networks and regional value chains with an "open, fair and transparent" business environment in the Indo-Pacific. Both countries enhanced this idea further in 2016 by identifying strategic convergence and synergy between India's Act East policy and Japan's EPQI. Japan's EPQI is a foreign policy initiative that focuses on greater connectivity between Asia and the rest of the world, including Africa,[59] whereas India's Act East policy emphasises on connectivity in the Indo-Pacific region, including a special focus on the neighbouring Southeast Asia. The AAGC contextualises how both Japan and India prime each other as global partners in a rapidly changing Indo-Pacific environment. India's Act East policy factors Japan as a "special" partner, while Japan's EPQI factors India as a key economic and strategic partner in its regional and global outreach. Partnership on infrastructure building and connectivity are accorded two important objectives in this strategic congruence.

Japan has been concerned about China's rising profile in Africa and maritime outreach in the Indian Ocean. Beijing's growing counter-piracy operations along the African coasts and participation in the UN Peacekeeping Operations (UNPKOs) and capacity-building exercises have been a serious cause of concern for Japan for some time. As a result, Japan has begun to show greater interest in Africa, primarily through security undertakings where Japan's Self-Defence Forces (SDFs) have played a key role in various counter-piracy operations, e.g. the UNPKO in South Sudan, and in expanding its first overseas base, from just an airfield to a military base, in Djibouti. In other words, Tokyo is aiming to pursue a more security-oriented partnership with Africa. Eclipsing the Chinese presence in Africa, mainly China's maritime reach with the African littoral states, is a crucial factor that Japan finds difficult to handle singularly. Tokyo's limited maritime outreach on the African coast has restricted its ability to emerge as a security provider in Africa. India has emerged as a natural partner in this Japanese endeavour.[60] This equally benefits India's strategic positioning in the region. Therefore, the AAGC signifies a growing strategic convergence between Japan and India in the Indo-Pacific.

On Tokyo's part, the attempt to establish a strategic connection between Asia and Africa, factoring India as a global partner, has a sequential route which was articulated by Shinzo Abe in his influential speech entitled "Confluence of the Two Seas" as far back as August 22, 2007, in the Indian Parliament. Abe had forcefully articulated that Japan and India along with countries like Australia and the US must establish strategic networking spanning the Pacific and Indian Oceans.[61] Thrusting on Japan's and India's ability to take greater "responsibility" in international affairs, he had stressed that the aim should be to nurture and enrich the Pacific and Indian Oceans as "Seas of clearest transparency".[62]

In the larger context of the AAGC, China's growing influence and the India-Japan growing global partnership, three points can be noted: *First*, the AAGC is at present an abstract idea that is based on an intercontinental framework, making it really an ambitious proposition. The AAGC arrives at a post-US "pivot to Asia" strategy, encouraging India and Japan to take a lead in regional affairs, factoring Asia and Africa. *Second*, the AAGC's strategic foundation is based on the power struggle over infrastructure, investment and connectivity, both in Asia and Africa. In this power struggle, an India-Japan strategic congruence is clearly emerging, to balance out the Chinese influence, including the flagship BRI. *Third*, the AAGC is a result of the Indo-Pacific security coalition led by India and Japan. Barring Africa as a continent, though the AAGC proposition is yet to directly involve a third country, the AAGC framework complements the changing security order in the Indo-Pacific region against unilateralism and authoritarianism. Importantly, the AAGC backs a rule-based order that is democratic and transparent.

NOTES

1. Aristotle Tziampiris, "Chapter 2: Balance of Power and Soft Balancing", *The Emergence of Israeli-Greek Cooperation*, Springer, Switzerland, 2015, pp. 21-30.
2. K. S. Bajpai, "Japan, India and the Balance of Power", *The Hindu*, January 27, 2014, at http://www.thehindu.com/opinion/op-ed/japan-india-and-the-balance-of-power/article5620518.ece (Accessed January 14, 2018).
3. Stephen Waltz, *The Origin of Alliances*, Cornell University Press, Cornell, 1987, p. 17.
4. K. S. Bajpai, No. 2.
5. This chapter is a revised and updated version of the author's earlier paper published in *Focus Asia*, a publication of the Stockholm-based Institute for Security and Development Policy (ISDP): Jagannath Panda, "The Asia-Africa Growth Corridor: An India-Japan Arch in the Making?", *Focus Asia: Perspective & Analysis*, No. 21, August 2017, pp. 1-11. Some section in this chapter are reprinted with permission.
6. The Silk Route is an ancient phenomenon. President Xi Jinping formally announced the two important components of the newly activated concept, i.e. Maritime Silk Road (MSR) and Silk Road Economic Belt (SREB) under the flagship "One Belt, One Road" in 2013. He announced the MSR in his speech to the Indonesian Parliament in October 2013 and SREB at the Nazarbayev University in Kazakhstan. See "Speech by Chinese President Xi Jinping to Indonesian Parliament", ASEAN-China Centre, October 3, 2013, at http://www.asean-china-center.org/english/2013-10/03/c_133062675.htm (Accessed January 20, 2018); "President Xi Jinping Delivers Important Speech and Proposes to Build a Silk Road Economic Belt with Central Asian countries", Ministry of Foreign Affairs of the People's Republic of China, September 7, 2013, at http://www.fmprc.gov.cn/mfa_eng/topics_665678/xjpfwzysiesgjtfhshzzfh_665686/t1076334.shtml (Accessed January 20, 2018).
7. This is based on the author's interaction with many experts in Japan, mainly from the National Institute for Defence studies (NIDS), Tokyo; Japan Institute of International Affairs (JIIA), Tokyo; Sofia University, Japan; National Graduate Institute for Policy Studies (GRIPS), Tokyo; and other think tanks and universities. In India, the author had interactions with officials from the Ministry of External Affairs (MEA), Indian Council for Research on International Economic Relations (ICRIER), Research and Information System for Developing Countries (RIS), etc.
8. "India-Japan Joint Statement during the Visit of Prime Minister to Japan", Ministry of External Affairs, Government of India, November 11, 2016, at http://mea.gov.in/bilateral-documents.htm?dtl/27599/IndiaJapan+Joint+ Statement + during+the+visit+of+Prime+Minister+to+Japan (Accessed January 14, 2018).
9. Ibid.
10. Ibid.
11. "Prime Minister's Speech at the inauguration of the Annual Meeting of the African Development Bank (AfDB), Gandhinagar", Ministry of External Affairs, Government of India, May 23, 2017, at http://mea.gov.in/Speeches-Statements.htm?dtl/28478/Prime+Ministers+Speech+at+ the+ inauguration+ of+the+Annual+Meeting+of+the+African+Development+Bank+AfDB+Gandhi nagar+May+23+2017 (Accessed January 14, 2018).
12. Liu Zongyi has noted that "the Asia-Africa Growth Corridor is a duplication of the 'Freedom Corridor' designed by Japanese Prime Minister Shinzo Abe"; and

that "Indian media foresee this as a 'counter' initiative to China's Belt and Road initiative". See Liu Zongyi, "Belt and Road Remains Open to India despite Absence at Recent Forum", *Global Times*, June 1,2017, at http://www.globaltimes.cn/content/1049599.shtml (Accessed 20 June 2017).

13. See, for instance, Avinash Nair, "To Counter OBOR, India and Japan Propose Asia-Africa Sea Corridor", *The Indian Express*, May 31, 2017, at http://indianexpress.com/article/explained/to-counter-obor-india-and-japan-propose-asia-africa-sea-corridor-4681749/ (Accessed January 15, 2018); "India, Japan Forge Ahead with Connectivity Project to Counter China's OBOR", *Business Standard*, July 30, 2017, at http://www.business-standard.com/article/current-affairs/india-japan-forge-ahead-with-connectivity-project-to-counter-china-s-obor-117073000073_1.html (Accessed January 15, 2018).
14. *Asia Africa Growth Corridor: Partnership for Sustainable and Innovative Development: A Vision Document*, Africa Development Bank Meeting, Ahmedabad, India, May 22-26,2017.
15. Ibid., p. 1.
16. Titli Basu, "Thinking Africa: India, Japan, and the Asia Africa Growth Corridor", *The Diplomat*, June 3, 2017, at http://thediplomat.com/2017/06/thinking-africa-india-japan-and-the-asia-africa-growth-corridor/ (Accessed July 23, 2017)
17. Chris Heathcote, "Forecasting Infrastructure Investment Needs for 50 countries, 7 Sectors through 2040", *World Bank Group: Infrastructure & Public-Private Partnerships Blog*, August 10, 2017, at http://blogs.worldbank.org/ppps/forecasting-infrastructure-investment-needs-50-countries-7-sectors-through-2040 (Accessed January 16, 2018).
18. Morten Lauridsen, "Africa Needs More Private Investment. Here's How to Make It Happen", World Economic Forum, October 23, 2017, at https://www.weforum.org/agenda/2017/10/how-to-boost-investment-in-africa/ (Accessed January 16, 2018).
19. "Quality Infrastructure: Building Trust for Trade", United Nations Industrial Development Organisation (UNIDO), May 2016, at https://www.unido.org/sites/default/files/2016-05/UNIDO_Quality_system_0.pdf (Accessed January 17, 2018).
20. India and Japan officially called their relationship a "special strategic and global partnership" under the *Vision 2025* plan in the Indo-Pacific region during Prime Minister Abe's visit to India from December 11-13, 2015. *Vision 2025* aims to uphold the "principles of sovereignty", "territorial integrity" and "peaceful settlement of disputes", among other issues. See *Joint Statement on India and Japan Vision 2025: Special Strategic and Global Partnership Working Together for Peace and Prosperity of the Indo-Pacific Region and the World*, Ministry of External Affairs: Government of India, December 12, 2015, at http://www.mea.gov.in/bilateral-documents.htm?dtl/26176/Joint_Statement_on_India_and_Japan_Vision_2025_Special_ Strategic_ and_ Global_Partnership_Working_Together_for_Peace_and_Prosperity_of_the_IndoPacific_R (Accessed January 17, 2018).
21. *Priority Policy for Development Cooperation: FY 2017*, International Cooperation Bureau, Ministry of Foreign Affairs, Japan, April 2017, at http://www.mofa.go.jp/files/000259285.pdf (Accessed January 17, 2018).
22. *Inaugural U.S.-India-Japan Trilateral Ministerial Dialogue in New York*, Media Centre, Ministry of External Affairs, Government of India, September 30, 2015, at http://mea.gov.in/press-releases.htm?dtl/25868 (Accessed February 23, 2018)

23. *Vision and Actions on Jointly Building Silk Road Economic Belt and 21st-Century Maritime Silk Road,* National Development and Reform Commission, Ministry of Foreign Affairs and Ministry of Commerce of the People's Republic of China, with State Council Authorisation, March 2015.
24. Xi Jinping, "Secure a Decisive Victory in Building a Moderately Prosperous Society in All Respects and Strive for the Great Success of Socialism with Chinese Characteristics for a New Era", Delivered at the 19th National Congress of the Communist Party of China, October 18, 2017, at http://www.xinhuanet.com/english/download/Xi_Jinping's_report_at_19th_CPC_National_Congress.pdf (Accessed February 23, 2018).
25. "Official Spokesperson's Response to a Query on Participation of India in OBOR/BRI Forum", Ministry of External Affairs, Government of India, May 13, 2017, at http://www.mea.gov.in/media-briefings.htm?dtl/28463/Official_Spokespersons_response_to_a_query_on_participation_of_India_in_ OBORBRI _ Forum (Accessed January 20, 2018).
26. Ibid.
27. "Cabinet Approves India's Accession to the Customs Convention on International Transport of Goods under Cover of TIR Carnets (TIR Convention)", Press Information Bureau, Government of India Cabinet, March 6, 2017, at http://pib.nic.in/newsite/PrintRelease.aspx?relid=158890 (Accessed January 20, 2018).
28. Jagannath P. Panda, "Beijing's 'One Belt, One Road' Diplomacy and India", *India-China Relations: Politics of resources, Identity and Authority in a Multipolar World Order,* Routledge, London and New York, 2017, p. 86.
29. "Asia's Dream: Linking the Pacific and Eurasia – Speech by Prime Minister Shinzo Abe at the Banquet of the 23rd International Conference on The Future of Asia", Prime Minister of Japan and His Cabinet, June 5, 2017, at http://japan.kantei.go.jp/97_abe/statement/201706/1222768_11579.html (Accessed January 20, 2018).
30. Charlotte Gao, "'Aimai': Japan's Ambiguous Approach to China's 'Belt and Road'", *The Diplomat,* November 22, 2017, at https://thediplomat.com/2017/11/aimai-japans-ambiguous-approach-to-chinas-belt-and-road/ (Accessed January 20, 2018).
31. "Japan and China Sign 23 Energy-saving, Environmental Cooperation Projects at Tokyo Meet", *The Japan Times,* December 24, 2017, at https://www.japantimes.co.jp/news/2017/12/24/national/japan-china-sign-23-energy-saving-environmental-cooperation-projects-tokyo-meet/#.WmMn7STlfFI (Accessed January 20, 2018).
32. "Asia's Dream: Linking the Pacific and Eurasia", No. 29.
33. Ibid.
34. "Japan-China Summit Meeting", Ministry of Foreign Affairs of Japan, April 23, 2015, at http://www.mofa.go.jp/a_o/c_m1/cn/page1e_000041.html (Accessed June 26, 2017).
35. Jagannath P. Panda, "Institutionalizing the African Reach: Reviewing China's and India's Multilateral Drive", *Journal of Asian and African Studies,* 52(6), 2017, p. 857.
36. Occasionally, the West has been warning Africa to be cautious about the "new colonialism" from China and India that is designed to enhance their trade and economic contacts in the continent, conveniently oblivious of its own overarching reach and exploitation of African resources over centuries. See D.H. Shinn, "Emerging Powers Expand Ties with Africa", *International Policy Digest,*

September 17, 2012, at https://intpolicydigest.org/2012/09/17/emerging-powers-expand-ties-with-africa/ (Accessed January 24, 2018).

37. Ibid.
38. L. Dittmer, "China and the Developing World", in L. Dittmer and G.T. Yu (eds.), *China, the Developing World, and the New Global Dynamic*, Lynne Reiner, Boulder, pp.1-12.
39. H. Wasserman, "China in South Africa: Media Responses to a Developing Relationship", *Chinese Journal of Communication*, 5(3), 2012, pp. 336-354.
40. Maguemati Wagbou, "Africa: a Bridge between Latin America and Asia", South-South Collaborative Programme, Occasional Paper Series, COD 11, 2008, pp. 5-10.
41. "Uniqueness of TICAD", Ministry of Foreign Affairs of Japan, April 13, 2016, at http://www.mofa.go.jp/af/af1/page22e_000767.html (Accessed January 24, 2018).
42. This is in contrast with the OECD-Development Assistance Committee (DAC) countries' overall net ODA percentage, which has increased in the same period (see Figure 2). The DAC currently has a total of 30 members, including Japan. China is not a member. See "DAC Members", Organisation for Economic Co-operation and Development (OECD), at http://www.oecd.org/dac/dacmembers.htm(Accessed June 26, 2017).
43. For example, see Ayako Mie, "With TICAD, Japan Pursues African Growth and Export Markets", *The Japan Times*, August 9, 2016, at http://www.japantimes.co.jp/news/2016/08/09/reference/ticad-africa-initiative-sees-japan-pursue-bigger-slice-economic-pie/ (Accessed June 26, 2017).
44. "Address by Prime Minister Shinzo Abe at the Opening Session of the Sixth Tokyo International Conference on African Development (TICAD VI)", August 27, 2016, Kenyatta International Convention Centre (KICC), Nairobi, Kenya, August 27, 2016, at http://www.mofa.go.jp/afr/af2/page4e_000496.html (Accessed June 22, 2017).
45. "Japan's Measures for Africa at TICAD VI: 'Quality and Empowerment'", Ministry of Foreign Affairs, Japan, at http://www.mofa.go.jp/files/000183835.pdf (Accessed June 22, 2017).
46. John Aglionby, "Tokyo Takes on Beijing in Africa, Claiming Quality over Speed", *Financial Times*, January 16, 2016, at https://www.ft.com/content/564df09e-824a-11e5-a01c-8650859a4767?mhq5j=e2 (Accessed June 22, 2017); "Database Reveals Extent of China's Aid to Africa", *The Japan Times*, May 1, 2013, at http://www.japantimes.co.jp/news/2013/05/01/asia-pacific/database-reveals-extent-of-chinas-aid-to-africa/#.WUvwCyTldlI (Accessed June 22, 2017); Ayako Mie, No. 43.
47. "Agenda 2063" is a strategic continental framework to bring socio-economic transformation across Africa over the next 50 years. Its primary objective is to emphasise on growth and development. See "Agenda 2063", African Union, at https://au.int/en/agenda2063/about (Accessed February 10, 2018).
48. See "Address by Prime Minister Shinzo Abe at the Opening Session of the Sixth Tokyo International Conference on African Development (TICAD VI)", No. 44.
49. "PM's Address at the Inauguration of the Annual Meeting of the African Development Bank", PMINDIA, May 23, 2017, at http://www.pmindia.gov.in/en/news_updates/pms-address-at-the-inauguration-of-the-annual-meeting-of-the-african-development-bank/ (Accessed February 10, 2018).

50. This was a programme through which India aimed to expedite trade and economic cooperation with seven sub-Saharan African countries, namely South Africa, Nigeria, Mauritius, Tanzania, Kenya, Ghana and Ethiopia. See "Focus Africa Programme", Government of India, at http://focusafrica.gov.in/focus_africa_programme.html (Accessed February 10, 2018).
51. Rajrishi Singhal, "Modi Resets India's Africa Strategy", *The Hindu Business Line*, November 17, 2015, at http://www.thehindubusinessline.com/opinion/modi-resets-indias-africa-strategy/article7888689.ece (Accessed August 2, 2017).
52. "Briefing by Secretary (West) on PM's Visit to Ethiopia and Tanzania", Ministry of External Affairs, Government of India, May 17, 2011, at http://mea.gov.in/in-focus-article.htm?3195/Briefing+by+Secretary+West+on+PMs+visit+to+Ethiopia+ and+Tanzania (Accessed March 6, 2016).
53. Rajrishi Singhal, No. 51.
54. H.H.S. Vishwanathan, "India-Africa Relations: Nurturing an Enduring Partnership", in Abhijnan Rej and Tanoubi Ngangom (eds.), *Common Futures: India and Africa in Partnership*, Observer Research Foundation, New Delhi, 2015, p. 12.
55. "Inaugural Address by Prime Minister at Second Raisina Dialogue", New Delhi, January 17, 2017, at http://mea.gov.in/Speeches-Statements.htm?dtl/27948/Inaugural_Address_by_Prime_Minister_at_Second_Raisina_Dialogue_New_Delhi_January _17_2017 (Accessed 10 February 2018).
56. "Full text: Vision for Maritime Cooperation under the Belt and Road Initiative", *Xinhuanet*, June 20, 2017, at http://www.xinhuanet.com/english/2017-06/20/c_136380414.htm (Accessed February 11, 2018).
57. Xi Jinping, No. 24.
58. "Full Text of Hu Jintao's Report at 18th Party Congress", Embassy of the People's Republic of China in the US, November 27, 2012, at http://www.china-embassy.org/eng/zt/18th_CPC_National_Congress_Eng/t992917.htm (Accessed February 12, 2018).
59. EPQI is an expanded version of the earlier designed PQI, which centres on "quality infrastructure investment", extending Japan's targeted area of infrastructure investment from Asia to the rest of the world, with particular emphasis on Africa. "The 'Expanded Partnership for Quality Infrastructure' Initiative Directed toward the G7 Ise-Shima Summit Meeting Announced", Ministry of Economy, Trade and Industry, May 23, 2016, at http://www.meti.go.jp/english/press/2016/0523_01.html (Accessed February 11, 2018).
60. Subhomoyo Bhattacharya, "Race for Supremacy: India, Japan Plan Alternative to Counter China's OBOR", *Business Standard*, May 16, 2017, at http://www.business-standard.com/article/economy-policy/race-for-supremacy-india-japan-plan-alternative-to-china-s-obor-117051501273_1.html (Accessed February 14, 2018).
61. "'Confluence of the Two Seas': Speech by H.E. Mr. Shinzo Abe, Prime Minister of Japan at the Parliament of the Republic of India", Ministry of Foreign Affairs of Japan, August 22, 2007, at http://www.mofa.go.jp/region/asia-paci/pmv0708/speech-2.html (Accessed February 14, 2018).
62. Ibid.

16

Japan, India and China on Africa: Global Ambitions and Human Resource Development

Kenneth King

The simmering competition amongst Japan, India and China can be illustrated from their human resource ambitions including in Africa. In respect of investment, China has been long in the lead with large, iconic projects going back to the 1970s. More recently, Japan, with its focus on quality investment, has signalled a desire to be more resilient and agile in respect of its long-standing development cooperation in Africa.[1] India, too, has had very lengthy, historical links with parts of Africa; but since 2008, it has had a much more active engagement, including exploring from November 2016 what would become the Asia-Africa Growth Corridor (AAGC) partnership with Japan in May 2017 to parallel what it sees as the ambitions of China's Belt and Road Initiative (BRI), including in Africa.[2]

On the soft side of investment in Africa, China's footprint has been very evident not only in its massive media investments in Africa, but also in its support of its language and culture centres, the Confucius Institutes, in the majority of African countries.[3] While Japan and India do not rival China's media and cultural investment, India regards itself as having a comparative advantage in information technology (IT) and has flagship examples of Pan-African networking in information technology; and Japan perceives its quality infrastructure ambitions for Africa as being intimately connected to quality human resource development (HRD) and quality information technology investment.

This chapter is particularly focused on the human resource dimensions of these three nations' engagement with Africa. This is because HRD and capacity building have long been critical elements in the interactions of Japan, India and China with Africa, going right back to the very beginnings of their diplomatic linkages with the continent. Equally, in their recent global ambitions, HRD remains a critical element. This is as true of the AAGC, in which Japan and India are the main players, as it is of the BRI. It will be important to review whether the current promotions of HRD by all three Asian nations remain faithful to their traditions of support to education and training, or whether they may become part of a global competition and rivalry within Africa.

The positioning of Africa in these latest global ambitions requires careful attention. All three Asian countries have had Pan-African instruments for their involvement with Africa. Japan's Tokyo International Conference on African Development (TICAD) is the oldest, reaching back to 1993, while China's Forum on China-Africa Cooperation (FOCAC) emerged in 2000. India's is the youngest of the three, with its India-Africa Forum Summits (IAFS) only emerging in 2008. At one level, the three Asian nations use a somewhat similar discourse in describing their African involvement. Even though one of them, Japan, is a member of the Organisation for Economic Cooperation and Development (OECD), they all make use of the discourse of 'mutual benefit' and thus aspire to see Africa as a partner rather than as a recipient. However, it can be argued that the language of capacity building has been more used by India and Japan in discussing their human resource engagements with Africa. This suggests a deficit of capacity in Africa even though all three Asian nations also use the more symmetrical discourse of 'people-to-people partnership'.

On the other hand, India, apart from being a donor to Africa, has also been the largest recipient of Japan's Official Development Assistance (ODA) loans for several decades, and these have been used, in part, for what might be called 'quality infrastructure' in India itself such as the Delhi Metro, and the very recently launched Ahmedabad-Mumbai high-speed rail corridor. This parallels directly Japan's experience in the 1960s when it was receiving World Bank loans for its bullet trains at the same time as it was beginning to provide Japanese grant aid and yen loans to the developing countries of Asia.[4]

The Crucial HRD Dimensions of AAGC and of BRI

Possibly because HRD has historically been a central plank in their engagement with Africa, as well as in the programmes of TICAD, FOCAC and IAFS, it appears also to be a key feature in the very conceptualisation of the AAGC and of the BRI. Obviously, these are very early days in the programming and development of these two global ambitions, but it may still be valuable to tease out some of their illustrations in foregrounding HRD. At least at the level of discourse and language, there seems to be some difference in the approaches to HRD of India and Japan in the AAGC and China in the BRI. A key issue must be whether these approaches towards Africa can remain complementary, or whether they can begin to involve competition and then rivalry. We turn first to the AAGC, but a preliminary point on the comparison should first be made. Though both the BRI and the AAGC have released general vision statements, which are the focus of this discussion, the Chinese Ministry of Education has also released a document specifically on the educational implications of the BRI. For the purpose of our comparison here, however, the focus is on the general vision papers of the two platforms.

AAGC: Development and Cooperation, Quality Infrastructure and Connectivity

In the case of the AAGC's *Vision Document*, which was produced through the collaboration of three Asian institutes and launched at the African Development Bank (AfDB) meeting in India in May 2017,[5] no less than two of its four pillars relate to HRD. These are 'enhancing capacities and skills' and 'people-to-people partnership'.[6] Intriguingly, the document claims that "the centrality of people to people [sic] partnership would be the unique feature of this initiative".[7]

The other two pillars are 'development and cooperation projects' and 'quality infrastructure and institutional connectivity'. At least one of these, however, contains major human resource implications. Thus, the pillar on development and cooperation projects picks out just three areas to illustrate its focus: agriculture and agro-processing; health and pharmaceuticals; and disaster management. But in its list of five key priorities, educational services are also included. Moreover, the executive summary of the *Vision Document* states quite categorically that the "AAGC will give priority to development projects in health and pharmaceuticals, agriculture and agro-processing, disaster management and skill enhancement".[8] Again, in introducing the scope of the pillar on development and cooperation projects, the *Vision Document* powerfully underlines the HRD element in this pillar by its reference to human capital, skill development and knowledge:

> Development and cooperation projects in identified sectors are significant for building productive human capital to reduce costs in

> the production blocks or economic centres. Skill development, knowledge centres, research and development, specialty medical treatment, are important components of AAGC.[9]

The pillar on quality infrastructure and institutional connectivity does not explicitly mention capacity building or HRD in laying out the several different dimensions of infrastructure development and connectivity that are planned; however, the pillar on enhancing capacity and skills does crucially mention the importance of the development of capacities to sustain infrastructure.[10]

HRD Pillars of Enhancing Capacities and Skills and People-to-people Partnership

It may be instructive to tease out the ambitions that lie behind these two pillars that appear explicitly to prioritise HRD.

According to the *Vision Document's* conceptual model, enhancing capacities and skills covers a rather large canvas: "Human resource training and education; vocational/industrial training centres; Pan Africa (sic) E-Network; develop capacities to sustain infrastructure; centres to share development experience".[11] Obviously, this is only an indicative listing, but several elements are suggestive. First of these is certainly the importance of maintenance skills and capacities, mentioned above, since the planned investment in quality infrastructure is unsustainable without these. Second is the sharing of development experience. What is not clear in this last short reference is whether this points to the two Asian nations sharing with Africa their experience of their own development as opposed to their experience of providing development aid to others. Equally, it is not clear whether this could also cover Africa's own experience of its development.

A third element of interest is the actual naming of India's well-known Pan African E-Network, which is termed a 'unique' example of institutional connectivity and distance learning between universities and hospitals in India and Africa, in respect of education and health.[12] It is perhaps surprising that there is not included here the equally well-known Japanese support to science and maths education across many African states. We shall return shortly to examine the African side of some of these AAGC plans, but open and distance learning is certainly no stranger to Africa, and notably the University of South Africa (UNISA) in Pretoria which has a history of more than 140 years, and currently has some 400,000 enrolled students.[13]

The section on Enhancing Capacities and Skills includes some very ambitious plans. But the overall message seems to be that Japan and India's capacities will be used to build up capacities in Africa. Right up front, it is suggested that the AAGC can be expected to intervene "to address the daunting challenge of unemployment and skills [in Africa], especially to design and implement project [sic]".[14] The text goes on to talk about education and skills development being very important areas for capacity building, and how, for instance, "India has advantage in healthcare sector, medical training and other capacities which can be shared in Africa, in partnership with Japan".[15] What is not alluded to in the document is that India is itself in the midst of a massive campaign ('Skill India') to build the capacity of more than 400 million of its own workers by 2022.[16]

It is further suggested that there may be a need for India and Japan to partner Africa in more specific areas such as mining and mineral exploration "for enhancing capacity and skills", even though it is also mentioned that this will help Africa to realise its own potential.[17] According to the document, HRD in these fields will be critical, and a crucial role can be played by the India-Japan collaboration. It adds that "India can also share its huge experience in mining and minerals sector".[18] It may seem a little disingenuous for this *Vision Document* to spotlight mining and minerals for capacity building in Africa when resource extraction in Africa has been such a theatre of competition and contestation in the continent. A final suggestion in the section on Capacities and Skills is for there to be Entrepreneurship Development Institutes in African countries. This too might be seen as proposing partnership with the globally well-known Entrepreneurship Development Institute of India, located in Ahmedabad, Gujarat.

Turning to the other pillar which seems closely linked to HRD – 'people-to-people partnership' – it might be expected that this would encourage a discourse of symmetry between the people of Africa and of Asia, but instead we find that the very first thing said about the scope of people-to-people partnership is that "there is need for systematic up-gradation[19] of local human resource" and that human potential can be improved "through capacity-building and training".[20] In other words, the understanding of people-to-people partnership seems to be one that is essentially asymmetrical, with Africa benefiting from the goodwill of India and Japan. This disparity in the conception of people-to-people partnership is confirmed by the assertion that there is the "whole field of education, skill development and cultural exchange which can be shared by India with Africa, in partnership with Japan".[21] It is perhaps surprising that, in turn, the opportunity for India and Japan to be enriched by cultural and educational exchange with Africa is also not mentioned. A further confirmation that people-to-people partnership in the AAGC is a distinctly one-way relationship is evident when it is argued that cooperation (with India and Japan) can "improve the current facilities and infrastructure and human resource conditions of universities in selected African countries".[22]

It is important to underline the fact that the AAGC comments about the priority of capacity building for Africa are not something new for agencies working in Africa, such as the AfDB. The AfDB's *Human Capital Strategy for Africa (2014-2018)* emphasises the critical need for HRD in a continent that "records the world's lowest school enrolment and quality".[23] It is not so much a question of denying these massive human capital deficits in Africa, as Mehrotra, drawing on the AfDB report acknowledges;[24] rather, it is a challenge for the AAGC to present the opportunities for people-to-people partnership with Africa in a way that genuinely acknowledges the mutual benefits associated with human capital development. We shall see shortly if China has a different approach in its BRI documents and plans.

Drawing together these different human resource threads that run through the current AAGC *Vision Document*, we see that though it is claimed that "the centrality of people to people (sic) partnership" is a "unique feature of this initiative", its conception of the relations between Asia and Africa seems far from symmetrical. These conclusions derive primarily from the AAGC *Vision Document* of May 2017. There will however be a more detailed *AAGC Vision Study* developed by the three research institutes associated with this present *Vision Document*, but through a 'joint study team' along with other centres and think tanks in Asia and Africa. It can be safely assumed that through such collaborative analysis more detailed work on the HRD dimensions of the AAGC initiative will become available as part of this *Vision Study*.[25]

Africa's Place in the AAGC Vision Document

Before leaving the AAGC and turning to the role of HRD in the BRI, it may be worth spending a moment reviewing the place of Africa in the AAGC *Vision Document* of May 2017. It has already been noted that Africa seems to be very much cast as the beneficiary of Indian and Japanese cooperation. This includes the positioning of Africa in both the pillars concerned with HRD. Beyond this, it may be noted that though there have been three Asian think tanks associated with the production of the AAGC *Vision Document*, mentioned at the outset of this chapter, there is no single African think tank identified with its development. Of course, it may be regarded as positive that the AAGC initiative was launched at the AfDB Annual Meeting which took place in India. But the AAGC launch was preceded by at least two India-Japan roundtables. The first of these, "Promoting Asia-Africa Economic Development", took place in New Delhi on January 12, 2017. There were 38 participants from the Governments of India and Japan, the three think tanks, as well as the Japan External Trade Organisation (JETRO), New Delhi and more generally from India. But there were no participants at all from Africa at this meeting.[26] A second meeting, specifically on Asia-Africa connectivity was held in Jakarta on April 21, 2017. This meeting had 28 participants from the Governments of India and Japan, the three think tanks, as well as from Indonesia, Singapore and Australia. Just two participants were from Africa – one from a think tank in Pretoria and the other a private consultant from Mozambique.[27] In other words, just two of the 66 participants at these two key meetings were from Africa, and neither of them were from Government or from a major think tank such as the Council for the Development of Social Science Research (CODESRIA) or the Organisation for Social Science Research in East and Southern Africa (OSSREA). The African Union was not represented either.

A preliminary conclusion from this level of minimal engagement with Africa in the production of the AAGC *Vision Document* would be that the role of African agency in this initiative seems to have been initially neglected. The AAGC *Vision Study* will need dramatically to change this perception through its joint study team if the initiative is to gain any lasting credence with the African policy and academic communities. Indeed, recently, there was a half-day meeting entitled "Asia Africa Growth Corridor Consultation: The Way Forward" organised by the Research and Information System for Developing Countries (RIS) in New Delhi on August 25, 2017, at which African participation was significant.[28] There was also a one-hour discussion meeting in RIS on "AAGC and the National Development Priorities of Tunisia", at which the Tunisian Ambassador to India gave a presentation on July 6, 2017. The detailed forward planning for the AAGC will need to await the development of its joint study team.

More generally, it will be intriguing to follow whether the new global HRD ambitions of Japan and India for Africa are significantly different from the education and training modalities which they have been pursuing for decades. In other words, will there be any attempt to develop a coordinated HRD strategy between Japan and India that will be markedly different from what they have been doing, on their own, bilaterally?

HRD within the BRI

Though the first proposals around the BRI go back to September and October 2013 in Central and South East Asia, the main document outlining the BRI is the *Action Plan on the Belt and Road Initiative* of March 2015. We accordingly start with examining the human resource dimensions of this key statement, and then look at a document of the Ministry of Education on the specifically educational dimensions of the BRI.

A crucial marker in the language about the historical Silk Road is the claim that it linked the major civilisations of Asia, Europe and Africa. What the document then terms the 'Silk Road Spirit' illustrates the very principles which are at the centre of the rhetoric about South-South cooperation. It is important to note that mutual learning is one of these principles: "Peace and cooperation, openness and inclusiveness, mutual learning and mutual benefit."[29] The focus is not so much about China building capacities in other countries but rather how to connect Asian, European and African countries more closely and promote "mutually beneficial cooperation".[30]

In the Background section of the BRI document, there is a strong emphasis on connectivity, as was seen in the AAGC *Vision Document*. However, it is noticeable that these connectivity networks and projects are thought to bring employment, educational and cultural benefits; they will

> create demands and job opportunities, enhance people-to-people and cultural exchanges, and mutual learning among the peoples of the relevant countries, and enable them to understand, trust and respect each other and live in harmony, peace and prosperity.[31]

The Principles of the BRI are said to be in line with the UN Charter as well as with the Five Principles of Peaceful Coexistence. It is frequently stressed that the "initiative seeks mutual benefit" for all those involved.[32] In the Framework section, there is an affirmation of the central concept of "mutual learning and mutual benefit", but, again, the emphasis is definitely not on what the BRI countries can learn from China, but rather the purpose is "to enhance cultural exchanges; encourage *different civilizations to learn from each other*; and promote mutual understanding, peace and friendship among people of all countries" (emphasis added).[33]

Under the section on Cooperation Priorities, there are several major sub-themes, such as "facilities connectivity", "unimpeded trade", and "financial integration", but the one of most direct interest to our HRD concern is "People-to-people bond". By contrast with the AAGC, where there seemed to be some clear asymmetry between India and Japan on the one hand and Africa on the other, the discourse of BRI is full of the key term "exchanges", as this initial goal makes very evident:

> We should carry forward the spirit of friendly cooperation of the Silk Road by promoting extensive cultural and academic exchanges,

> personnel exchanges and cooperation, media cooperation, youth and women exchanges and volunteer services, so as to win public support for deepening bilateral and multilateral cooperation.[34]

In the specifically educational arena, the BRI text talks of sending "more students to each other's countries", and promoting "cooperation in jointly running schools". In the health training sphere, there is discussion of "jointly" addressing public health emergencies. This is not to say that there is no mention of China's readiness to "provide medical assistance and emergency medical aid to relevant countries", but there is a strong emphasis on exchange and joint action.

The same is true of the theatre of science and technology; the predominant discourse is of working together and of mutual learning:

> We should increase our cooperation in science and technology, establish joint labs (or research centers), international technology transfer centers and maritime cooperation centers, promote sci-tech personnel exchanges, cooperate in tackling key sci-tech problems, and work together to improve sci-tech innovation capability.[35]

Even in the complex worlds of youth employment, entrepreneurship training and vocational skills development, the language is not about China providing the ideas, the funding or the infrastructure, but rather about the importance of integrating "existing resources to expand and advance practical cooperation between countries along the Belt and Road".[36]

Another whole area is that of culture, media, the arts, heritage and sports. Here too, the text is all about joint action and collaboration.

One field where historically there has been much less symmetry is in the provision of scholarships to study in China. In the case of Africa, for instance, China's historical provision of long- and short-term scholarships and training awards to Africa has been very substantially more than Africa's offer of scholarships and training to China. Here, all that is said in the BRI text is that China will provide 10,000 government scholarships to the countries along the Belt and Road every year.

Other sources and commentaries put this figure into perspective. For example, since the start of the Study in China Programme in 2010, the number of international degree students in China had soared to 164,694 by 2014. And of these, no less than 96,240 were from Belt and Road countries.[37] Apart from these very significant numbers, there will also be BRI students who are on China Scholarship Council (CSC) awards. The latter are part of China's 'aid' programme, but it has been the case for many years that self-funded international students in China outnumber those on CSC awards, even for Africa. It can be assumed therefore that the figure of 10,000 scholarship students annually mentioned above will be a small proportion of the total international students from BRI countries. In fact, the number of China Scholarship students from BRI countries rose from 9,368 in 2010 to 19,485 in 2014. In other words, the BRI scholarship students made up almost a fifth of the total BRI international students in China. So the great majority of BRI students are coming to China on their own resources. This underlines the point that international study in China is not predominantly an aid phenomenon.

It is important, however, to underline that international education is seen by China as an absolutely central part of the BRI process and planning. Indeed, one scholar of international and comparative education has stated that "Education Action is not only an important part of the Belt and Road initiative, but also the basis of the Belt and Road Initiative".[38] Illustrative of this importance is the fact that the Chinese Ministry of Education on July 13, 2017, issued a publication, in Chinese, specifically on the Belt and Road, entitled *Education Actions to Promote the Joint Construction of the Belt and Road*. A Chinese scholar has argued that:

> The document points out that, under the framework of South-South cooperation, the Chinese government will scale up education aid through coordinating the resources to train teachers, scholars and various types of skilled personnel for the Silk Road countries. In one word, One Belt One Road wants to invest in people and create benefits for people.[39]

The English version of this same publication provides an extraordinary comment on the educational ambitions associated with this initiative. The language is full of the terminology of joint learning, joint exchanges and research, and of Chinese students going to BRI countries, and vice versa. In the final paragraph, the language epitomises the ideals of collaboration and mutuality, and is a long way from the discourse of Chinese capacity building or of aid:

> The Ministry of Education of China proposes that we, the Belt and Road countries, channel our energies and enthusiasm into action, scale up efforts to align our strategic plans and coordinate our policies, explore new mechanisms and models for educational cooperation and exchange, further deepen educational cooperation and exchange, and ensure the quality and effectiveness of all such initiatives. Based on principles of mutual understanding, mutual trust, mutual assistance and mutual learning, we shall join hands to promote the development of education and closer people-to-people ties.[40]

It should be noted that there is also planning for HRD specifically for the marine side of the BRI. A document that parallels and updates the *Action Plan* we have been examining looks particularly at all the connectivities and exchanges on the marine side: *Vision for Maritime Cooperation under the Belt and Road Initiative*.[41] This too envisages "marine knowledge and cultural exchange". There will be a Marine Scholarship Programme which will bring individuals to China for research and training. But equally there will be efforts undertaken to "implement marine knowledge and cultural exchange and integration programmes".[42]

It is interesting to note that the maritime document particularly picks out the potential of think tank cooperation amongst the many countries located across the maritime silk road:

> Enhancing cooperation among think tanks. Dialogue and exchange among the think-tanks of the countries along the Road will be encouraged, joint research on the alignment of strategies and policies undertaken, and major initiatives launched, in order to provide intellectual support for the 21st Century Maritime Silk Road. China supports domestic think-tanks in developing strategic partnerships with counterparts along the Road and relevant international organizations in efforts to set up a 21st Century maritime Silk Road think-tank alliance.[43]

It would not be appropriate to leave this analysis of the BRI without looking briefly at the language of its chief architect, President Xi Jinping. His speech at the opening ceremony of the Belt and Road Forum for International Cooperation in May 2017 is replete with the discourse of learning together across the BRI countries.

Very early in this key discourse, the President turns to the sub-theme of 'Mutual learning', powerfully emphasising that "the ancient silk routes were not for trade only, they boosted flow of knowledge as well".[44] In the five years since 2013 when he first raised the silk road concept in Kazakhstan and Indonesia, the President talks of progress having been made on just four major 'connectivities': "Enhanced infrastructure connectivity, increased trade connectivity, expanded financial connectivity, and strengthened people-to-people connectivity." The last covers cooperation in education, health, culture and science. It is best captured in his own words:

> These four years have seen strengthened people-to-people connectivity. Friendship, which derives from close contact between the people, holds the key to sound state-to-state relations. Guided by the Silk Road spirit, we the Belt and Road Initiative participating

> countries have pulled [sic] our efforts to build the educational Silk Road and the health Silk Road, and carried out cooperation in science, education, culture, health and people-to-people exchange. Such cooperation has helped lay a solid popular and social foundation for pursuing the Belt and Road Initiative.[45]

Beyond these activities of cooperation and exchange, the 10,000-person scholarship programme is mentioned, as noted earlier, along with "special Silk Road scholarships to encourage international cultural and educational exchanges". But educational and cultural cooperation appears to be absolutely central to the delivery of the overall vision. It is worth noting that this collaboration encompasses not just schools and universities but cooperation among think tanks:

> We should establish a multi-tiered mechanism for cultural and people-to-people exchanges, build more cooperation platforms and open more cooperation channels. Educational cooperation should be boosted, more exchange students should be encouraged and the performance of cooperatively run schools should be enhanced. Think tanks should play a better role and efforts should be made to establish think tank networks and partnerships.[46]

What is intriguing about the overall vision of the Belt and Road is that when it comes to the interaction of different civilisations, the President takes the moral high ground, and makes it clear that exchange and 'mutual learning' are critical to delivering on other mutual benefits:

> Fifth, we should build the Belt and Road into a road connecting different civilizations. In pursuing the Belt and Road Initiative, we should ensure that when it comes to different civilizations, exchange will replace estrangement, mutual learning will replace clashes, and coexistence will replace a sense of superiority. This will boost mutual understanding, mutual respect and mutual trust among different countries.[47]

Indian Counterparts

While there is no exact parallel to China with the Indian Prime Minister's engagement with the AAGC, there have been plentiful commentaries on the significance of the Japan-India cooperation since the declaration of the AAGC in India in May 2017. It was however surprising that in the slew of agreements between Japan and India announced during Shinzo Abe's visit to India on September 13-14,2017, there was no explicit endorsement of the next stage of the AAGC.[48] Indian commentators are, however, aware that "no doubt comparisons will be made regarding the merits of the Indo-

Japanese and Chinese initiatives".[49] Sure enough, a leading security analyst, Pradhan, has listed a whole series of critical differences and distinctions between the two platforms. Amongst these, there is the assertion that the AAGC has been more consultative, involving various stakeholders in Asia and Africa, whilst the Chinese initiative has been 'centrally designed';[50] the Chinese project is designed to serve Beijing's interest, but the AAGC is for the common benefit of all; allegedly, China's BRI is to generate employment for Chinese companies, while by contrast the AAGC is designed to create work for the local population.[51] There are several more claims and comparisons; but it is clear that there is seen, at least by Pradhan, to be a distinct rivalry between the two platforms.

Although there is certainly evidence that some of the media, particularly in India, do read the AAGC as a counter to China's BRI,[52] it is also worth noting that this competition can be exaggerated. There are at least some indications that Japan and China are moving to mend their relations.[53]

Concluding Remarks on AAGC and BRI

The fora to launch AAGC and BRI took place within two weeks of each other in Ahmedabad, India, and in Beijing in May 2017. Arguably, they are at very different stages of development. The conceptualisation of BRI has been available since 2013, even if March 2015 marked its formal full text version. Already there have been detailed commentaries on it from around the world, including from McKinsey.[54] By contrast, the AAGC principally has the *Vision Document* which we have analysed in some detail. What is not yet available is the detailed *Vision Study* which is being worked on currently by a joint task team.

Even in this preliminary and somewhat uneven comparison of the documentation from the two platforms, we have underlined a number of significant contrasts within the sphere of human research development. For one thing, the AAGC document has been produced by a series of three think tanks, all of them based in Asia; there does not seem to have been any significant African participation in its production, or in the two preliminary round tables in India and Indonesia. Significantly, there was no preliminary round table in Africa. Of more concern is that the AAGC, despite having Asia-Africa in its title, has not been developed with the help of any major African think tank. There has, however, been a meeting in Delhi with substantial African participation during the summer of 2017, as mentioned earlier. No details are yet available from that.

Possibly, one of the consequences of this pattern of developing the key text of the AAGC without significant African agency is that Africa is largely portrayed as a recipient of expertise, technology, experience and aid from India and Japan. Hence 'capacity building' is mentioned throughout the AAGC text; it simply does not appear in the text of the *Action Plan on the Belt and Road Initiative* delivered in late March 2015, or in the more recent *Education Action Plan*.

Even though these are vision documents and not detailed implementation plans, their language may still be indicative of how Africa is positioned in the global ambitions of these three Asian nations, at least as presented in the *Vision Document*. The emphasis on the antiquity of the great civilisations of Asia, Europe and Africa, and of the importance of exchange and mutual learning is one of the central features of the BRI. By contrast, the AAGC, despite its assertion of the centrality of people-to-people partnership, appears to focus on the deficits of Africa and on the needs for the "systematic up-gradation of local human resource".[55]

Doubtless, a great deal will change as the AAGC develops its *Vision Study* and as BRI moves to tease out the HRD implications of the BRI for the countries of the East African coast and the rest of the continent. But for the moment, it may be acknowledged that these initial documents of AAGC and BRI have a somewhat different feel in terms of their language and discourse. This has important implications for how these documents and the ambitions within them are read in Africa.

Last Word on the Bigger Picture of Japan, India and China in Africa

The history of these three Asian nations' engagement has been essentially bilateral, despite having their increasingly well-known respective Pan-African platforms in TICAD, IAFS and FOCAC. Their involvement has changed over time, as has been shown in Panda's analysis of the AAGC.[56] In addition, their historical traditions of working in Africa have been affected by their dynamic current heads of state, who are anxious to make a difference in their respective global relationships, and specifically the work in Africa.

Undoubtedly, it has proved easier to put flesh on the bones of India and Japan's long-standing bilateral activities in relation to Africa than on the outline of their shared intentions from the AAGC *Vision Document*. The very positive histories of both their bilateral and Pan-African HRD programmes and projects in Africa are not altered by the particular wording of a single document. In other words, the preliminary comparisons with the BRI around such terms as capacity building and people-to-people exchange must remain tentative until the AAGC's vision is turned into an action plan through the work of its joint study team. The same will doubtless be the case with the role of African agency and consultation in the AAGC. The AfDB's positive assessment of India and Japan as bilateral investors in Africa will need to be carried over into what they execute together through the AAGC. The practical and conceptual challenge for the AAGC is to create a programme that is more than a mere amalgam of their on-going bilateral actions such as India's Pan-African e-Network and Japan's science and maths initiatives in Africa.

The same practical and conceptual challenge faces China's BRI: how does the BRI add value to the existing HRD investments of China in Africa whether in their Confucius Institutes or their wide-ranging scholarship and training programmes? So, for all three Asian nations, the very success and visibility of their on-going bilateral HRD engagements with Africa may prove to be the biggest challenge to their rebranding of their new initiatives as specifically the AAGC or BRI.[57]

NOTES

1. K. King, "Lenses on 'Japaneseness' in the Development Cooperation Charter of 2015: Soft Power, Human Resources Development, Education and Training", JICA-RI Working Paper No. 135, JICA Research Institute, Tokyo, November 2016.
2. For valuable background on the development of the AAGC in relation to the BRI, see J. Panda, "The Asia-Africa Growth Corridor: An India-Japan Arch in the Making?", *Focus Asia, Perspective & Analysis*, No. 21, Institute for Security and Development Policy, Stockholm, August 2017.
3. K. King, "Confucius Institutes in Africa: Culture and language without Controversy?", in Kathryn Batchelor and Xiaoling Zhang (eds.), *China-Africa relations: Building Images through Cultural Cooperation, Media Representation and on the Ground Activities*, Taylor and Francis, London, 2017, pp. 98-112.
4. K. King and S. McGrath, *Knowledge for Development: Comparing British, Japanese, Swedish and World Bank Aid*, Zed Books, London, 2004, p. 157.
5. The three think tanks behind the *Vision Document* were Research and Information System for Developing Countries (RIS) in New Delhi, Institute of Developing Economies-Japan External Trade Organisation (IDE-JETRO) in Chiba, Japan, and Economic Research Institute for ASEAN and East Asia (ERIA) in Jakarta.
6. *Asia-Africa Growth Corridor: Partnership for Sustainable and Innovative Development: A Vision Document*, African Development Bank Meeting, Asia-Africa Growth Corridor (AAGC), Ahmedabad, India, May 22-26, 2017, p. 7.
7. Ibid., p. 1.
8. Ibid.
9. Ibid., p. 9.
10. Ibid., p. 7.
11. Ibid.
12. Ibid., p. 5.
13. For background on UNISA, see "The Leading ODL University", University of South Africa (UNISA), at http://www.unisa.ac.za/sites/corporate/default/About/The-leading-ODL-university.

14. *Asia-Africa Growth Corridor*, No. 6, p. 11.
15. Ibid.
16. A. Sharma and K. King, "'Skill India': The 'modification' of skill development in India", in S. McGrath, J. Papier, M. Mulder and R. Suart (eds.), *International Handbook of Vocational Education and Training for the Changing World of Work*, Springer, New York, forthcoming (2018).
17. *Asia-Africa Growth Corridor*, No. 6, p. 11.
18. Ibid.
19. The use of the term "up-gradation" suggests that this part of the AAGC text has been drafted in India.
20. *Asia-Africa Growth Corridor*, No. 6, p. 11.
21. Ibid., p. 12.
22. Ibid.
23. *The Bank's Human Capital Strategy for Africa: 2014-2018*, African Development Bank, Abidjan, 2014, p. iv.
24. S. Mehrotra, "Asia-Africa Cooperation in Human Resource Development", RIS Discussion Paper 218, RIS, New Delhi, 2017.
25. *Asia-Africa Growth Corridor*, No. 6, p. 15.
26. Ibid., pp. 28-29.
27. Ibid., p. 30.
28. For the programme of the half-day meeting, see http://www.ris.org.in/asia-africa-growth-corridor. There are as yet no papers available from the meeting.
29. "Preface", *Action Plan on the Belt and Road Initiative*, National Development and Reform Commission, Ministry of Foreign Affairs and Ministry of Commerce, People's Republic of China (PRC), Beijing, March 30, 2015 (updated).
30. Ibid.
31. "Background", *Action Plan on the Belt and Road Initiative*, National Development and Reform Commission, Ministry of Foreign Affairs and Ministry of Commerce, PRC, Beijing, March 30, 2015 (updated).
32. "Principles", *Action Plan on the Belt and Road Initiative*, National Development and Reform Commission, Ministry of Foreign Affairs and Ministry of Commerce, PRC, Beijing, March 30, 2015 (updated).
33. "Framework", *Action Plan on the Belt and Road Initiative*, National Development and Reform Commission, Ministry of Foreign Affairs and Ministry of Commerce, PRC, Beijing, March 30, 2015 (updated).
34. "Cooperation Priorities: People-to-people Bond", *Action Plan on the Belt and Road Initiative*, National Development and Reform Commission, Ministry of Foreign Affairs and Ministry of Commerce, PRC, Beijing, March 30, 2015 (updated).
35. Ibid.
36. Ibid.
37. B. Liu, "Education for International Degree Programme Students from Belt and Road Countries: Status, Problems and Countermeasures", PowerPoint presentation at the International Seminar on the Belt and Road Initiative and 2030 SDGs in Education, Zhejiang Normal University, Jinhua, May 7, 2017, slide 6.
38. Ibid., slide 4.
39. S. Lou, "Aligning FOCAC, SDGs and One Belt One Road", *NORRAG News*, 54, 2017, p. 88.
40. *Education Action Plan for the Belt and Road Initiative*, Ministry of Education, Ministry of Education (MOE), PRC, Beijing, 2016, Section 6.

41. *Vision for Maritime Cooperation under the Belt and Road Initiative*, State Council, PRC, Beijing, June 20, 2017.
42. Ibid., 4.4.
43. Ibid., 4.5.
44. Xi Jinping, Speech at the Opening Ceremony of the Belt and Road Forum for International Cooperation, May 12, 2017, 2, at http://news.xinhuanet.com/english/2017-05/14/c_136282982.htm (Accessed November 14, 2017).
45. Ibid., 3.
46. Ibid., 5.
47. Ibid., 5.
48. For the full text of the meeting, see "India-Japan Joint Statement during Shinzo Abe's Visit: Full Text", *The Indian Express*, September 14, 2017, at http://indianexpress.com/article/india/india-japan-joint-statement-during-shinzo-abes-visit-full-text-narendra-modi-bullet-train-mous-4843849/.
49. R. Beri, "India's New Initiative in Africa: The Asia-Africa Growth Corridor", *IDSA Comment*, Institute for Defence Studies and Analyses, 2017, at https://idsa.in/idsacomments/indias-new-initiative-in-africa-asia-africa-growth-corridor_rberi_130617 (Accessed November 14, 2017).
50. S.D. Pradhan, "Asia-Africa Growth Corridor: A Positive Initiative", *Chanakya Code* (Blog), *The Times of India*, October 28, 2017, at https://blogs.timesofindia.indiatimes.com/ChanakyaCode/asia-africa-growth-corridor-a-positive-initiative/ (Accessed November 14, 2017).
51. Ibid.
52. R. Davis, "India-Japan Asia-Africa Growth Corridor Is Partial Response to Chinese One Belt and One Road (OBOR) Initiative", *Foreign Policy and Domestic Politics* (Blog), November 28,2017, at https://bobdavisblog.wordpress.com/2017/11/28/28-november-2017-india-japan-asia-africa-growth-corridor-is-partial-response-to-chinese-one-belt-and-one-road-obor-initiative/ (Accessed November 30, 2017).
53. M. Rich and J. Perlez, 2017. "Wary of U.S., Japan and China Move to Mend Ties", *The New York Times*, November 20, 2017, p.4.
54. *One Belt, One Road: From Dialogue to Action*, McKinsey, New York, April 2015.
55. *Asia-Africa Growth Corridor*, No. 6, p. 11.
56. J. Panda, No. 2.
57. For a similar challenge (where the BRI and AAGC are not mentioned), see C. Alden, *New Actors, New Models, New Outcomes? African Countries' Engagement with China and Other Development Partners in Achieving the SDGs and Agenda 2063*, Oxfam Research Report, Oxfam, Oxford, 2017.

17

Realising 'Make in India': Port-led Development in the Indian Ocean

Titli Basu

Prime Minister Narendra Modi's 'Make in India'[1] initiative aimed at transforming India into an economic pole of global growth holds promise; however, it needs to be complimented with world-class infrastructure and enhanced regional connectivity, both within India and beyond. Improved regional connectivity will facilitate in integrating the economy with dynamic regional value chains, in accessing emerging markets and in sourcing energy supplies and raw materials to fuel India's economic engine. Infrastructure plays an instrumental role in stimulating economic development by linking connectivity gaps, plummeting trade costs, and accelerating networks with the resource-rich regions. Given this, promoting regional connectivity has emerged as one of the central themes in Modi's economic policy and foreign policy.

While Indian strategic thinking has traditionally had a continental underpinning, maritime strategists have for long urged to expand the strategic mind space to embrace the oceanic aspect. India is situated at the heart of the Indian Ocean which hosts vital sealanes and serves as an engine for global growth and prosperity. Subsequently, "after almost a millennia of inward and landward focus', India is 'once again turning gaze outwards and seawards", which has been argued as "the natural direction of view for a nation seeking to re-establish itself, not simply as a continental power, but even more so as a maritime power".[2] India is a maritime nation not just drawing from history, when it enjoyed extensive maritime linkages with Africa, Gulf, Mediterranean, South East Asia and the Far East, but also owing to its geophysical and geopolitical setting which makes it reliant on sealanes.

Prime Minister Modi argued that "India's quest for economic prosperity through oceans is a part of our larger efforts to transform India".[3] This chapter critically analyses the significance of Indian Ocean highways, connecting critical geo-economic and geostrategic sub-regions, in facilitating Prime Minister Modi's economic development agenda pursued through his signature 'Make in India' initiative, which aims to enable India as a global manufacturing hub. Regional connectivity constitutes one of the key themes of Modi's foreign policy – whether it is the "Act East" policy, "Connect Central Asia" policy, "Neighbourhood First" policy or linking the Indo-Pacific through Asia-Africa Growth Corridor. This chapter situates Modi's 'Make in India' initiative in the Indian Ocean theatre and evaluates some of the key port-related projects India has pursued, including Chabahar and Sittwe, amongst others, in its maritime neighbourhood.

While most of these port related projects predate Modi administration, but India's growing economic potency, diplomatic capital and strategic ambitions has led Prime Minister Modi to articulate India's vision for the Indian Ocean region. This vision aims at improving capabilities to protect land and maritime interests; growing economic and security cooperation in the littoral; supporting collective action while dealing with natural disasters and maritime security threats; endorsing sustainable regional development through a web of political and economic partnerships; and upholding maritime rules and global norms.[4] The vision enunciated in Modi's Security and Growth for All in the Region (SAGAR) encompasses some of the key issues such as buttressing intra-ocean trade and investment, nurturing blue economy, infrastructure and connectivity, including improving port connectivity among the Indian Ocean littoral states – and securing sealanes from non-traditional and traditional threats to ensure unimpeded movement of goods and ideas.

Indian Ocean as an Anchor in Modi's 'Make in India'

Indian Ocean performs an instrumental role in Modi's pursuit for economic development. Tapping the shipping lanes as a primary means of extending India's connectivity and trade networks with the international market on one hand and sourcing energy resources critical for national development through major energy sea-lanes, running from the Hormuz Strait and Bab-el-Mandeb into the Indian Ocean and beyond, on the other is critical to achieving Modi's economic agenda. Projections from the International

Monetary Fund (IMF) reflect that India is expected to grow at 7.4 percent in 2018 and 7.9 percent in 2020.[5] According to the US Department for Agriculture Economic Research Service (USDA ERS) projections, Indian economy is likely to grow annually at an average 7.4 percent, amounting to US$6.84 trillion by 2030.[6] Meanwhile, Niti Aayog estimates that India will be a US$7.2 trillion economy by 2030, developing at a rate of 8 per cent.[7] To sustain the economic momentum, there is enormous need for energy. The *India Energy Outlook* published by International Energy Agency (IEA) in 2015 argued that oil and gas production cannot keep up with the growth in demand. It further suggested that by 2040, India's dependence on oil imports will rise above 90 percent.[8] India, with a demand of 4.1 million barrels per day, already overtook Japan to emerge as the third largest oil consumer after the US and China in 2015.[9]

Table 1: IMF World Economic Outlook Projections

	Projections			*Difference from July 2017 WEO Update*[1]		*Difference from April 2017 WEO*[1]	
	2016	*2017*	*2018*	*2017*	*2018*	*2017*	*2018*
World Output	3.2	3.6	3.7	0.1	0.1	0.1	0.1
Advanced Economies	1.7	2.2	2.0	0.2	0.1	0.2	0.0
United States	1.5	2.2	2.3	0.1	0.2	-0.1	-0.2
Euro Area	1.8	2.1	1.9	0.2	0.2	0.4	0.3
Germany	1.9	2.0	1.8	0.2	0.2	0.4	0.3
France	1.2	1.6	1.8	0.1	0.1	0.2	0.2
Italy	0.9	1.5	1.1	0.2	0.1	0.7	0.3
Spain	3.2	3.1	2.5	0.0	0.1	0.5	0.4
Japan[2]	1.0	1.5	0.7	0.2	0.1	0.3	0.1
United Kingdom	1.8	1.7	1.5	0.0	0.0	-0.3	0.0
Canada	1.5	3.0	2.1	0.5	0.2	1.1	0.1
Other Advanced Economies[3]	2.2	2.6	2.5	0.3	0.1	0.3	0.1
Emerging Market and Developing Economies	4.3	4.6	4.9	0.0	0.1	0.1	0.1
Commonwealth of Independent States	0.4	2.1	2.1	0.4	0.0	0.4	0.0
Russia	-0.2	1.8	1.6	0.4	0.2	0.4	0.2
Excluding Russia	1.9	2.9	3.3	0.4	-0.2	0.4	-0.2
Emerging and Developing Asia	6.4	6.5	6.5	0.0	0.0	0.1	0.1
China	6.7	6.8	6.5	0.1	0.1	0.2	0.3
India[4]	7.1	6.7	7.4	-0.5	-0.3	-0.5	-0.3
ASEAN-55	4.9	5.2	5.2	0.1	0.0	0.2	0.0

Source: *World Economic Outlook: Seeking Sustainable Growth Short-Term Recovery, Long-Term Challenges*, IMF, October 2017.

In order to achieve the development targets outlined by Prime Minister Modi, including elevating the contribution of the manufacturing sector to 25 percent of the gross domestic product (GDP) by the year 2025, India needs uninterrupted supply of energy to fuel the development engine. *BP Energy Outlook 2017* underscores that India's energy consumption increases by 4.2 percent every year, faster than every major economy in the world. Energy demand growth at 129 per cent overtakes China at 47 per cent, Brazil at 41 per cent and Russia at 2 per cent. Oil consumption will escalate from 4.1 million barrels per day in 2015 to 9.2 million bpd in 2035. *International Energy Outlook 2016*, US Energy Information Administration (EIA), argued that Non-Organisation for Economic Co-operation and Development (OECD) Asia, including China and India, will account for more than half of the world's total increase in energy consumption over the 2012 to 2040 projection period.

India sources crude oil through the Indian Ocean, transporting from the Persian Gulf and Africa. In 2015, the EIA estimates reflected that India sourced 58 percent of imported crude oil from the Middle East (especially from Saudi Arabia and Iraq) and 19 percent from Africa (especially from Nigeria). Given this, the 2015 Indian Maritime Security Strategy identifies the Persian Gulf and its littoral, Gulf of Oman, Gulf of Aden, Red Sea, East Coast of Africa littoral, Arabian Sea, Bay of Bengal, Andaman Sea and their littoral regions including the choke points in the Indian Ocean as India's primary areas of maritime interest.[10]

Beyond energy security, Indian Ocean as an important channel for trade has a significant role in attainment of Modi's Make in India initiative. Indian Ocean connects India with the major global economic engines, including Southeast Asia, Eastern and Southern Africa. Today, 50 per cent of international container traffic and one-third of global cargo traffic transit through this critical maritime space. Moreover, 90 percent of India's trade by volume and oil imports are done through the seas. India's exclusive economic zone of 2.4 million square kilometres stresses the economic connotation of the Indian Ocean.

As a major highway connecting vast geographies for international trade, Indian Ocean contributes as a facilitator connecting domestic manufacturing hubs and industrial corridors with the markets of Southeast Asia and Africa. To attain this objective, it is important to connect infrastructure that bridges inland Asia and Africa with the Indian Ocean rim in order to improve the viability of regional ports. Hence, infrastructure building and connectivity both within India and beyond is one of the major themes of Prime Minister Modi's development policy. While connectivity

Figure 1: Oil – Major Trade movement 2016 (Unit: Million Tonnes)

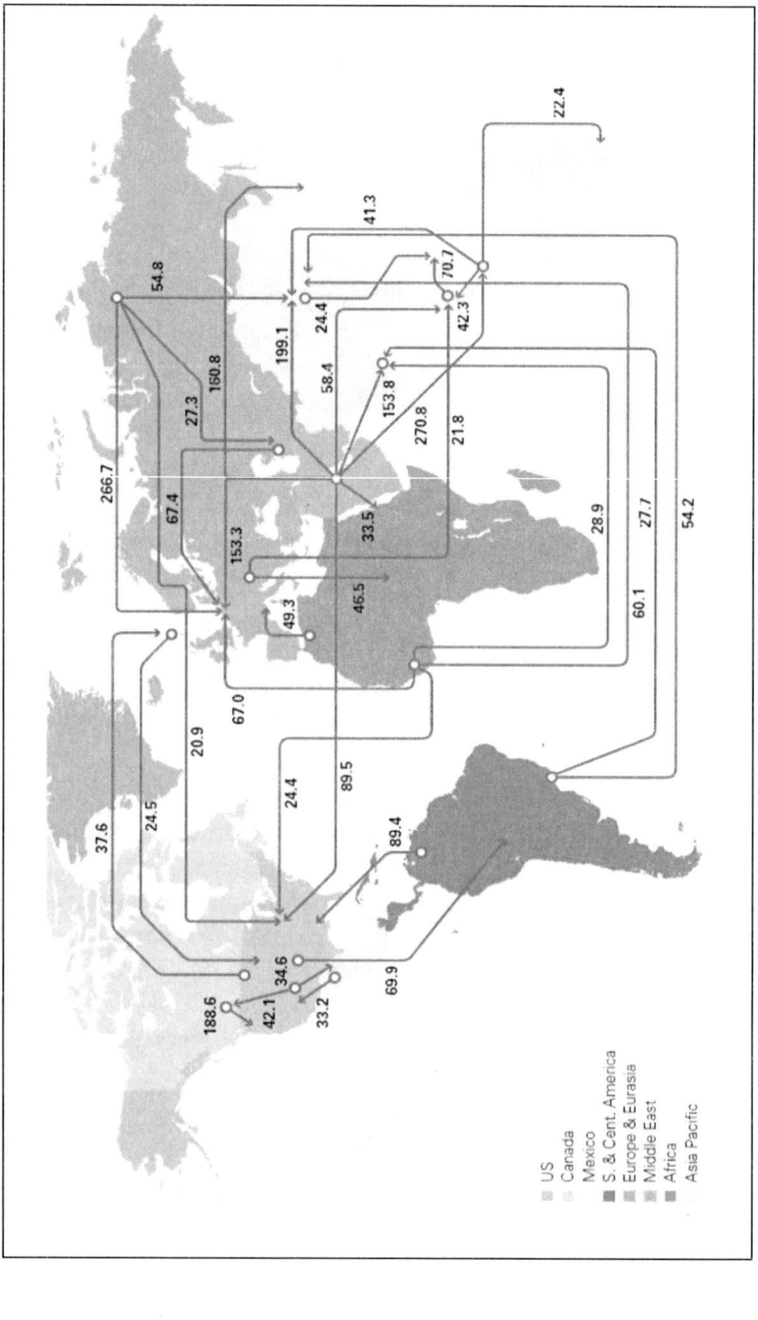

Source:*BP Statistical Review of World Energy*, June 2017.

issues have implications for regional security concerns, India's approach is founded on "norms of transparency, good governance, commercial viability, fiscal responsibility and respect for sovereignty and territorial integrity".[11]

To support the Make in India initiative, New Delhi is bolstering connectivity and enhancing export competitiveness by developing port-proximate industrial clusters. Within the Sagarmala Programme, 415 projects have been mapped across India at an estimated cost of US$ 123 billion from 2015-2025. The key objective is port modernisation and new port development, port connectivity enhancement, port-linked industrialisation and coastal community development. Coastal economic zones (CEZs) hosting industrial clusters are aligned to industrial corridors, for instance, the Delhi-Mumbai Industrial Corridor (DMIC) and Chennai-Bengaluru Industrial Corridor (CBIC), which will enable port-linked industrialisation. India aims to improve exports to US$900 billion by 2020 from US$ 465 billion in 2014-15 through port-linked industrialisation.[12] India has identified 189 port modernisation projects at an estimated cost of US$ 21 billion; 170 connectivity enhancement projects at an estimated cost of US$ 35 billion; and 33 port-linked industrialisation projects at an estimated cost of US$ 65 billion. Following the challenges related to port saturation and developing strategic ports to seize economic opportunity, six new port locations have been identified, including in Vadhavan, Enayam, Sagar Island, Paradip Outer Harbour, Sirkazhi and Belekeri.[13]

In addition, India is building Dedicated Freight Corridors (DFCs), along the eastern and western routes, at an estimated cost of US$ 12 billion with the aim of transporting goods at an economical and faster pace from the industrial heartlands to the ports to support Modi's Make in India initiative. The Western DFC (WDFC), running from JNPT to Dadri through Vadodara-Ahmedabad-Palanpur-Phulera-Rewari, passes through Haryana, Rajasthan, Gujarat, Maharashtra and Uttar Pradesh, and will link the Eastern Corridor at Dadri. The WDFC is focussed on container traffic from JNPT and Mumbai Port in Maharashtra and Pipavav, Mundra and Kandla in Gujarat.[14]

India is building infrastructure to support its planned Industrial Corridors, which is critically dependent on top-notch infrastructure and transport facilities to support a robust business ecosystem. There are five Industrial Corridors in the making, including the DMIC encompassing Uttar Pradesh, Haryana, Rajasthan, Madhya Pradesh, Gujarat and Maharashtra; CBIC covering Tamil Nadu, Andhra Pradesh and Karnataka; Bengaluru-Mumbai Economic Corridor (BMEC); Amritsar-Kolkata

Figure 2: Ports, Industrial Corridors and Connectivity

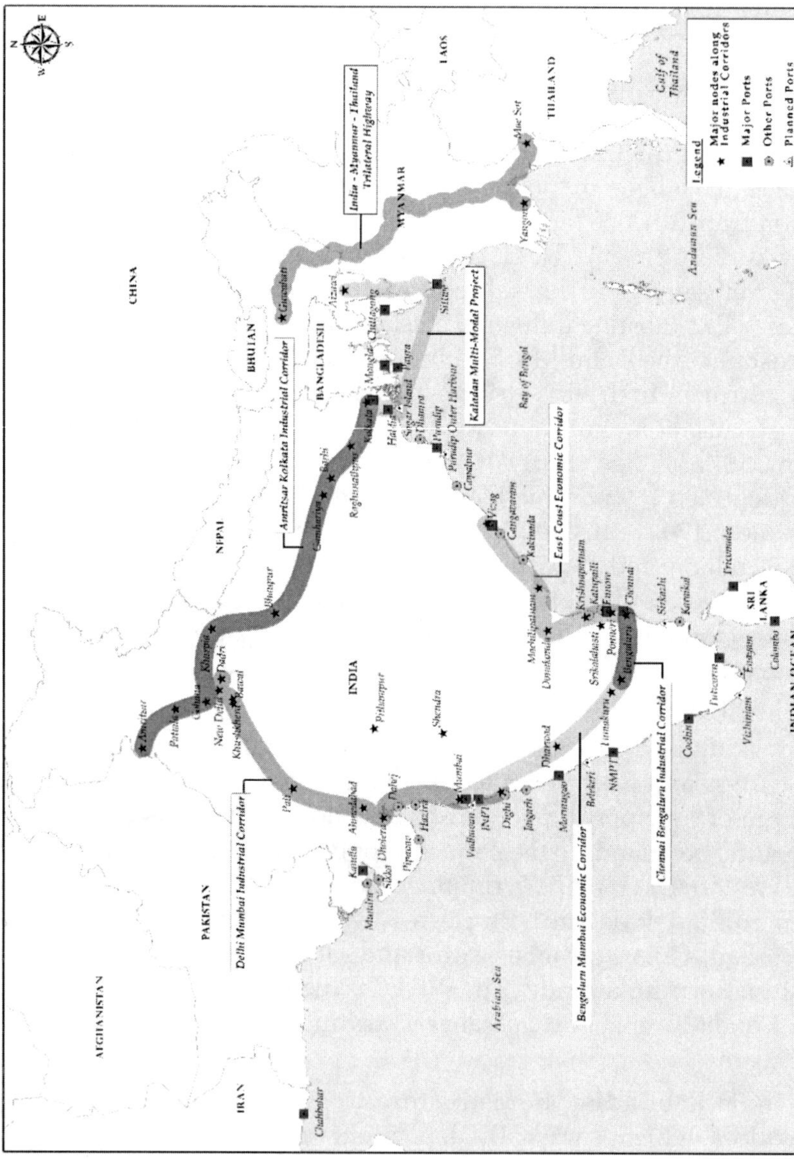

Source: GIS Lab, IDSA.

Industrial Corridor (AKIC) passing through Punjab, Haryana, Uttarakhand, Uttar Pradesh, Bihar, Jharkhand and West Bengal; and East Coast Economic Corridor (ECEC) encompassing West Bengal, Odisha, Andhra Pradesh and Tamil Nadu.[15]

Given that 95 percent of India's trade by volume is conducted through the maritime route, it is imperative to develop India's ports and trade-related infrastructure and further connect it with the Indian Ocean and beyond to accelerate growth in the manufacturing industry and to assist the Make in India initiative. Infrastructure is critical in facilitating economic growth by linking connectivity gaps, easing expenses and boosting linkages with the resource-rich nations and gaining access to emerging markets.

Connecting with the Indian Ocean Neighbourhood

To realise the objectives of Modi's economic development agenda, it is critical to tap the potential of the Indian Ocean highways. Promoting robust regional connectivity ambition lies at the core of Modi's key foreign policy initiatives, including the Neighbourhood First, Act East Policy, Africa Policy and Think West Policy. Pursuing the ambition of a free and open Indo-Pacific, India is engaging in several ambitious infrastructure and connectivity projects both bilaterally and in cooperation with like-minded countries. Africa has been accorded importance by the leadership, besides exploring prospects of cooperation in priority regions including South Asia, Southeast Asia and adjoining countries like Iran and Afghanistan.[16]

'Connect Central Asia' through Chabahar Port

Strategically situated Chabahar Port, often touted as India's gateway to Afghanistan, Central Asia and Europe, is at the fulcrum of India's connectivity ambition in the region. Chabahar Port offers India an alternative access route to Afghanistan making use of New Delhi's investment in Zaranj-Delaram road on the one hand and a direct sea-road access route into Central Asia on the other. Chabahar's strategic location also enables India to "skirt any challenges posed by developments in the Persian Gulf and Strait of Hormuz".[17] The operationalisation of the first phase of the Shahid Beheshti Port at Chabahar in December 2017 will complement the International North South Trade Corridor (INSTC), to be operational in 2018. It is argued that Chabahar together with the INSTC is likely to augment trade worth up to US$ 170 billion from India alone.[18] The INSTC, a land- and sea-based multi-modal transport corridor, was founded by India, Russia and Iran with the objective of connecting the Indian Ocean and Persian Gulf to the Caspian Sea to offer a shorter transit passage between Russia and India via Iran.

Figure 3: Access through Chabahar

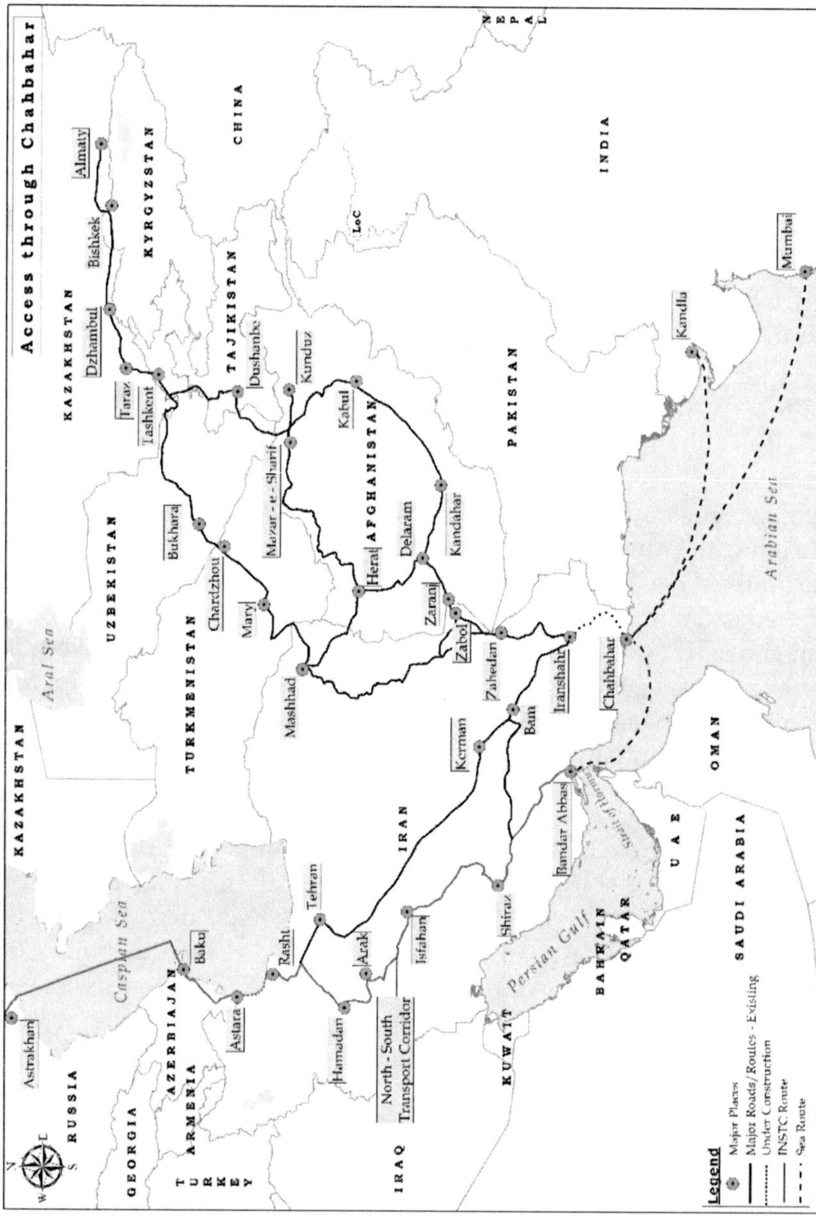

Source: GIS Lab, IDSA (map not to scale).

Chabahar would offer the landlocked Central Asian nations with a condensed land route to carry out engagements with the economies of the Indian Ocean. Moreover, connectivity through Chabahar Port is competitive with regard to reduced delivery time, lower cost and market access to and from Eurasia. In May 2016, India-Iran-Afghanistan Trilateral Agreement to establish International Transport and Transit Corridor was signed following which a commercial contract was signed between India Ports Global Private Ltd, a consortium of Jawaharlal Nehru Port Trust and Kandla Port Trust, and Iran's Arya Banader for the development and operations of Chabahar Port.[19] In October 2017, India shipped wheat consignment from Kandla Port in Gujarat to Afghanistan via Chabahar Port.

India has committed to construct two terminals and five berths with cargo handling for a decade in Chabahar. India Ports Global would revamp a 640 metre long container handling facility and rebuild a 600 metre long container handling facility. It will also invest in modernising ancillary infrastructure by setting up four rail-mounted gantry cranes, 16 rubber-tire gantry cranes, two reach stackers, two empty handlers and six mobile harbour cranes. India has agreed to equip and operate two berths in Chabahar Port first phase with capital investment of US$ 85.21 million and annual revenue expenditure of US$ 22.95 million on a 10-year lease.[20] India has committed US$235 million line of credit for Chabahar Port development since 2015. Once upgraded, Chabahar's capacity would escalate to 8 million tons from the current 2.5 million ton capacity.[21]

While India has invested in developing the Chabahar Port for decades, the project has suffered following sanctions imposed on Iran for its controversial nuclear programme. Notwithstanding the sanctions, India invested US$135 million to construct the Zaranj-Dilaram highway in 2009 connecting the Kabul-Herat highway to Chabahar Port. Subsequently with President Obama's 2015 Iran Nuclear Deal and easing of sanctions, Japan had demonstrated its interest[22] in supporting connectivity through Chabahar. The 2016 India-Japan Joint Statement underscored the prospects of cooperation "in the development of infrastructure and connectivity for Chabahar".[23] However, with the Trump administration's overturning of the Iran policy, Japan as a formal alliance partner of the US is weighing the costs and benefits of such a collaboration.

Acting East through Myanmar

Southeast Asia has emerged as an important growth pole in world trade. From 2007-2015, the Association of Southeast Asian Nations (ASEAN) registered an annual average growth rate of 5.3 percent. Collectively, the

ASEAN economy was the third largest in Asia, with a population of 629 million, in 2015.[24] But India has been unable to tap the full potential of the region owing to inadequate infrastructure for physical connectivity. Robust connectivity between ports is an indispensable catalyst to facilitate smoother maritime linkage between Southeast Asia and India and unfold greater opportunities for integrating into the regional value chains. There is a need to boost a multi-modal and multi-tier approach for ASEAN-India connectivity including through the sea route along the Mekong-India Economic Corridor (MIEC) which depends on the indispensable role of the Dawei Port in Myanmar and land route along the Trilateral Highway (TH)/Asian Highway (AH1) connecting Thailand, Myanmar and India. There is policy deliberation on extending the TH to Cambodia, Lao PDR and Vietnam. As India's economic engagement is expanding in Southeast Asia, including Indonesia, Malaysia, Myanmar, Thailand and Vietnam, it needs to reduce both its expenditure and time required in transporting through feeder routes.[25]

Myanmar presents maritime linkage between Southeast Asia and India across the Bay of Bengal. In 2016, India completed the Sittwe Port in the Bay of Bengal as a part of the Kaladan Multimodal Transit Transport Project whose key objective is to create access to the Bay of Bengal for the landlocked north-eastern states of India. Under the waterways component of the multi-modal project, Port and Inland Water Transport (IWT) terminal at Sittwe and related infrastructure/back up facilities; IWT/trans-shipment terminal and related facilities at Paletwa; navigational channel along Kaladan river from Sittwe to Paletwa and six self-propelled IWT vessels have been completed.[26] Sittwe Industrial Park is located near the Sittwe Port, which is being developed by India. Furthermore, India, grasping the importance of strengthening connectivity through Myanmar, has engaged in discussing the possibilities for cooperation on the Dawei Deep Sea Port and special economic zone projects with Nay Pyi Taw[27] and Bangkok.[28] The MIEC involves integrating the four Mekong countries connecting Ho Chi Minh City with Dawei through Bangkok and Phnom Penh and further linking it to Chennai, boosting trade and connectivity on the one hand and reducing dependency on the congested Malacca Strait on the other. As India's natural partner for development, Japan is engaged in developing Dawei in cooperation with Myanmar and Thailand. Both countries should explore the opportunities for bilateral cooperation in Myanmar aimed at establishing improved economic network through connectivity.

Connecting with 'Neighbourhood First'

Augmenting regional connectivity and improving cross-border infrastructure to facilitate regional trade and investment constitutes one of the fundamental pillars of Modi's Neighbourhood First Policy. India features as one of the key development assistance partners in its neighbourhood extending grants and loans.[29] India has invested in several projects including railway modernisation, inland waterways, coastal shipping and upgrading of ports in Bangladesh, which is likely to grow at 6.9 percent in the fiscal year 2018, according to the Asian Development Bank (ADB) forecast. India has extended three lines of credit worth US$ 8 billion to Bangladesh. Dhaka has used the first line of credit amounting to US$ 862 million, which has been invested in building infrastructure including roads, railways, bridges and inland waterways including procurement of one dredger for Mongla Port and construction of Khulna-Mongla Port Rail Line.[30] In addition, second lines of credit of US$ 2 billion and third Line of Credit of US$ 4.5 billion[31] have been extended, and 17 projects have reportedly been identified, including upgrading the ports of Payra, Chittagong and Mongla, making more roads four lane, upgrading of airports, increasing railway lines and building dedicated economic zones.[32]

The operationalisation of the 2015 Coastal Shipping Agreement and transhipment of goods via the Ashuganj River Port under the Protocol on Inland Water Transit and Trade (PIWTT) have strengthened connectivity aimed at facilitating trade. The Coastal Shipping Agreement has shrunk the shipping times from about a month to a week.[33] Under this agreement, the first cargo ship sailed from Chittagong to Vishakhapatnam in March 2016. Further strengthening infrastructure and connectivity, India and Bangladesh have invested in establishing an Inland Container Port (ICP) at Ashuganj and upgrading the road between Akhaura Land Port and Ashuganj to four lanes.

While Sri Lanka has emerged as one of the key hubs straddling the Indian Ocean shipping lanes, India has intensified its engagement with Colombo by way of several infrastructure projects including reconstruction of the Kankesanthurai Port into a commercial port and developing Sri Lanka's first liquefied natural gas (LNG) terminal near Colombo in a joint venture with Japanese and Sri Lankan companies.[34] Meanwhile, New Delhi is keen on jointly developing the Trincomalee Port project and the Eastern Container Terminal of the Colombo Port.[35] Since the Colombo Port handles over 70 percent of the transhipment cargo to and from India and is situated at a strategic point in the global sea trade, India is competing for the Eastern

Container Terminal. In this regard, Container Corporation of India (Concor) has formed a consortium with APM Terminals B.V., John Keells Holdings and Maersk Line to bid for the development of the East Container Terminal. With regard to the Kankesanthurai project, four phases of the rehabilitation, out of the six, have reportedly been completed including dredging and hydrographic survey. With US$ 45.27 million extended in fresh assistance in January 2018, the last two phases will focus on the rehabilitation of the breakwater and existing pier, construction of a new pier for commercial cargo handling and installation of port infrastructure facilities.[36] Reinforcing economic cooperation, India has signed a Memorandum of Understanding (MoU) for Cooperation in Economic Projects with Sri Lanka which enables India to cooperate on infrastructure projects such as port, petroleum refinery and other industries in Trincomalee, including jointly operating and managing oil storage tanks in Trincomalee under a 50-year lease agreement and development of road segments including Mannar-Jaffna, Mannar-Trincomalee and Dambulla-Trincomale Expressway under Indian investments.[37]

Linking Indo-Pacific through Asia-Africa Growth Corridor

While India has been a beneficiary of Japanese Prime Minister Shinzo Abe's Extended Partnership for Quality Infrastructure (EPQI) with high-speed rail, industrial corridors and urban mass rapid transport systems playing an instrumental role in redefining national infrastructure and complimenting Modi's Make in India, both leaders have mapped the Indo-Pacific theatre for furthering bilateral cooperation. Conceptualisation of the Asia-Africa Growth Corridor (AAGC) in cooperation with Japan is a pragmatic initiative. The goal is to coordinate bilaterally and with other countries for developing better regional economic linkages, connectivity and facilitating industrial networks employing collective capabilities. The May 2017 AAGC Vision Document underscores pursuing joint initiatives in various sectors, including infrastructure, manufacturing, and connectivity, consistent with the development priorities of Africa and the Sustainable Development Goals.[38] The central idea is to combine India's experience and understanding of the African market with Japan's technological know-how and capital for a "win-win scenario"[39] in realising the growth opportunities in the African market.

Following the launch of the AAGC, the Asia-Africa Growth Study is being conducted currently and a report is likely to be submitted to the stakeholders in 2018, outlining "the next steps for sustainable and innovative development, as well as partnership between Asia and Africa through AAGC".[40] Founded on a consultative and inclusive approach, the idea of AAGC is aimed at cultivating the value chains, integrating and developing a competitive economic bloc, thereby accelerating Africa's and Asia's development trajectory. However, translating the idea into deliverables will require India and Japan to conceive joint projects aiding capacity building, infrastructure and connectivity, synergising their resources and capabilities and, most importantly, ensuring the efficient implementation of these projects to demonstrate bilateral commitment to the African partners.[41]

Thinking Africa

India's stakes in Africa, besides strategic complementarities, are shaped by the emerging markets in the continent which also serves as an important source for natural resources. Africa's GDP is likely to reach US$3.6 trillion by 2020, and estimates indicate that the market would expand to US$1.4 trillion by 2020.[42] Indian industry argues that the manufacturing sector, including automotive industry, has potential. India-Africa trade amounts to US$70 billion, and Indian investments in Africa amounts to US$35 billion,[43] most of which is focused in Southern and Eastern Africa. Africa's energy resource has emerged as an alternative source of imports as India is attempting to diversify its supply beyond the Middle East. India's development partnership cooperation with Africa is underscored by the commitment of US$8 billion lines of credit between 2008 and 2011. Moreover, at the India-Africa Forum Summit in 2015, India pledged an additional US$10 billion worth of concessional credit. Africa receives roughly 53 percent of the operative credit lines which are used in varied projects, including agriculture, irrigation, food processing, rural electrification, information technology and infrastructure.[44]

India is exploring opportunities to share its know-how on building roads, airports, ports, railways, economic zones and industrial corridors with Africa. India's Essar Ports Ltd is developing a 20 million tonne capacity coking coal loading terminal at Beira Port in Mozambique as a Public-Private Partnership (PPP) project. A 30-year concession agreement is signed with the Mozambique government. This project will be implemented on Design, Build, Own, Operate and Transfer (DBOOT) approach through a subsidiary, the New Coal Terminal Beira (NCTB). The NCTB is a joint venture of Essar and Portos e Caminhos de Ferro de Moçambique (CFM) on a 70-30 stake.[45] The first phase of the terminal, at an estimated cost of $275 million, is likely to be operational by 2020. The aim of the NCTB is to function as the evacuation point for shipping coal from Tete province and provide for the Indian markets. In addition, the NCTB can be utilised as an outlet for the landlocked hinterland nations, including Zimbabwe,

Zambia, Democratic Republic of the Congo, Malawi and Botswana, and presents the shortest route to India.[46]

Securing the Global Commons

To drive India's economic development through the waters of the Indian Ocean and for a sustainable Indian Ocean economic revival, India together with other regional stakeholders needs to ensure that "these waters must not only be better connected but they should remain free from non-traditional and traditional threats ... that all stake holders abide by a rules-based global order".[47] As India embraces the responsibility for securing this critical maritime space in cooperation with other regional stakeholders, Prime Minister Modi has infused momentum in strengthening security cooperation including anti-piracy, maritime security and Humanitarian Assistance and Disaster Relief (HADR) operations in the maritime neighbourhood.

Drawing from the strength of the Indian Navy's operational footprint, the Indian leadership, including former Prime Minister Manmohan Singh, has argued that India is well positioned to become a net provider of security in its immediate region and beyond. Moreover, the military leadership has underscored that the Indian Navy has been "mandated to be a net security provider to island nations in the Indian Ocean Region".[48] India is being perceived as a security provider by the US, Japan and several other regional players. The 2017 National Security Strategy published by the Trump administration outlined that the US will deepen strategic partnership with India and "support its leadership role in Indian Ocean security and throughout the broader region".[49] The previous US administration under Obama argued the case of deepening cooperation with India in safeguarding maritime security and ensuring freedom of navigation and over flight throughout the region, including the South China Sea.[50]

While New Delhi launched the Indian Ocean Naval Symposium with the objective of promoting multilateral naval and maritime security cooperation among regional countries, it also maintains a robust framework of bilateral and multilateral military exercises, including the Milan and Malabar exercises involving the US, Japan and India, to enhance interoperability between the navies of the three democracies and strengthening trilateral cooperation in the Indo-pacific region. Meanwhile, India has a monitoring station in Madagascar with the aim of enhancing the domain awareness of the Navy and help in securing the Indian Ocean sealanes. India intends to establish a network of coastal surveillance radars, including eight in Mauritius and Seychelles, six in Sri Lanka and 10 in

Maldives. India has instituted a trilateral security framework at the national security advisors' level with Sri Lanka and Maldives with the objective of boosting cooperation on maritime security issues.

In 2015, Prime Minister Modi signed an MoU with Mauritius for Improvement in Sea and Air Transportation Facilities at Agalega Island with the objective of "setting up and upgradation of infrastructure for improving sea and air connectivity at the Outer Island of Mauritius" that will improve the opportunities for the local communities and "enhance the capabilities of the Mauritian Defence Forces in safeguarding their interests in the Outer Island".[51] Furthermore, Modi signed another MoU with Seychelles for Development of Facilities on Assumption Island, which is pending ratification in their Parliament.[52]

In February 2016, Prime Minister Narendra Modi enunciated India's approach to the Indian Ocean as:

> The oceans, especially the Indian Ocean, occupy a vital place in India's national security and economic prosperity. The waters of the Indian Ocean touch the shores of over 40 countries ... it also serves as a strategic bridge with the nations in our immediate and extended maritime neighbourhood ... The Indian Ocean Region is one of my foremost policy priorities. Our approach is evident in our vision of 'Sagar', which means 'Ocean' and stands for – Security and Growth for All in the Region. We would continue to actively pursue and promote our geo-political, strategic and economic interests on the seas, in particular the Indian Ocean.

The Way Forward

The unfolding power play between India and China, as each pursues its national interest and competes for influence, is increasingly shaping the Indian Ocean as strategic centre of gravity. Some scholars argue that as China follows its plan in the Indian Ocean without making attempts to "co-opt India as a partner", it may be challenging for Beijing to curve a favourable geostrategic environment.[53] As Xi Jinping pursues Chinese rejuvenation with the 21st Century Maritime Silk Road and makes deep inroads into the Indian Ocean with port development in Cambodia's Sihanoukville, Myanmar's Kyaukphyu, Chittagong in Bangladesh, Sri Lanka's Hambantota, Pakistan's Gwadar and several projects in the African coast, India is keen to assume greater responsibility towards securing and further supporting regional mechanisms for collective security and economic integration in the Indian Ocean. The objective of Maritime Silk Road strategy is to advance China as an economic, political and maritime power in the Indian Ocean and neighbouring region.[54] As Chinese debt trap diplomacy[55] is unfolding in the neighbourhood, India has stressed the significance of building connectivity through a consultative and transparent process founded on good governance, commercial viability, fiscal responsibility and respect for sovereignty and territorial integrity.[56]

For decades, India's Indian Ocean Policy suffered from political neglect owing to the continentalist orientation of the leadership. But China's forays in the Indian Ocean compelled India to weigh the implications on its own maritime security which further strengthened India's resolve to utilise its "natural geographic advantages in the littoral".[57] However, "walking the strategic talk", and translating the political vision into concrete deliverables has remained a challenge for India.[58] As Prime Minister Modi pursues India's quest to become a leading power, India will first have to lay a strong economic foundation by discarding the legacy of insular policies. As Indian economy embarks on the journey to integrate with global markets and production networks under Modi's Make in India programme, political elites rationalise the inevitable seaward alignment. While India's reliance on India Ocean trade and energy highways will intensify in the coming decades to sustain its growth momentum, India will benefit from further investing energy and capital in supporting regional connectivity linking South, Southeast and Central Asia in order to achieve regional economic integration. India under Modi has reflected strategic innovativeness and intensified efforts in creating a network of strategic partnerships, based on shared universal values and norms, to exercise strategic influence and protect its interests in the Indian Ocean, which serves as the "pathway of peace and prosperity for all".[59]

NOTES

1. Aimed at laying a strong foundation for the Indian economy and nation-building process, Prime Minister Narendra Modi initiated the Make in India programme in September 2014. While Indian economy is currently founded on the robust services sector, Modi's objective is to make India into an international design and manufacturing hub and boost the contribution of the manufacturing sector to 25 percent of the gross domestic product (GDP) by 2020. To this end, 25 thrust sectors are identified, including automobile, electronic systems, electrical machinery, chemicals, biotechnology, pharmaceuticals, construction, railways, ports and shipping, roads and highways, renewable energy, oil and gas and defence manufacturing, among others. The 'Make in India' programme is centred on four pillars: new processes, new infrastructure, new sectors and new mindset.
2. Pranab Mukherjee, "Speech for the Admiral A. K. Chatterjee Memorial Lecture", Press Information Bureau, Government of India, June 30, 2007, at http://pib.nic.in/newsite/erelease.aspx?relid=28921 (Accessed January 15, 2018).

3. "Text of PM's address at International Fleet Review 2016", Press Information Bureau, Prime Minister's Office, Government of India, February 7, 2016, at http://pib.nic.in/newsite/PrintRelease.aspx?relid=136182 (Accessed January 20, 2018).
4. "Text of the PM's Remarks on the Commissioning of Coast Ship Barracuda", Press Information Bureau, Prime Minister's Office, Government of India, March 12, 2015, at http://pib.nic.in/newsite/PrintRelease.aspx?relid=116881 (Accessed January 20, 2018).
5. "Real GDP Growth: Annual Percent Change", IMF Data Mapper, International Monetary Fund, October 2017, at http://www.imf.org/external/datamapper/NGDP_RPCH@WEO/OEMDC/IND (Accessed January 15, 2018).
6. Raj Kumar Ray, "India's Economy to become 3rd Largest, Surpass Japan, Germany by 2030", *Hindustan Times*, April 28, 2017, at http://www.hindustantimes.com/business-news/india-s-economy-will-become-third-largest-in-the-world-surpass-japan-germany-by-2030-us-agency/story-wBY2QOQ8YsYcrIK12A4HuK.html (Accessed January 17, 2018).
7. "Economy to Grow over 3-fold to $7.25 Trillion by 2030: Arvind Panagariya", *The Economic Times*, April 24, 2017, at economictimes.indiatimes.com/articleshow/58330421.cms?utm_source=contentofinterest&utm_ medium = text &utm_campaign=cpp (Accessed January 17, 2018).
8. *India Energy Outlook: World Energy Outlook Special Report*, International Energy Agency, 2015, at https://www.iea.org/publications/freepublications/publication/IndiaEnergyOutlook_WEO2015.pdf (Accessed January 17, 2018).
9. "India Becomes Third Largest Oil Consumer", *The Hindu*, September 16, 2016, at http://www.thehindu.com/business/Industry/India-becomes-third-largest-oil-consumer/article14391860.ece (Accessed January 17, 2018).
10. "Ensuring Secure Seas: Indian Maritime Security Strategy", Integrated Headquarters, Ministry of Defence (Navy), October 2015, at https://www.indiannavy.nic.in/sites/default/files/Indian_Maritime_Security _Strategy_Document_25Jan16.pdf (Accessed January 20, 2018).
11. Sushma Swaraj, "Address by External Affairs Minister at Third Raisina Dialogue", Ministry of External Affairs Government of India, January 17, 2018, at http://www.mea.gov.in/SpeechesStatements.htm?dtl/29362/Address_by_External _Affairs_Minister_at_Third_Raisina_Dialogue_New_Delhi_January_17_ 2018 (Accessed January 20, 2018).
12. "Developing Ports: Sagarmala Project", Make in India, at http://www.makeinindia.com/article/-/v/developing-ports-sagarmala-project (Accessed January 20, 2018).
13. "Sagarmala Programme", Press Information Bureau, Ministry of Shipping, Government of India, March 9, 2017, at http://pib.nic.in/newsite/PrintRelease.aspx?relid=159037 (Accessed January 20, 2018).
14. "Connecting The Country: Dedicated Freight Corridors", Make in India, at http://www.makeinindia.com/article/-/v/connecting-the-country-dedicated-freight-corridors (Accessed January 20, 2018).
15. "Industrial Corridors", Press Information Bureau, Ministry of Commerce & Industry, Government of India, November 16, 2016, at http://pib.nic.in/newsite/PrintRelease.aspx?relid=153692 (Accessed January 20, 2018).

16. Titli Basu, "Thinking Africa: India, Japan, and the Asia-Africa Growth Corridor", *The Diplomat*, June 3, 2017, at https://thediplomat.com/2017/06/thinking-africa-india-japan-and-the-asia-africa-growth-corridor/ (Accessed January 23, 2018).
17. "Lok Sabha Unstarred Question No. 2723, Development of Chabahar Port", Ministry of External Affairs Government of India, January 03, 2018, at http://www.mea.gov.in/lok-sabha.htm?dtl/29311/question+no2723+ development +of +chabahar+port (Accessed January 20, 2018)
18. P. Stobdan, "India Gears up to Enter the Eurasian Integration Path", *IDSA Issue Brief*, June 7, 2017, at https://idsa.in/issuebrief/india-gears-up-to-enter-the-eurasian-integration-path_pstobdan_070617 (Accessed January 22, 2018).
19. "Lok Sabha Starred Question No.192, Development of Chabahar Port", Ministry of External Affairs Government of India, March 15, 2017, at http://www.mea.gov.in/lok-sabha.htm?dtl/28138/QUESTION + NO192 + DEVELOP MENT+OF+CHABAHAR+PORT (Accessed January 22, 2018).
20. "1st Phase of Strategically-important Chabahar Port Inaugurated", Press Trust of India (PTI), December 3, 2017, at http://www.ptinews.com/news/9289194_1st-phase-of-strategically-important-Chabahar-port-inaugurated (Accessed January 19, 2018).
21. "Chabahr Port - A New Transit Gateway for Afghanistan", Aid for Trade, Organisation for Economic Co-operation and Development (OECD), 2017, at https://www.oecd.org/aidfortrade/casestories/casestories-2017/CS-61-NTP-MIP-Chabahar-port-New-transit-gateway-for-Afghanistan.pdf (Accessed January 22, 2018).
22. Suhasini Haidar, "Japan Pitches for Chabahar Port", *The Hindu*, May 8, 2017, at http://www.thehindu.com/todays-paper/tp-national/japan-pitches-for-chabahar-port/article18405900.ece (Accessed January 22, 2018).
23. "India-Japan Joint Statement during the visit of Prime Minister to Japan", Ministry of External Affairs Government of India, November 11, 2016, at http://mea.gov.in/bilateraldocuments.htm?dtl/27599/IndiaJapan+Joint+ Statement + during+the+visit+of+Prime+Minister+to+Japan (Accessed January 22, 2018).
24. "ASEAN Economic Community at a Glance", ASEAN Secretariat, at http://asean.org/storage/2012/05/Binder-AEC-at-a-Glance.pdf (Accessed January 22, 2018).
25. ASEAN-India Maritime Connectivity Report, ASEAN-India Centre RIS, 2014, at http://www.mcrg.ac.in/Logistics/Report_Final_Print_Martitime_connectivity.pdf (Accessed January 20, 2018).
26. "Lok Sabha Unstarred Question No.6280 Kaladan Multi-Modal Transit Transport", Ministry of External Affairs, Government of India, April 12, 2017, at http://Mea.Gov.In/Loksabha.Htm?Dtl/28382/Question_No6280_ Kaladan_ Multimodal _ Transit_Transport (Accessed January 20, 2018).
27. "Joint Statement by India and Myanmar on the State visit of Prime Minister of India to Myanmar", Ministry of External Affairs, Government of India, May 28, 2012, at http://www.mea.gov.in/bilateraldocuments.htm?dtl/19893/Joint + Statement+by+India+and+Myanmar+on+the+State+visit+of+Prime+ Minister + of+India+to+Myanmar (January 20, 2018).
28. "Joint Statement on Prime Minister's Visit to Thailand", Press Information Bureau, Prime Minister's Office, Government of India, May 30, 2013, at http://pib.nic.in/newsite/PrintRelease.aspx?relid=96311 (Accessed January 20, 2018).

29. "Remarks by Foreign Secretary at Indian Ocean Conference", Ministry of External Affairs, Government of India, September 1, 2016, at http://www.mea.gov.in/SpeechesStatements.htm?dtl/27356/Remarks_by_Foreign_ Secretary _at_ Indian _Ocean_Conference_September_01_2016 (Accessed January 20, 2018).
30. "List of Projects under the US$ 800 Million Indian LOC to Bangladesh", High Commission of India, Bangladesh, March 25, 2014, at https://www.hcidhaka.gov.in/pages.php?id=1239 (Accessed January 20, 2018).
31. "India-Bangladesh Joint Statement during the State Visit of Prime Minister of Bangladesh to India", Ministry of External Affairs, Government of India, April 8, 2017, at http://www.mea.gov.in/bilateraldocuments.htm?dtl/28362/India ++ Bangladesh+Joint+Statement+during+the+State+Visit+of+Prime+Minister + of+ Bangladesh+ to+India+April+8+2017 (Accessed January 23, 2018).
32. Suhasini Haidar and Kallol Bhattacherjee, "Delhi, Dhaka exchange 22 Deals", *The Hindu*, April 8, 2017, at http://www.thehindu.com/news/national/delhi-dhaka-exchange-22-deals/article17894933.ece; "India and Bangladesh Sign 22 Agreements, Discuss Water Sharing", *The Wire*, April 9,2017, at https://thewire.in/122402/india-bangladesh-relations-talks/ (Accessed January 23, 2018).
33. "Trade Gets a boost from Coastal Shipping Line", *The Daily Star*, November 3, 2016, at http://www.thedailystar.net/business/trade-gets-boost-coastal-shipping-line-1308523 (Accessed January 23, 2018).
34. "India Gets LoI from Sri Lankan Govt. to Set-Up LNG Terminal in Sri Lanka", Petronet LNG, September 6, 2017, at https://www.petronetlng.com/NewsContent.php?newsid=440 (Accessed January 23, 2018).
35. Dipanjan Roy Chaudhury, "India in Race for Colombo Port Project", *The Economic Times*, June 8, 2017, at https://economictimes.indiatimes.com/news/politics-and-nation/india-in-race-for-colombo-port-project/articleshow/59043489.cms (Accessed January 23, 2018).
36. "India Gives $45.27 Million Aid to Develop KKS Harbour in Sri Lanka", *The Economic Times*, January 12, 2018, at https://economictimes.indiatimes.com/news/defence/india-gives-45-27-million-aid-to-develop-kks-harbour-in-sri-lanka/articleshow/62472575.cms (Accessed January 23, 2018).
37. Devirupa Mitra, "India, Lanka Tread Cautiously on Trincomalee Deal, Say Oil Tank MoU 'Only a Road Map", *The Wire*, April 28, 2017, at https://thewire.in/129616/india-lanka-trincomalee-ioc/ (Accessed January 23, 2018).
38. Titli Basu, no. 16.
39. Atul Ranjan, "JETRO to Push Japan-India Business Collaboration in Africa", *The Japan Times*, February 5, 2017, at http://www.japantimes.co.jp/news/2017/02/05/national/jetro-push-japan-india-business-collaboration-africa/ (Accessed January 23, 2018).
40. "Lok Sabha Unstarred Question No.2694, Asia-Africa Development Corridor", Ministry of External Affairs, Government of India, January 3, 2018, at http://www.mea.gov.in/loksabha.htm?dtl/29306/question+no2694 +asiaafrica +development +corridor (Accessed January 13, 2018).
41. Titli Basu, no. 16.
42. Harshavardhan Neotia, "Africa, A Land of opportunity", Media Coverage (*The Hindu Business Line*), Federation of Indian Chambers of Commerce and Industry

(FICCI), July 7, 2016, at http://www.ficci.in/ficci-in-news-page.asp?nid=11444 (Accessed January 13, 2018).

43. "Imperatives that Drive African-Indian Engagement Are Based on Our Shared Challenges, Common Interests, and Perceptions of Mutual Benefit: Vice President", Press Information Bureau, Vice President's Secretariat, Government of India, February 21, 2017, at http://pib.nic.in/newsite/PrintRelease.aspx?relid=158594 (Accessed January 13, 2018).
44. Waheguru Pal Singh Sidhu, "Africa: The Indispensable Continent for India?", *Africa in Focus,* Brookings, November 3, 2015, at https://www.brookings.edu/blog/africa-in-focus/2015/11/03/africa-the-indispensable-continent-for-india/ (Accessed January 23, 2018).
45. "Essar Ports Signs Concession Agreement With Mozambique Government To Develop New 20 Mtpa Coal Terminal In Beira Port", ESSAR, August 4, 2017, at https://www.essar.com/essar-ports-signs-concession-agreement-mozambique-government-develop-new-20-mtpa-coal-terminal-beira-port/ (Accessed January 13, 2018).
46. "Essar Ports Ventures Overseas with Mozambique Coal Terminal Deal", *The Hindu Business Line,* August 4, 2017, at http://www.thehindubusinessline.com/economy/logistics/essar-ports-signs-concession-pact-with-mozambique-for-coal-terminal/article9802840.ece (Accessed January 13, 2018).
47. Sushma Swaraj, "Address by External Affairs Minister at the 2nd Indian Ocean Conference", Ministry of External Affairs, Government of India, August 31, 2017, at http://mea.gov.in/SpeechesStatements.htm?dtl/28907/Address+by+External +Affairs+Minister+at+the+2nd+Indian+Ocean+Conference+August+31+2017 (Accessed January 23, 2018).
48. "Indian Navy-Net Security Provider to Island Nations in IOR: Antony", Press Information Bureau, Ministry of Defence, Government of India, October 12, 2011, at http://pib.nic.in/newsite/PrintRelease.aspx?relid=76590 (Accessed January 23, 2018).
49. "National Security Strategy of the United States of America", The White House, December 2017, at https://www.whitehouse.gov/wp-content/uploads/2017/12/NSS-Final-12-18-2017-0905.pdf (Accessed January 23, 2018).
50. "US-India Joint Strategic Vision for the Asia-Pacific and Indian Ocean Region", Ministry of External Affairs, Government of India, January 25, 2015, at http://www.mea.gov.in/bilateralocuments.htm?dtl/24728/USIndia_Joint_Strategic _ Vision_for_the_AsiaPacific_and_Indian_Ocean_Region (Accessed January 23, 2018).
51. "List of Agreements/MoUs signed between India and Mauritius during the Visit of the Prime Minister to Mauritius", Ministry of External Affairs, Government of India, March 11, 2015, at http://www.mea.gov.in/bilateraldocuments.htm?dtl/24900/List_of_AgreementsMoUs_signed_ between_India_and_Mauritius_during_the_visit_of_the_Prime_Minister_to_Mauritius_March_11_2015 (Accessed January 22, 2018).
52. Devirupa Mitra, "Why Seychelles Has Been 'Very Slow' in Removing Hurdles for India's Assumption Island Project", *The Wire,* January 10, 2018, at https://thewire.in/212476/seychelles-slow-removing-hurdles-indias-assumption-island-project-leader-opposition/ (Accessed January 23, 2018).

53. David Brewster, "India and China at Sea: A Contest of Status and Legitimacy in the Indian Ocean", *Asia Policy*, 22, July 2016.
54. Jagannath Panda, "Maritime Silk Road and the India-China Conundrum", *Indian Foreign Affairs Journal*, 9 (1), January–March 2014.
55. Brahma Chellaney, "China's Debt-Trap Diplomacy", *Project Syndicate*, January 23, 2017, at https://www.project-syndicate.org/commentary/china-one-belt-one-road-loans-debt-by-brahma-chellaney-2017-01?barrier=accessreg (Accessed January 16, 2017).
56. Sushma Swaraj, No. 11.
57. C. Raja Mohan, "Modi and the Indian Ocean: Restoring India's Sphere of Influence", *ISAS Insights*, 277, March 20, 2015, at https://www.files.ethz.ch/isn/189804/ISAS_Insights_No._277__Modi_and_the_Indian_Ocean_20032015163047.pdf (Accessed January 6, 2017); C. Raja Mohan, *Samudra Manthan: Sino-Indian Rivalry in the Indo-Pacific*, Oxford University Press (South Asia Edition), New Delhi, 2013.
58. Abhijit Singh, "India's Indian Ocean Paradox", *ORF Commentary*, September 8, 2017, at http://www.orfonline.org/research/india-indian-ocean-paradox/ (Accessed January 16, 2017).
59. "Text of the PM's Remarks on the Commissioning of Coast Ship Barracuda", Press Information Bureau, Prime Minister's Office, Government of India, March 12, 2015, at http://pib.nic.in/newsite/PrintRelease.aspx?relid=116881 (Accessed January 17, 2017).

18

India's Transformed 'Continental-Nautical' Strategy: Rebooted Connectivity-Based Infrastructure-Compact

Dattesh D. Parulekar

In an increasingly interconnected and interdependent global order, marked, by the metamorphosing locus, trajectory and configuration of trade, investment and financial flows, and also underpinned by emergent normative challenges, posed, by an inflection of the proverbial 'East' and the putative 'South', assailing and counteracting the narrative and template of entrenched Anglo-Saxon contours and parameters of global governance, and tenor of institutional firmament, the strategic balance and equilibrium has been relocating, through the progressive erosion of the inveterate primacy of the Euro-Atlantic space, devolving to the rising salience of the Asian expanse, propelling the Asian sovereign-triumvirate of China, India and Japan to proverbial cynosures of attention and acclaim. As preponderant regional sentinels, characterised, by unique civilisational identities, distinct politico-social ordering, differentiated national economy priorities, distinguishing developmental patterns, and wedged traditions of regional perceptions and global outlook, contributing to variegated mutual power asymmetry, the interplay, of the remit of their bilateral interaction and scope of triangulated equations, in all its complexity and cross-currents, of trenchant competition, melded, with compulsively-ordained sensibilities for pluralised cooperation, straddles, the dialectic gamut of existential security dilemmas, blending, with virtuous economic imperatives, set against, the strategic context of mutating geopolitical concourse of circumstances and reconfiguring geo-economic hue, spanning the arc of continuum-terrain, from the continental 'Eurasian' swathe to the maritime 'Indo-Pacific' vector.

Notwithstanding the longstanding anecdotal and empirical vintage of the phenomenon of 'infrastructure', constituting an innate and integral dimension to robust national development and tangible socio-economic emancipation, the conceptual and operative construct of iconic infrastructural development, undergirding cross-border, regional and transcontinental connectivity initiatives, has only recently peregrinated onto the canvass of a nation's strategic calculus, referenced to the extant. In contemporaneous times, extra-territorial infrastructural schema, vividly represented by protracted-gestation investments across sovereign frontiers, and communitarian and gregariously crafted trade, transportation and strategic sectors corridors, constitutes, the luminous modern-day premise for deliberated foreign policy and statecraft ideation; conditions, enlightened diplomatic engagement and outreach; underpins, pragmatically expanded vistas of mutually beneficent economic interchange; pervades predominantly, on the unfolding hue of developmental financial assistance; characterises, potentially incisive sub-regional and regional cooperation mechanisms; and fosters effective prospects for win-win outcomes, through pan-regional and trans-regional collaboration and compact.[1] This said, there is no diminishing or supplanting the bell-weather principles, underwriting a cogent and sound trailblazing infrastructure investment framework; the sine-qua-non elements to successful vicissitudes of sovereign-mooted infrastructural designs, whether operationalised nationally, or forayed across territorial frontiers; embodied in clairvoyant and coherent long-horizon and medium-term supple strategic planning, abidingly redoubtable political commitment, steady and sustained financial stream and congruently aligned and seamlessly coordinated 'actor-stakeholder' perceptions.[2]

Perspectives and the discourse around infrastructure reside, at the intersection of multiple debates, from the feasibility of silos classification of infrastructure, as being quintessentially securitised or eminently economic, rendered arguably a misnomer in present times, where the comprehension of the 'strategic' perfunctorily encompasses the pervasiveness of the security and economic dimensions of initiatives, particularly when undertaken in the maritime realm and/or along border territories, as, notwithstanding the ostensible domesticity of such physicality-binge, it can cut both ways, in perception-stakes, emboldening nationalist sentiments at home, but sparking anxieties, restiveness and alarm, across sovereign boundaries, potentially precipitating portents for conflict and crises, than enhancing prospects for security, stability and productivity, a tough call indeed, in times, when cross-country and cross-regional corridors are being increasingly showcased and broadly appreciated, as harbingers of prosperity and symbols of multilateral amity and plural comity amongst states. Debates also abound over the conventional notions of physical elements of infrastructure, having to contend with newer forms of infrastructural-build, anchored in technological imbue and import, instilling scientific temper, inculcating ingenuity and spurring innovation towards disrupting to transform. Contentions are equally rife over determinations of a threshold level of infrastructural focus and investment, in a country or across a region, to act as a catalysing change-agent, propelling infrastructure, from its infirmities of criticality to acquiring and attaining a certain critical-mass, transitioning an economy and engineering a society, from a mundane level of existence to an elevated plane of performance, enabling the alleviation of impoverishment, amelioration of the job-less growth syndrome and imparting an improved quality of life to the target populace.[3] This said, one cannot but underscore the overriding considerations of exercising due diligence and adhering to fiscal-prudence, towards warding off the unmitigated catastrophe of unbridled infrastructural splash and splurge, epochal to ensuring that sovereign-exponents are not left hoist-with-their-own-petard, in riding the damning crest of an impishly promoted, unsustainable and difficult to leverage, purported infrastructural revolution.

Revamping Indian Infrastructure: Reforming to Transform, with a Strategic World View

In the two decades plus since New Delhi unshackled the labyrinthine fetters on its socialistically moored economy, in the compulsively witting embrace of a liberalised economic reform framework, growth, though generically impressive, has exasperatingly ebbed-and-flowed, seldom acquiring the sustained trajectory of high index that would see it quantum-leap and comprehensively transform the national socio-economic milieu, akin to the salutary Chinese experience of the late 20th and early 21st century. Notwithstanding the multitude of inhibiting factors – ranging from the constraints and gripes of decision-making within a federal democratic polity, to the quirks and idiosyncrasies of governing coalitions, to the debilitating epochs of policy-paralysis in governance – it's the apparent dysfunction in envisioning and implementing benchmarks on ensconcing and proliferating infrastructure, both nationally and across the immediate South Asian concentric, that remains the recurrent Achilles heel. In an enveloping environment, harbouring the propensity to perceive good economics as constituting gawky politics, ostensible prioritisation of populist social and financial welfare measures commended a relative abiding short-shrift to infrastructure development, reflecting the abject inability to efficaciously address significant historical deficits in archaic trunk-infrastructure (roadways, rail-lines, power-grids, ports, etc.) and bridging wrenchingly enduring gaps in outmoded critical infrastructure systems, consequently impeding and impairing, existential processes of industrialisation, urbanisation, transportation and logistical development, rural-uplift and beyond. Furthermore, the obsessive fixation on a singularly growth induced and conditioned development model, rather than a focus and emphasis on fostering a diversified development paradigm, reinforcing growth, precipitated the engendering of dichotomously imbalanced national economic advancement, the disparity evidenced in Western and Southern India being at the vanguard, whilst the Northern and Eastern sections of the country, languishing as an arguable laggard; not to mention the remote North-Eastern vector, which despite its strategic geographical location of contiguity to China, spurring sporadic geopolitical contestations, and its coterminous adjacency to continental South East Asia, beholding geo-economic opportunities on the horizon has, owing to lackadaisical and impervious national neglect, wallowed in obscure detachment to obvious pyrrhic detriment.

When extrapolated to the accosting regional-setting, the enervating experience of such long stemming flippancy and ennui in statecraft, towards the putative near-abroad, has rendered New Delhi grappling to shape and stay-on-top of regional dynamics, most notably, in the infrastructure-spatial, but broadly, in reference to strategic transpiring by failing to requisitely and optimally harness the dint of its geographical centrality, within South Asia, in pursuing incontrovertible geostrategic primacy for itself. Far from being a forerunning progenitor of strong, integrative cross-border and intra-regional linkages, coalesced around logistical hubs, commercial and civilian itinerant activities and pivotal capacity-building domains, and spearheading institutionalisation of political affinity, diplomatic convergence, trade and investment exchanges for the region, within and without of the South Asian Association for Regional Cooperation (SAARC), it now has to poignantly contend with the vexatious prospect of an inexorable and comprehensive Chinese strategic involvement, pervasively punctuating its avowed South Asian sphere of influence, in definitive courtship of sovereign-protagonists, through a medley of surfeit of financial blandishments, substantive commercial infrastructure-bolstering ventures in capacitive strategic sectors, blooming developmental compact and steadily fomenting security cooperation, exerting mortal strains on India's tenor of strategic pre-eminence, its scope for strategic manoeuvre, the wherewithal to protect and preserve its vital national interests and to legitimately exude and project benign and coercive power in the region.

Prime Minister Modi's ascension, from regional iconoclast to national helm-ship, during May 2014, rode the crest of a resoundingly popular mandate at the hustings; in good measure, the upshot of his munificently laced assurances on the campaign-stump, of tectonically revolutionising the situation and stock of country-wide infrastructure, towards fundamentally addressing the rudimentary infirmities and structural anomalies, bedevilling the national economy, going beyond the till then internalised governance creed, of subjecting and exerting palliative gambits, to tend to momentary stutters, and a virtual fait accompli acceptance of cyclical trends in infrastructural transformation. This notwithstanding, his impressive track record of delivering multi-layered infrastructural growth at the bedrock of diversified and inclusive broad-sheet development in his home state of Gujarat, which he adroitly stewarded for over a decade such that the province, routinely characterised as the industrial locomotive and entrepreneurial engine of the country, witnessed significant uptick in social indicators of human development; was the wringing benefactor of an unprecedented agrarian boom, due to enduring solutions *sussed* in respect of irrigation, water-conservation and sufficiency; and stood testament to progressive urban rejuvenation and renewal, in that the capital city of Ahmedabad found itself pegged, behind the twin cities of Chengdu and Chongqing, in the pecking-order, for most urbanising centres worldwide, in terms of sustainable development and the improving quality of life of its residents.[4] While merely scaling up such empirically grounded experiences to national conceptualisation and actualisation, through instituting mechanisms for their resolute and time-bound implementation, would be passé and par-for-the-course, in his new capacity, what has in fact been refreshing is the Modi dispensation's pertinacity to fuse these convictions in radical infrastructural ramp-up, nationally, with the qualitative foreign policy and diplomatic goals of the 21st century Indian statecraft, distilled in the form of a legitimate quest for incontrovertible regional leadership within South Asia; plausible ambitions, to craft and carve-up a burgeoning productive role, across a wider perimeter of its existential strategic environs in the immediate and extended neighbourhoods; and comprehensible aspirations, for greater integration and substantive intertwining, within the persisting and emerging regional and continental economic and security frames, segueing into the international architecture.

A fervent strain of economic nationalism that puts a premium on infrastructure to lay the foundations for a new Indian economy and society, is complemented by enlightened pragmatism, anchored in the dogged pursuance of pluralised diplomacy and the genuine search for stability and productivity in mutually beneficent and multifaceted relationships with major global powers, established continental powers and regional and sub-regional peers and rivals alike. The thought process, sub-serving such disposition, holds that to harness the full extent of India's growth and developmental processes, propelling its unmitigated comprehensive regional and continental rise going forward, would need a phase of peace dividend and preservation of the balance of power, rather than a cataclysmic upending of it, just yet. Ensuring these objectives would entail New Delhi to concurrently engage in strong bilateralism, but also constructive and sagacious multilateralism, in respect of mutual relationships, regional engagements, and as a sovereign-actor, advocating rules-based regimes and open-ended regionalism initiatives in persisting and emerging strategic architectures, eschewing susceptibility, to its potentially dislocating fault lines and pitfalls.

At a time of Asia's well documented geo-economic rise, in heft and pelf, with still 400 million people deprived of electricity, 300 million sans access to clean drinking water and as many as 1.5 billion out of bounds from sanitation facilities, its aggravated requirement for investible resources to usher in and radiate social and industrial development, across sovereigns, in certain less developed sub-regions is equally well acknowledged.[5] Emerging economies such as China and India, despite their remarkable tenors of economic transformations, are also poster boys in their own differentiated right to the phenomenon of imbalanced and inequitable growth and development across their domestic landscapes, although Beijing, with its pronounced financial muscle, possesses the means to underwrite its inclinations for a reoriented and recalibrated development trajectory and altered coordinates. India, in comparison, has the potential to emerge as the alternative pole to China; some would adduce, it is singularly primed to do so. Yet, while the formidability of an unforgivingly treacherous neighbourhood is endlessly touted, it's the greater convolute challenge of connecting the world's largest democracy, a premier economy in celerity, with a burgeoning, aspirational middle class and the brimming younger genre of talent, but tethered to a miniscule proportion of trade and investment integration, globally, to regional and global markets, via road, rail and sea links, the dint of which has often tamped down its ambitions for global acclaim. Cut from a different loin are the likes of Japan, South Korea, Singapore and those from the Gulf Cooperation Council

(GCC), vested with abundant finances, but heralding saturated markets at home, hence, in search of opportunities across investment-craving growth-horizon zones, offering attractive remuneration, consequently gravitating such investible surpluses.[6] India's inchoate infrastructure, in a concerted bid to turn storied, under its present leadership, offers prime propitious circumstances, through the manifold scale of projects, size of the market, demand for strategic resources, opportunities for human resource development and attractive returns, all enablers, to scooping up such investible funds, looming around, towards shoring-up its chequered volatility at financing projects, marred by erratic public-investment, sub-serving populism rather than the strategic, and constricted private-investment, stressed by inventory over-capacity and saddled indebtedness.

With the Asian continent, estimated, to requite, up to US $27 trillion, over the 2016-2030 epoch, with eight-tenths of the infrastructure funding emanating from public sector avenues and multilateral agencies, and 60 per cent of all funding emanating from the Chinese banking system,[7] India's incumbent dispensation has its finger on the pulse in identifying eminent strands to its seminally envisioned infrastructural initiatives, cogitated and being given vent, through an 'in-out' philosophical strategy, whereby the internalised dynamics surrounding infrastructural development are conditioned by external involvement, through financial deployment, technological appropriation and dissemination of allied expertise and best practices experiences, even as the improving level of such national infrastructure would allow New Delhi the bandwidth to in turn leverage such development in its immediate neighbourhood and across a wider realm in pursuance of forking-up strategic influence, measured by enhanced trade and investment ties, facilely accessible transportation and transit options and augmented economic and societal interchange. With the feature of 'connectivity', the key to determining the relevance or redundancy of infrastructural development, which in turn constitutes the backbone to deliver an economy and society out of the mire, one can observe varied strands to the Modi-led infrastructural plan for India to revamp its national scene, as also to reboot its strategic regional and global outlook, coalesced around infrastructure initiatives. The Modi regime has over the past three years predominated its focus and unleashed overwhelming energies, in ploughing massive investments into critical verticals of the nation's 'connectivity-economy', in a wider perceptive frame, embracing the conventional physical elements in earnest, but by no means to the exclusion of the social and the softer dimensions of it. This has translated itself into a comprehensive, bottom-up modernisation of the patently archaic and creaking Indian Railways, one of the world's largest rail-line networks, yet, in a distinctly moribund infrastructural state, due to decades of appalling neglect, since Independence; a significant paving of rural roads, at a hair-razing clip of 120 km a day, as also the humungous task of electrifying over 18,000 villages, and the unveiling of the real-time prospect of illuminating 40 million households, endemically deprived, since the advent of Independent India, through the lustrous solace of a basic power connection; the reconceptualisation of cities and revolutionising of townships, into chic modern urban centres, exuding the attributes of access and mobility, consumption and operational efficiency, integration of services, and sustainable living; holistically integrated industrial hubs, aligned with dedicated freight corridors, and tethered to ramped-up port facilities.

India's South Asian Infrastructural Gambit: From Fragmented-to-Composite Framework in 'Neighbourhood First'

Despite enjoying immutable geographical centrality, coupled with the welter of antiquated and entrenched cultural affinities and historical links, within the South Asian regional subset, New Delhi, through acts of omission and commission, has been perpetually grappling with the challenge of efficaciously translating this factual oddity into veritable, unparalleled, geopolitical and geo-economic primacy for itself, through substantive consolidation of ties with fellow sovereign-protagonists, regardless of the obviously whopping power differential, in virtually all elements of national power, contributing to an inherently lopsided, asymmetry in engagement. Notwithstanding blame, which can be liberally shared, juxtaposing as the informal territorial gendarme, the onus and responsibility invariably lies at India's altar, to envision, conceptualise and solicitously wean South Asian countries into multilateral, region-wide cooperative and integrative initiatives, through purposeful political discourse, outcomes-oriented diplomatic dialogue, mutually-beneficent economic interchange and bolstering strategic cooperation, ideally coalesced around a viable and sustainable framework for convergence in robust infrastructural development in all its spheres and dimensions.

Yet, as the Modi premiership dawned, New Delhi found itself confronting a vexatious spectre, of antagonised or alienated contiguous neighbours, feeling slighted and let down by the former's apparent indifference, intermittent instances of inane muscle-flexing and the abject lack of benign leadership towards the region and its welfare, to the extent that even an understood 'zero-problem' neighbour such as Bhutan had felt estranged, due to an inexplicable cut-back in fuel subsidies, by India.[8] This seemed particularly vacuous, since South Asia, on the evolving cusp of changing politic-economic realities of greater democratisation and marked inclinations for economic integration, has emerged centripetal to externally conditioned, open-ended processes of regionalism, allowing sovereign-constituents, the latitude, to beneficently engage with extra-territorial continental powers, endeavouring to deepen their strategic footprint across the region, collaterally threatening to alter the core regional identity and profile of South Asia in the bargain. The sub-region of South Asia mirrors such living dichotomies, in that, despite being one of the faster growing sections of Asia, even outpacing the perfunctorily bustling East Asia, it ranks lower than Sub-Saharan Africa, in terms of intra-regional trading exchanges and investment linkages, representatively reflected in its stunted exports to the gross domestic product (GDP) metric, for instance, not to mention other allied indices.[9] While one could speak to the plethora of political contretemps, such as the India-Pakistan foibles, the social lacerations, as reflected in the polarising ethnic cauldron, or the fact of fragile states and porous borders, precipitating a cornucopia of subversive internal and external security vexations, holding the space back, it cannot detract from the omission and commission in pioneering, piloting and pursuing region-wide integration initiatives across a sub-continent that is blessed with strategic location, encompasses huge young and aspirational classes of population and avariciously craves for massive physical and social infrastructural facelift, proffering scale for resources deployable and size of markets to be harvested and harnessed.

Reinventing the dial was the need of the hour, and the new federal dispensation in India has manifested the penchant for being inventive and imaginative in recasting and reconfiguring relations with South Asian neighbours, encapsulated in its newly christened 'Neighbourhood First' policy-framework, the underlying goals of which are to recoup ceded strategic space, to bridge the credibility-gap, regionally construed and plausibly perceived, on account of multiple inordinately procrastinated or reneged-upon ventures, and to acquire progressive incandescence in the socio-economic trajectories of smaller South Asian countries, by substantiating commitments and proffering a new paradigm of infrastructure-development, anchored in facets of continuity and change, but punctuated on a wider canvass of hard, soft and virtual components of connectivity. The first vestige, of this shake-up in policy-outreach, soon became evident, with the Indian Prime Minister throwing down the gauntlet to the scientific fraternity at the Indian Space Research Organisation (ISRO) during a visit in mid-2014, followed by a unilateral pronouncement at the SAARC Summit in Kathmandu that same year, that India would voluntarily develop a totally cost-free communications satellite for gratuitous utilisation, by all countries of the SAARC community, carrying the initial moniker of a 'SAARC' Satellite, later mutated, to that of a 'South Asia' Satellite, upon Pakistan, nixing itself. The dint of the conceptualisation to crystallisation of this gregarious gesture, within a span of three years, leading to its formal unveiling and launch, earlier this year, was particularly instructive, in that it came in the historical backdrop of India, having once declined newly liberated Bangladesh's plea to use India's satellite facility, on account of bureaucratic perception of a security threat, besides being quite salutary, in the current context, where South Asian self-reliance in space technological capability is on the march, with the likes of Sri Lanka and Maldives having already elicit access to satellite infrastructure from China, and Bangladesh and Nepal being indulgent down this path.[10] This commissioned regional satellite, with its wide array of applications, enabling remote-sensing governance to natural resources mapping, and instrumentality for higher-education, telemedicine, early warning and information dissemination against climactic cataclysms, autonomous broadcasting, etc., has seminally helped to dissipate the crescendo of criticism fielded at New Delhi, for its hitherto earlier capriciousness; besides chiming with the overt yet subtle manifestation of India's globally acclaimed cutting-edge capacities in the domain of space technologies for human emancipation in a manner that serves to project its confidently exercised, decisive but benevolent leadership, in a region, that is equally being nudged by a 21st century India into enlighteningly comprehending, the broadening ambit of infrastructure development, with its myriad dividends and spin-offs, for socio-economic advancement, transcending and traversing, beyond conventionally conceived, but undimmed, ground-based physical connectivity, the import of which was hardly lost on the participating sovereign-protagonists.

In similar vein of canniness and pragmatic street-smartness, Prime Minister Modi has taken it upon his administration, to grasp the nettle in consummating, eminently low-hanging infrastructure possibilities in the neighbourhood, by earnestly endeavouring to spearhead, the resurrection of New Delhi mooted, but yawningly-stalled infrastructure projects, through lending a renewed thrust to alleviating the pendency of road-building and hydropower projects, across the Eastern vector, in the form of the East-West Postal Highway and the Pancheshwar Multipurpose Power Development ventures in Nepal, for example, successively pledged, by predecessor dispensations, prior to the turn of the century and since, but, which hadn't met with traction, denuding New Delhi's credibility and stock all these years, and detrimentally paling in attractive comparison to expeditious delineation and time-bound execution of projects by Beijing.

In contiguous Bhutan, the Modi infrastructural strategy is founded in iterative reaffirmation and conviction-smitten assurances of accelerating the development of major hydropower facilities, beholding as much as 10,000 MW of capacitation, in an incentivising mutually-beneficial framework, bringing hard-capacity and revenue-accrual to Bhutan, alright, but equally importantly, serving as potential elixir for the Eastern corridor of India, most notably, the impoverished and backward states of Uttar Pradesh and Bihar, as also the boxed-in region of the North East, whose industrial, urban and civilian developmental needs have remained enduringly stymied, due to sustained inadequacy of electricity generation and sparse supply, but whose tectonic transformation, could now be conveniently powered, through the constructed labyrinth of cross-border power production and transmission infrastructure.

In neighbouring maritime Sri Lanka, New Delhi under Modi has been astir and trenchant, in a conscious and concerted attempt to preclude the Indian Ocean country from being strategically co-opted by Beijing, under the latter's tutelage of oceanic machinations. Apart from the perfectly understandable wringing tactical commitment made to the development of the Colombo Port project, which had been contracted to the Chinese, in a desperate bid to redeem matters, on the back of the self-wrought Hambantotta fiasco and establishment of major oil-storage depot and LNG plant in addition to the port development at the key transit node of Trincomalee, it's the robust commitment, both financial and operative, to rebuilding the war-lacerated Tamil predominant Jaffna region, by provisioning for low-cost housing facilities and the affording of a US $318 million line-of-credit towards laying of a dedicated railway line connecting the region to the Sri Lankan heartland, with a view to unlocking the untapped potential of the North-Eastern section of the Emerald Island and mainstreaming this region within overall economic advancement and progress, and preventing the recurrence or relapse of the region to secessionist insurrection and violence, going forward, has resonated powerfully, being a refreshing aspect of Indian infrastructural development designs, lately, appearing to resist, remaining beholden to a one-size-fits-all generic approach to the region, wedding itself instead to the merits of a distinctly customised and nationally tailored foray instead.[11]

Confronted with the intractable adversarial nature of its relations with Pakistan, with bleak prospects for a northward turn, anytime soon, India has presciently resigned itself to the long persisting precluding limitations of sweeping, institutional-based regionalism, embodied in the auspices of the still-born and largely defunct SAARC framework, a coagulating view in the region, which finds grist-to-the-mill, through Islamabad's stubborn stonewalling of successive collectivised connectivity initiatives, pertaining to seminal Transportation and Transit for Trade-facilitation arrangements, landmark Regional Energy Cooperation accords and an elaborate, region-wide partnership in bringing home a dedicated Railways Corridor. Under such impeding regional dynamics, the idea of forging mini-lateral sub-regionalism has found broached favour as a necessitous virtue in New Delhi, conceptualising the disaggregation of the South Asian region into functional geo-strategic clusters of a Himalayan, Peninsular and Maritime South Asia, intimately interacting and engaging, whether conterminously or in overlap, with a hub-power India, mutually devising and collaboratively appropriating representative initiatives, purveying economic cooperation and ushering integration, underpinned by a congruent combination of hard and soft infrastructural connectivity schemes. Such a sapient approach facilitates intensifying, coordinated and cohesive regional cooperation, circumventing a forestalled SAARC and the discerning pitfalls of its prohibitively high threshold for consensus, through the nurturing of ostensibly collegial and consultatively positioned mechanisms of well-targeted, reductionist and expansionist sub-regional formulations, such as the Bangladesh, Bhutan, India and Nepal (BBIN) quadrilateral and a reactivated Bay of Bengal Initiative for Multi-Sectoral Technical and Economic Cooperation (BIMSTEC) constellation, that encompasses the Eastern South Asian sovereigns, alongside an outreach to formally non-South Asian, but objectively socio-economically connected sovereign-entities, such as Myanmar and Thailand. Such subaltern formats of sub-regional cooperation offer viable avenues for consummating efficacious integration, albeit, within a subset frame, through focussed modes of infrastructural connectivity, imparting enhanced economic, social and cultural interface, and fostering a compositely intertwined, regional identity and profile, offering realistic prospects for tangible, optimal benefits to communities and societies for mutual development and comprehensive empowerment across borders. For instance, the four-power sub-regional BBIN initiative, reposed of the objectives of developing trading and North-South directional communication channels has, through the formalisation of the Motor Vehicles Agreement in June 2015, accomplished traction in mitigating the factors hindering seamless regional transportation, underpinned by a dedicated electronic tracking system, whereby thorough-faring motor vehicles would be recipients of an online access permit to the territory of the Member-States, with the Customs Clearance being only implemented, upon arrival at destination, thereby significantly reducing the delivery durations. While the institution of this seamless technological regime speaks to the Indian wherewithal, the allocation of over a billion dollars by New Delhi, towards construction of a 558 km road network, weaving Bangladesh, Bhutan and Nepal, destined for completion in 2018, with half of the funding spouting from the Asian Development Bank, estimated to spike regional trading turnover by 60 per cent, points to an Indian commitment to advance the duality of physical and technological connectivity, in gelling measure. This said, in qualitative terms, India of late has been decidedly spendthrift for the right reasons, through its pledged commitments of significantly higher fiduciary sums of Export-Import (EXIM) Bank's Lines-of-Credit, transitioning from the multiple millions into the multiple billions, extended to the likes of Nepal, Bhutan and Bangladesh in particular, and designated, for specific infrastructure pertinent investments of structural and human capacity-building, not to mention, improving its track-record of eliciting the public and private sectors to rendition of the same hymn-sheet in project implementation for a better bang-for-the-buck.

Infrastructure at the Frontlines: Buffeted Strategic Frontier, Buttressed Periphery, Bolstered Effective Buffer

In close conjunction, the second strand of the Modi-inspired unfolding transformation relates to the prioritised development of infrastructure in forward areas, border locales and coastal territories, be they remote and far-flung spaces, or more main-landed coordinates. It's seldom lost on anyone that a nation beholding an aggregated land-border, in excess of 15,000 kilometres, a predominant portion of which is either overtly contested, subtly restive or innately porous, for that matter, concomitant to a straggled coastline of close to 7,500 kilometres has to elusively appraise and outstandingly appreciate the epochal character of robust infrastructural development, defined in terms of transportation and logistical links, as also the existential demands of multi-layered civilian infrastructure, something that ought to have been a no-brainer. Since the inception of the Modi government, India has incontrovertibly deployed its shoulder to the wheel of endeavour and accomplishment, in earnestly realising principally hard-infrastructure, but also soft-wiring across the meandering swathe of both the North East, which is a proverbial gateway to continental South East Asia, and the pivotal state of Jammu & Kashmir.

It's a truism to aver that for over five decades, India has ignored its frontier infrastructure requirements, majorly, along the 4,056 kilometre winding, disputed border with China. And far from being oblivious happenstance, this galling deficiency of vulnerable proportions is the upshot of the national elite being facetiously sworn, until recently, to a blissful perception that sidestepping the acquisition of hard core strategic depth in forward areas would constitute effective area-denial and potential ingress to its historical adversary, with whom it enjoys a ducks-n-drakes relationship in matters of militaristic posturing. While such befuddling sanguinity neither mellowed Chinese utterances of territorial claims, across into Arunachal Pradesh, nor tamed their robust, boundary-skirting physical build-up, it nevertheless left India, who has long been wary of Chinese disposition to creepy territorial encroachment, and its tacit manipulation of insurgent outfits against India, throughout the region, holding the rough end of the wedge, in terms of its woeful inadequacy in defence preparedness and vacuous smothering of its own legitimate developmental aspirations, leaving it hamstrung and disadvantaged across the swathe of the Seven Sisters of the North-East, home to 45 million inhabitants, covering nine per cent of the nation's landmass, yet contributing a measly three per cent, to the national GDP.

Under Modi, this was primed to change, both in terms of the rhetorical narrative and the operational script. In the archetypal mould of an unapologetic nationalist and a compunction-free, infrastructure-smitten evangelist, in pursuance of uncorking the latent potential of this utterly landlocked North Eastern region, a repository of abundant natural resources, in that apart from harbouring the conventionally known sources of coal, limestone and gas-based deposits exists the largely untapped potential for engendering up to a staggering 60,000 MW of hydro-electricity, thereby hemming in the promise of economic and trade opportunities, vide powering, not just itself, or the lagging Eastern states within the Indian Union, but equally potent to transmitting these solacing benefits to the less developed and poorer geographical and demographic sections of girdling continental South Asian and South East Asian countries, all along the land-based Mekong Corridor, but with the quirky facet of its outer perimeter almost unanimously opening itself out to an assertive and self-indulgent China on its head and to the genial but porous continental South East Asia, flanking it, has invariably been viewed through the predominating security lens, counselling lesser infrastructure development not more than through working to liberate it from its enveloping and stifling, intra-regional security constraints. The persisting bane of the Indian state has been its ardent tardiness in prosecuting the multiplicity of road and rail projects, prejudicing connectivity through the region, exemplified in the torturous progress of 73 designated road projects, 46 of which are mandated under the Ministry of Defence, and the 27 rest tasked to the Ministry of Home Affairs. Until 2012, which constituted the ordained deadline, in respect of 61 border area roads, a disheartening confluence of incompetence, venality and rigmaroles conspired to leave just 15 projects completed, a further seven having seen the light of day, up until 2016, with the remaining primed for fulfilment, a full nine years behind schedule, in 2021, notwithstanding the US $900 million worth of road contracts, awarded by the Modi government, in 2016-17. In stark contrast, whether through the expedited completion and dedication of the long-in-the-works, hugely strategic nine plus kilometres vehicular bridge, spanning the Brahmaputra, proffering vital underfoot and heavy purveying access from Assam into Arunachal Pradesh, or the grandiosity of a 2,000 kilometres highway for the frontline Tibet-bordering state, envisaged at an exchequer tab of US $6 billion, or its immediate common sense executive missive of relaxing environmental norms within 100 kilometres of the Line of Actual Control (LAC), facilitating the swift development of up to 6,000 kilometres of frontier roads, all of them, against the debilitating backdrop of the largely frustrated fortunes of 28 different railway lines, having met with implementation-stasis since 2010, is evidence of the Modi regime having gotten reliably and delectably footloose in its professed conviction, in foundationally transforming, within truncated timelines, the subset landscape, termed by the Prime Minister as the 'Ashta-Lakshmi', through erecting and beefing-up the whole gamut of strategic infrastructure, aimed at meeting the emanating panoply of challenges and opportunities along the security-economic axis.

Such has been the radical shift, that the region, which, coinciding, arguably stoking, even reinforcing, the ruling BJP's rising political fortunes across the electoral map of the North-East, has received top-billing priority in terms of generously earmarked funding, expeditiously granted executive policy approbations, better harmonised inter-ministerial and inter-agency coordination, as also the streamlining of administrative machinery, both at the federal and provincial levels, driving various infrastructure connectivity ventures, encapsulated, in the proactive laying of 750 kilometres of railway track, over different stretches across the regional subset, to an inter-state broad-gauge rail-track, stringing all State Capitals, through 2020. At the heart of an overwhelming 10,000 kilometres of webbing road connectivity projects, lies the federal dispensation's fervent commitment, to supplanting the excruciating visage of narrow pot-holed serpentine roads, meandering their course, with the paving of all-weather road stretches, besides, integrating the button-holed North East, within the ambitious initiative of two national trunk-road corridors, spanning 7,300 kilometres, dotting the length and breadth of the country, wherein, the 3,000 kilometres East-West Corridor would connect Porbandar in Gujarat to Guwahati in Assam, via the 'Chickens Neck' stretch (Siliguri Corridor) in West Bengal.

In consonance with the considered belief that infrastructure does not exist in a vacuum, but militates, embedded, within a sustaining community and thriving society, the Government of India seems an avid protagonist, to adopt and act on the recommendations of the commissioned study report, that has proposed a slew of trade-enhancing and multi-vectored connectivity-establishing proposals, be undertaken, under the aegis of the BBIN and BIMSTEC frameworks, involving delineating and actualising, scores of freight carrying routes traversing the region, including those, which would conjoin all North-Eastern state capitals, estimated to futuristically account for approximately eight-tenths of the aggregated freight flows peregrinating the cross-border and inter-regional North-Eastern Corridor (NEC). Such comprehensive sentiment, has underwritten the jumpstarting of marquee power generation projects, such as the 726 MW Palatana power project in Tripura, with the deliberated potential to not only power the landlocked state, but also light up parts of neighbouring Bangladesh. This said, the assertive promotion of infrastructure building, towards realising the captive ecological and tourism potential of the salubrious North East, not just internally, but weaved in cooperation with Nepal, Bhutan and even South East Asian nations, through the envisioning of an integrated cross-border and cross-regional 'Buddha-Circuit', and a prospective 'Ramayan-Circuit', with Sri Lanka, Indonesia and Thailand, not to mention the pioneering and showcasing of organic-farming, in verdant, rustic Sikkim, are solidly rooted in cultural comity smitten connectivity and through creating self-sustaining livelihoods, and epitomises the innovative and imaginative vent, meeting New Delhi's infrastructure thrust and drive in the region, beyond the inveterate and ubiquitous permeation of security dynamics, in discourse and template. Not to be left behind by any stretch, the state of Jammu and Kashmir, has also witnessed the incumbent government's temporal and operational emphasis, through the sanctioning and undertaken implementation of a phalanx of infrastructure projects, most notably, the completion and inauguration of the 11 kilometre long highway tunnel, at an altitude of 1,200 metres, conjoining Udhampur and Ramban towns, to a half hour drive, besides, the audacious enterprise of an under construction railway track, at highest elevation, 360 metres aloft the Chenab river, aimed at establishing real time rail connect of the nation with Kashmir, not to mention, substantive hydro-power and road construction projects, to the tune of Rs. 971 billion and Rs. 800 billion. It's self-evident, that cogent, all-weather road and rail connectivity would reflexively convert the North-East into India's window to lucratively trade and enact vibrant societal interchange with neighbours, yet, through decades of policymakers' apathetic neglect, the region has remained isolated and replete with spartan transportation, anaemic trade facilitation and denuding communication-related bottlenecks, diminishing its capacity to serve as an authoritative strategic-frontier, buttressing periphery and effective buffer-zone, all the more inexcusable in an era, where connectivity has emerged, as the critical, centripetal theatre to all and sundry, Geopolitics and Geo-strategy.

Maritime Infrastructure Connect: Strategic Depth to Normative Discourse, Tactical Activity, Regime Architecture

If over three million square kilometres of continental dimensions has historically evoked the paramount constancy of policymakers' attention and mind-space, sentient of its mortal fault lines and morbid pitfalls, then how not, and why shouldn't, the echelons within the national policy establishment accord prima-donna priority to the nation's enduringly disregarded maritime topography, of nine states and four union territories, panning-out across a 7,500 kilometres coastline, flanked by close to 1,200 island-formations, in virtual archipelagic chains, jutting out into the Indian Ocean, and beholding an Exclusive Economic Zone, in excess of two million square kilometres? The foregoing immutable geographical facets, point as much, to an unforgivingly conspicuous sea-blindness and abject strategic abdication, as it shimmers and shingles, the boundless, pristine potential, presented to a peninsular India, to effectively shape the normative discourse, tactical activity and institutional architecture, going forward, across an expansive oceanic vector and maritime realm, in arguable fluidity of strategic symmetry, but whose visage is fast changing, with the contending deepening footprint of an extra-territorial, ambitious China, being tugged at its coattails, by a renewed and resurgent, nationalist Japan, and the pervading presence, of an albeit, recanting and hedging US. Under such enveloping conditions of major power plurality, subjective attributes of legendary sea-faring traditions, impeccable credentials of democracy and sterling human diversity, in paradigmatic terms, can take New Delhi only as far; it's the objective, actionable components, of a dynamic Indian Ocean Region (IOR) vision and consequent strategy, which would be moot, to accomplishing national interest, through addressing national developmental needs, and corralling a legitimate strategic sphere of influence, placing it, at the unfolding centre of gravity.

Amidst the certitudes of US-China geostrategic rivalry, riven across the vast Indo-Pacific, China-Japan maritime showdown, festering in the Western Pacific, and China-South East Asian countries faceoff, rearing-up intermittently, in the South China Sea, India, with its dominant position in the middle of the India Ocean, astride strategic sea lanes of communication (SLOCs), and, with its extended geography of the islands, straddling some of the busiest shipping corridors, through its broader political acceptability, burnishing benign economic footprint and genial diplomatic stock, and progressively enhancing capability of its military, disposing as a net security provider within the IOR, can, through the significant ramp-up of strategic infrastructure, in its vicinity, and across its coordinates of perceived and desired influence, emerge as a veritable geostrategic partner, consolidating its standing within the IOR, and exerting a potentially 'swing-state' influence across the Indo-Pacific, the dint of which is hardly lost on the Prime Minister, who was formerly the Chief Minister of a frontline maritime state, within the Union, astutely comprehending the 'in-out' complementary of hinterland-coastal mechanics, interfacing with externalities of territories abutting.

There is no gainsaying that the green-shoots have been encouraging, in so far as the Modi government having undertaken to cover its bases across the trinity of fronts, of normative articulation in pursuance of a concordant strategic regional discourse, procreation and realignment of geostrategic assets, in buttressing strategic postures, and purposeful diplomatic outreach, to exhort the sculpturing of a robust, overarching regional regime and architecture, by delineating a dynamic, innovative and sustainable template coined Security and Growth for All in the Region (SAGAR), to address the fundamental geopolitical and geo-economic shifts, transpiring in its maritime environment, a function of the overwhelming reliance of national economies upon seaborne commercial interchange, the arterial nature of SLOCs in the IOR for regional and continental prosperity, and the ineluctable strategic stakes of the global growth engine, China, in ensconcing itself in the IOR towards surmounting its First Island Chain and Malaccan dilemmas, closely followed by the peer leading light economies of the Asia-Pacific, also drawn to the IOR by receptive and responsive resonance to their own resources and markets-based, strategic imperatives.

The Indian Government's decision to make the holistic development of the nation's myriad island outposts its concomitant top-priority, identifying no fewer than 10 of them for well-rounded infrastructure-based socio-economic development and multi-modal and multi-vectored capacity-building, prominently encapsulated, in the capstone rostering of Rs. 15,000 crore (US$2 billion) of infrastructural investments across the entire elongation of the Andaman and Nicobar chain, leading into 2020, implies, being unequivocally sold on the proposition of effecting a decisive and tangible strategic footprint across the emergent strategic theatre of competition and influence.[12] With the multitude of Rs. 3,000 crore (US$ 450 million) strategic road connectivity projects, commissioned, on and across the islands, under the Special Purpose Vehicle, the National Highways and Infrastructure Development Corporation Ltd, (NHIDCL), besides the North-South island conjoining bridges and an inter-island railway track, underscores the recognised virtue for strategic power projection, leveraging an island chain, which long houses the Tri-Services Forces Command, was at the vanguard of dispensing yeomen good offices during the post-Tsunami Humanitarian Assistance and Disaster Relief (HADR) clarion call and sits in close proximity of the arterial lifeline of the Malacca straits, giving strategic depth to India, to influence benign but critical Chinese commercial shipping and the not-so-innocuous naval manoeuvres.[13] The improved connectivity in the Northern stretches of the Andaman and Nicobar Islands (A&NI) chain creates leverage in terms of easy reach to continental South East Asian community, proffering huge benefits in terms of convenience of shipping, benign maritime economy development and harnessing the sea and ocean resources, through energy, fishing and scientific and technological exploration practices for sustainable living, the key to the Maritime Security and Blue Economy template of Prime Minister Modi, besides signifying that extending India's maritime infrastructural remit, and resourceful control over its islands, is neither singularly countervailing nor exclusively reductionist, instead, equally, inclusive and cohesive.[14] The innovative focus on cultivating myriad island entrenched tourism facilities and requisite infrastructure, drawing on pioneering Singaporean experiences, dispels notions of an islands infrastructure outreach swaddled in unvarnished security considerations, emphasising the beneficence of such maritime frontier infrastructural development for community empowerment, not just locally or nationally, but in cooperation, collaboration and compact with tourist hot-spot nations in the East.

For over three centuries, the Indian Ocean region has been inhabited by foreign powers, amidst conspicuous Indian passivity to such endeavours. This is set to change, as New Delhi decides to rise to the occasion, deepening economic and security cooperation with maritime neighbours, with an avid and conscious willingness to tangibly engender and strengthen their capacities and enhance capabilities. While China cannot be wished away from continental or oceanic spaces of South and East Asia, owing to its preponderant trade and investment ties with countries of the region, it's Beijing's penchant for port-construction and island-swooping overtures, which has New Delhi disconcerted. From missives to building ports in Myanmar and Bangladesh in the Bay of Bengal, to capitalising on Indian lackadaisicality, which forsook Hambantotta and virtually handed out

Colombo port, in Sri Lanka, to the recent overtures to Maldives, over concerted footprint on its Ihavan island, has New Delhi's hackles raised to the looming prospect of being infrastructurally cordon-sanitared alright, but also strategically straitjacketed. Modi's response has been a decisive outreach to coastal and maritime nations of South and East Asia, offering his own infrastructural packages, even not averse to doing it collaboratively with Japan, but more importantly, exercising suasion on these countries to stave off such captivating Chinese financing and sassy infrastructural build, towards preserving their national solvency, sustaining national ownership and ensuring community belonging, all of which stands threatened, through the medium of externally imposed Chinese interests centric initiatives. The renewed befriending of crux-located, tiny island states of Mauritius and Seychelles in the Western IOR, along a differentiated axis of infrastructure development-based solidarity, and proposals, to develop strategic capacitive infrastructure, through increased air and sea connectivity, modes of civilian infrastructure and adducing strategic assets, such as radars for effective reconnaissance and surveillance, on the leased islands of Agalega (Mauritius) and Assumption (Seychelles), gives India important leverage, at critical points along the maritime expanse, its best route, to effectively deterring, what is an increasingly pervading Chinese presence, all along the maritime corridors.

The maritime sphere has been integral to national power and national development of the powers that be, yet, one could not greater underscore its epochal character in current times. With up to nine-tenths of its value of trade, seven-tenths of its volume of trade and as much as one-half of its external GDP emanating from amphibious commercial and merchandise thoroughfare, it's not hard to fathom, why an India which under Modi has made increasing participation in regional and global trade, production and investment networks, the raison d'être for its external orientation, should seriously undertake acquiring strategic depth, across the IOR, on-setting with a reappraisal of its sovereign cartography. The long beleaguered coastal landscape, afflicted by an abysmally low level of mechanised and modernised infrastructural development, retarding growth and developmental processes at home, but also adversely impinging on trade augmentation and integration, not to mention the high logistical costs associated with doing business in India, and turnaround times for docking and berthing at ponderous Indian ports, falling way short of international standards in terms of costs, efficiency, sustainability and safety, a dint exemplified, in India ranking a lowly 35th in the World Bank's Logistics Performance Index, and attendant costs exacting, a prohibitively high Rs. 25 lac crore or 19 per cent of GDP.[15] With a view to lending a sure-footed enduring impetus to anodyne commercial interface with hub regions in the neighbourhood and beyond, the fortunes of Indian ports and concomitant areas, are sought to be potentially revolutionised, through the marquee 'SAGARMALA' project, envisioned by Prime Minister Vajpayee, only to be imperviously shelved during the United Progressive Alliance (UPA) regime, and now to be pioneered in a comprehensive and integrated hue, by Prime Minister Modi, through a staggering aggregated spend, to the tune of US $120 billion, originally envisaged over a decade, now proposed to be expended in half the time span, encompassing ambitious port development, coastal areas community development, coastal road connectivity and dotting industrial centres, premised on revamping and sprucing the quadrant of national strategic levers, viz. optimised multi-modal transportation network towards winnowing the cost of domestic cargo, attenuating the time and cost of export-import cargo logistics, whittling down costs for bulk industries by locating them in proximity of the coast, and proffering an impetus to export competitiveness, by establishing discrete manufacturing clusters near ports.[16] All of these, and more, are an attempt to redeem chunks of existing infrastructure, across the swathe of the nation's heartland, redundant in their isolated existence, but which, if mainstreamed and scaled-up, through comprehensive and compact connectivity, can be the crucible to assured foundations of steady economic growth trajectory.

India's 'Act-East' Schema: Mainstreaming Infrastructure for 'Hinterland – Near-Abroad' Connectivity Continuum

Foreign policy and diplomacy, across dispensations, presiding over mature celebrated democracies, routinely embodies elements of continuity and change, yet, when a country sets its date with a leader driven by telegenic vision and ardent conviction, it's not untoward to expect seminal departures in policy vent, even within a predating forged framework. As Prime Minister Modi endeavours to propel Indian foreign policy, out of its somnolence, into perceptible proactivity, one section of marked change has been the reorientation and retooling of New Delhi's 'Look-East' policy, fostered in the immediate wake of the advent of a globalised world, in which India sought to vibrantly engage the economically dynamic region of South East Asia and East Asia, through deepened trade and commercial ties. Despite the progressive involvement of India, within the politico-diplomatic architecture of the ASEAN region, through the inception of mutual Sectoral, Dialogue and Strategic Partnerships, through the 1990s, trade flows grew manifold, but within a largely transactional straitjacket, whilst investment flows were more tactical than strategic in character. Amidst the conception and fostering of Comprehensive Economic Cooperation and Comprehensive Economic Partnership Agreements (CECA and CEPA) with East Asian juggernauts of the likes of Japan and South Korea, and the conclusion of a long drawn out negotiated Free Trade Agreement with ASEAN, come 2010, which has found 55 per cent of its trade volumes transiting the South China Sea, and Singapore accounting for its largest foreign direct investment (FDI) provider, New Delhi had still struggled to consolidate ties with peers across the Eastern vector, in terms of ensuring that its canvass of economic engagement hemmed in elements of strategic interlocking and intertwining stake holding in the investment domain.[17]

The paramount measure of power in the 21st century, is unmistakably, infrastructure-based and connectivity-driven, in all hues and persuasions, specifically referenced to global structural networks, trade flows, capital markets and the realm of the digital socio-economy. In the concomitant global economic environment of a protectionist pushback and hidebound, insular and recanting sovereign economic policies, as also the apparent desultoriness and drift in negotiations over concluding regional and trans-regional behemoth integration pacts, the new norms of the production economy are no longer the function of comparative cost advantage alone. Instead, the measure of economic competitiveness and vitality of a sovereign entity stands benchmarked by the account of contribution, which national economies or their firms therein exert, within the unfolding regional and global production and logistical value chains. Standalone manufacturing facilities aside, it's the integrating quality of one's production edifice, which weighs disproportionately, in present-day trade and investment exchanges.[18] Notwithstanding India's significant comparative advantages across the gamut of information technology and information technology-enabled services, it's the deficits in strong manufacturing and logistical capacities across hard and soft infrastructure connectivity, shorn of quality, frugality and sophistication, undermining global competitiveness, which is the bugbear stymieing it from gainfully and productively participating in value radiating, regional production-networks in the continuum eastern neighbourhood. Confronted with the daunting spectre of assertive Chinese commercial activity and increasing presence in connectivity infrastructure and production and logistics integrating corridors, through South East Asia, kindling prospects for economic entrenchment, morphing to the latter's girdling dependency, New Delhi's legendary weaknesses leave it grossly disadvantaged, in terms of benefitting from investment in lower production cost economies of Mekong Delta countries such as Myanmar, Cambodia and Laos PDR; acquiring access to a potentially swelling market for Indian firms and their wares; circumventing the bulwark of ostensibly protectionist measures through investing in production and exporting facilities from the region; ameliorating the nation's voracious appetite for cheaper and reliable foreign energy sources, from within proximity; and ferreting opportunities to augment its manufacturing base and engendering viable employment avenues.

Through the re-coinage of the nation's framework for engaging and interchanging with its Eastern flank, vide the modalities of recast interactions, reconfigured agendas and recalibrated relationships, Prime Minister Modi has sought to re-imagine the tangible presence of India and the countries of East and South East Asia in each other's strategic calculus and popular consciousness; has endeavoured to re-envision what progressively constitutes India's eastern neighbourhood, expanding geographical cartography and coordinates much beyond conventional stereotypes notions of bridgehead South East Asia and beachhead South East Asia to casting a dragnet, as far and wide as Mongolia in North Asia and Australia in the Southern East Asian littoral, and as proximate to home as coterminous Eastern South Asia, concurrently deepening relations with economic and technological powerhouses of Japan and South Korea, respectively. Identifying this extended geostrategic space as being critical to Indian national development and nation-building, as much as being pivotal to finding traction for Indian foreign policy and national security objectives in consummating regional and continental peace and security and ushering in a widening arc of prosperity, Prime Minister Modi has set the stall out on a convivial pitch for multidimensional infrastructural connectivity, cross-cuttingly important, standalone infrastructural project development and nationally enjoined trunk and arterial infrastructural-build, with and within the newly contoured region, prospectively interlocking with the Indian North Eastern section, and potentially seamlessly aligning along the long running Eastern corridor of India, leading down the Southern coast. Needless to state, this has implied, reinvigorating and rejuvenating the steeped hard-connectivity initiatives of the Trilateral (India-Myanmar-Thailand) Highway and the Mekong-India Economic Corridor (MIEC), on the one hand, with rekindling momentum for homestead flagship projects, such as the Delhi-Mumbai Industrial Corridor (DMIC) and the Dedicated Freight Corridor (DFC), on the other, complemented and supplemented by the pressing imperative to quantitatively and qualitatively scale up the crisscrossing labyrinth of multimodal and intermodal linkages, in respect of the geographically shut-out North East and multimodal operations out of Southern India.[19]

Integral to the prioritisation of the Mekong sub-region, within the overarching template of the Modi government's Act-East policy schema, the unfolding India-Myanmar-Thailand (IMT) trilateral highway project, the singular land connectivity initiative between India and the Mekong set of countries, commissioned at New Delhi's behest back in 2010, has long been touted as part of the renewed thrust to institute physical connectivity with the wider South East Asian region, given Prime Minister Modi's proposal to extend the trilateral highway through the C-M-L-V countries – Cambodia, Myanmar, Laos and Vietnam. However, the 1360 km trilateral road tract, pegged at a cost of US $150 million, has been beset by slipping timelines on account of bureaucratic disjuncture and administrative muddle, which has seen the due date extended from 2015 to 2020; the work culture related incoherence of multi-layered development of varying stretches of the arterial road, across the trinity of sovereign protagonists; the formidability of ensuring that link roads within the North Eastern states or the poorer provinces of Myanmar, afflicted by ethnic unrest and subversive insurgent virulence, keep pace with the grandiloquence of the hallowed trans-boundary connectivity initiative; and the perceived qualms, whether skeletal and primitive levels of border management, customs controls and the ilk, can effectively leverage the trunk road transportation and transit corridor to greater formalisation of trade and increased cross-border volumes of commercial interchange.[20] To New Delhi and Modi's chagrin, Beijing's infrastructural machine has been at full-tilt-to-the-hilt, aggressively courting the Mekong region sovereigns into its orbit of strategic influence, in terms of economic interests and access to the Indian Ocean expanse, through tangible integration, brought on by the incisive execution of a dense web of multiple roads and multi-speed railway connect, patchwork quilt of energy pipelines, pathways of inland-water transportation and collateral development along the Lancang-Mekong corridor, offshore industrial relocation towards cross-border cooperation, technological and financial intertwining, etc., diluting New Delhi's strategic objectives, its latitude for operation and manoeuvre and trajectory of salience and prominence.

Buffeted with river-waters aplenty, providing the historical backdrop to the narrative of popular connectivity, India, with its inland navigable channels to the tune of 14,500 km, has, most inexplicably, remained oblivious to this dimension to its national development, which, if harnessed, posits material spin-offs for voluminous, cost-effective cargo transportation, tangible logistical infrastructure development, promotion of new inner-line industrial townships as hubs and mainstreaming many a local community based economies, inland and hinterland. Studies have vividly documented the potential for robust inland water transportation development to significantly denude costs, in comparison to road-lines and railways, in the movement of goods, the dint of which stands emphatically appreciated by Prime Minister Modi, making it an emblematic dimension to his national development strategy and the fulcrum of his intra and inter-regional connectivity infrastructure enterprise. While having enacted legislative mutations at home to designate as many as 111 rivers navigation channels as national waterways, and pronouncing an intent to holistically develop transportation and allied infrastructure, spanning 30 of them by 2020, New Delhi has taken this mission cross-border and into the deep reaches of the extended sub-region, resurrected in compact with Dhaka, long quiescent national waterways, to circumvent the cumbersome road network in instances, as well as to amplify the latter in other cases. The potential for weaving transnational rivers, such as the Ganges and the Brahmaputra, into viable sub-regional and regional waterways framework, could prospectively witness strengthened inland connectivity, leading to a blossoming water corridor, between the states of Assam and Meghalaya in India, with Bhutan and Nepal, in the upper Himalayan reaches, and Bangladesh, nestled, at the coastal frontier of the maritime Bay of Bengal, ushering in much vaunted access to locked-up resources, unexplored markets and communities in opacity. While the internal elements of inland water connectivity are increasingly comprehended, they would be rendered redundant, beyond a point, as a dimension to transportation corridors, within the multilateral regional context, without the adequacy of resplendent maritime-based connectivity, through reinforced shipping links and substantive cross-ports productive interface, utilising the dimensions of the waters, straddling the Eastern and Southern coastline of India, with the full length of coastal boundaries, of continental East South Asia and South East Asia. With New Delhi and Dhaka recently concluding a bilateral Maritime Shipping Agreement, as also a Coastal Shipping Agreement, leading to drastically reduced transportation costs, paving the way for full-blown commercial and security impelled mutual maritime interaction and interchange, the trail has been blazed, for expanding such an arrangement into a regional framework, for full scale and diversified maritime cooperation, within the reincarnated BIMSTEC setting, incorporating the countries of Sri Lanka, Myanmar and Thailand into a new flavour of sub-regionalised Eastern South Asia-South East Asian inter-regionalism, with India as the lynchpin to its conception, expansion and prospective consolidation.

It's heart-warming to witness the incumbent Indian Government's pertinacious policy drive and concerted operational push, to palpably bolster mainland India's connectivity, through its maritime component, with its primitively developed North-East region, and to economically and industrially lesser developed mortals along the Mekong stretch, whose intra-locale, trade, business and societal links have remained retarded, due to prohibitive connectivity, compounded by the otherwise exacerbating factors of asperities of terrain and harsh climactic conditions. New Delhi's current strategic gambit is plonked in the development of alternative multi-modal transportation corridors in an interlocking hue, such that they constitute strong cross-cutting and cross-fertilising sub-regional and inter-regional connect. With the emergence of Yangon, as its strategic anchor, maritime connectivity between Kolkata and Sittwe ports in India and Myanmar, and road-inland waterway connectivity, vide the Kaladan Multi-Modal Transit Transportation (KMMTT) project, is emblematic, in being ordained to proffer an alternative, albeit detouring route for purveying of goods to North Eastern India, connecting to the deep states of Manipur and Mizoram in particular, through the Western section of Myanmar. At the heart of the KMMTT idea, lies twin components of development of the port and accosting inland water transportation facilities, between Sittwe and Kaletwa, along the Kaladan river in Myanmar, and a further leveraging highway from Kaletwa to the Indo-Myanmar border, connecting to Mizoram state, not to mention the furrowing of a navigational channel, the creation of trans-shipment terminal and construction of inland water transportation barges, all of which would enable local employment generation in ancillary activities, invaluable income generation for local communities, and beneficent long-term infrastructural development of the locales and the wider regional subset. Notwithstanding the economic advantages, replete in the initiative, the project is also strategic, from a security vantage-point, in that, it allows for a reduction in dependency on the availing of roads, through the slender Chicken's Neck stretch of the Siliguri Corridor, and whose potential vulnerability to adversarial machination, stood eminently exposed during the recent Sino-Indian military standoff, at the Doklam tri-junction.

In similar vein of critical import to regional economic cooperation and regional security ordering lies the much touted Mekong-India Economic Corridor (MIEC), integrating the Mekong countries of Myanmar, Cambodia, Laos PDR and Vietnam with India, principally through yin-n-yang of road and rail network connectivity, but equally through cooperative developmental infrastructure of energy exploration and piping, alternatively sourced power-generation and transmission, industrial and logistics facilities, geared for low and competitive cost manufacturing of intermediates and production components, comprehensive and integrating port and port-accosting-area infrastructural upgrade and optical fibre cable networking for digitisation and solutions-based technological entrenchment.[21] Buttressed by the Modi cabinet approbating US $75 million in 2016 towards augmenting regional economic footprint, coming on the heels of the Prime Minister's unilateral announcement of a billion dollars towards boosting physical and digital connectivity between India and ASEAN, this corridor, when completed, is expected to ramp-up trade with India, by whittling down travel distances between India and MIEC countries, besides weeding-out supply-side bottlenecks. Notwithstanding, given the emphasis of the corridor on expanding the manufacturing base and outbound trade interchange, notably with India, though by no means foreclosed, the corridor would provide meaningful opportunities for the constituent South East Asian countries to carve-up a solid economic and industrial base themselves, although one would query their chances at availing world-class infrastructure, given the challenges inherent in Indian patronised infrastructural projects, neither completing in time nor delivering the top-notch felinity and finesse that is deserving of such big-ticket ventures. This said, the corridor would enable the economies of ASEAN and India to integrate further and potentially collectively emerge as a regionally cohesive and globally competitive economic bloc, a distinct prospect, building on their political affinities, and diplomatic convergence, over a range of sub-regional, regional and global strategic dossiers.

With India's longstanding dependence on externally sourced energy resources, overwhelmingly reliant on the tempestuous Middle East, and its recent propensity to diversify sources of supply towards achieving uninterrupted flow and steady pricing, the prospect of harvesting meaningful magnitude of energy resources from a relatively halcyon close vicinity cannot but be inviting. With all South Asian nations reflecting deficient power supply, on account of underwhelmed capacity and underperforming distribution systems across agrarian and industrial usage, and drawing predominantly from ecologically vitiating forms of coal and hydrocarbons, the largest consumer India could well do with optimally harnessing, albeit embryonic stage capacities, across the twin continental sub-regions of Eastern South Asia and South East Asia, with the wherewithal to procreating between 70,000 to 1,00,000 MW of hydro-electricity, through its North East, in conjunction with the Himalayan states of Nepal and Bhutan, in equal measure. Consonantly, the Indian State has begun responding to the pertinent investment requirements of the region, not just in creating captive-power, but also in the infrastructure for bringing it on-stream, through cogently interlinked, bilateral, trilateral and regionally permeating power-grids, across Nepal, Bhutan and Bangladesh, a vestige of symbiotic interdependence that would indemnify sustainable energy utilisation at commercial and societal levels in the sub-region. Extending this intra-Eastern South Asian cobweb of power connectivity to dip into the pristine untapped reservoirs of thermal and hydro-power generation in Myanmar could conveniently facilitate the interlinking of the dual sub-regions into a viable undistinguished and seamless 'Energy Corridor', fuelling dynamic economic advancement, although the seemingly plausible logic and wisdom of dusting off and reviving erstwhile mothballed projects, such as the tri-nation gas-pipeline initiative, between India, Bangladesh and Myanmar dating back to the 1990s, would necessitate enlightened political and policy pragmatism and partaking in trans-regional prosperity, a long elusive trait, but which may be finding resonance in changed conditions.[22]

While countries have long moved up the economic pecking-order, driven by traditional elements of hard infrastructure connectivity, in the conventional Industrial Revolution age, the post Industrial Revolution epoch is placing new demands on restructuring economies and societies towards meeting vaulting national aspirations and strategic ambitions along a non-linear, exponential trajectory. Nowhere is this better exemplified than in the virtual universalisation of technology, and its induction and incorporation into myriad dimensions of governance and strategic asset creation, within and beyond sovereign borders. India, with its resourcefully acquired soft skills in information technology and enabled services, in the post-liberalisation environment, since the advent of the Modi regime, accelerated and pioneered flagship projects, aimed at streamlining governmental disposition, benignant interface with its subjects and efficacious dissemination of services, through the increasing use of technology, the most representative aspect of which has been the massive foundational work at digitisation of content, processes, systems and solutions, across economic and social sectors, from manufacturing to skill development, and dispense of Education and provisioning for Healthcare, in an era, where Data is being venerated as the new Oil. However, developing societies and emerging economies are blighted by the dearth of an enabling IT infrastructure, in terms of sufficient bandwidth capacity, contingent upon the paving of a functional and tensile optical fibre network. Himself a huge proponent of the new infrastructural revolution built around Information, Digital and wider Technological connectivity, complementing the established hard connectivity domains, Prime Minister Modi, through his Highways-to-I(Information)-ways mantra, has been assiduously advocating and piloting, digitalised solutions and last-mile tech-connectivity cooperation across South Asian and South East Asian countries, in a manner that allows New Delhi to exercise sub-regional leadership and cultivate its legitimate regional sphere of influence, but accomplished through consultative, collegial and collaborative means of beneficent socio-economic emancipation, not through the instrumentality of hegemonic paternalism and cooperative frameworks, exuding exploitation, insubordination, and rendering a handmaiden.[23] India-Bangladesh cooperation has been archetypal in this regard, laying the plinth of a dedicated Information Technology corridor, with Dhaka exporting its surplus bandwidth to the hollowed-out Indian North East, connecting Tripura and itself, through the intermediaries of Agartala and Akhaura, a model that could be replicated, as a sub-region spanning or region-wide regime.

Infrastructure in the Western Theatre – From Strategic Dilemmas to Strategic Opportunities in Connectivity

For Indian strategic policy-planners, the conceptual frame for engagement with the Western Asian theatre, viz. the Middle East, has oscillated between containing abidingly metastasising malevolence and subversive virulence on the one hand, and representing national interest imperatives of ensuring energy security, tending to the primordial welfare and well-being of the expatriate Indian citizenry, and endeavouring to curtail Islamabad's stock across the region, on the other. As for Central Asia, the region, though initiated to India since ancient times, harking back to historical and civilisational links during the Silk Road exploits, had fallen off New Delhi's strategic map, so-to-speak, with the subset's profoundly landlocked features and its perception as the Russian backyard subsequently morphing into fortified ties of economic, commercial and financial dependency upon China, conditioning a stunted level of engagement with India since their independence in the early 1990s. With Afghanistan, catapulted, back into an infamy of prominence, post 9/11, and the country witnessing the return of the plurality of global and regional players in a post-Taliban epoch, visages of a new Great Game, ordered around infrastructural development and connectivity structures, aimed at unlocking the vast untapped potential of the Central Asian Republics (CARs) in terms of harnessing its huge deposits of strategic natural resources, from minerals and metals to hydro-electricity and the ilk, and mainstreaming the region, within Asia's overall rise, has surfaced.[24]

While enlightened bipartisan consensus across the political spectrum has ensured that New Delhi sat out the United Nations (UN) approbated intervention in Afghanistan, which would have drawn it into hands-on management of the degenerative security situation in the country, it has instead, across 116 projects spanning 31 provinces and US $3 billion in developmental aid, concentrated its activities on ushering in capacity-building development, both through constructing road infrastructure, vide its Border Roads Organisation, provisioning for social sector infrastructure, committing to establishing schools and hospitals, and even imparting professionalised training to the newly raised Afghan National Army and Police forces. Despite the knowledge that Islamabad has been pulling out all the stops to continually subvert Indian presence in Afghanistan, New Delhi has not only remained steadfast, in its beneficent footprint, translating its contribution to Afghan institution-building, through the construction of the Afghan National Parliament in Kabul and training legislators and administrators, and to economic and social reconstruction, through the consummation and dedication of the 42 MW hydroelectric Salma Dam in Herat, but, in appreciation of its prospective strategic role, has pursued wider and cross-sectional physical connectivity infrastructure, indulgent, in anticipation of a time, when a more peaceful and democratic Afghanistan would constitute the most viable transit corridor for Indian commercial and strategic interchange with the Central Asian region, besides indemnifying against Pakistan's regressively destabilising involvement.

However, this isn't to contend that Indian endeavours towards the region have not displayed their fair share of foibles. After long pursuing the fraught twin initiatives of the Turkmenistan-Afghanistan-Pakistan-India (TAPI) natural gas pipeline and the Iran-Pakistan-India (IPI) gas pipeline, both floundering, largely due to Pakistan's obstructionism and dissuading security concerns, New Delhi has settled on ferreting trade and transit routes, circumventing Islamabad, which has made the foraging for access through Iran via Afghanistan into Central Asia as the most eminently feasible option. Yet, as has been customary, with many an Indian strategic initiative in the extant, the long festering time horizon has often undercut the productivity of such missives, with the seminal Chabahar deep-sea port and port area development project in Iran, in perpetuating limbo, since its announcement during Prime Minister Vajpayee's tenure, and listlessly drifting through the Dr. Manmohan Singh years, when stresses of the US-Iran nuclear imbroglio impinged on its timorous and diffident pursuance, only to get jumpstarted in any earnestness since Prime Minister Modi ascended to the helm of affairs, and upon much exasperation by Tehran, with the urgency of the situation and the dearth of strategic counter-valance becoming apparent, stemming from China's all-weather Gwadar port, off Pakistan, entrenching itself and stepping-up operations, sticking out a sore thumb, in India's western frontier. Similarly, the International North-South Transport Corridor (INSTC) venture, envisaged at the turn of the century, with a view to enabling and facilitating robust freight thoroughfare and expanded volumes in commercial exchanges, with markets in Russia and across Europe, through the 7,200 km long incisive, multi-modal connectivity from Iran, hiving through Central Asia, the Caucuses, the Caspian, all the way to Moscow and beyond, at mitigated costs to the tune of 30 per cent, and through significantly reduced traversable distances, pegged at 40 per cent shorter, than the Northern Europe and the Mediterranean route, has wallowed, until its recent dust-off and resurrection by Prime Minister Modi's government.[25]

Under Modi, India has assumed much vaunted proactivity in piloting connectivity initiatives in its Western neighbourhood, pledging US $500 million and even transmitting the first tranche of the Line of Credit, to the tune of US $150 million for the warm water Chabahar port, situated in the Gulf of Oman, and within 72 km from Gwadar, offering New Delhi a great foothold in the vicinity of the energy chokepoints and across the strategic sea lanes of communication in the Western Indian Ocean. In what is now a tripartite agreement, concluded between India, Iran and Afghanistan, its formalised mutual development of road and rail networked trade corridor connectivity, from Chabahar across Zahedan (1380 km), onwards to Zaranj (200 km) and further on to Delaram (200 km), to feed off the benefits of the Chabahar port and its accosting port area development, which, by most accounts, has an Indian petrochemicals facility in store. While this opens up the sluice gates to accessing Central Asia, this connectivity project also liberates US$684 million worth of India-Afghanistan trade, from the retrograde interposition of Pakistan. With Japan gazing further West and given its new found keenness to embrace the CARs, Tokyo has been willing to underwrite the financial commitment to comprehensive and conclusive development of the Chabahar facility, a shot in the arm for India, which often grapples with mobilising the requisite fiduciary resources to pull its weight. This said, Indian connectivity outreach must be tempered by reality and has to be contextualised against the eye-popping Chinese commitment to develop the 3000-km-long China-Pakistan Economic Corridor, initially pegged at US$46 billion, now swollen to US$54 billion dollar infrastructure corridor, tying up Kashgar in Western China with Gwadar in Pakistan, hiving Pakistan Occupied Kashmir (PoK), through a bunch of unfolding and prospective trunk infrastructural projects, from road and rail pathways to industrial centres and logistics hubs, power plant grids, water systems, etc., although serious misgivings persist, all round, over the pecuniary credence of this venture, despite professed Chinese commitment, that this remains an ineluctable geopolitical project, carrying arguably unflinching political sanction.[26]

Significance of the Western Asian region in the foreign policy matrix of India cannot be greater underscored, in so far as India's foreign policy and national security is conceptualised, as comprising of sets of ever widening concentric circles around a central axis of historical and cultural commonalities. The security, stability and prosperity of a internally cohesive Central Asia, integrating beyond, is imperative for India's peace and economic development. However, the proof of the pudding is always in its eating, and the crucible of hallowed Indian intent, of cultivating a vast network of physical and digital connectivity, that extends from Eurasia's northern corner to Asia's southern shores, focussed on its strengths in sectors such as small business and enterprise, digital connectivity, pharmaceuticals, medicine and health, construction and service. India's efforts to forge a close strategic partnership rests as much on how it takes its physical connectivity initiatives to their logical conclusion in a time-bound manner, transcending geopolitical competition and regional rivalries, as much as it does on its permeating deployment of soft power by offering cooperation and aid in capacity building, knowledge transfer, people-to-people contact and bolstering its developmental and humanitarian assistance.[27]

India-China-Japan: Strategic Posturing and Positioning through Competing Narratives at Infrastructure-Building

The Asian continent is no homogenous monolith; if anything, the copious territoriality dovetails unprecedented heterogeneity. Intrinsic duality inhabits every nook and turn of its expansive dimensions, from a mosaic of incandescent and nondescript natural resources endowed regions to those fundamentally starved and staunched-off such strategic resources, yet, making for dynamic markets; from regions critically located at the crossroads and corridors of continuing thoroughfare to those geographically landlocked and bottled-up, pining for mobility and access; from regions of outrageous lucre and affluence, but boasting authoritarianism, weak governance and stifled human development indicators, to those coveted democracies, heralding vibrant demographics and lodestar governance practices, yet impugned by the onerousness of satiating the exponentially rising expectations of an ever burgeoning aspirational class. In current drift, the continent is a proverbial patchwork-quilt of grandiose connectivity initiatives, spearheaded by regional and trans-regional sovereign-power potentates, whose cartography criss-crosses the landscape, reshaping sub-regional, regional and continental geopolitical dynamics and recalibrating geo-economic realities, in terms of sourcing resource-markets to meeting the domestic demand for strategic commodities and investable fisc and harnessing product-markets for national exports, consequently, redefining the balance of power framework, through competing risk-n-reliance driven, diversified multi-alignment. Each of the trinity of countries in question bring to bear across their respective militating orbits and axis, and appreciated statist spheres of endeavour and influence, dichotomous credentials, in envisaging and executing paradigms of infrastructure-building, emanating from individualised captive national strengths, honed strands of professional expertise and wherewithal for experiential extrapolation and export.

On the one hand, a globally ascendant and continentally surging China, buttressed by its swiftly growing treasure-trove of engineering eco-system and buffeted by humungous financial bling to boot, not to mention the pervasive niftiness of its establishment to expeditiously envision, conceptualise and consummate gargantuan potentially game-changer, trans-boundary and cross-continental, hard-wired infrastructural initiatives, is able to accomplish traction, borne of the coveted attributes of size, speed and skill. Nevertheless, in the archetypal nature of a nascent exponent's hit-n-miss blitz, it has to intermittently contend, with palpable popular resentment and perceptive pushback, on certain of its misfiring outbound projects, which default on delineated timelines, err, in conforming to gilt-edged quality and environmental standards, and are culpable of inducing, unsound and odiously disruptive commercial financial models, inundating targeted, co-opted countries of operation. Almost juxtaposed, in stark contrast, is an eminently rising India, which, motivated by traditional solidarist considerations and a comporting impulse, has conventionally endeared itself to the sweep of the developing comity of nations, through procreating modest physical and social infrastructure and mentoring benign soft-wired projects, anchored in beneficent human capacity building and goodwill, radiating grass-roots societal and community empowerment. Yet, it has equally found it formidable to shrug-off the seemingly self-inflicted, pervasive reputation for arguably stunted and parochial politico-diplomatic imagination and blinkered strategic appreciation of the yeomen role of infrastructure in catalysing human and community transformation, at home and abroad, a dilettante demeanour, steeped in wishy-washy and prevaricating sovereign commitment, an enduring odyssey of invariably stuttering financial support, and generally tardy, slothful implementation, leading to inordinately procrastinated infrastructural initiatives. A resurgent, re-engaging Japan, for its part, makes for a curious dossier, in that, even whilst long enjoying an enviable pedigree for pioneering and fructifying perfunctory and futuristic, world-class infrastructure, domestically and overseas, leveraging, its fecund financial and verdant technocratic base, drawing on a niche, industrial-urban technological complex, epitomising meticulous perfection and exuding exceptional excellence, it has nevertheless punched below the radar in reticent emblazoning of its stellar cutting-edge technology-imbued physical capacity-building proficiency and prowess, across foreign shores, transcending and traversing beyond, the ordained regime of ODA mandated investments.

The superficially cordial yet subcutaneously tense Sino-Indian relationship stands laden with multiple layers of competition and cooperation, marred by the occasional confrontation and imbued with the sporadic sprinkle of collaboration. Conditioned by the baggage of historical friction and shaped by widening asymmetry, in the measure of their comprehensive national power, equations, have lately been defined by the respective trajectories of their infrastructure-binge and connectivity-labyrinths, across their contiguous and extended neighbourhoods, with China, on account of its huge financial muscle, the irrepressibility of its logistical-technical infrastructure machine, and plausible ambitions of consolidating its major power standing, through the conceptualising and pioneering of sub-regional, regional, continental and transcontinental strategic initiatives, underwritten by its infrastructure investment institutions and forums, is holding a palpable ascendant edge, vis-à-vis India. This said, the fervent nationalist and comporting pragmatic streak in Prime Minister Modi, recognising the limits to strategic engagement, yet, advocating the overriding need for a stable and productive curated strategic-partnership, has distilled the relationship with China, along the infrastructure vertical, in three interlinked impulses, moulding consequent policy responses; an unequivocal appreciation of the undiluted sanctity of India's sovereign borders, both continental and maritime, mandating a robust buffeting and buttressing of Indian strategic preparedness, along dimensions of military and civilian infrastructural build-up, across contested and frontlines terrains; the imperative to engage China, with a view to exploring the potential vistas for harnessing the iconic elements of their domestic infrastructural transformation, and instrumentalising something similarly revolutionising, across the dimensions of landscape, back home; and articulating assertively and moving assiduously, to non-countenance, if anything, actively counteract, adversarial attempts, at compelling India to cede strategic space in legitimate spheres of influence, even endeavouring to recoup, ground squandered. Such a trilateralised approach speaks to why New Delhi, despite not being able to overcome, mostly reasonable, though sometimes exaggerated notions, of China's potentially successful pitching for big ticket national infrastructure projects, portending deleterious ingress, has nevertheless been the founding member of the Chinese conceptualised and spearheaded Asian Infrastructure Investment Bank (AIIB), portraying such apparently curiosity evoking effusive endorsement of the dyed-in-the-wool Chinese institution, as linear to securing invaluably significant avenues for arguably concessional infrastructure financing at home. This said, the sobering realisation that trammelling the predatory Chinese infrastructural blitz, imperilling to overwhelm land-based and maritime-ensconced South Asian neighbours, or curtailing such Middle Kingdom impelled connectivity push, across its own delineated extended spheres of influence in South East Asia, the Indian Ocean Region and the West Asian theatre would necessitate a multilateral bulwark, has driven New Delhi into a tightening embrace of witting partners, such as the more overt likes of Japan and Vietnam, and the more subtle likes of Singapore and Myanmar, even as the more complex South Asian pushback to Chinese regional penetration, from Sri Lanka and Bangladesh, can cut both ways, of disposing truant to Beijing, allaying Indian concerns, on the one hand, also, opportunistically feeding-off, playing the Asian gladiators, off each other.

India and Japan have long engaged each other, through the prism of donor Japanese investments, deployed, in seminal developmental and consumer industrial projects, under the ODA framework; however, the form exuded a proclivity for Japanese condescension, and subjected India to an arguably 'patron-client' relationship. In much contrast, the present-day environment is more matured and edified, in that Tokyo now approaches its investments in Indian flagship projects, pitches for big ticket infrastructure ventures in India and stakes itself out across Indian regions, in a manner that does not implicitly regard India as a supplicant; to the contrary, such investments form an integral part of the budding and blossoming strategic partnership, coalesced around collaboration in logistics development, critical infrastructure systems and arterial infrastructure connectivity in frontier areas and maritime outposts. As New Delhi's 'Act-East' strategy mates with Tokyo's vision for the 'Confluence of the Two Seas' (Indo-Pacific) and Modi's inexorable drive for 'Make-in-India' and flagship national infrastructure building chimes with Abe's 'Expanded Partnership for Quality Infrastructure' (PQI) commitment, the mutual desire of either protagonist to foster and preserve a secure, stable and prosperous continental and maritime Asian space, based on universal respect for cardinal principles of immutable sovereignty, multilaterally enjoined norms of collectivised demeanour and consensually concurred rules of engagement, and open-ended regionalism based on primacy for sovereign autonomy, national self-reliance and an intimate sense of national stake holding and local belonging, has injected a sense of strategic trust, breeding qualitatively enhanced strategic thrust in Japanese investments into India, and the scope and scale of persisting and prospective collaborative endeavours, in third countries and external sub-regions.[28] Japanese International Cooperation Agency's (JICA) US $610 million commitment, for Phase I of the North East Road Network Connectivity Improvement initiative, the benefactor of which would be the remote states of Meghalaya and Mizoram, though a small speck, in the estimated US $48 billion requirement for enhancement of rickety road connectivity and transportation network in the region, is salutary for its considered alacrity, in the face of international funding agencies disinclination to underwrite investments in perceived territories of contestation between India and China. Similarly, New Delhi has solicited and acquiesced to Japanese investments in the sovereign maritime outpost of the Andaman and Nicobar islands, where the latter is developing power generation infrastructure for now, but could get escalated, should New Delhi decide to revisit its decision not to involve an outside sovereign to carve-up sensitive infrastructure, either on the islands or out in the North East too.

India, China and Japan proffer alternative paradigms and exude competing narratives in the showcasing and peddling of their infrastructure development activity, most emblematically, across the connectivity dimension of things. Yet, neither of the protagonists would allow their intense competitive edge to vitiate their mutually beneficent bilateral relations. Despite the absence of strategic trust in their schmooze, both New Delhi and Beijing covet their equations, albeit for wholly different reasons; Beijing wants to continue exploiting the lop-sided lucrativeness of its growing trade with New Delhi, and possibly co-opt the latter into the extravagance of its Belt and Road Initiative (BRI), so as to legitimise the Maritime Silk Road (MSR) pathway, by then touting the endorsed presence of the world's largest democracy, and a rising regional economy, as validation of its characterisation of the transcontinental geostrategic initiative as 'cooperative' in nature.[29] India, for its part, would brook none of this, over time allowing its muted, circumspect and equivocating response to the BRI, to morph into more categorical demur, fully sentient of the non-existence of any element of partnership in the exercise, and vexed by Beijing's callousness to its sovereignty related sensitivities and strategic sensibilities, even as New Delhi continues to stress dialogue on the subject and maintains ambiguity on the Bangladesh-China-India-Myanmar (BCIM) corridor project, given that it realises that effective connectivity solicits capital and China's unparalleled deep pockets are a potential boon for its own strategic national infrastructural development. This apart, the India-Japan mooted Asia-Africa Growth Corridor strategy, which emanates at one level from the mutually conceived Indo-Japan Vision 2025, stressing consultative and collegial project development in cross-continental third countries, premised on attributes of sovereign-autonomy, inclusivity, sustainability and collating capacity, though presented as a direct ideational and futuristically operational challenge to the Chinese BRI, unlike New Delhi, it did not keep Tokyo from participation in the marquee Inaugural Belt and Road Summit in Beijing, earlier this year, or for the Japanese-led Asian Development Bank (ADB) and the Chinese-led Asian Infrastructure Investment Bank (AIIB), to explore mutually collaborated investments.

Four factors motivate connectivity initiatives for modern-day India within a rising Asia, viz. the appraisal and appreciation of India's growing importance as an investment destination and a buoyant trading market, and as a repository of competent, white-collared workforce; the attributes of size and scale and the intangibilities of its eclectic society, which marks it down as the singular counterbalancing force to overweening Chinese regional dominance; New Delhi's growing realisation of the thriving possibilities in greater economic and societal interchange within Asia, and the spin-offs from its incontrovertible economic rise; New Delhi's fervent desire to shed its marginalisation within Asia, long hemmed in as a South Asian sub-regional entity, and instead, create a sphere of political and economic influence across near and extended neighbourhoods within Asia, in pursuance of addressing geopolitical considerations, transport and connectivity concerns and long-term political and sub-regional stability objectives.[30] Now, with the intended collectivisation of aggravated discomfiture and nettle over the astonishing spectre of Beijing's politically-sanctioned, region-smothering and continent-encompassing, indomitable infrastructure-carving juggernaut, rampantly fording its way, virtually unmatched, hence untrammelled, hemming countries across the overland and maritime domains into its politico-diplomatic, economic and security corral, through the audacity and expanse of its Belt-and-Road Initiative, and, in the refreshing context of New Delhi's long-elusive but-for-once fervent desire to significantly boost its domestic industrial-and-logistical development, tangibly burnish its relatively feckless regional diplomacy and veritably course-correct its apparently plateaued national credibility, across geopolitical and geo-economic coordinates of vital national interest, by assertively stepping up its infrastructure gambit, mooted and presided over by its dynamic incumbent nationalist federal dispensation, Tokyo, under its own nationalist helm-ship, has found the latitude to substantively foray not just to countries in the Asia-Pacific, but to consciously forage for avenues to outreach and ensconce itself across the abounding Indo-Pacific; whether, of its own accord, or, in consultative and collegial volition, with like-minded peers, besides India, as in, the slew of common-cause making entities within the ASEAN, and the sovereign ilk, strewn across the Indian Ocean, Afro-Asian littoral.

Under Prime Minister Modi, India has not necessarily done all new things; however, has definitely begun doing things differently, whether through the imaginative devising of the instrumentality entity of the NHIDCL, tasked with end-to-end structured and time-bound development of most of the strategic road connectivity projects, or in greater and better attuning of the work of the Development Partnership Administration (DPA) of the Ministry of External Affairs, constituted in 2012 towards purging lingering bottlenecks and lacunae, and reorienting the profile of developmental infrastructural profile and presence abroad. But as long as the focus of Indian infrastructure does not mate directly with the national development goals of the target countries, no matter how qualitatively refined, may the envisaged projects be, they will pale in comparison, thereby, keeping India's strategic national interests, tamed. There is no gainsaying that India's outreach and comporting overtures meld with the societal requirements of the 21st century, yet, it ought not to come at the expense of 20th century infrastructural deficiencies of physical connectivity, a pervasive visage across the Asian landscape, and where China is viewed more favourably.

NOTES

1. "Infrastructure for a Seamless Asia", Joint Study by the Asian Development Bank (ADB), Manila, and the Asian Development Bank Institute (ADBI), Tokyo, 2009, at https://www.adb.org/sites/default/files/publication/159348/adbi-infrastructure-seamless-asia.pdf.
2. Ibid.
3. Dr Kevin Lu, "Financing Asia's Infrastructure Gap: New Ideas for the Public and Private Sectors", Luncheon Address to the ASIA-INC Forum, Brunei, November 26, 2013, at https://centres.insead.edu/global-private-equity-initiative/research-initiatives/documents/financing-asia-infrastructure-gap.pdf.
4. Joel Kotkin, "The World's Fastest Growing Cities", *Forbes Magazine,* October 07, 2010, https://www.forbes.com/2010/10/07/cities-china-chicago-opinions-columnists-joel-kotkin.html.
5. *"Bridging Global Infrastructure Gaps", McKinsey Global Institute, June 2016.*
6. Aladdin Rillo and Zulfiqar Ali, "Public Financing of Infrastructure in Asia: In Search of New Solutions", *Policy Brief* 02, Asian Development Bank Institute (ADBI), Tokyo, 2017, https://www.adb.org/sites/default/files/publication/297481/adbi-pb2017-2.pdf.
7. Laura He, "Private Finance Expected to Fill the Gap in Funding Asian Infrastructure Projects", *South China Morning Post*, July 06, 2017, http://www.scmp.com/business/markets/article/2101583/private-finance-expected-

fill-gap-funding-asian-infrastructure.

8. Sachin Parashar and Sanjay Dattal, "Ties Strained as India Cuts Fuel Subsidy to Bhutan", *The Times of India*, July 06, 2013, https://timesofindia.indiatimes.com/india/Ties-strained-as-India-cuts-fuel-subsidy-to-Bhutan/articleshow/20936874.cms.
9. Nilova Roy Chaudhary, "Connectivity in South Asia: Projects and Prospects", *India Strategic*, March 2017.
10. Srinivasa Prasad, "India's South Asia Satellite Is Fine, but China Is Way Ahead in Wooing Neighbours in Space", *First Post*, May 05, 2017, http://www.firstpost.com/tech/news-analysis/indias-south-asia-satellite-is-fine-but-china-is-way-ahead-in-wooing-neighbours-in-space-3702329.html.
11. Nilanthi Samaranayake, "India's Key to Sri Lanka: Maritime Infrastructure Development", *The Diplomat*, September 09, 2017, http://thediplomat.com/2015/03/indias-key-to-sri-lanka-maritime-infrastructure-development/.
12. Manu Pubby, "Border Infrastructure: Modi Government driving Strategic Projects with Radical Changes", *The Economic Times*, May 16, 2015, https://economictimes.indiatimes.com/news/economy/infrastructure/border-infrastructure-modi-government-driving-strategic-projects-with-radical-changes/articleshow/47303236.cms.
13. "Ensuring Secure Seas: Indian Maritime Security Strategy", Naval Strategic Publication (NSP) 1.2, Indian Navy, October 2015, https://www.indiannavy.nic.in/sites/default/files/Indian_Maritime_ Security _ Strategy_ Document_25Jan16.pdf.
14. Sonali Mittra, "Blue Economy: Beyond an Economic Proposition", *ORF Issue Brief* 173, March 2017, http://cf.orfonline.org/wp-content/uploads/2017/03/ORF_IssueBrief_173_BlueEconomy.pdf.
15. Surya Sarathi Ray, "Infrastructure: How SAGARMALA Project Can be a Shot in the Arm for the Economy", *Financial Express*, November 21, 2016, at http://www.financialexpress.com/economy/infrastructure-how-sagarmala-project-can-be-a-shot-in-the-arm-for-the-economy/450802.
16. "SAGARMALA Project to be Completed in 5 Years", *Economic Times*, April 15, 2016, at https://economictimes.indiatimes.com/news/economy/infrastructure/sagarmala-project-to-be-completed-in-5-years/articleshow/51826345.cms.
17. Pradumna B. Rana and Chia Wai-Mun, "LEP2: Phase Two of South Asia's Look-East Policies", *SIS Commentary*, 47, March 21, 2013.
18. B. Bhattacharyay, R. Nag and M. Kawai, *Infrastructure for Asian Connectivity*, Edward Elgar, Cheltenham, 2012.
19. Prabhir De, "India's Emerging Connectivity with Southeast Asia: Progress and Prospects", Asian Development Bank (ADB) Working Paper Series No. 507, December 2014.
20. Prabhir De and J. K. Ray, "India-Myanmar Connectivity: Current Status and Future Prospects", Institute of Foreign Policy Studies (IFPS), Kolkata, India, 2013.
21. Fukunari Kimura and So Umezaki (eds.), *ASEAN-India Connectivity: The Comprehensive Asia Development Plan, Phase II*, ERIA Research Project Report No. 07, 2010, http://www.eria.org/RPR-2010-7.pdf.
22. Prabhir De and M. Majumdar, "Developing Cross-Border Production Networks between India's North-Eastern Region of India, Bangladesh and Myanmar: A

Preliminary Assessment", Research and Information System for Developing Countries (RIS), New Delhi, 2014.

23. Parag Khanna, "With Connectivity Comes Growth", Mint, September 26, 2017.
24. A. Sahgal and V. Anand, "Strategic Environment in Central Asia and India", in Nirmala, J (ed.), *Reconnecting India and Central Asia Emerging Security and Economic Dimensions,* Central Asia-Caucasus Institute & Silk Road Studies Programme, 2010, at www.silkroadstudies.org/new/docs/publications/1004Joshi-V-Strategic.pdf.
25. Bhavna Dave, *Resetting India's Engagement in Central Asia: From Symbols to Substance*, RSIS Policy Report, January 2016, https://www.files.ethz.ch/isn/196264/PR160202_Resetting-Indias-Engagment.pdf.
26. Ibid.
27. Micha'el Tanchum, "Modi and the Sino-Indian Game for Iranian Gas: The Indian Prime Minister Makes His Opening Move in a Mini 'Great Game'", *The Diplomat,* July 17, 2015, http://thediplomat.com/2015/07/modi-and-the-sino-indian-game-for-iranian-gas/ post-sanctions.
28. Titli Basu, "India, Japan and Confluence-of-the-Two-Seas: Ten Years On", *Institute for Defence Studies and Analyses (IDSA) Issue Brief*, September 13, 2017.
29. Sundeep Kumar, "Why India's Decision to Not Endorse China's New Silk Road Project Is Wise Foreign Policy", Chennai Centre for China Studies, May 17, 2017, http://www.thenewsminute.com/article/why-indias-decision-not-endorse-chinas-new-silk-road-project-wise-foreign-policy-62181.
30. Rupa Chanda and Sasidaran Gopalan, "Understanding India's Regional Initiatives with East and South East Asia", *The Asian Pacific Economic Literature,* 23(01), May 2009, http://journals2.scholarsportal.info/details.xqy?uri=/08189935/v23i0001/66_uiriweasa.xml.

19

The Belt and Road Initiative and Southeast Asia

Munmun Majumdar

China's President Xi Jinping announced the One Belt One Road (OBOR) also known as Belt and Road Initiative (BRI) during his tour of Central Asia in September 2013, which is an ambitious and complex transport corridor project. He unveiled a complementary vision – the 21st Century Maritime Silk Road (MSR) in an address to the Indonesian parliament during his official visit the same year. Broadly, the BRI[1] has two components – the Silk Road Economic Belt (SREB) and the MSR, which allows China to expand business and influence over an area that includes both land and sea. The Eurasian land corridor connects China to Europe through central Asia, while the MSR at sea connects China to the European market through South China Sea, Indian Ocean and the Mediterranean.

Alternatively, OBOR's Digital Silk Road component will see China's enterprises building telecommunication infrastructure, providing network services and selling communication devices that will not only help realize the Digital Silk Road. At the same time enable China to address the deficit that is there in several OBOR countries through overseas investment in digital infrastructure.[2] Strategically, telecommunication cables built by Chinese firms would amount to host countries subjecting themselves in increased electronic surveillance.[3]

In sum, the goal of the BRI is to connect China with Asia, Europe and Africa through a network of railways, highways, oil and gas pipelines, fibre-optics lines, electric grids and power plants, seaports and airports, logistic hubs, and free trade zones. The estimated investment cost for realizing this project is US $4-8 trillion.

The vision on maritime cooperation outlined by the White Paper (MSR Vision 2017) is largely a reiteration of the vision for the Silk Road Economic Belt and 21st-Century Maritime Silk Road proclaimed in March 2015 Belt Road Initiative (BRI Vision 2015).[4] Unlike the original blueprint for the belt and road initiative that had just one belt on land and one road at sea, the 2017 white paper on Maritime Cooperation under BRI envisages three oceanic passages.[5] One way of explaining the expanding maritime prospect on BRI is that since China relies heavily on external trade it is important for China to protect its trade routes.[6] Therefore, through the MSR it aims to secure its expanded sea-lanes and defend its global outreach.

Choosing regional leader Indonesia[7] (First among the equals), which also strategically links the Pacific and Indian Oceans, as the venue to officially announce MSR is a pointer to the importance attached by China to Southeast Asia and to maritime connectivity. The MSR proposed maritime trade to be promoted by developing transport routes, ports and other modern maritime infrastructure.[8] China's path to the sea is distinguished by seaborne commerce followed by naval development.[9] Considering that fact that 90 percent of global trade is carried through the sea route, and that the region constitutes significant sea-lanes for China's maritime trade, maritime connectivity with Southeast Asia would logically play a major role.

Southeast Asia is geographically, ethnically and culturally diverse region. The level of development is different for each constituent country. The varying degree of economic dependence on China makes economic considerations influence the relations between the individual ASEAN countries and China.[10] Similarly, each member of ASEAN responds to the tension in the South China Sea through the lens of its national interest, and China takes advantage of the fact that this prevents the ASEAN from arriving at a common position. For instance, Myanmar, Laos, Cambodia are not claimant states and do not have a direct stake in the conflict. They want stronger ties with China and do not want to jeopardize their economic interests by taking a position that is not favorably seen by. Thailand and Singapore are indifferent. Indonesia is concerned since China's claims overlaps part of its EEZ. Among the claimants Malaysia and Brunei considering the large volume of trade with China, would like to avoid tension so that they can carry on trade with China smoothly. Vietnam and Philippines are more vociferous and active. While Hanoi's strategy of applying pressure on Beijing has leaned towards internationalization of the dispute rather than seeking any sorts of eventual bilateral compromise. Rising nationalism in Vietnam and anti-China sentiments ensure that Sino-Vietnam cooperation, especially with regards to joint economic projects will be closely monitored and influenced by public opinion and civil society in Vietnam.[11] Philippines under Rodrigo Duterte in the recent past adopted a more pragmatic approach towards China. Rodrigo Duterte's June electoral victory coincided with the issuance by the UN Convention on the Law of the Sea (UNCLOS) Permanent Court of Arbitration (PCA) long-awaited ruling on Manila's arbitration case against Beijing's claim to maritime sovereignty in the South China Sea (SCS). The new president in Philippines promptly volunteered to "set aside" the verdict, and even announced his admiration for China and dissatisfaction with America.[12] Other Southeast Asian nations have for the most part avoided public mention of the PCA ruling for fear of offending Beijing, a vital trade partner.

For the ASEAN countries, regional economic integration plays a very important role in mitigating external uncertainties and global economic vulnerabilities.[13] They are divided on the extent to which they should welcome the BRI. For example, the developing countries of Southeast Asia such as Laos Cambodia who are also long term strategic allies of China are enthusiastic about the BRI, others such as Vietnam and Indonesia are cautious in their approach although they require aid from China to address their infrastructure deficit. And China has offered the much needed investment for connectivity related infrastructure construction to accelerate industrial and economic growth. [14] The official blueprint released by the Chinese government in May 2015, clearly stated that Southeast Asia is one of the priority regions for the improvement of physical connectivity under the BRI framework.[15] It is for these reasons that countries such as Vietnam while skeptical of the proposal do not want to be left behind and miss the opportunities for economic development.[16] Therefore, China's proposal paradoxically presents both threat and opportunities for the region. It is for these reasons that its success in achieving its objectives in Southeast Asia will be conditioned to a large extent on the internal dynamics there.

Southeast Asia is also significant since it serves to establish secure sea routes, offers alternative routes to seaports for China's landlocked provinces and creates alternative supply routes overland that will ensure continued access to markets abroad. In view of the fact that the actualization of this initiative can come about only with connectivity by both land and sea[17] this region is also included in China's grand design to develop transport links and industrial parks.[18] The initiative will take advantage of China's 3,889-kilometer border with Myanmar, Laos and Vietnam, running overland through Malaysia to Singapore as proposed in the China-Indochina Peninsula Corridor, one of the six economic corridors envisioned in the program.[19] The land-based routes afford Beijing new outlets to the sea thereby letting China to increase its links to the sea to facilitate the flow of goods. For example, in order to decrease its dependency on the Malacca Straits, China has been engaging with Myanmar in the construction of a deep-sea port in Kyaukphyu.[20] It is for these reasons that the vision statement categorically mentions Yunnan Province as a Chinese gateway to the Greater Mekong[21] region as a part of China's policies wherein the BRI has been marketed as a regional plan to accommodate ASEAN countries growth strategies.[22]

The regions geographical proximity to China, and that Southeast Asia will be the first stop on the MSR outside of China, makes it crucial to the success of the project. Given that ASEAN is economically important for China, the regions growing markets, manufacturing hubs and abundant natural resources offers Beijing opportunities. As such, a key focus of the belt and road initiative is ASEAN's burgeoning economies, with ASEAN-China trade is projected to increase from US $366.5 billion in 2014 to a target of US $1 trillion in 2020.[23] The fact that Xi met President Rodrigo Duterte and President Joko Widodo individually[24] reiterated the importance that China gives to the region for the successful implementation of the BRI.

President Xi Jinping highlighted five guiding principles of BRI at the first Belt and Road Forum (BRF) in Beijing held on 14 May 2017, namely: for it be a road for peace; a road of prosperity; a road of opening up; a road of innovation; and a road connecting civilizations.[25] The initiative however, came under scrutiny when European Union officials voiced their apprehension over transparency, labor and environment standards together with India's non-participation due to sovereignty issues concerns as the China-Pakistan Economic Corridor (CPEC) transits the Indian Territory in Pakistan Occupied Kashmir.[26]

BRI makes it certain that connectivity will be critical and the MSR is perceived to play a vital role in strengthening economic linkages between ASEAN member countries and China as well as among the ten ASEAN members. Thereby, bringing together two of the world's most dynamic economic regions. Given that the Southeast Asian countries are situated directly in the middle of the MSR's path and as a part and parcel of China's reaching out policy, the strategic implications for the ASEAN countries are significant.

Implications for Southeast Asia

(A) Economic

The tide of state-guided overseas capital investment as a part of the "going out" policy[27] was to secure energy and raw materials by channelizing domestic savings abroad.[28] Over the years China's reasons to invest its capital surplus overseas have grown. Herein the BRI is seen as an attempt to further redirect surplus capital and industrial overcapacity that can at the same time address the prevalent structural problem of the Chinese economy. And hence expected to be a key pillar of its going out strategy and a crucial driver for the country's long-term ambitions.[29]

The slowdown of Chinese economy and its planned restructuring demand the opening of new markets. Besides, focusing on building infrastructure will help stimulate the economy of China's remote regions, reduce domestic capital surplus and developing countries that are on the path of the BRI will be the market outlets of Chinese import.[30] The result is a new era of cooperation where China extends economic aid to meet its own development needs while simultaneously serving the development needs of recipient countries. The transfer of industrial capacity and world-class infrastructure would enable development in sectors where they have less comparative advantage. This venture defining new economic cooperation fits the two Silk Roads because countries along the routes are developing countries that do not have suitable infrastructure.

There is no doubt that China's investment into infrastructure developments and connectivity plans are useful for the development of the ASEAN Economic Community (AEC) as improving connectivity is also a key component of the AEC project. The present inadequate port capacity and roads in the region pose a major hurdle in the expansion of intraregional and interregional trade.[31] Even though the MSR taps into regional connectivity aspirations it remains to be seen whether the Southeast Asian proposal and China's Silk Road project are compatible.

While The ASEAN Economic Community is bringing the ASEAN economies together these countries welcome the BRI that offers further integration by developing physical infrastructure, with a pinch of salt. Although the initiatives hold the potential to address the infrastructure deficit, and lift industrial development, they view the long-term trajectory of their economic ties with China with caution. The reason being the difference in the economic scale between China and the Southeast Asian countries, which creates asymmetric interdependence that goes in China's favor. Together with the fact that China's military superiority gives China additional leverage over its neighbors. Even though China has stated that infrastructural investments do not imply political constraints, these countries fear that China may establish its economic and political dominance to dictate and that would undermine their foreign policy decisions too. As a result even if the BRI promises several benefits and aid from China they are doubtful that Beijing's intentions are benign.

The concerns raised are not without basis. The ASEAN China relationship is not a balanced one where ASEAN registers a substantive trade deficit with China. Besides, ASEAN invests more in China, but at a much slower pace than China's capital inflow into the region. The share of ASEAN's trade with China in its total external trade has increased over the years. China's FDI in Southeast Asian countries especially in countries such as Laos, Cambodia and Myanmar is much greater than before.[32] China's rise has enabled what Andrew Baker said as ideational shift in the construction of world political and economic order.[33] What is striking is that China's economic growth[34] has profoundly changed the structure of the regional political economy by causing most Southeast Asian economies to become significantly reoriented into a regional production network centered on China.[35] This makes the Southeast Asian countries even more vulnerable.[36] Hence, raising added concerns.

As mentioned earlier that certain Southeast Asian countries such as Laos, Cambodia[37] support the initiative, mainly for economic reasons, especially its infrastructure development and production-capacity cooperation elements. There are apprehensions voiced from other quarters such as Vietnam, which has had lukewarm political ties with China for decades. And China's aggressive moves in South China Sea (SCS) have sharpened that divide even more. Tension also prevails between Myanmar and China over Chinese funded dam and port projects in the country.[38] Likewise, Indonesia is also increasingly getting uncomfortable over China's actions in the SCS. [39] Additionally, apart from corruption and growing anti Chinese sentiments[40] there are problems related to financial deliveries and sustainability of constructing the investment projects.

The exclusion of Prayut Chan-ocha from the BRI Summit in May 2017 is yet again a reminder of how China's charm offensive that offers carrots applies the stick that compelled Thailand to adopt the Decree No.30/2017 on 15 June 2017 to accommodate China's interest.[41] Similarly, keeping Singapore out is also Beijing's way of showing its angst over Singapore's position in The Hague Tribunal's 2016 decision against China's claims on SCS, together with developing its ties with Washington in a way that does not align with Beijing's intents. Therefore, there is mounting concern that

China's geo-economic[42] influence will see Beijing resorting to economic retaliation to settle its political differences with neighboring countries.[43]

China's policies therefore, arouse suspicion and countries of the region feel that in time to come they may be forced to reciprocate China regional and global interest.[44] As a fall out the Southeast Asian countries are cautious of China's intent at the same time they do not want to be left out of the benefits that derive from the initiative. Implementing the belt and road agenda will therefore, requires a high level of mutual cooperation, transparency, understanding and trust. Unless that happens it would be difficult to realize common development and prosperity.[45]

(b) South China Sea Issue

While ASEAN governments continue to view China's policy with some measure of suspicion especially in light of Beijing's growing assertiveness in terms of its energy resource exploration, maritime claims and frequent military activities in the South China Sea,[46] at the same time China undoubtedly is also major power in the eyes of ASEAN.[47] China has declared an Air Defense Identification Zone (ADIZ) in the East China Sea during November 2013. China is yet to clearly establish any claim on ADIZ in the South China Sea, but there is no guarantee that it would not do so. While China's naval capability dwarfs other Asian countries capabilities.[48] The combined amalgamation of growing militarization with terraforming, the rise of the activities of the little blue men has given a new strategic dimension to this body of water that gives China a dominant position while continuing to reaping the benefits of increased economic ties with its Southeast Asian neighbors. Even though the ASEAN countries are engaged with China in a conflict management process they are at the same time alarmed because the PLA is armed with greater power of coercion [49] and has taken unilateral actions over the years to assert its claims in the SCS that go against the spirit of the 2002 Declaration on the Conduct of Parties in the South China Sea. So the sea that geographically binds China and maritime Southeast Asia also constitutes a space, that has become an area of competing territorial and maritime claims[50] that is in turn further complicated with the participation of extra-regional powers.

China's rejection of the ruling of the Permanent Court of Arbitration, in July 2016, has added concerns for the Southeast Asian countries. These countries fear that since there are no enforcement provisions in this convention, so there is nothing to prevent China from continuing to expand its presence in the South China Sea. And China's insistence on the sovereign interpretation of rights beyond the reach of international jurisdiction has left the smaller countries to feel vulnerable. It is clear to them that China will not turn to international tribunals to resolve sovereignty disputes. Therefore, they fear that without the protection of international legal norms and institutions in case of disputes with China they will be forced to accommodate with China's interest. More so since, China has the power and means to force its intent either through aggression, economic sanctions or by offering economic aid. It is not surprising then that they are apprehensive about who will apply international law with objectivity when China's interests conflict with those of its neighbors, as in the South China Sea.

Although China has propagated the idea of China's peaceful rise,[51] what must not be lost sight of is that corollary in China's peaceful development simultaneously embraces that China will fight for its core interests;[52] which includes Chinese claims in the SCS.[53] In other words, China reserves the right to use force if anyone denies Chinese territorial claims or other core interests. With unsettled issues of sovereignty and sovereign jurisdiction over the disputed islands in the SCS, uncertainty looms large about the intent of the MSR – whether the MSR would be used to foster mutually beneficial ties or under the guise of the MSR China will further its geostrategic objectives and project its economic and maritime power[54] that may not be in consonance with the interest of the ASEAN countries. And that China would use its military leverage to advance their stay and use commerce as a tool to expand its geopolitical and geostrategic influence. Since there is skepticism about furthering economic interdependence without addressing the South China Sea disputes, then resolving the SCS dispute will continue to remain as a preliminary to further cooperation with China. Until then it is likely that ASEAN will continue to harbor misgivings about the mismatch in China's pronouncements and actions. As for China it would be in its favor not to attend to regional security concerns while brushing the disputes in the SCS under the carpet and carry on business as usual, but the question is can the Southeast Asian countries can afford to do so?

(C) Undermining the ASEAN Way and ASEAN Unity?

ASEAN is unsure of Beijing's desire in laying out a vision of regional order that is indeed in contrast to the *ASEAN way*.[55] The Chinese approach to regional integration is different from ASEAN-style regionalism in important respects.[56] China promises prosperity in association with its own continuing growth and development. The core-periphery relations, practice of reciprocity in China's bilateral diplomacy, regional decision-making, and membership status differs from ASEAN's unique set of values and the kind of multilateralism that ASEAN has entertained.

For China spreading its influence in the area fulfills its vision of establishing a Sino-centric Order. Xi Jinping chose the term "Community of Common Destiny" during his October 2013 tour of ASEAN countries to express a vision of China-centered regional community.[57] ASEAN countries are worried that they will need to accommodate to the values and interest of China to avoid the loss of rights and privileges in the Community of Common Destiny sponsored by China".[58] Specifically in the case of China and ASEAN conflict management process in the SCS, questions have been raised about the utility of consensus diplomacy often referred to as the "ASEAN way". What makes the ASEAN countries anxious about is China laying the terms by virtue of its might and see China retaliating if countries do not conform to its views.[59] Thereby leaving the cardinal principles of *Musjawarah* and *Mufakat* (consultation and consensus) that have been ASEAN's core guiding principles since its formation redundant.

Considering disparate goals of its potential partners Beijing has so far pursued bilateral deals with the countries of Southeast Asia individually to realize its ambitions for overland connectivity. In Laos it has met with success. In Myanmar and Vietnam however, China failed to materialize the vision for parallel rail lines. But in conducting the MSR initiative within a bilateral framework there is the possibility of countries in the region to compete with each other for BRI loans, in which case bilateral arrangements with China may bypass the existing ASEAN mechanisms. Such a practice will undermine ASEAN's relevance to its members as well as regional affairs. Thereby strengthening the growing concern that China might use economic incentives as a tool to engulf these countries in a cooperation that will threaten the ASEAN way and ASEAN unity.[60] In this sense, these countries fear that MSR may erode ASEAN unity.

In the past China has been able to draw a wedge between the ASEAN members and in preventing ASEAN from tackling the SCS dispute with a united front.[61] This found expression when member states failed to reach an agreement on issuing a Joint communiqué [62] in the 45th ASEAN Ministerial Meeting in Phnom Penh in July 2012. And again following the 49th ASEAN Ministerial Meeting in Vientiane in July 2016, in the absence of any mention of the Permanent Court of Arbitration's (PCA) legal ruling in favor of Philippines against China regarding the control over disputed waters in the SCS. Both these instances revealed not only a lack of political will among ASEAN members to forge a united stand, but was also an illustration of China's ability to exercise its economic and strategic ability to divide the countries in the region. Therefore, despite the fact that they have an immense stake in maintaining good relations with China, they are uneasy of China's attempt at playing member states against one another. More importantly, the absence of consensus in the decision making structure for the execution of BRI makes them wary since it undermines its consensus principle and the *ASEAN way*.

Conclusion

The Belt and Road strategy is an important driver for China's long-term development strategy, foreign policy etc. The ASEAN countries see the initiative as an opportunity to fill critical gaps in their infrastructure, at the same time they are wary of the consequences stemming from of becoming excessively dependent on China. The lack of key information, operational strategy, terms of reference and detailed work plan for trade partners in the BRI have aroused suspicion. And together with China's assertive actions in the SCS over the years have eroded trust to a great extent. As a result, the Southeast Asian countries are not confident enough to go along without probing about either the intended benefits of BRI or China's strategy.

In order to mitigate the risk for ASEAN economies therefore, steps should be taken to strengthen their own economic integration, diversify their economies etc and highlight the fact that just as the ASEAN are beneficiaries of Chinese aid so is China a beneficiary of its investments in Southeast Asia. And that China is benefitting more from market access in Southeast Asia than visa versa. While the ASEAN countries are apprehensive of the Chinese intransigence in the SCS, it would be in their interest to maintain centrality, speak in one voice and weave the SCS issue as an integral part of the implementation of the MSR. Additionally stress on the compulsory requirement for a correlation between China-ASEAN economic interdependence and dispute settlement in the South China Sea.[63]

Unlike Deng Xiaoping who advocated, "hide your strength and bide your time,"[64] the current leadership is advocating a stronger foreign policy to achieve the great "Chinese dream."[65] China's success in achieving this dream will however, depend on taking that one step to dispel the fear that its project will lead to China's domination in Asia. At the same time, address the hurdles and put forth a clear operational strategy for the entire project that would explain the benefits and rules of engagement with the Southeast Asian countries. Only then the initiative would be able to capitalize on the opportunities that the geography common to China and Southeast Asia presents.

NOTES

1. J.P. "What is China's belt and road initiative? The many motivations behind Xi Jinping's key Foreign Policy, *The Economist*, May 15, 2017.
2. Sanchita Basu, "OBOR's Digital Connectivity Offers Both Benefits and Risks", *ISEAS Perspective*, August 14, 2017.
3. *Ibid*
4. National Development and Reform Commission, Ministry of Foreign Affairs, and Ministry of, and Commerce of the People's Republic of China, "Vision and Actions on Jointly Building Silk Road Economic Belt and 21st-Century Maritime Silk Road," National Development and Reform Commission, March 28, 2017, at http://en.ndrc.gov.cn/newsrelease/201503/t20150330_669367.html
5. This includes the originally envisaged China-Indian Ocean-Africa-Mediterranean Sea Blue Economic Passage; the blue economic passage of China-Oceania-South Pacific travelling southward from the South China Sea into the Pacific Ocean; and, a future blue economic passage to Europe via the Arctic Ocean. Full text of the Vision for Maritime Cooperation see June 20, 2017, at http://englisj.gov.cn/archive/publications/2017/06/20/content_2814756918.
6. In September 2015, China's National Development and Reform Commission (NDRC), Foreign Ministry and Ministry of Commerce (MOFCOM) announced that the scheme's official English name is 'The Belt and Road', or 'B&R'
7. "Chronology of China's Belt and Road Initiative", *Xinhua News*, March 28, 2015, at http://news.xinhuanet.com/english/2016-06/24/c_135464233.htm. (Accessed on 02.08.2016).
8. Peter Roell, "China's Maritime Silk Road – An Ambitious Undertaking", ISPSW Strategy Series, Issue No. 423, May 3, 2016, at http://www.css.ethz.ch/content/dam/ethz/special-interest/gess/cis/center-forsecurities-studies/resources/docs/423_roell_SLOC.pdf (Accessed on 02.08.2016).
9. Andrew S. Erickson, Lyle J. Goldstein and Carnes Lord eds., "China Goes to Sea: Maritime Transformation", *Comparative Historical Perspective* (Annapolis: Naval Institute Press, 2009), p. 345.
10. Nargiza Salidjanova, Jacob Koch-Weser and Jason Klanderman, "China's Economic Ties with ASEAN: a country-by-country analysis", US-China Economic and Security Commission, 17 March 2015, at http://origin.www. uscc.gov/sites/default/files/Research/China's%20Economic%20 Ties% 20with%20ASEAN.pdf (Accessed 2 February 2016).
11. Chinese investments became the target for popular protests and vandalism after Beijing deployed an oil-drilling rig in waters near Hoang Sa/Paracel Islands claimed by Vietnam in mid-2014.
12. However, on November 7, 2016, despite his earlier rhetoric against the US and the alliance, President Duterte suddenly gave his consent for the conduct of a joint US-Philippine military exercise and for implementation of the Enhanced Defense Cooperation Agreement signed in 2014.
13. Hong Yu, "China's Belt and Road Initiative and Its Implications for Southeast Asia", *Asia Policy*, Number 24, July 2017, pp. 117-122.
14. Hong Yu, "Infrastructure Connectivity and Regional Economic Integration in East Asia: Progress and Challenges," *Journal of Infrastructure, Policy and Development 1*, No.1, 2017, pp. 44-63.

15. National Development and Reform Commission, Ministry of Foreign Affairs, and Ministry of Commerce of the People's Republic of China (PRC), "Vision and Actions on Jointly Building Silk Road Economic Belt and 21st-Century Maritime Silk Road," March 28, 2015, at http://en.ndrc.gov.cn/newsrelease/201503/t20150330_669367.html. (Accessed on 30 May 2015).
16. Although both the Philippines and Vietnam have disputes with China in the South China Sea, both countries actively supported, rather than opposed, the AIIB, which was first proposed by China and will have its headquarters in Beijing. Both countries attended the signing ceremony of the memorandum of understanding on establishing the AIIB on 24 Oct. 2014. See Xinhua, October 24, 2014, at http://news.xinhuanet.com/world/2014- 10/24/c_1112965880.htm. (Accessed 5 April 2015).
17. The long list of intra-ASEAN and ASEAN-China agreements related to connectivity demonstrate its importance for trade and security are the 2004 MoU on Transport Cooperation, 2007 ASEAN-China Maritime Transport Agreement, sister port agreements etc.
18. The State Council of PRC, "Full Text: Action plan on Belt and Road Initiative", at http://english.gov.cn/archive/publications/2015/03/30/content_281475080249035.htm.
19. Jonathan Holslag, "China's Road to Influence", *Asian Survey*, 50(4), 2010, pp.641-662.
20. Shannon Tiezzi, "Chinese Company Wins Contract for Deep Sea Port in Myanmar", *The Diplomat*, January 01, 2016, at http://thediplomat.com/2016/01/chinese-company-wins-contract-for-deep-sea-port-in-myanmar/ (Accessed on 03.08.2016).
21. The Greater Mekong sub-region includes 6 states of Cambodia, Yunnan Province of China, Laos, Myanmar, Thailand and Vietnam.
22. http://news.xinhuanet.com/English/2015-08/06/c_134484989.htm.
23. Zheng Yiran, "China-ASEAN trade to hit $1t by 2020", *China Daily*, 16 June 2017.
24. Ministry of Foreign Affairs (PRC), "President Xi Jinping Meets with President Rodrigo Duterte of the Philippines," May 15, 2017, at http://www.fmprc.gov.cn/mfa_eng/zxxx_662805/t1462704.shtml. Ministry of Foreign Affairs (Indonesia), "President Jokowi Meets President Xi Jinping to enhance Strategic Partnership Cooperation," May 15, 2017, at http://www.kemlu.go.id/en/berita/Pages/president-jowoki-meets-president-xi-enhance-strategic-partnership.aspx.
25. Speech at the Xi Jinping, Work Together to Build the Silk Road Economic Belt and The 21st Century Maritime Silk Road, speech by President Xi Jinping at the Opening Ceremony of the Belt and Road Forum for International Cooperation, May 14, 2017, at http://news.xinhuanet.com/english/2017-05/14/c_136282982.htm.
26. Ministry of External Affairs, Government of India, "Official Spokesperson's Response to a Query on Participation of India in OBOR/BRI Forum," at http://www.mea.gov.in/media-briefings.htm?dtl/28463/official+spokesperso... "When declining China's invitation to participate in the Belt Road Forum in Beijing in May, 2017, India had stated: We are of firm belief that connectivity initiatives must be based on universally recognized international norms, good governance, rule of law, openness, transparency and equality. Connectivity initiatives must follow principles of financial responsibility to avoid projects that would create

unsustainable debt burden for communities; balanced ecological and environmental protection and preservation standards; transparent assessment of project costs; and skill and technology transfer to help long-term running and maintenance of the assets created by local communities. Connectivity projects must be pursued in a manner that respects sovereignty and territorial integrity".

27. General Secretary Jiang Zemin spoke about the strategy of encouraging those "overseas investments where our nation enjoys comparative advantages." When the CCP convened the 15th Congress in 1997. In 2001, Premier Zhu, in his policy address to the People's Congress, officially used the term "going global" strategy for Chinese firms.
28. Charles Wolf, Jr., Xiao Wang, and Eric Warner, *China's foreign aid and government-sponsored investment activities: Scale, content, destinations, and implications* (Santa Monica, CA: RAND National Defense Research Institute, 2013), at http://www.rand.org/content/dam/rand/pubs/research_reports/RR100/RR118/RAND_RR118.pdf.
29. Brahma Chellaney, "China's Debt-Trap Diplomacy", Project Syndicate, January 23, 2017, at https://www.project-syndicate.org/commentary/china-one-belt-one-road-loans-debt-by-brahma-chellaney-2017-01?barrier=accessreg (Accessed on 12 August 2017).
30. Richard Scott, "China's Maritime Silk Road project advances", *Hellenic Shipping News*, 12 July, 2016, at http://www.hellenicshippingnews.com/chinas-maritime-silk-road-project-advances/ (Accessed on 7 August 2016).
31. Hong Yu, "Infrastructure Connectivity and Regional Economic Integration in East Asia: Progress and Challenges," *Journal of Infrastructure, Policy and Development 1*, No.1, 2017 pp.44-63.
32. Foreign Direct Investment Statistics, ASEAN, February 2017 table 27, at http://asean.org/storage/2015/09/Table-27_oct2016.pdf (Accessed on 14 August 2017).
33. Andrew Baker, "The New Political economy of the Macroprudential Ideational Shift", *New Political Economy*, Volume 18, Issue 1, 2013, pp.112-139.
34. See Justin Yin Lifu, New Structural Economics: A New Framework for Rethinking Development and Policy, The World Bank, Washington, D.C., 2012, at http://siteresources.worldbank.org/DEC/Resources/84797-1104785060319/598886-1104951889260/NSE-Book.pdf
35. Evelyn Goh, "The Modes of China's Influence", *Asian Survey*, Vol. 54, Number 5, 2014.
36. Yong Deng, "China: the post-responsible power", *The Washington Quarterly*, Winter 2015.
37. ALE, William: China's Maritime Silk Road Gamble. In: *The Diplomat*, April 22, 2015. http://thediplomat.com/2015/04/chinas-maritime-silk-road-gamble/. See Vannarith Chheang "Cambodia Embraces China's Belt and Road Initiative" *ISEAS Perspective*, Singapore, July 6, 2017.
38. Mike Ives "A Chinese-Backed Dam Project Leaves Myanmar in a Bind", *New York Times*, March 31, 2017. Thomas Fuller, "Myanmar Backs Down, Suspending Dam Project", *New York Times*, September 30, 2011.
39. South China Sea; Indonesia renames part of maritime economic zone in defiance of Beijing, 15 July 2017 at http://www.abc.net.au/news/2017-07-15/south-china-sea-territory-renamed-by-indonesia/8711346 (Accessed on 13 August 2017).

40. See at http://www.reuters.com/article/us-indonesia-election-china/in-indonesia-labor-friction-and-politics-fan-anti-chinese-sentiment-idUSKBNI7KOYG
41. S44 invoked for Thai-Chinese railway", *Bangkok Post*, June 14, 2017, at http://www.bangkokpost.com/news/general/1269743/s44-invoked-for-thai-chinese-railway
42. Geo-economics is seen as an interlinkage of international economics, geopolitics and strategy, at http://www.chathamhouse.org/system/files/publications/twt/WiB%20YQA%20Geoeconomics.pdf
43. See at http://www.reuters.com/article/lotte-china/as-missile-row-drags-on-south-koreas-lotte-still-stymied-in-china-idUSL3NIJC3BA
44. Kavi Chongkittavorn, "Pushing East Asia Summit to new level", *The Strait Times*, November 11, 2014.
45. "Chronology of China's Belt and Road Initiative", *Xinhua News*, March 28, 2015, at http://news.xinhuanet.com/english/2016-06/24/c_135464233.htm (Accessed on 31 July 2017).
46. Denny Roy, "Southeast Asia and China: Balancing or Bandwagoning", *Contemporary of Southeast Asia*, Vol.27, No.2, 2005.
47. Alice D. Ba, "Who's Socializing Whom? Complex engagement in Sino-ASEAN relations", in Amitav Acharya and Richard Stubbs eds.,Theorizing Southeast Asian Relations, Routledge, 2009.
48. Andrew S. Erickson, "New US Security Doesn't Go Far Enough on South China Sea", *Wall Street Journal* (website), August 24, 2015, at http://www.blogs.wsi.com/chinarealtime/2015/08/24/new-asia-pacific-maritime-security-strategy-necessary-but-insufficient/ (Accessed on 19 September 2015).
49. Ian Storey, " China's Terraforming in the Spratlys: A Game Changer in the South China Sea?" *ISEAS Perspective*, #29, 23 June 2015.
50. Overlapping claims made by China, Vietnam, Malaysia, Brunei, the Philippines, and Taiwan.
51. China's Peaceful Rise: Speeches of Zheng Bijian 1997-2004, at https://www.brookings.edu/wp-content/uploads/2012/04/20050616bijianlunch.pdf (Accessed on 13 August 2017).
52. "Xi Jinping Explains the Principled Bottom Line in China's Peaceful Development," *Xinhua Online*, January 30, 2013, at http://www.chinanews.com/gn/2013/01-31/4535125.shtml (Timothy Heath, "Diplomacy Work Forum: Xi Steps Up Efforts to Shape a China-Centered Regional Order," *China Brief*, Vol. 13, issue 22 (November 7, 2013), at http://www.jamestown.org/single/?tx_ttnews[tt_news]=41594&no_cache=1#.VJGRfqbdVRA
53. In 2009, speaking at the US-China Strategic and Economic Dialogue, State Councilor Dai Bingguo defined China's core interests in the following way: "First Round of the US-China Economic Dialogue: Other Important Issues Discussed Besides the Moon," China News Online, July 29, 2009, at http://www.chinanews.com.cn/gn/news/2009/07-29/1794984.shtml (
54. Full Text: China's Military strategy-Xinhua1 English.news.cn," at http://news.xinhuanet.com/english/china/2015-05/26/c_134271001.htm. See also Phillip C. Saunders et al, The Chinese Navy: Expanding Capabilities, Evolving Roles (Government Printing Office), 2011, pp.109-11.

55. Danny Quah, "Is the ASEAN Way the Right Way?" *ASEAN Insight*, at http://aseaninsight.economist.com/2015/07/28/is-the-asean-way-the-right-way/ (Accessed on 13 August 2017).
56. David Arse, "China's Two Silk Roads: Implications for Southeast Asia", *ISEAS Perspective*, #2, January 22, 2015.
57. "China vows to build community of common destiny with ASEAN," *Xinhua*, October 3, 2013, at http://news.xinhuanet.com/english/china/2013-10/03/c_132770494.htm (Accessed March 21, 2014). "Xi Jinping: Let the Sense of Community of Common Destiny Take Deep Root in Neighbouring Countries," Ministry of Foreign Affairs of the People's Republic of China, October 25, 2013. http://www.fmprc.gov.cn/mfa_chn/zyxw_602251/t1093113.shtml
58. David Arase, "China's Two Silk Roads: Implications for Southeast Asia", *ISEAS Perspective*, #2, January 22, 2015.
59. See Oda OpdalZachrisen, "China's political use of economic ties in territorial disputes. A comparative case study of Japan's and the Philippines reactions" Master Thesis in Political Science Norwegian University of Science and Technology, Trondheim June 2015. "How relationship between China and Philippines affect Trade", *Waltham Trade Policy Review*, April 17, 2016.
60. David Arase, "Explaining China's 2+7 initiative towards ASEAN", *Trends in Southeast Asia*, #4, 2015.
61. Asean nations fail to reach agreement on South China Sea, 13 July 2012, *BBC News*, at http://www.bbc.com/news/world-asia-18825148 (Accessed on 3 December 2016).
62. Carlyle A. Thayer, "ASEAN's Code of Conduct in the South China Sea: a litmus test for community building?", *The Asia Pacific Journal*, at http://www.japanfocus.org/carlyle A-Thayer/3813/article.html (Accessed on 12 September 2012).
63. Munmun Majumdar, "Analyzing Indonesia's Policy in the South China Sea," *Indonesian Quarterly*, Vol. 44, No. 3 (2016) pp.224-238.
64. For an analysis of China's changing foreign policy, see "Less Biding and Hiding," *The Economist*, December 2, 2010, at http:// www.economist.com/node/17601475.
65. See President Xi Jinping's speech at the 12th meeting of the National People's Congress, March 2013, at http://news.xinhuanet.com/english/china/2013-03/17/c_132240367.htm.

Index